Scene Technology

Scene Technology

Third Edition

Richard L. Arnold
Northern Illinois University

PRENTICE HALL,   Englewood Cliffs, New Jersey 07632

Library of Congress Cataloging-in-Publication Data

ARNOLD, RICHARD L.
    Scene technology / Richard L. Arnold. — 3rd ed.
        p.   cm.
    Includes bibliographical references and index.
    1. Theaters—Stage-setting and scenery. I. Title.
PN2091.S8A7 1994
792'.025—dc20   93-16748
ISBN 0-13-501073-X   CIP

Acquisitions editor: Stephen Dalphin
Editorial/production supervision and interior design: Barbara Reilly
Copy editor: James Tully
Cover design: Robert Farrar-Wagner
Manufacturing buyer: Mary Ann Gloriande
Prepress buyer: Kelly Behr
Editorial assistant: Caffie Risher

Cover photo: Setting for *The Persecution and Assassination of Jean Paul Marat as Performed by the Inmates of the Asylum of Charenton under the Direction of the Marquis de Sade* produced at Northern Illinois University and designed by Scott Marr. (Photo by George Tarbay)

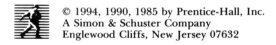 © 1994, 1990, 1985 by Prentice-Hall, Inc.
A Simon & Schuster Company
Englewood Cliffs, New Jersey 07632

Printed in the United States of America
10 9 8 7 6 5 4 3 2

ISBN   0-13-501073-X

Prentice-Hall International (UK) Limited, *London*
Prentice-Hall of Australia Pty. Limited, *Sydney*
Prentice-Hall Canada Inc., *Toronto*
Prentice-Hall Hispanoamericana, S.A., *Mexico*
Prentice-Hall of India Private Limited, *New Delhi*
Prentice-Hall of Japan, Inc., *Tokyo*
Simon & Schuster Asia Pte. Ltd., *Singapore*
Editora Prentice-Hall do Brasil, Ltda., *Rio de Janeiro*

Contents

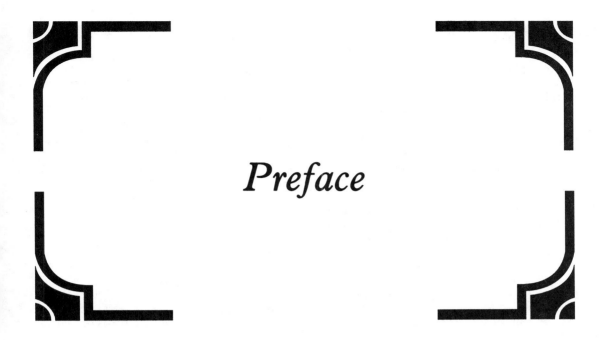

Preface

It is inherently exciting and challenging that each theatrical production is different, that each has its own dramatic circumstances and its own physical needs. This compels the scene technician to approach each production with a new and fresh orientation. The dissimilarity of one production to another means that there are new problems to solve and staging principles and methods to be applied to different performance situations.

There are infinite solutions to production problems. Whether rummaging through the trunkful of traditional practices or exploring new and innovative technologies, the technician must be inventive and creative while remaining sensitive to the specific needs of the performance. The goal is to find the best solution to a problem, the simplest, the most efficient, and the most reliable. What is required is a considerable breadth of knowledge, a precision of craftsmanship, a spirit of exploration, and a keen imagination. This

is the viewpoint underlying the focus of this text.

In addition, it is clearly acknowledged that contemporary scenic media includes all of the performing arts, whether live or recorded. While reference to live theatre tends to dominate discussion, a text on this subject cannot be exclusive for the foundations of scene technology; that is, its functions and practices are fundamental to all the performance fields. This book tries to examine a range of contemporary principles and general practices rather than a specific scenic approach, a few technical hints, or how-to recipes. Each chapter aims to introduce the reader to an area as a foundation for understanding and experience in the field. The selected reading lists are intended to stimulate further study and exploration.

The state of scenic art and craft is rapidly changing owing to the growth and increased application of modern technology, and we have much to learn from other technologies and crafts. A persistent curiosity helps us expand our knowledge and sharpen our technical skills. Only by maintaining interest in a variety of technical fields—as well as keeping abreast with scenic production practices through books, journals, and professional meetings—can we expand the materials, tools, and techniques at our disposal. This is the impetus that leads to better production solutions.

Much of our individual professional development and inspiration can be attributed to our teachers, professional colleagues, and outstanding students. I have been blessed with the finest in each of these categories. They are responsible for the positive accomplishments of my work and the intense interest in this field that ultimately led to the preparation of this text. Any notable contributions in this book can be considered a tribute to their encouragement, stimulation, and guidance over the years.

Many individuals gave valuable assistance in the development of this project. In particular, I wish to thank Alexander Adducci, Samuel Ball, Ned Bowman, Kenneth Bunne, Susan Christensen, Roy Christopher, Robert A. Dahlstrom, Walter S. Dewey, Richard Dunham, Leonard Harman, Richard L. Hay, Thomas Hines, Richard M. Isackes, Thomas Korder, Darwin Reid Payne, and Barbara Sellers. Thanks are extended to *Dramatics Magazine* and *Theatre Design and Technology* for permission to reprint material. I am also grateful for the assistance provided by a number of firms, organizations, and educational institutions. These include De-Sta-Co; The Great American Market; Hoffend and Sons, Inc.; Jerit/Boys Inc.; J. R. Clancy Corporation; Jules Fisher Associates; Martha Swope Photography; Masonite Corporation; MGM/UA Entertainment Company; National Association of Fire Equipment Distributors; Northern Illinois University; Northwestern University; Pacific Conservatory of the Performing Arts; Peter Albrecht Corporation; Rosco Laboratories; Ross Associates and Flood, Meyer, Sutton and Associates; Stardust Hotel; Up-Right Scaffolds; United States Institute for Theatre Technology; Virtus Corporation; and Williams/Gerard Productions. Special thanks also go to William M. Price (Northern Illinois University) and Dale Seeds (The College of Wooster) for reviewing my manuscript. In addition, my appreciation is extended to the editors who have been very helpful in the realization of this work, Steve Dalphin and Barbara Reilly. Finally, I am especially indebted to my wife for her valuable preparation and editorial assistance and to Mark, Marcia, and Rick, who throughout their lives have accepted my passion for scenic illusion with benevolent support.

Richard L. Arnold

Scene Technology

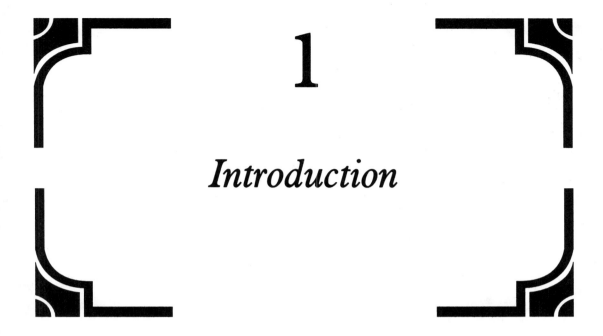

1

Introduction

In its most historical and narrow meaning, the word *scenery* refers to drops, draperies, and framed screens used as a background for performers on the stage. Modern design and technology, however, have broadened and expanded the means of providing scenic embellishment so that the term *scenery* is inadequate to describe the production setting found in contemporary performing arts.

Modern design practice is a rich mixture of styles and forms often created with the aid of new technical materials and mechanical devices. *The scene* or *the environment* are more meaningful and accurate terms to describe contemporary stage effects. In productions using minimal settings, stage properties often provide the greatest contribution to the scene; lighting has matured as a powerful means of creating environment; and the medium of radio demonstrated the potential of sound as a device for establishing significant settings. The word *scenography* encompasses the full range of audiovisual elements that establish the artistic unity required by the scene.

In reflecting contemporary practice, the terms *scene* and *environment* are used frequently in this text. The word *scenery* is employed, of course, but in its broad implication. Scene technology refers to the fabrication and operation of a setting including scenery construction, the rigging and shifting of scenery, scene painting, stage properties, and special effects. While some scenic values of sound and lighting are explored, an extensive examination of these fields along with costume and makeup is omitted from the focus of this book.

THE SCENIC MEDIA

It is no exaggeration to say that there has been an enormous expansion in the field of theatrical entertainment in the 20th century. Once prominent only in key metropolitan centers, theatre, opera, and dance have spread throughout the United States. Milwaukee, Houston, Seattle, Minneapolis, San Diego, Washington, D.C., and other cities now boast resident professional theatre companies. Similar growth has been evident in ballet and dance troupes. Dinner theatres scattered throughout the country offer popular fare, and small dedicated groups experimenting with new forms of drama have sprung up to be labeled "off-off Broadway" or "off-loop" theatre. A revival of interest in providing cultural opportunities for the citizenry has encouraged relatively small communities to preserve old theatres or to build impressive new buildings as performing arts centers for local productions as well as for national touring companies. Musical theatre, including opera, book musicals, revues, and the unique musical extravaganzas performed in the Las Vegas showrooms, is widely popular. Summer stock, summer package shows, and resident companies still provide off-season entertainment. Community and high school theatre continues to thrive, and the college and university theatre has increased both in number and in quality of performance. It is difficult to find any community far removed from some sort of live stage entertainment. Even more available are feature motion pictures and television dramas, specials, series, and related programing. For selected audiences, industrial theatre ranges from slick business promotion presentations to full-scale theatrical productions. Another particularly American development is the theme park, which not only displays numerous live and recorded performances but also wraps its audiences in lavish and magical settings.

Scenery is an integral feature of all of these presentations. To be sure, the wide range and level of production attests to considerable diversity of decorative treatment, from the simplest to the most sophisticated. The nature of the performance, the type of stage facility, and the creative skills of the personnel are only a few factors influencing production settings. Some entertainment fields, especially the television and film media, find a few particular production techniques and materials especially suitable for their needs. But despite these differences, general scenic practices are, for the most part, common to all of the entertainment media.

TECHNICAL PRACTICE

Scene technology differs from other technical fields in several profound ways. First of all, it is an *inclusive* endeavor, utilizing the knowledge and skills of many industrial arts and crafts. Technicians must have an array of craft skills and understand the use of tools and materials of diverse trades. This includes an ability for self-teaching and for keeping abreast of new technologies.

Scenic practice is also *accumulative*. Methods of operation and construction techniques change and expand with the development of technology resulting in both new solutions and improvements to existing practices. But, like the magician's art, old effects are never discarded. They often are used again in new ways and in different applications.

This creativity, unique to scene technology, is present in the work of all the artists and craftspeople in the performing arts, for the resulting effort of scene technicians, like the entire work of art, is an *illusion*. While a setting often must be functional (one aspect of reality), it is intended primarily to be expressive in other ways; that is, to seek intellectual and emotional responses from an audience. Illusion makers must be inventive and imaginative to devise workable solutions for scenic effects.

Finally, scenic practice is *demanding* and *exacting*. A stage effect must perform accurately and consistently. Nothing is more obvious and distracting than a technical error;

and, unlike the resourceful live performer, a stage effect cannot cover up a mistake. Scenery sometimes employs simple materials, and benefits by distance from the audience or by the limited vision of a camera; yet fitting two 14-foot flats snugly together approximates the tolerances of the smaller scale of a cabinetmaker. An illusion may be achieved with the most advanced and complicated tools and materials or merely by "a paper moon and cardboard sea," but only if the construction is executed with care and precision will the technology succeed.

CHARACTERISTICS OF THE SCENIC ENVIRONMENT

In serving the performance, the scene takes many forms, has a range of functions, and specifies numerous practical demands for the technician. Obviously, a knowledge of the performing arts, their historical and contemporary modes and conventions, is necessary to understand the purposes of the scenic environment. Technicians execute their tasks more effectively when they know how scenic effects serve the performance. Need for this knowledge is emphasized here by a review of some of the characteristics of scenery.

Ways of Describing Settings

Scenery is categorized in many ways. The designer thinks of the environment as meeting a specific and unified image or concept of the drama or performance. The result is often a particular emphasis on mood, functionalism, the specificity of reality, decorativeness, or another design value. These values are sometimes labeled in general terms as styles of design, ranging from realism to more nonrealistic or presentational forms.

On the other hand, the technician is likely to identify a setting in terms of the types of

scenery it embodies. We may refer to the predominant form of the scenery (for example, a platform set consisting largely of levels, ramps, and stairs), to the scene changing function of a set (for example, a unit set), or to the type of construction (for example, a skeletal setting). Modern theatre inherited pictorial wings and drops from the 18th and 19th century practice. The box setting developed in the era of Naturalism. More suggestive and symbolic settings—unlocalized levels, skeletal and fragmentary structures—originated in other times and circumstances.

Unlike staging in previous centuries, modern staging utilizes a wide range of types of scenery. The choice is based partially on the function or purpose served by a setting in a particular production. The choice may be made evident by the nature of the performance, by the environmental information or attitude to be expressed, by the form of the stage, or by the particular media. Three-dimensional, realistic scenery is often required by the relative proximity of scenery in intimate theatres, film, and television. More emphasis on spectacle is demanded for other types of performances.

Basically, a setting has a unique communication and service function for each production. Some dramas use the barest fragments of scenery that are complete scenic statements if not complete enclosures.

Contributions of the Technical Elements

Recognizing that scenery has a function, it is helpful for the technician to be aware of how it serves the total production. Scenery serves in a variety of ways, varying considerably by culture and historic time. Essentially, the setting should "illuminate" the drama, heightening the audience's awareness and response to the text. It may do this by conventional ways of revealing the inner life of the drama, by a mixture of experienced images of the past, or even by creating tension or opposition to energize the audience to the drama.

In general, scenery provides four distinct contributions that assist, reinforce, and intensify the performance. Perhaps the most essential is the contribution of the setting in *aiding the performers*. It does this by emphasizing the performer through elevation, color, appropriate framing, and clarity of visibility. Scene design is a spatial art, providing appropriate spaces for the physical action of the actors, which makes possible effective performer groupings, actions, and patterns of movement. The setting is also an important means of *intensifying the mood* of the production. This strengthens response to the pattern of emotions that grow and develop in a drama. It is useful for scenery to *reinforce the style* of a production, the special manner of expression that orients and unifies the audience to the point of view of the dramatic action. Finally, scenery must often *convey information* vital for the understanding of the unfolding story. This information includes facts about the time and place of the action, the circumstances of the occasion, the characters, and character relationships.

Special Requirements of Scenery

In contrast to other crafts, the service that scene technology must provide the production results in a number of special requirements. These often dictate the construction methods, the selection of tools and building materials, the shop layout, and the methods of construction operation. The following list outlines some of these requirements.

1. Scenic elements must be faithful to the designer's plan and must function in performance as conceived.
2. A setting must be strong enough to serve the performance adequately and to be handled

FIGURE 1–1   Frequently, when scenery serves the performers effectively, it is inconspicuous and unobtrusive. Scene from *Romeo and Juliet* at Northern Illinois University. Scene design by the author.

and moved easily without damage. Portions conceived to be "practical" (used in a particular way by the performers) or to bear weight require special durability.

3. In appearance and service, the construction of a setting must be governed by the proximity of the audience or camera so the illusion is not destroyed.

4. A setting must be lightweight, built in units, packageable, and compactly storable.

5. Scenery is intended for limited usage for a given performance run, but must often be reused, altered, or preserved for adaptation in a future production.

6. A setting must usually be transportable and conceived for quick and easy handling in a scene shift.

7. Scenery must be low in cost, planned in keeping with a minimal production budget.

8. Scenic effects must be reliable and easily repeatable in their production functions.

9. Scenic elements in use and handling must not jeopardize the safety of performers or crew members.

10. Scenery must be constructed in a short period, often in 3 to 5 weeks.

SELECTED READINGS

ALBRIGHT, A. D., WILLIAM P. HALSTEAD, and LEE MITCHELL, *Principles of Theatre Art* (2nd ed.). Boston: Houghton Mifflin, 1968.

ARONSON, ARNOLD, *American Set Design.* New York: Theatre Communications Group, 1985.

BAY, HOWARD, *Stage Design.* New York: Drama Book Specialists, 1974.

BELLMAN, WILLARD F., *Scene Design, Stage Lighting, Sound, Costume & Makeup* (rev. ed.). New York: Harper & Row, 1983.

BURIAN, JARKA, *The Scenography of Josef Svoboda.* Middletown, CT: Wesleyan University Press, 1971.

GILLETTE, J. MICHAEL, *Theatrical Design and Production* (2nd ed.). Mountain View, CA: Mayfield, 1992.

PAYNE, DARWIN REID, *The Scenographic Imagination.* Carbondale and Edwardsville, IL: Southern Illinois University Press, 1981.

2

Production Organization and Operation

A production is a highly collaborative art. Many people are involved in its creation: a producer, a director, a company of performers, designers, production crews, craftspeople, and sometimes a musical director, musicians, dancers, a choreographer, numerous assistants, and many others. Each person contributes in a special way to the realization of the collaborative effort. An effective organization is necessary to accomplish and coordinate successfully the hundreds of tasks needed to mount a production.

Scenery, like all other elements in the production, has no independent life of its own. Elements not fused into the performance experience are likely to be conspicuous and distracting. This inevitably affects the success of the production. Scene technicians, members of the production team, have responsibility to the common effort and an ob-

ligation to be supportive of the aims and needs of the production.

PRODUCTION ORGANIZATION

Every production effort requires an organizational structure for the distribution of responsibilities. This provides for efficiency of operation and establishes a clear line of authority. The size of the production program and the professional or nonprofessional status are just two factors leading to differences in organization structure. In many professional efforts, an association is formed solely for an individual production with a staff composed of freelance specialists, union technicians, and the personnel of a scenic construction company. Other companies, such as resident theatres, have a permanent staff and an assortment of specialists. Mod-

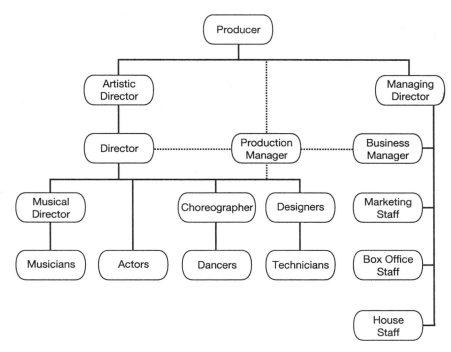

FIGURE 2–1   General production organization.

erate- and small-sized organizations have smaller production staffs with multiple duties assumed by their personnel.

The general organizational chart, Figure 2–1, illustrates the lines of authority and the responsibilities and duties of production individuals. At the administrative level is the *producer*, an individual or governing board of an organization, who initiates the production and has ultimate responsibility for contractual, financial, promotion, and operation of the undertaking. Organizations with a season of productions are frequently managed by two individuals, an *artistic director* and a *managing director*, who oversee, respectively, the artistic quality and the business functions of the company.

An individual production is under the leadership of the *director*. This person carefully coordinates the production with a specific interpretation and production goal to achieve a single unified work of art. Working with the designers in production conferences, the director seeks to develop a unified production concept. Guided by the concept, the *designers* translate the underlying meanings and qualities of the script into line, form, color, and texture. Under the best circumstances, the director and the design team are able to inspire and be inspired by each other, which results in an exciting and unified event.

The *production manager* is an important coordinator assisting the production team within the established plans of the company administration. This includes preparation of the **production calendar** (see sample calendar in Figure 2–2), which schedules the design period, production meetings, design and production deadlines, rehearsal and construction periods, and technical and dress rehearsals. Knowledgeable of time and

PRODUCTION CALENDAR	
Servant of Two Masters	

DESIGN CONFERENCES	
Aug 19	Production Conference I
Sep 3	Production Conference II
Sep 9	Production Conference III
Sep 16	Production Conference IV
Sep 23	Final Designs

REHEARSAL AND CONSTRUCTION PERIOD	
Sep 30–Oct 5	
Oct 7–Oct 12	
Oct 14–Oct 19	
Oct 19	Last day to add props
Oct 21–Oct 26	
Oct 28	Set load-in
Oct 28–Nov 2	
Nov 4	Run through for crews

TECHNICAL AND DRESS REHEARSALS	
Nov 5	1st Technical
Nov 6	2nd Technical
Nov 7	3rd Technical
Nov 8	1st Dress
Nov 9	2nd Dress
Nov 10	Final Dress

PERFORMANCES	
Nov 11	Opening Night
Nov 17	(no performance)
Nov 23	Last Night / Strike

FIGURE 2–2 Sample production calendar.

work requirements, the production manager strives for efficiency within the limitations of the facility, budget, and personnel resources of the production. The composite calendar of a multiproduction organization reveals the overlapping calendars of all productions and how they share facilities, personnel, and other resources.

A production is designed and planned in a series of conferences before rehearsals begin. The production team consists of the director, the designers, the technical director, the stage manager, the musical director, the choreographer, and sometimes heads of the technical areas. Effective collaboration results in a production plan and final designs that satisfy the artistic as well as the physical and budget limitations established by the organization. Of course, artistically, the communication process is not always easy or entirely successful. This fact has encouraged the establishment of a single master designer, known as the *scenographer*, who develops a unified aesthetic concept for a production. This is a common practice in Europe, although professional practice in the United States has moved toward specialized designers for scenery, costumes, lighting, and, in recent years, sound. The scene technician must work closely with the scenic designer or scenographer, a relationship in this collaborative art that also requires effective communication. It is essential that the scene technician understand the vision of the designer, know how the setting is to function in the production, and assist the designer in achieving the aesthetic result. Creativity is possible only with technical knowledge and achievement. This relationship of art and technology is also embodied in the concept of scenography.

The scene designer is responsible for the design of the stage settings and properties. While collaborating is necessary with the costume designer and lighting designer, the design of the setting often is a dominant factor in the total visual effect of the production. In most professional productions, scenic designers must belong to the United Scenic Artists Union, which requires an extensive examination in the field. In television and film, this position is usually called the art director or production designer. Designers often have assistants and drafters in preparing renderings, models, and drawings.

THE TECHNICIANS

Technicians have specific duties and responsibilities in the technical areas of scenery, properties, lighting, sound, special effects, and costumes. Often crews involved in the preparation phase (building the show) are different from the crews that run the performances. The different titles and functions of these individuals are indicated on the organization of technical staff in Figure 2–3.

The *technical director* (TD) supervises the execution of the technical elements of a production. Responsibilities may also include preparation of working drawings, mounting of the setting, and supervision of the techni-

cal rehearsals. This position is particularly associated with educational theatre and resident theatre companies that have permanent staffs. In college theatre, this task is sometimes assumed by the scenic designer or lighting designer. The TD may also act as the shop manager; that is, maintaining equipment and supplies and, with the help of department heads, supervising the construction and rigging of scenery, props, sound effects, and special effects.

FIGURE 2–3 General organization of the technical staff.

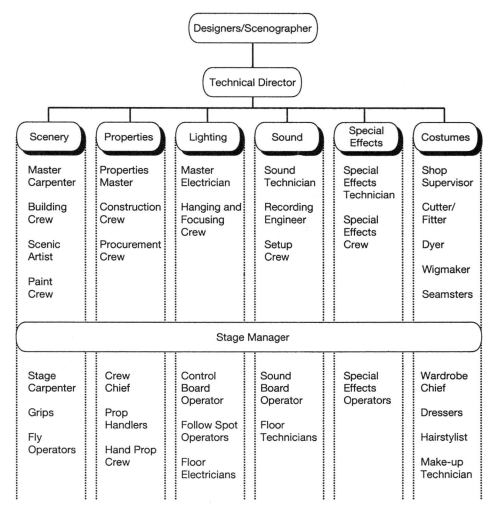

Scenery construction is supervised by the *master carpenter*. After becoming familiar with the working drawings, the master carpenter schedules the work and then assigns it to other carpenters, assistants, and building crews who may have special skills in plastics, metalworking, cabinetmaking, and other crafts. In professional theatre, the construction of scenery is often contracted to a scenic studio, which has a regular staff of construction carpenters. Production organizations with in-house shops will employ a permanent master or key carpenter and staff of workers. In these situations the master carpenter is frequently the shop manager or supervisor. On the running crew, the *stage carpenter* is in charge of rigging and shifting scenery during final rehearsals and performances. This includes responsibility for the load-in of a show and supervising the stage crew. The crew is assigned specific tasks. Some may serve as grips, that is, as stagehands responsible for moving equipment on the floor, as the curtain operator, or as fly operators in charge of flying scenery during a scene shift.

Responsible for developing a property list and supervising the property personnel is the *property master*. This person consults regularly with the director and the scene designer. Some of the property crew are assigned to scout and procure props for the approval of the property master, the scene designer, or designer's assistant. Others construct props and furniture as specified by prepared drawings and instructions. The prop crew for the running of the production may be given specific authority to handle floor props in a shift or to take charge of hand props or set dressings. They are rehearsed and assigned duties by the property supervisor with the assistance of the technical director and the stage manager.

All lighting is set up and operated by a crew of electricians following the developed light plot of the lighting designer. The crew is supervised by the *master electrician*, who may also be assigned to prepare instrument schedules and cue sheets. During rehearsals and performances some members of the crew are assigned as controlboard operators, as follow-spot operators, or as floor technicians. Following the plan of the sound designer, the *master sound technician* selects sound equipment and prepares, selects, or creates sound effects for the production. Assistance is provided by a sound crew, which may include a sound recorder and a sound operator. *Special-effects technicians* plan, create, and rig all special-effect devices. In television and film, special-effects departments are sizable and include a variety of assistants, pyrotechnicians, and other specialists.

BUILDING THE SHOW

To be an effective production technician, one needs to acquire the knowledge and skills in the crafts of the field. This comes only from proper instruction and supervised experience. In educational theatres, the production workers are often students assigned to the crew for a learning experience. For effective learning and for the safety of the student, close supervision is necessary. It is best if the student works along with a supervisor or other experienced worker. This type of instruction will assure that each step, technique, and tool process is understood and fully explained. Safety is vitally important in the shop. No one should use a tool alone without prior instruction. The student should provide evidence of knowledge of power tools before working in the shop. Ideally, prior classroom and laboratory instruction should have been undertaken. The potential for risk must be carefully understood by all crew members. Safety policies and regulations should be posted in the shop, and everyone should know of his and her responsibilities in the safety process. Having acquired the basics of tools and materials, crew experiences will continue to provide training in the more complex processes of the technology.

Crew heads must be fully aware of the operation of their shops. This includes preparation of work schedules, estimation of time and costs, methods of purchasing, stocking of supplies, equipment maintenance, etc. In addition, they need to cultivate qualities of effective management. Good planning, organization, and discipline are necessary to create a production of quality and artistic merit. Efficiency is an important ingredient in the production work. Shop time should be well spent; wasted or idle time and construction mistakes require costly and time-consuming corrections. Crew members should report for work on schedule and be released promptly at the end of the work period. Crews appreciate when their time is used productively and with minimum of unplanned overtime sessions.

A friendly, understanding, and personable environment should be established. More can be accomplished with a content and cooperative crew than a disgruntled and unhappy one. Thus it is important that crew members know how the objects they are constructing serve the action of the production. They will better appreciate the importance of their work and the use of the object or effect on stage. Their interest and pride in creating the scenery will be increased. This often requires a review of the appropriate drawing with the crew and a careful expla-

FIGURE 2–4 For the dramatic action to play successfully, a myriad of scenic details must be well planned, carefully assembled and constructed by the shop crew, and smoothly managed by the running crew. A scene from *Crimes of the Heart* at Northern Illinois University. (Photo by George Tarbay)

nation of the job and techniques to be employed. The crew head monitors the progress of the work and checks on quality to make certain the project is moving along on schedule. Decisions involving problems that arise during the construction process usually require the advice and approval of the shop manager or technical director.

RUNNING THE SHOW

Throughout the production, the *stage manager* is a key person in the management and operation of the show. The stage manager attends all rehearsals, working closely with the director, and develops the production book, assists in rehearsals, prepares schedules, and serves as liaison to all production areas. Beginning with the first technical rehearsal, the stage manager takes over the management of the production. For large shows there is often a production stage manager who supervises other stage managers and assistants. A professional production stage manager is responsible for maintaining the original direction of the performance and has authority in recasting and in rehearsing replacement actors.

In preparing for the first technical rehearsal, crew heads work with the stage manager to arrange the use of the backstage space for all crews and technical elements. They will determine the location of prop tables, scenery storage area, booths for quick costume changes, and traffic patterns for cast and crews. Good preparation will permit the technical rehearsals to run smoothly. If there are extensive or complicated shifts and cueing, it may be best to have a cue-to-cue rehearsal or a technical rehearsal without the cast. Crew members should report at least an hour before rehearsals and performances to set up the technical elements and run equipment checks before the opening of the show. The preshow checklist should detail these items and include mopping the

stage floor and arranging scenery and props for the first scene.

It is usually the task of the stage manager to plan the actual scene shifts. A **scenery shift plot** is prepared for each setup and change. A shift must be carefully sequenced for the proper order of events—which tasks must be accomplished first to allow others to follow. Sometimes the walls of the setting must be opened to remove furniture, and walls must be stripped of set dressings before they are moved offstage. **Spike marks** of colored tape or paint are needed to mark the location of each setting and its furniture. Similarly, offstage storage areas for each set and property item should be carefully selected and spiked. This often requires arranging items in a compact and safely stacked position that will not interfere with the shift and location of other scenery. Items must be returned to their storage locations to avoid unexpected clutter, interference with traffic patterns, delays and confusion in scene shifts, and injury to people or property. A scene shift is developed through repeated rehearsals under actual conditions of the performance. At first, shifts should not be hurried; but, as the tasks are learned, speed and coordination improve, and soon the movement of cast and crew will develop into a consistent routine. Shifts are usually timed, and efficiency is improved, if necessary, to keep within the allotted time for the scene change. Any difficulties that arise must be worked out before the next rehearsal and individual crew assignments amended or altered. The crew should review cues, update their job lists, and be advised on how to handle any repairs or emergencies. Dark clothing and quiet shoes should be worn by the crew to reduce the chances of being seen or heard in a scene shift. A no-curtain scene change requires a well-rehearsed and choreographed shifting plan that is attractive to watch and holds the attention of the audience until the next scene begins. At the end of the rehearsal or performance, cleanup tasks are assigned to the crew, props are put away, and the stage is readied for the next performance.

A scene shift will become a smooth and efficient operation if the crew steadfastly follows simple precautions.

1. Get ready and in position well in advance of the command to shift.
2. Prepare scene and prop items in easily handled loads. Padded baskets or boxes may help to remove assorted dishware or other objects.
3. Waste no motions. Do not go off or on stage empty-handed if it can be avoided.
4. Move rapidly but not so hurriedly as to endanger others. Actions must be reliably repeatable.
5. Maintain the established routine. Changes in the order of events may upset the coordination of the shift.
6. Keep an accurate list of your assignments, and have it handy for reference.
7. Be alert to difficulties and potential solutions in a shift, and inform the crew head so efficiency can be improved.
8. Avoid delays and holdups. Find expedient ways to double-check the setup and precise means of signaling to start the shift promptly and to indicate its completion.

Property Plots

Properties are often numerous, frequently small items, and extremely important to the business of the actors. Every prop should be traceable in a series of lists, charts, and plans detailing its placement and handling during a production. Nothing should be left to chance. This results in the need for well-prepared prop plots.

The Setup Plot. A setup plot is prepared for each scene of the performance to indicate the location of each property. A ground plan or chart is a common way to describe the set props in the setting. Furniture and large props must be marked on the set in the specified colored spike marks. Hand and decorative props are listed by location—on the table, on the mantel, and so on (see Figure 2–5). Prop tables are used for hand props offstage. A minimum of two tables, one on each side of the stage, is necessary. Frequently, a table is needed near each entrance to the setting. A chart lists the location of each prop on the table, or the tabletop can be covered with brown kraft paper and the location of each prop outlined with a felt-tipped pen. If the actor does not have the opportunity to come to the prop table, it may be necessary to hand the prop to the actor before he or she enters the scene. The setup plot must include all the tasks to be performed before the scene begins.

The Shifting Plot. This plot lists the changes of props between scenes in a production (Figure 2–6). The shifting plot must indicate what is removed from the stage, what is brought onstage, and the changes in location of props already on the set. A shift that must be accomplished in a blackout or in a very short time will require special planning and extra rehearsal time. Choreograph movements of the crew to achieve the greatest efficiency in time and effort. Careful planning is essential to prevent damage and injury. Movement should be planned to avoid an actor or a stagehand colliding with a prop person carrying a handful of props.

The Storage and Cleanup Plot. At the end of the performance, all props must be accounted for, inventoried, and placed in a secure place until the next performance. They must be found on stage where they have been placed, or where actors have been assigned to leave them. It makes little sense to waste valuable time searching for hand props, and it is absolutely senseless to be required to replace a prop that cannot be found. Lockable cabinets are used to secure props between performances. A good storage plot indicates precisely the listing of props on each shelf of the prop cabinet. This makes the inventory process easy. Traveling productions have special prop boxes designed with padded niches to house the

The Gentleman from Athens Act I,
Scene I (use red spike marks)

Furniture:

Sofa—RC
Armchair—DR
Coffee table—DR
Drum table—C
Wing chair—C
Writing table—LC
Straight chair—LC
Straight chair—UC
Hallway table—UR
Liquor cabinet—UR

On the writing table:

Briefcase
Pen and ink set

On the fireplace mantel:

2 candelabra

On the hall table, UR:

2 supper trays, dishes, food (Daniel)
Letter (Lee)

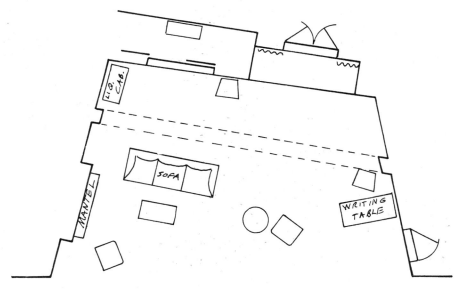

FIGURE 2–5 The property setup plot.

Shift: Act I, Scene 2 to Act II, Scene I
(use yellow spike marks)

Remove:

2 supper trays, dishes, food
Briefcase
Letter
Sofa

Bring on:

Fancy desk
3 telephones on desk
Legal papers on desk
Bottle of cognac on liquor cabinet
Calendar on desk
Bust of Socrates on desk

Move:

Up-center chair to behind desk

FIGURE 2–6 The property shift plot.

props and protect them in shipping. A list of the contents is often placed in the box lid or labeled in the compartments. Finally, a number of cleanup tasks must be included on the list. These include washing dishes and doing similar chores.

AFTER THE PRODUCTION

After the last performance, the stage usually must be cleared of scenery for the next event. Removing a setting is called a **strike**. If the production is going on to another theatre, this means dismantling the set for loading onto a vehicle for transport. Often, though, it is at the end of the run and the scenery will not be used again for this show. In this case, the strike removes the scenery but preserves components and materials for future use. Striking the set is a careful dismantling and not the destruction of the scenery. Many components are standard units—flats, platforms, etc.—which have cost-saving value to the company. Units that contain salvageable materials are disassembled for lumber, fabric, and hardware. Properties should be removed first before dismantling the scenery. They must be returned to storage or, if rented or borrowed, returned to their owners without delay. A strike requires careful planning by the technical director, shop technicians, and production crew heads to determine the order of activities and the assignment of crew duties. The work must be closely supervised and organized. Rushed and frenzied activity endangers the safety of workers.

THE PROFESSION

Scene technicians are a diverse group. Some may prepare themselves with a broad training in a variety of technical skills for employment where such diversity is required. Some may seek to become specialists for such careers as carpenters, scenic artists, property specialists, special-effects operators, etc. Others may strive for positions in management to become shop supervisors, technical directors, production managers, etc. Depending on their interests, skills, and diversity, traditional employment is available in live theatre (drama, dance, opera, musical revues), in television, in film, or in educational theatre (secondary school, college, university). But that is not all. Employment for those with technical abilities in theatre is not limited to the standard entertainment fields. Trained technicians are sought for technical opportunities related to industrial theatre (company meetings, sales promotions, new product introductions), convention booths, TV commercials, museum exhibits, cruise ship entertainment, and amusement/theme park entertainments.

Various organizations and publications offer valuable service to technical craftspeople. Many excellent books and journals are published directly pertaining to the many technologies in the field or are valuable resources for the technician. Professional associations assist members to keep abreast of current practices and developments in the field through journals, newsletters, workshops, seminars, conferences, and other activities; and contacts can be made with others in the profession for informal exchanges helpful in expanding knowledge and skills and in career advancement. Employment in some professional positions frequently requires union membership. Unions provide protection for workers and negotiate contracts. Although unions do not find work for their members, employment in many professional fields is improved by having a union card. One of the largest unions for technicians is the International Alliance of Theatrical Stage Employees and Moving Picture Machine Operators of the United States and Canada (IATSE), more commonly known as the IA.

SELECTED READINGS

BURRIS-MEYER, HAROLD, and EDWARD C. COLE, *Scenery for the Theatre* (rev. ed). Boston: Little, Brown, 1971.

CARTER, PAUL, *Backstage Forms*. New York: Broadway Press, 1990.

KATZ, JUDITH A., *The Business of Show Business*. New York: Harper & Row, 1981.

STERN, LAWRENCE, *Stage Management* (4th ed). Boston: Allyn & Bacon, 1992.

Technical Periodicals

Art Hazards News. Center for Safety in the Arts, 5 Beekman Street, New York, NY 10038.

Journal of the SMPTE. Society of Motion Picture and Television Engineers, 6706 Santa Monica Blvd., Hollywood, CA 90038.

Lighting Dimensions. P.O. Box 425, Mount Morris, IL 61054-0425.

Theatre Crafts. 135 Fifth Avenue, New York, NY 10010.

Theatre Design and Technology. U.S. Institute for Theatre Technology, 10 W. 19th Street, Suite 5A, New York, NY 10011-4206.

3

Scenic Drawings

Before scene construction actually begins, a planning process to design and describe the setting must be followed. The artistic conception, the first step in the planning process, is the task of the scenic designer and is revealed through a rendered design. With the help of the scene technician, approved designs are translated into construction terms. Until an environment has been completely visualized and dimensionalized, it is wasteful of time and materials to begin construction. Scenic designers and technicians employ a system of graphic representation to solve the artistic problems of the shape, appearance, and location, and the method of construction, for the scenic and property elements. Designs and the accompanying mechanical drawings are the result of this necessary planning process and serve as the means of communication required to actualize the setting. Learning this graphic language and developing skills in drafting are fundamental necessities for all work in scene technology.

TOOLS AND MATERIALS FOR DRAFTING

The Drawing Surface

Drawing boards and **drafting tables** are specially made to provide a smooth and warp-resistant structure for drafting. Treat them with care. They need protection from water, excessive heat, and physical damage. The side boards or metal edges used for the head of the T-square must be kept true and undamaged for drawing accuracy. A vinyl or heavy paper drawing board cover is a valuable acquisition. When attached to the drawing surface, it provides a surface toughness that resists dents and holes made by

17

drawing instruments. The drawing board or table should be slightly larger than the largest size of drawing paper used.

Basic Drafting Tools

Horizontal lines are drawn with the **T-square**. The head of the square is placed along the left side of the drawing board and held securely while lines are drawn along the top edge of the blade (Figure 3–1). T-squares with clear plastic edges are smoother than all-wooden blades, and they permit adjacent lines to be seen. The T-square should be long enough for the size of the paper but should not be longer than the width of the drawing board or table. Drafters who are left-handed should place the head of the square along the right edge of the board. In drawing lines with the T-square, beware of the extreme end of the blade because it has a tendency to waver.

The **45° triangle** and the **30°–60° triangle** are standard for drawing angles in drafting. The better ones are made of clear, nonyellowing plastic, which is scratch resistant and retains good edges. The 8-, 10-, and 12-inch sizes are the most common for scenic drawings. Vertical and angled lines are drawn by placing a triangle firmly against the upper edge of the T-square. Some experience is needed to learn how to hold the T-square

FIGURE 3–1 Drawing board and T-square.

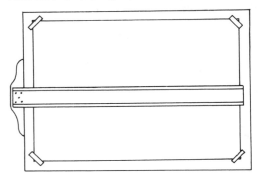

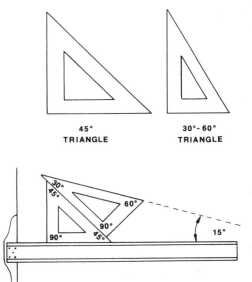

FIGURE 3–2 Triangles used in drawing.

and triangle securely to achieve true parallel lines in a drawing. By using these two triangles in combination, a variety of angles in 15° increments can be formed (Figure 3–2). An **adjustable triangle** is useful for drawing other angles. The blade has an adjustable gauge from 0° to 45°. Also valuable is a plastic **protractor**, which is used for laying out or measuring angles.

Irregular curves are produced by tools commonly called **French curves** (Figure 3–3). They are available in a variety of sizes and shapes. On a drawing, special points are first established for an irregular curve. Then, an appropriate arc on the French curve is found to produce the curve desired. **Templates** are thin plastic tools used to increase the speed and accuracy of drafting. There are templates, in a variety of scales, to aid in drawing many items. Circle, square, ellipse, and furniture templates are particularly useful for scenery drawings.

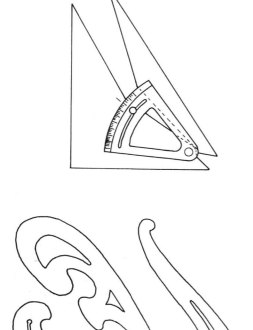

FIGURE 3–3 Adjustable triangle and French curves.

Drawing Instruments

Instruments for drawing include compasses and dividers (Figure 3–4). **Bow compasses** are needed to draw circles and arcs. Both a small and a large one are desirable. An extension bar is a needed attachment for the largest circles. Some compasses can be fitted with either lead holders or ruling pens. **Dividers** have two metal points and are used to provide precise measurements for transfer to a drawing or to divide a line into equal parts. Drawing instruments may be acquired individually or in instrument sets.

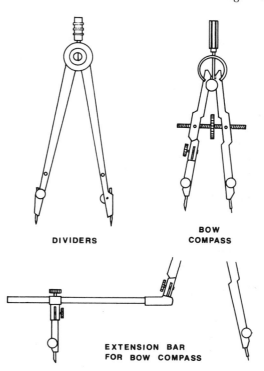

DIVIDERS

BOW COMPASS

EXTENSION BAR FOR BOW COMPASS

FIGURE 3–4 Drawing instruments.

Architect's Scale Rule

Most drawings are reductions of actual proportions of scenic objects. An **architect's scale rule** is used to achieve this. The triangular-shaped rule is the most common. It contains eleven different scales plus a full foot ruler. On each face of the rule there are two scales, so it is important to learn to read the proper numbers and lines. Find the scale with a 1 appearing on the left edge of the ruler (Figure 3–5). This is the 1″ = 1′-0″ scale. To the left of the 0 on this scale is a foot divided into inches and fractions much like a standard ruler. To the right of the 0 is a row of numbers—1, 2, 3, and so on—representing feet. To measure 2′-6″ in this scale, you would begin at the 2-foot mark and move left past the 0 to the 6 on the

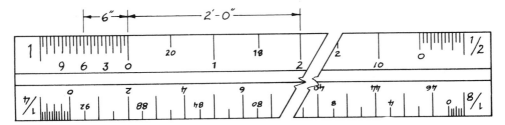

FIGURE 3–5   Architect's scale rule (triangular type).

divided foot scale. Note that the ½″ = 1′-0″ scale begins at the other end of this rule face and the foot measurements read to the left of the 0 in a row of numbers nearer the edge of the rule. Do not confuse these two different rows of numbers when using the scale rule. If you have not used a scale rule before, you will need to practice reading the scale with a variety of measurements.

Drawing Materials and Aids

There are a variety of **drawing papers**. The better ones are suitable for both pencil and ink and have a slight matte surface to hold the line shapes. Vellum, which has 100% rag content, is the most common. It can be used for overlay and for reproducing copies. The paper is held to the drawing board with drafting tape or drafting dots. Paper 18″ × 24″ and 24″ × 36″ are the most used sizes for scenic drawings.

Wooden drawing pencils, lead holders, and **mechanical pencils** are used for drafting (Figure 3–6). Lead holders handle thick leads, which must be kept sharpened to a conical point by a **lead pointer**. Mechanical pencils contain leads of drawing thickness and are available in 0.3 mm, 0.5 mm, 0.7 mm, and 0.9 mm sizes. Graphite lead is categorized in degrees of hardness: 9H (extremely hard), 8H, 7H, 6H, 5H, 4H, 3H, 2H, H, F, HB, B, 2B, 3B, 4B, 5B, 6B, and 7B (very soft). Soft lead is used primarily for sketching rather than drafting. Lead that is too soft smears easily; lead that is too hard tends to leave dents in the drawing surface.

Medium to medium-hard leads, such as H, 2H, 3H, and 4H, are satisfactory for most mechanical drawings. A **sandpaper paddle** is used to keep pencil leads to pinpoint sharpness. Pencil leads on compasses are sandpapered sharp by flattening the lead on the outside edge like the point of a chisel.

No drafter can do without a **soft eraser**, the softest possible, to remove lines and keep the drawing clean. Smudges can be removed

FIGURE 3–6   Drawing pencils and point sharpeners.

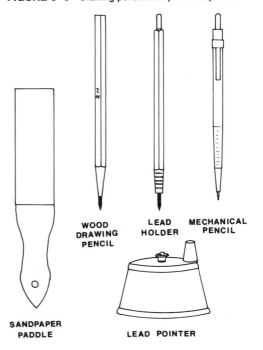

WOOD DRAWING PENCIL

LEAD HOLDER

MECHANICAL PENCIL

SANDPAPER PADDLE

LEAD POINTER

by a **dry cleaning pad**, and a **drafting brush** will remove loose graphic and eraser crumbs. Attempting to clean a drawing with your hand usually results in smears. When extremely clear copies are sought, drawings are finalized in ink. This is done by either ruling pens or technical drawing pens. Inking a drawing is a long, cautious process and requires considerable skill. It is not essential for most scenic drafting.

The materials and tools described are the essential items needed for drafting, and they are relatively low in cost. Large production centers and designers or technicians with extensive production schedules may find complete instrument sets and more elaborate equipment to be a good investment. For instance, the parallel straightedge replaces the T-square, and the drafting machine replaces both the T-square and the triangles. These are precision equipment that require frequent checks to assure accuracy and alignment. However, they enhance both the ease and the speed of the drafting process.

DRAFTING PRACTICE

Developing drafting skills takes experience. To be able to draw clean, easy-to-read, and accurate drawings requires a knowledge of drawing tools, a mastery of drafting techniques, and the development of good drafting habits. For precision and service, quality tools are essential. Know how to use, clean, adjust, and store them properly. An architect's scale rule should be used for measuring only. If used for drawing lines, the calibrated edge can be damaged, which will reduce accuracy in reading dimensions. Similarly, the usefulness of a T-square and triangles can be destroyed if they are used as straightedges for cutting paper with a knife. Learn to use all tools properly. It will take practice to hold the T-square and triangles while drawing firm, clean lines. Pencils must be sharpened frequently while drawing to assure uniformity of lines.

Cleanliness is essential in drafting. Before beginning a drawing project, be sure all equipment is clean. Remove all eraser and dust particles from the drawing board, and wipe tools with a clean cloth. If necessary, use a damp cloth on triangles and other tools, then remove the water with a dry cloth. Keep the drawing clean during the drafting process. Do not sharpen pencils over the drawing. Wash your hands occasionally, and keep the paper and equipment clean. Even the oil and perspiration of your hands will add smudges to the drawing.

Before starting a drawing, the proper scale should be chosen and the object to be drawn should be centered on the paper. It is good practice to draw in all the object lines very lightly at first. It is easy to erase light lines. Once the object has been fully drawn, erase unneeded lines and the pencil dots used to locate the outlines. After checking the drawing for accuracy, the final lines can be drawn in the proper line weight.

DRAFTING CONVENTIONS AND SYMBOLS

Just as no language can be mastered without a uniform vocabulary, graphic communication requires a set of commonly understood conventions and symbols. Clarity and consistency are vital in technical drawings for exact and efficient communication. Drafting methods used in the various architectural and engineering professions have many similarities but also differences. These differences are a result of drawing needs that require special conventions and symbols. Thus, standards or guidelines are established to provide a common graphic language for a specific field. A set of standards serves as a model for efficient communication. Scenery is a specialized field with a need for a consistent graphic language. The drafting conventions and symbols presented in this chapter adhere to the standards for scenic design and technical production established by the Graphics Standard Board of the United States Institute for Theatre Technology (USITT).

Lines

Lines are given specific meanings in a drawing. They are drawn in different patterns and different thicknesses (weights)[1] as can be seen in Figure 3–7.

Figure 3–8 provides an example of the use of these lines in a drawing.

Lettering

Hand lettering is a skill that each drafter must develop. Characters must be easy to read and capable of being drawn easily and rapidly. The single-stroke uppercase Gothic style is most suitable for this purpose (Figure 3–9). Learn through practice how to perfect the strokes needed to create legible and uniform letters. Upper and lower guidelines may be helpful in achieving consistency in height. Lowercase letters should not be used unless necessary to conform with other established graphic standards.

Dimensions

As with letters, numerals must be drawn precisely to prevent miscommunication and costly errors in construction. Sevens should not be mistaken for nines, nor fives for sixes. Learn to form numbers accurately. Dimensions greater than 1 foot are separated into feet and inches, the foot indication with a single apostrophe followed by a dash and inches with a double apostrophe, as follows: 2'-6", 7'-0", 9'-7½". Dimensions less than 1 foot are presented with no foot indication, such as, 10", ¾", 8½". Note that fractions are reserved for inches alone. To indicate the heights of platforms and stair treads above the stage, the heights are given in inches, circled, and located near the center of the

platform or tread. Where space is not sufficient for dimensions, they should be placed nearby, parallel with the lower edge of the paper and directed to the location by a leader line. Examples of dimensioning in

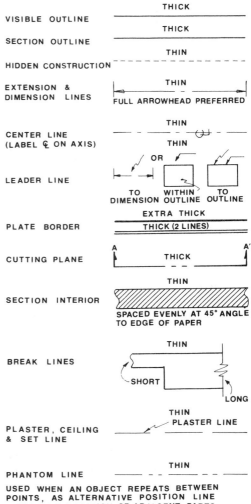

FIGURE 3–7 Types of lines used in drawing.

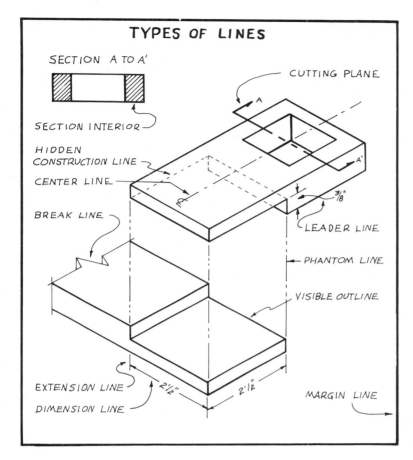

TYPES OF LINES

SECTION A TO A'

SECTION INTERIOR

HIDDEN
CONSTRUCTION LINE

CENTER LINE

BREAK LINE

EXTENSION LINE

DIMENSION LINE

CUTTING PLANE

A

A'

3/8"

LEADER LINE

PHANTOM LINE

VISIBLE OUTLINE

2½"

2'|½"

MARGIN LINE

FIGURE 3–8 Types of lines.

this and other circumstances are shown in Figure 3–10. Whenever possible dimensions should be located on only two sides of an object and logically grouped. They should be placed to be read from left to right and from bottom to top parallel with the lines of the object.

FIGURE 3–9 Lettering.

ABCDEFGHIJKLM
NOPQRSTUVWXYZ

Title Block

Drawings are labeled with a title block located either in the lower right corner or in a strip along the bottom of the drawing. The location of the block should be consistent throughout the entire set of drawings for a project. The following information should be included in the title block:

1. Name of the production and, if appropriate, the act and scene
2. Name of the producing organization and theatre or both
3. Drawing title

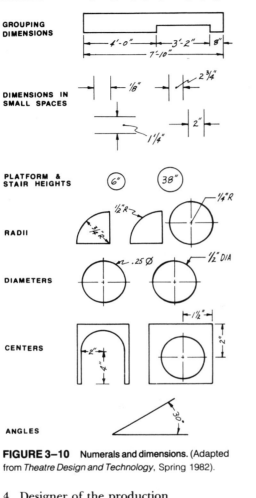

FIGURE 3–10 Numerals and dimensions. (Adapted from *Theatre Design and Technology*, Spring 1982).

4. Designer of the production
5. Drafter, if different from the designer
6. Drawing number
7. Predominant scale of the drawing
8. Date of the drawing
9. Approval of drawing, if applicable

Symbols

Symbols are used for the convenience of identifying objects that have some standard-

ization in shape and size. A symbol has an accepted meaning so the drafter is saved unnecessary written explanations. Figures 3–11 and 3–12 list the scenic symbols recommended by the USITT Graphics Standard Board. A furniture template contains some

FIGURE 3–11 Drafting symbols for ground plans.

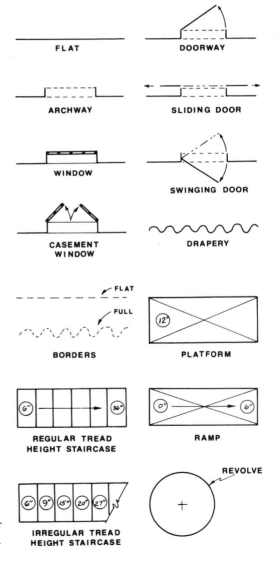

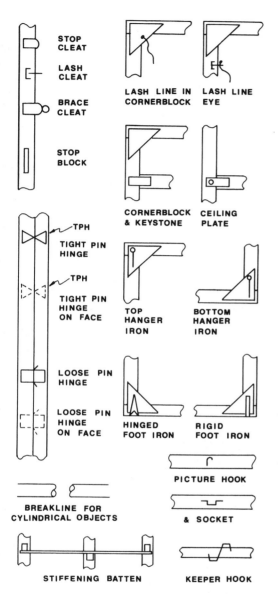

FIGURE 3–12 Drafting symbols for construction drawings.

a cutting plane usually at a height of 4'-0" above the stage floor or at whatever height is necessary to provide the most descriptive view of the setting. Objects such as fireplaces, shelves, and other built-in units not standardized in size or style should be drawn at a sectional cutting plane of 4'-0" or any other view that would be most descriptive. Objects on the drawing located above the 4'-0" cutting plane should be drawn with a hidden construction line. This includes chandeliers, ceiling beams, drapery borders, and scenery flown overhead for use in other scenes.

THE PLANNING PROCESS

Dramatic production has become a vast collaborative art over the years as design specialties have expanded and as growth in modern technology has multiplied the number of craft areas. This has increased the difficulty of achieving unity in the aesthetic solution for a production that successfully reinforces the inner meaning of the play and its communication to the audience. Production philosophy places emphasis on the need for a synthesis of all design and technology areas to a single and commanding design goal. The term *scenography* embodies this concept. Whether or not there is a single scenographer (or master artist) who conceives the total artistic effect in scenery, lighting, and costumes, individual designers and technicians must work together in a truly collaborative way to achieve artistic unity. Scenography stresses the close relationship of the designer and the technician if for no other reason than the extreme difficulty for a designer to be proficient in all areas of modern technology. Technicians must be aware of the aesthetic goal of a production and assist the designer with knowledge of materials and techniques, which can lead to imaginative design solutions. This becomes of particular importance during the design and planning process.

patterns that can be accepted as symbols. However, generalized shapes such as bookcases and tables may require labeling for clarity. The ground plan (also called a floor plan) is a horizontal sectional drawing with

The Design

Once the creative concept has been crystalized, the scenic designer (or scenographer) describes the setting by means of a **colored perspective sketch** or a **three-dimensional model** or both. The sketch is sometimes preferred because of the additional time and effort necessary to build a satisfactory model in wood, clay, or cardboard. A model is also bulky and sometimes fragile for the extensive use it must have. Nevertheless, models are often the best choice, especially for settings that are complex in construction, contain multiple acting levels, or must be shifted or rearranged. Since it is scaled in three dimensions, a model is an easier way to visualize the actual setting. A model is especially valuable for directors, producers, and others who have difficulty conceiving space from a perspective rendering. In any case, the sketch or model should be complete enough to be a full representation of the setting. It should give a descriptive view of the style and type of architecture and decoration; the arrangement of doors, windows, and scenic elements; the choice and selection of furniture and properties; and the color and texture of all visible items. It serves as a valuable aid to the director, the actors, the entire staff, and the technicians as to the appearance the scene will take.

Part of the design process is the preparation of a number of scaled mechanical drawings. In fact, some information gained in mechanical drawings is usually required before completion of the perspective sketch or model. It is often a chicken-and-egg question whether the sketch or model is created first because each designer works in a different way. One of the first things to learn before creating a finished design is the space provided by the stage: the height, width, and depth of the area. Some of this relates to the need to provide for the location of a setting that is appropriate for audience sight lines in a theatre. **Sight-line drawings** consist of

FIGURE 3–13 Designer's perspective sketch. The setting for *Noises Off*, designed by the author.

a horizontal sectional drawing and a vertical sectional drawing (Figure 3–14). These show the actual space on the stage and the location of the extreme seats of the auditorium. The setting must conform to the space limitations of the facility and be visible to the live audience. Sight-line drawings can be created more rapidly by using tracing paper overlays on master drawings of the facility. Master drawings should contain all information about the stage, including location of all rigging and permanent scenic equipment.

The **ground plan** and **front-elevation** **drawings** are indispensable drawings of the designer. The ground plan assists the designer in determining the space and arrangement of the setting on the stage floor (Figure 3–15). This includes the location and widths of all scenic elements, furniture arrangements, masking units, window and door backings, and the offstage space for property and scene storage. Sight lines from the extreme seats should be drawn in to guide the designer in composing the plan of the setting. The ground plan must be complete and accurate. It will be of use to the

FIGURE 3–14 A horizontal plan and vertical sectional drawing reveal the extreme sight lines governing the location of a setting and the masking elements.

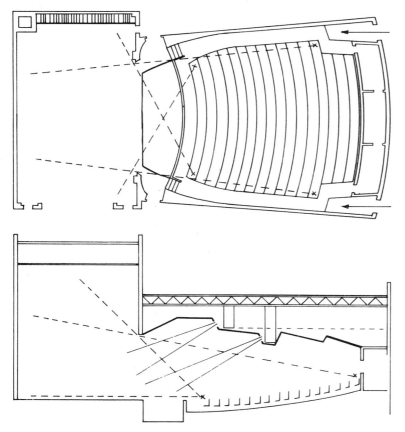

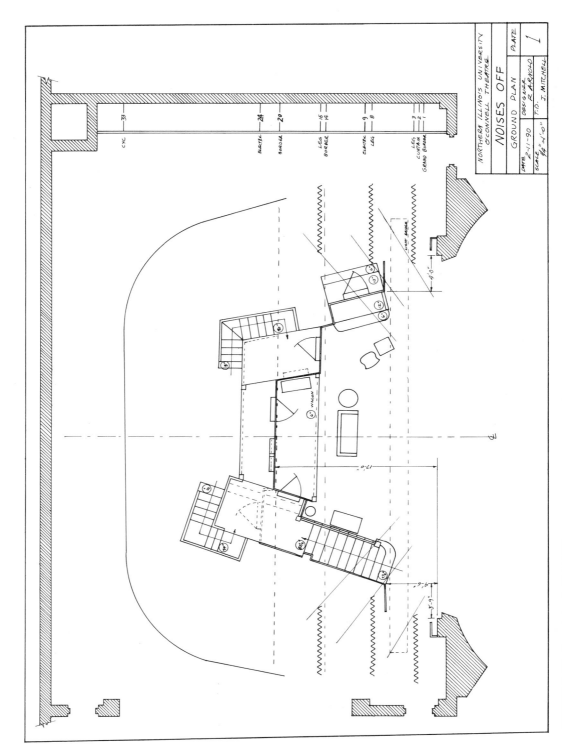

FIGURE 3–15 Ground plan for *Noises Off*.

director in blocking the action, to the lighting designer in determining the light plot, and to the property and scene technicians.

The sectional drawing is a section view of the setting on stage along the center line. It shows audience sight lines and reveals the trim heights of the masking and the angles and locations for lighting the set (Figure 3–16).

Front elevations are scaled mechanical drawings showing the front views of all the scenery. The setting is flattened out, and

FIGURE 3–16 Sectional drawing for *Noises Off*.

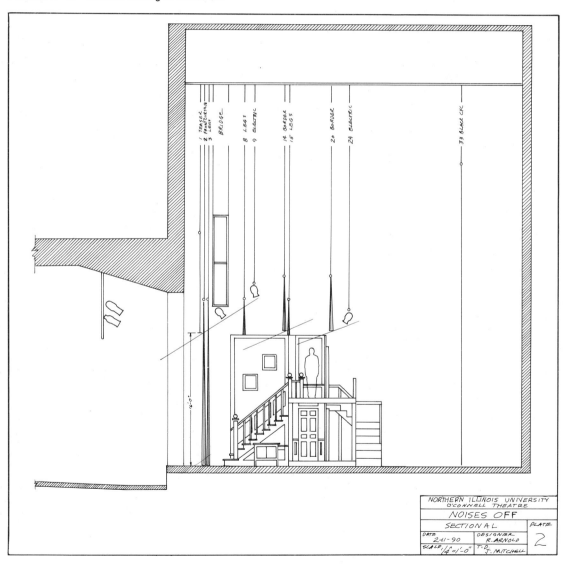

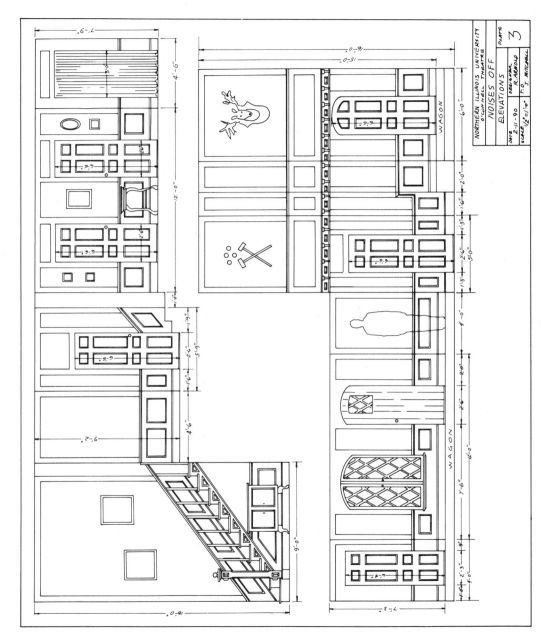

FIGURE 3–17 Front elevation drawing for *Noises Off*.

each visible surface is drawn in a single plane (Figure 3–17). With knowledge of the width of scenic elements as determined by the ground plan, the designer concentrates on designing the vertical proportions and relationships of the various parts of the setting in exact dimensions. The designer is concerned with the composition of areas: the size and nature of the decoration, wallpaper patterns, and architectural trim. Elevations include window draperies, wall hangings, set dressings, and furniture or objects placed on or against the walls.

The ground plan and elevation drawings are usually drawn on a scale of ¼″, ⅜″, or ½″ = 1′-0″. However, this scale is inadequate to describe the details of a fireplace, a door panel, architectural trim, and similar small items. Furthermore, three-dimensional objects require more complicated drawing techniques. These items are described in **detail drawings** in a scale of ¾″, 1″, or larger. A two-dimensional detail is the simplest to draw (Figure 3–18). The object is drawn in detail, and a scaled grid is superimposed over it to help the technician scribe the design directly on the construction material. A three-dimensional object must be described in a multiview drawing such as orthographic projection or isometric drawing. These types of drawings are considered later in this chapter.

The scenic designer is also responsible for **painter's elevation drawings**. These drawings are scaled front elevations rendered in color to aid scenic artists in the layout and painting of the scenery. They include the proportions, colors, appropriate highlight and shadow tones, wallpaper designs, cartooning, and ornamentations. Their necessity is increased when the designer is not the chief scenic artist. They often include actual paint samples. Elevations for a drop or a detailed ornament will require gridding in 1′-0″ intervals for transferring the design to the canvas unless it can be cast onto scenic surfaces by lighting projection.

FIGURE 3–18 Detail drawing showing the flat cutout of a mirrored hat rack.

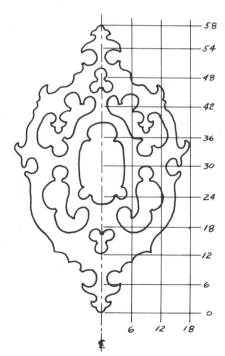

The Construction Drawings

While the designer's plans fully describe the setting, they do not inform the shop technicians how it is to be constructed. Construction drawings are needed to provide the building details and specifications. These drawings are scaled rear elevations of the scenery that reveal the nature of the construction (see Figure 3–19). When drawing rear views from the front elevations, the drafter must not forget to reverse the order of the walls to achieve true rear elevations. Construction drawings provide information on all materials, hardware, and methods of construction. This includes all joining, bracing, stiffening, rigging, and shifting details. Dimensions must be complete and accurate.

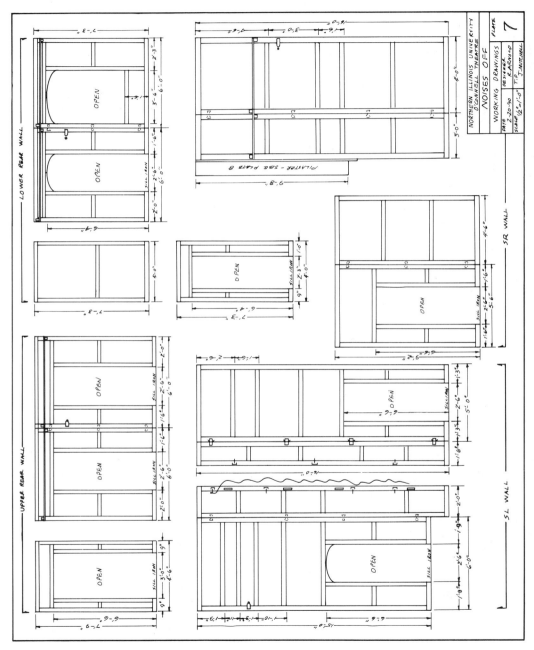

FIGURE 3–19 Construction drawings.

The scenery must be separated into small units that are appropriate for transporting, handling, and shifting. The methods of assembling these units must be indicated. Symbols are used to identify standard construction details. Specifications and notes should be provided on the drawing for describing special construction, unfamiliar procedures, and materials. The completeness of detail on working drawings will depend upon the experience of the shop personnel and the established construction practices of the shop.

MULTIVIEW DRAWINGS

Because paper is essentially two dimensional, special methods must be used to show the various sides of a three-dimensional object. **Orthographic projection** is one of the simplest ways of accomplishing this. This type of drawing views the object from more than one location. Each plane of the object is drawn from a different location. For instance, the top view is seen looking directly

down on it, the front view is seen directly from the front, and so on. Usually three views—top, front, and one side—are sufficient to detail the object, but complex shapes may require other views as well. When a top, front, and one side are adequate, the drawing paper is divided into four equal areas (see Figure 3–20), and the views are drawn in. Lines are projected by T-square and 45° triangle to eliminate repeated measuring with the scale rule.

Several other types of multiview drawings present a solid object in a more pictorial way. Chief among these is **isometric drawing**, which views the object at an angle to expose three sides simultaneously. A vertical line and a 30° angle to the right and the left form the isometric axes on which this drawing method is based. All lines parallel with these lines are formed the same way and can be measured with the scale rule (see Figure 3–21). Lines not parallel with the isometric axis must be located by drawing parallel lines and measuring to find points where the nonisometric lines are located. Curves and arcs require special construction. An isometric

FIGURE 3–20 Orthographic projection drawing of a bench.

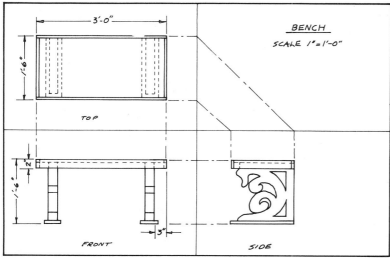

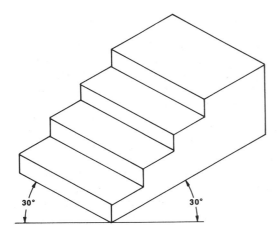

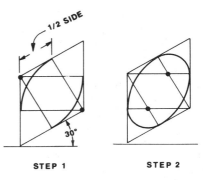

STEP 1   STEP 2

FIGURE 3–22 Drawing isometric circles.

FIGURE 3–23 Oblique and cabinet drawings.

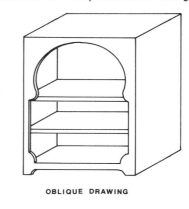

OBLIQUE DRAWING

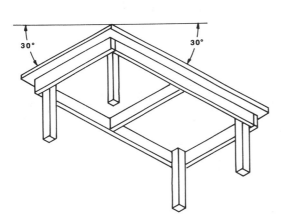

FIGURE 3–21 Isometric drawings.

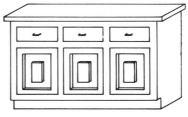

CABINET DRAWING

circle can be formed by four arcs. First draw a parallelogram that will enclose the circle. Lines are extended from the two largest corners to the center point of the opposite sides of the square. A compass placed at those corners can draw arcs between those lines. The small arcs are drawn by placing the pivot of the compass at the intersection of these lines (see Figure 3–22). Isometric drawings also can be positioned to show the front, end, and bottom of an object. Dimen-

sion lines on isometric drawings should parallel the lines of the object.

The **oblique drawing** is similar to isometric except one side is shown in full front view parallel to the plane of the paper. The other side is at a 30° or 45° angle. This type of drawing is particularly useful for objects with considerable detail on one face and less on the others. The side with the greatest detail is chosen for the front view. The drafting approach is much the same as for an isometric drawing. A variation of oblique drawing is called **cabinet drawing**. The same drawing procedure is used, but the receding side is reduced to half its length to eliminate the effect of distortion. This drawing is appropriate for objects that have considerable length in one dimension. Figure 3–23 shows examples of oblique and cabinet drawings.

REPRODUCTION OF DRAWINGS

Usually several copies of designer's and technician's drawings are needed for the production staff. A number of reproduction methods are available, including traditional blueprinting. One common process, called whiteprinting, is affordable and easy to achieve. A whiteprinter uses sensitized paper for printing. The translucent paper original is placed on top of the coated whiteprint sheet to pass through an ultraviolet light source for printing. The whiteprint paper is then developed by exposure to ammonia vapor. The result is a blue or black line drawing with a white background. Most whiteprinters have means of adjusting print speed for different types of paper.

COMPUTER-AIDED DRAFTING

The development of computer technology has made possible the use of the computer as a valuable tool in the development of

FIGURE 3–24 The finished setting on stage. A scene from *Noises Off* at Northern Illinois University. (Photo by George Tarbay)

drawings. Computer-aided drafting and design (CADD) systems were once limited entirely to large mainframe computers with vast memory capabilities. Now, however, technology has made CADD software available for affordable microcomputers and is improving in sophistication. The computer speeds up the work of drafting, thus allowing more time for the planning and testing of ideas. As information is fed into the computer, the graphic material is stored for later use. Portions of the drawing can be enlarged for the development of the smallest details. Changes and alterations can be made, and all data can be brought together into the final document. This eliminates errors in drafting by hand and shortens the process of drafting. Structures can be rotated for study of many views and be enhanced by multiple-layer or overlay views to coordinate complex details.

A variety of CADD software is available ranging from relatively low-cost to expensive systems according to what and how much they are able to accomplish. Some are designed primarily for two-dimensional drawing; others for three-dimensional, perspective, or color renderings. Most are designed for use with the IBM or Macintosh family of microcomputers. The IBM computers and IBM-compatible computers are strongly favored by many business and industrial users for their speed and flexibility. The Macintosh units with their pull-down menus and ease of operation are somewhat more user-friendly. Some software programs, such as *Autocad*, are popular and available for either IBM or Macintosh systems.

Figure 3–25 is a construction drawing created with *MacDraft*, a basic, inexpensive CADD software for the Macintosh com-

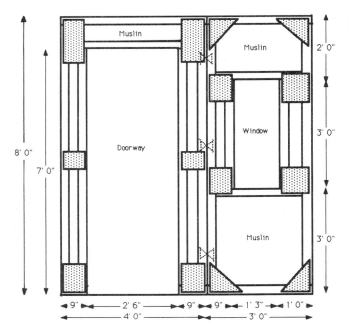

FIGURE 3–25 A construction drawing produced with *MacDraft* software.

puter, and printed on a dot-matrix printer. This simple software creates scaled drawings, dimension lines, circles and arcs, a zoom feature to add small details, and permits the rotation of objects. Adding fill patterns (notice the cornerblocks and keystones) makes it possible to clarify different parts of the construction. Another CADD program, *WalkThrough,* by the Virtus Corporation, is an interesting program especially for the designer. In a very short period of time, a designer can develop a three-dimensional model and explore or test ideas and basic design concepts. Any conceivable vantage point can be achieved as the perspective rendering can be turned to any view desired. Figure 3–26 is a view of *Walk-Through*'s basic screen, showing the palette of tools and modifiers, a view window revealing a ground plan or top view, and "walk

view" window showing a three-dimensional view of the setting. As changes are made in the view window, the three-dimensional view is immediately altered.

The CADD systems are competing more and more with manual drafting and design processes. They are useful for scenic, lighting, and costume designers as well as scene technicians. Easy modifications permit the designer and director to meet together at a work station to view visual ideas and test alterations instantly. Also, CADD menus provide the most frequent command options in the drafting process. In addition, the user can usually customize or program the system by storing in the "library" graphic symbols or items that can be quickly called up for placement in a drawing. Repeated items once created can be located anywhere in the drawing. This eliminates many time-

FIGURE 3–26 The *Walk Through* screen showing the tool palette, a ground plan, and a perspective view of a setting. Scene design by **Darwin Reid Payne.** (Courtesy of the Virtus Corporation and reprinted courtesy of *Theatre Design and Technology*)

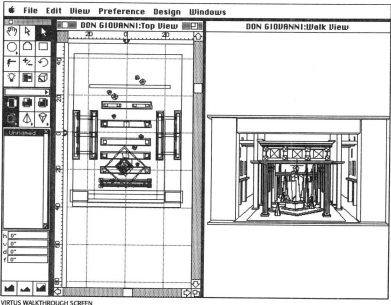

VIRTUS WALKTHROUGH SCREEN

consuming and repetitive tasks for the drafter. The computer stores all information and, unlike a manually drawn plate, it is easy to change, alter, and correct mistakes on the monitor. Time is then available to test alternative solutions and designs or to make modifications of previously made drawings. The computer itself determines dimensions and places them on the drawing on command. Some CADD systems can be programmed to produce on the drawing a cut list (list of lumber or other material by measured lengths) and a bill of materials such as hardware and other items required in construction. This is making CADD software a practical and indispensable drafting tool in many shops. The final document can be produced on regular printers or, as is best for large drawings, on pencil or ink plotters.

SELECTED READINGS

DORN, DENNIS, and MARK SHANDA, *Drafting for the Theatre.* Carbondale and Edwardsville, IL: Southern Illinois University Press, 1992.

FRENCH, THOMAS E., and CHARLES J. VIERCK, *A Manual of Engineering Drawing for Students and Draftsmen* (9th ed.). New York: McGraw-Hill, 1960.

PARKER, OREN W., *Sceno-Graphic Techniques* (3rd ed.). Carbondale and Edwardsville, IL: Southern Illinois University Press, 1987.

ROSE, RICH, *AutoCad Onstage.* White Hall, VA: Betterway, 1990.

ROSE, RICH, *Drafting Scenery for Theatre, Film and Television.* White Hall, VA: Betterway, 1990.

SWEET, HARVEY, *Graphics for the Performing Arts.* Boston: Allyn & Bacon, 1985.

WYATT, WILLIAM F., *General Architectural Drawing.* Peoria, IL: Chas. A. Bennett, 1969.

4

Safety and Health

That theatrical production work may be "hazardous to your health" is a fact recognized by anyone who has the slightest experience in the field. The stage and studio are cluttered with scene-related equipment of all kinds. Machinery and work stations hang above, to the sides, and often below the performance area. The great diversity of crafts that are involved in contemporary scene technology requires numerous, varied, and potentially dangerous shop facilities, tools, and scenic materials. Power demands (electricity, air, and hydraulics) have greatly increased in recent years. Modern technology and chemistry have provided new construction materials and processes that create new and different hazards to health. In fact, we are just beginning to learn the long-term dangers of noise, vapors, and air-borne particles. Additionally, an auditorium by its very nature attracts large numbers of people, thereby necessitating maximum safety pre-

cautions. Accidents and hazardous conditions are generally the result of ignorance, carelessness, and haste. Only a concerted effort by each artist and craftsperson can provide an environment appropriate for human safety and quality health.

SAFETY CODES AND REGULATIONS

The development of safety standards and practices historically began in the United States as the concern of private or nonprofit service organizations, groups formed by those intent on improving safety in the home, on the street, and in the workplace. The National Safety Council is one of the leading safety organizations. Others include the American Society of Safety Engineers, the National Board of Fire Underwriters, the National Fire Protection Association (NFPA), and the American National Standards Institute (ANSI). In many of these organizations, standards of safety are developed by consensus. ANSI, for instance, establishes consensus standards by creating working committees composed of members representing all groups and agencies who are involved and would be affected by the standard. When created, these standards are published and circulated to the particular industry or groups. They are only advisory unless adopted as a regulation by a governmental agency.

Building Codes

Most cities and counties have ordinances governing the design, construction, quality of materials, use, and maintenance of building structures. The purpose of these building codes is to establish minimum construction standards for the safety, health, and property of the citizenry. With the exception of a few major cities that prepare their own codes, most city and county codes are adopted from one of several model codes. Developed, published, and promoted by service organizations, these model codes are known as the Uniform Building Code, the Basic Building Code, the National Building Code, and the Southern Standards Building Code. Building codes are revised every few years.

National Electric Code

The National Electric Code is a comprehensive set of electric safety practices developed by the National Fire Protection Association. This model code has no legal basis by itself, but these standards are usually adopted entirely or in part by local and state governments for enforcement in their geographic areas.

Product Safety

The Underwriters Laboratory, Inc., associated with the National Fire Protection Association, has long been influential in the safety of electrical equipment. The UL label

FIGURE 4–1 In the creation of a scenic environment for a production, many safety and health precautions are to be taken. Setting for *Parsifal* at the Bavarian State Opera National Theatre, Munich, Germany. Designer: Gunther Schneider-Siemsson. (Photo by Alexander F. Adducci)

is granted to electrical equipment that, in extensive tests, meets minimum standards of safety. Manufacturers submit items of equipment to Underwriters Laboratory and pay for the cost of the testing procedures. As a result, the vast majority of electrical tools and products on the market are UL labeled, indicating that they meet protective standards when installed and operated in the correct fashion.

A history of injuries and accidents caused by consumer products led to a congressional act in 1972 that established the Consumer Products Safety Commission. This is a federal regulatory agency that examines consumer products for potential danger and injury to individuals. It has the power to ban unsafe products from the market.

Occupational Safety and Health Administration

In 1970, the enactment of the Occupational Safety and Health Act established a federal agency specifically dealing with safety in the workplace. The Occupational Safety and Health Administration (OSHA) was charged with developing safety and health standards for industry and enforcing these standards through inspections and penalties. Initially, OSHA adopted existing major consensus standards, including those developed by ANSI and the NFPA. This legislation was aimed at achieving uniformity in safety regulation among state and local governments and industry. OSHA's authority is extremely broad, covering construction practices, building design, fire protection, ventilation, electrical equipment, industrial protective equipment, machinery usage, noise and light exposure, air contaminants, and sanitary conditions.

A new awareness of safety and health conditions and practices has resulted from this legislation. Both employer and employee are obliged to be aware of safety standards and to put them into practice.

Another federal agency formed by the same act is the National Institute for Occupational Safety and Health (NIOSH). This organization functions to conduct studies and research leading to the development of criteria for occupational health and safety standards.

FIRE SAFETY

Fire can result from the use of open flame without taking proper precautions, from the improper storage of combustible materials, from inadequate wiring or failure in electrical equipment, from failure of a structure to comply with fire codes, and from improper fire safety and prevention practices.

The Physical Facility

Properly designed and constructed buildings for performances have special requirements for the safety of occupants. A number of theatres, auditoriums, and other public assembly halls have been sources of well-known and unfortunate disasters in the past. With this history, building and fire codes require construction practices and preventative devices for the dangers of smoke, fumes, fire, and panic:

Fire-retardant construction: The use of fire-resistant materials, fire walls to contain the spread of fire, fire-retardant paint, plaster, and coatings rated to withstand heat for a specific period of time.

Fire containment and control devices: Sliding and rolling fire doors and fire curtains to contain fire spread. Ventilation systems and smoke vents to direct the fire by exhausting smoke and fumes. These are often activated by heat-melting fusible links or other thermal devices.

Fire extinguishing equipment: Automatic sprinkler systems, fire extinguishers, stand pipes, and hoses for early suppression of fires.

Detection and warning equipment: Fire detection systems, fire alarms, smoke and thermal detectors.

Appropriate means of egress: A specific number, location, and size of exits; panic hardware on doors; a particular audience seating plan and capacity; carefully designed aisles and passageways to provide rapid and unobstructed egress to the outside.

An emergency lighting system: In a power failure, emergency lighting helps an audience leave the building. Emergency lights are usually powered by batteries. They include exit signs, aisle lights, and lighting in lobbies, stairs, passageways, and all other rooms leading to the building exit.

In an auditorium facility, responsibility for audience safety rests with the house staff. However, everyone working in the building has an obligation to the maintenance and safety of its operation. Neglect is often the greatest hazard.

Safety Practice

The Facility and Its Accommodation for Safety. It is important to learn the function and purpose of the code requirements and protective equipment to be prepared to cope with life-threatening hazards that might occur. All protective equipment and devices such as fire extinguishers, fire alarms, and emergency lights require regular maintenance. Aisles and passageways to exits must be kept clear and unobstructed. Exit doors should not be chained or locked, and all safety and warning signs should be observed. Fire doors should not be locked or blocked open. Obstructing or tampering with these fire devices could be disastrous. The chance of fire is also lessened if no-smoking areas are honored and if ash containers are checked regularly.

Provide a Setting That Is Fire Resistant. Fire codes normally require that all scenery and set decorations be treated for fire resistance. The term most used is *flame-proofing*, which, if taken literally, would be impossible to achieve. What is called for is the treating of flammable materials with a *flame retardant*. When applied properly, the treated material will not support a flame; that is, it will burn but will extinguish itself when the source of the flame is removed. It will be necessary to consult your local fire code to determine what materials must be "flameproofed" and the type of flame retardant that is acceptable.

Generally, all standard scenery (wood, fabric, and so on), curtains, draperies, furniture, and other decorative materials (such as artificial flowers and foliage) must be treated for fire resistance. All regular stage draperies, wings, and borders must also comply with this requirement. One of the standard tests for determining flame retardance uses the flame from an ordinary wooden match. The test must be conducted in a draft-free area. The match is held to the material for twelve seconds. If the scenery does not burn, carry the flame, or glow once the lighted match is removed from the substance, it passes the test satisfactorily. See your fire inspector for the particular type of test required by the local fire code.

Flame-retarding services can be provided by a professional company that is licensed to meet fire protection standards. It is usually best to use this service when purchasing new draperies, drops, scrims, and cycloramas for your stage. Professional companies have the equipment to properly treat large and heavy fabrics, and the finished product will bear a tag of certification. Although they cost a few cents a yard extra, it usually is advantageous to buy scenic muslin, canvas, cardboard, and other materials already treated with flame retardant. This saves valuable time for the technical staff. Fortunately, an increasing number of products used in scenery and in the display field are available already flame retardant.

The most common scenic materials can be treated in the scene shop. This will save the higher cost of materials that are pre-treated. The easiest method is to purchase already prepared fire-retardant compound. Be sure it meets the local code standards and is correct for the particular material to be treated. The National Fire Protection Association publishes a number of formulas for flame-treating materials. The compound is mixed into solution thoroughly with hot water and applied by brush, spray tank, or immersion. Sometimes the compound can be mixed into the sizing solution or with the prime coat of paint.

Application of a flame-retardant compound does not automatically guarantee flame-retarding properties. It may take some experimenting to be certain the solution has saturated the material sufficiently. Complicated systems are required to perform accurate tests of flammability. However, the wooden match field test as prescribed by the fire inspector can usually verify the success of the treatment. Another application of the compound may be necessary for satisfactory fire retardancy. It is also sometimes difficult to determine the nature of the fabric and therefore the compound that is correct for the material.

Most types of synthetic fabrics, plastics, artificial flowers, and real foliage usually require a different type of compound. Learn the appropriate flame-retardant solution for these materials and how to apply them. In addition, you may want to do samples first, because flame retardants may stain or ruin the appearance of some materials. Flame retardants only last for a few years.

Humidity and temperature cause a deterioration of the flame-retardant crystals. Washing and dry cleaning will remove them. Therefore, scenery and fabrics will need to be treated again either by your group or by a professional firm.

Small prop items are often exempt from flame treatment, as are costumes, wigs, and makeup materials. However, these items are often made from highly flammable materials. It is wise to know in advance what risk they have. The smallest fire or ember from a cigarette, an ash tray, or a lighted candle can create a hazard.

Be Prepared to Act in Emergencies. Valuable time is wasted if everyone is not ready to act immediately when a threatening event occurs. A telephone should be convenient with a list of emergency phone numbers attached for prompt action. Everyone should know the location of emergency exits and escape routes and the location of the fire alarm station and how to operate it. Be sure you have instructions on how to manually activate the fire curtain, the smoke vents on the roof, and the fire doors.

While the chief aim is avoiding the outbreak of fire, there may be times, even in the best operated theatres, when a fire will start. Everyone must be ready for such an emergency. This means knowing how to use the fire suppression equipment. Sometimes the best that can be achieved is to control the spread of the fire until the arrival of fire personnel. Portable fire extinguishers often make the difference in preventing real tragedy. Fire code standards specify in detail the location, number, type, and size of extinguishers in a given room. They must be located conspicuously in well-traveled areas and be readily accessible and available. The number and size of the units are determined by the degree of hazard (light, ordinary, or extra) that exists in the facility. The code requires that all extinguishers be inspected, tested, and maintained at specified intervals. Fires are classified in hazard groups. The three most common follow:

Class A Fires in ordinary combustibles such as wood, cloth, paper, and trash.
Class B Fires in flammable liquids such as gasoline, oil, paints, and grease.
Class C Fires involving electrical equipment. If electricity is turned off, the fire is reclassified A or B.

Fire extinguishers are typed according to the fire classifications for extinguishing effectiveness. Some types are approved only for class A fires, some for A and B or B and C, and some for all three. Pictorial fire classification symbols are now required on all fire extinguishers (Figure 4–2). All three symbols will appear on each extinguisher. A symbol printed in blue reveals that it is safe

USE ON "A" FIRES

USE ON "A / B" FIRES

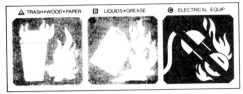

USE ON "B / C" FIRES

USE ON "A / B / C" FIRES

FIGURE 4–2 Fire extinguisher picture-symbols.

to use the extinguisher on this class of fire; a symbol in black with a red line through it indicates that it would be dangerous to use the extinguisher on this class of fire. Extinguishers are of several types (water, foam, carbon dioxide, and dry chemical) and are operated in different ways; you will need to learn how to use them. Often the local fire inspector will be willing to give advice and even provide instruction. Several types of fire extinguishers have been recently banned by OSHA, including the inversion types, which have failed to pass improved hydrostatic tests because they are subject to explosion hazards. Should you have any

doubt about the appropriateness of extinguishers, consult the fire inspector or safety officer.

Standpipe and hose systems are also frequently provided on the stage. They are available for occupants to use unless labeled for use by trained fire personnel only. There are several types. Learn how the water is supplied and how they are best used.

PHYSICAL SAFETY

Injuries are sometimes caused by tools and equipment that are not in safe operating condition. Even more widespread is people's using tools and materials incorrectly or without adequate safety precautions. While this may result from a lack of knowledge in the proper use of tools and the failure to read safety instructions, it is often simple failure to adopt known safety precautions in our practice and in our working mind-set. We are also becoming aware that physical and emotional stress are factors that can lead to personal injury. Because of the influence of stress, alertness in our work habits and productivity varies from individual to individual.

Stage Equipment

Permanent equipment on the stage most commonly includes a rigging system to suspend and fly scenery and lighting instruments overhead by counterweights, power winches, or hydraulics. Other equipment may include elevator lifts, revolving stages, motorized light bridges, and wagons. Equipment of this nature operating over heads, along the floor, and under feet has considerable potential for injury. Most such equipment is a custom installation, designed and constructed for that facility alone. Unfortunately, a set of uniform standards does not exist to provide some assurance regarding the safety of a rigging system. If you have doubts about your stage equipment, have it examined by a qualified theatre consultant or engineer.

Inspections of Stage Equipment. It is advisable to inspect rigging and other stage equipment at least once a year. This is the time to lubricate bearings and replace worn components. A sample checklist for safety inspection of a counterweight rigging system is shown in Figure 4–3.

Use and Maintenance of Staging Equipment. No one should be allowed to operate stage equipment without a period of training and supervision. Curiosity often encourages the neophyte to release a rope lock or play with winch controls. This must be prevented until the individual has received complete instruction on the use of the equipment. Many professional rigging firms provide written instructions on the use and maintenance of the equipment they install. If not, contact the installer for this information. The best firms are safety-minded and, if nothing else, are sensitive to life-threatening situations that might reflect on them.

One of the first things to learn is the load capacity of the equipment. On a counterweight or winch rigging system, this is determined by the size and rated strength of the components and the construction of each line set. The load capacity of each rigging system should be conveniently posted by the operating controls. The weight of the scenery should never exceed the allowable stress of any of the components that support it. A safety factor of 8–1 is minimal for rigging systems (never exceeding, for instance, a 250-pound load on a cable with a breaking strength of 2000 pounds). The loading capacity of a line set is usually expressed as a distributive load. A point or concentrated load must be considerably less to avoid exceeding the working stress of an individual cable, sheave, cable clips (Crosby clamps), or other component.

Equipment operation and maintenance go hand in hand. Never wait until inspection time to check the system for safety. It must be a constant practice. Look for frayed fibers on manila rope, or shiny cable, sure signs that replacement is needed. Are there sufficient cable clips, and are they attached properly (saddles on the live end)? Is the cable rubbing against the side of the loft block groove? These and other warning signs are examined in Chapter 13. Safety means observing for all indications of danger.

Safety Precautions. Safety procedures should be established for all equipment on the stage. Include such basics as keeping the rope locks on and turning off the power to winches when they are not in use. A work light should be left onstage overnight, especially when there are platforms on stage, an open trap, or an open orchestra pit. Working areas above the stage—the gridiron, the fly gallery, the loading platform, catwalks, and tall ladders or scaffold units—are of special concern. The stage below must be cleared of people when crews are working in these areas. Learn to respond to the call "Heads up," given whenever an object is lowered to the floor. Before working in areas above the stage, crew members should empty their pockets and secure tools with short lines to their waists. Even the smallest item gains tremendous velocity when falling to the floor and can do enormous damage. Consider the use of hard hats when working in these areas. Safety lines on spotlights, gel frames, and other equipment overhead are becoming common safety practices.

The process of hanging and removing scenery from a line set is a special concern. An unbalanced counterweight line can be extremely hazardous if the overweight side of the line is in a position to fall to the floor. If this happens, battens banging against the underside of the gridiron can fall, cables can break, and the chance of preventing injury is slim indeed. With the standard counterweight system, which has a loading platform hung beneath the gridiron, the procedure is precise. When *hanging* scenery, (1) lower the

SAFETY CHECKLIST FOR A COUNTERWEIGHT RIGGING SYSTEM

Theatre _____   Date _____

Condition/Approval

Locking Rail
  Bolts, welds, rivets
  Tension sheaves
  Rope locks

Operating Lines
  Rope condition: breaks, cuts,
    kinks, abrasions
  Terminations

Lift Lines
  Condition: wear, abrasions
  Terminations: cable clips,
    swages, thimbles
  Trim chains
  Turnbuckles
  Fleet angles to blocks
  Obstructions in flight

Counterweight Arbors
  Top & bottom plates
  Rods and nuts
  Spreader plates
  Lock plates
  Wire guide slots or T-bar
    fibre guides

Guidance System
  Wire tension & terminations
    (wire guide system)
  T-bar tracks & attachments
    (T-bar system)

Head Blocks
  Mounting clamps/bolts
  Sheave condition
  Spacer bars
  Bearings
  Axles

Loft Blocks & Mule Blocks
  Mounting clamps/bolts
  Sheave condition
  Spacer bars
  Bearings
  Axles

Pipe Battens
  Straightness, bends
  Splices & bolts/rivets
  Trim chains

FIGURE 4–3 Safety checklist for a counterweight rigging system.

batten to its lowest position at floor level, (2) attach the scenery to the batten, (3) clear the stage beneath the loading platform, and (4) add an estimated number of counterweights to the arbor and carefully test the counterbalance. When *removing* scenery, (1) lower the batten and scenery to the floor, (2) clear the stage beneath the loading platform, (3) remove those counterweights, which were added for the weight of the scenery, and (4) remove the scenery.

Shop Equipment

Tool Maintenance. A regular maintenance program is necessary to keep tools safe to operate. Tools need to be kept in repair, properly aligned, lubricated, blades and bits sharpened, attachments secured tightly, and, in short, functioning in top form. Electrical connections should be properly grounded and in good repair to prevent short circuits and electrical shock. At no time should tools be used without their appropriate safety guards and protective attachments. Large power tools need adequate shop space so the operator is not unduly restricted in using the tool in a safe manner.

Operating Tools Safely. First and foremost, no tool should be operated until an individual has been properly trained in its operation. The process is simple and threefold: (1) read tool instructions, (2) witness a demonstration of the tool, and (3) be supervised in your first few uses of the tool. Each tool has its own list of safety instructions. Instructional manuals will provide operational, maintenance, and safety information.

Most safety precautions are common sense. Tools should be used for their *intended purpose only*. Check the condition of a tool before using it (a hammer with a chipped head or a loose handle should not be used). Examine the material carefully (knots or nails in the wood may cause a problem). Power tools often provide the greatest hazard. What follows is a list of safety precautions for power tools:

1. ***Do not force tools.*** Let tools work at their own speed; never rush a job.
2. ***Disconnect tools.*** Unplug electric tools and remove the air hose from pneumatic tools when changing blades or other accessories.
3. ***Protect cords and hoses.*** Keep electric cables and air hoses away from the moving parts of the tool. Never carry a tool by the cord or disconnect it from a receptacle by a yank on the cord.
4. ***Watch your hands.*** Use push sticks when finishing a cut across a table saw, and avoid cutting small pieces of material that bring your hand too near a saw blade.
5. ***Secure work.*** Whenever applicable, use a vise or clamps to hold work. Then both hands are free to operate the tool.
6. ***Use tool guards and accessories.*** Keep guards in place and use rip fences and crosscut guides to prevent kickbacks.
7. ***Avoid distractions.*** Do not be distracted or distract anyone else using a power tool.
8. ***Alcohol, drugs, and medication.*** Do not operate power tools while under the influence of alcohol, drugs, or medication.
9. ***Do not leave a tool running unattended.*** Turn the power off and stay with the tool until it comes to a complete stop.
10. ***Use proper accessories.*** Only use blades and accessories that are designed or recommended for the power tool.
11. ***Maintain tools.*** Keep blades sharp and tools serviced properly at all times.
12. ***Ground all tools.*** Prevent shock by using grounded wiring, and avoid body contact with grounded surfaces.
13. ***Do not use tools in a dangerous environment.*** Avoid working with electrical tools in damp locations. Keep the work area well lit.
14. ***Do not overreach.*** Avoid overreaching. Maintain proper footing and balance when using power tools.
15. ***Know the tools.*** Know how to use them, adjust them, and service them.

Stepladders are necessary for work in the shop and on stage. Use stepladders only in completely open positions with all four legs on the floor. Never leave tools, hardware, or paint containers on the upper steps of the ladder. Use only the step side of the ladder;

never climb the back side. Tall A-frame ladders usually require two people to secure them from tipping. Finally, avoid upsetting the balance of a ladder by climbing to the top step or reaching out too far to one side.

Protective Clothing. Proper clothing should be worn in the shop. The type of dress must fit the nature of the work. Loose-fitting clothing is definitely inappropriate for work with power tools, which can grab the fabric and quickly draw the operator into the machinery. Nonabsorbing aprons are appropriate when working with chemicals and plastics. Welding aprons and other clothing must be heat resistant. Be sure feet are protected. Steel-toed shoes or protective shoe caps are best while working with metal or other heavy materials. Thin rubber soles are not appropriate in the shop, and at no time should a person go barefoot. Hair that is shoulder length or longer should be tied back and covered. Jewelry, such as rings and bracelets, should be removed for shop work.

HEALTH PROTECTION

Toxic materials are found everywhere in theatre production. They are basic staples in the smallest and in the largest producing group and in all the technical crafts. Only in recent years have we begun to accept the seriousness of the hazards they provide. We are exposed to them through chemical solutions, dusts, and vapors. Damage is caused when toxic materials enter the body. This occurs in three ways:

Inhaling. Vapors, fumes, dusts, and sprays are inhaled into the lungs. Chemical vapors will begin immediately to damage the lungs; mists and dusts may take longer. We breathe in airborne shop dusts and the mist caused by spray painting. The smallest particles usually cause the greatest damage. Welding fumes, and the vapors from solvents and from the chemical reaction in heating plastics are particularly hazardous.

The result is often one of several lung disorders such as emphysema and chronic bronchitis. Further, some toxic materials may enter the blood stream to affect other organs, such as the liver, the brain, and the kidneys.

Ingesting. Toxic materials often enter the mouth by dirty hands when smoking, nail biting, and eating. Paint, glue, and solvents on the hands and under fingernails are commonly ingested in this manner. Mucus in the lungs from inhaled mists can be coughed up and ingested by swallowing.

Skin Contact. Many chemicals such as benzene, toluene, and methyl alcohol directly penetrate the skin and enter the blood stream. Others weaken the protective layers of the skin sufficiently to allow other toxics to be absorbed. Sores, cuts, and breaks in the skin provide a clear passage for many substances into the body.

Exposure to a lot of toxic material will often cause an *acute* illness. Because it occurs within a short time after a sizable exposure, an acute effect is easily related to the exposure. Intense absorption of some solvents, for instance, may result in nausea, dizziness, headache, mental disorientation, or irritation to the eyes and nose. More insidious, however, are *chronic* illnesses. These usually result from exposure to one or more toxic substances over a long period. Individual doses of exposure may be extremely small, but their effect to the body will accumulate over many years. The symptoms will vary from person to person and are more difficult to diagnose. Chronic exposure may result in damage to the lungs, liver, skin, or nervous system or in psychological depression or irritability. Cancer is a common chronic illness and can result from some solvents and carcinogens (cancer-causing substances) such as benzene, asbestos, and carbon tetrachloride.

We live in a world filled with chemical poisons. They are used in contemporary manufacturing, in the arts, and even in food processing. When used safely and in moderate amounts they are often not harmful. The amount of toxicity will vary from substance to substance. A number, including lead, asbestos, and benzene (bensol) are highly toxic and have been banned in many commercial products.

Proper Ventilation

Effective ventilation is one of the most needed defenses against toxic hazards.

At the minimum, a roof or window exhaust fan combined with an open door or window to provide replacement air is essential. The best solution is a local exhaust system as specified by a qualified engineer. One system includes a hood, and sometimes a wraparound enclosure, as is typical of spray painting booths. The exhaust system used must suit the nature of the fumes. Heavier-than-air fumes naturally fall to the floor. A ventilation system that pulls them up into the work area would only increase the problem. A shop should never be tied into the general building ventilation (or dilution) system, which allows pollutants to be mixed with other air and be recirculated throughout the building. A local exhaust system traps and exhausts toxic materials before they can spread in the room. The more enclosure provided, the more thoroughly the contaminants can be removed from the air. A source of fresh or makeup air must be provided for an exhaust unit to function. It is particularly important that the makeup air be located behind the worker so the contaminants are directed away from the breathing zone of the worker.

Another ventilation feature, either replacing or in addition to the exhaust hood, is an accordion-like flexible-hose inlet. The end of the hose can be placed within inches of the work and suck the contaminants into the exhaust unit. Because these systems localize the work to a small area, they can be highly effective. They usually can provide sufficient air flow to satisfy the most dangerous pollutants found in the average scene shop.

Sawdust exhaust collection systems attach to woodworking tools to remove sawdust to an outside bin. These are most desirable. Paint spray booths are needed for aerosol spray work. When spraying water-based paints on large scenic units, wear a good respirator and have sufficient room ventilation. If a large surface must be painted with a more hazardous paint, do it with a brush or roller. Here is one last caution: Ventilation systems, no matter how effective, do not replace respirators. Always wear them.

The Hazards of Materials

A decided help in protecting ourselves is knowing the hazards of the materials we use. Proper precautions are more likely to be taken and less hazardous techniques might be found in working with the materials. Whenever possible, substitute less toxic substances for highly toxic ones. A variety of paints, solvents, inks, and dyes are used in the theatre. There are some toxic ingredients in nearly all of them. Some pigments and dyes are more hazardous than others.

Reading the labels on products is a help. However, many materials have labels that are incomplete or lacking in appropriate information. More information can be learned from *Material Safety Data Sheets* (MSDS). OSHA requires manufacturers to prepare data sheets on hazardous products. The manufacturer or the distributor is required to make these available upon request. Material Safety Data Sheets provide information on product ingredients, physical data, fire and explosive information, health hazard data, suggested first aid, and precautionary information. It is essential to acquire the MSDS information to know how to work safely with materials.

Modern paints often contain additives such as fillers, stabilizers, preservatives, and plasticizers. While the paints themselves may be relatively safe, we do not always know the hazards of these added chemicals. Spray-painting, which mists the air with tiny particles, is more hazardous than brushing or rolling.

Premixed paints and dyes are safest to use. Dry powdered forms are more dangerous and should be mixed only where a local exhaust system is available or in a glove box. Solvents are all toxic in some degree in liquid or vapor states. They can cause skin diseases and damage internal organs. It is best to use the least toxic solvent whenever possible or replace them with water-based products.

Plastic resin systems are most hazardous in the polymerization process when a new molecular structure is created. Most of the chemicals involved are highly toxic. In handling and pouring chemical ingredients, guard against splashes and vapors. Polyurethane foam systems use isocyanate cross-linkers, which are very hazardous to the respiratory system. Even sanding, cutting, or heating the final product releases deadly hydrogen cyanide, carbon dioxide, and other gases. Good ventilation and adequate face, hand, and nose protection are essential.

Although prohibited now in most products, asbestos still remains in many theatres in insulated wiring, gloves, old fire curtains, soundproofing, insulation, and old instant papier mâchés. When it becomes "friable" (deteriorates and releases fibers into the air), it is a known carcinogen. Methods have been established to remove, isolate, or encapsulate asbestos by specially trained workers.

The most common air-borne substance in shops, sawdust, can cause allergies. Woods treated with additives, pesticides, and preservatives can produce toxic dusts. Knowing whether lumber in your shop is chemically treated is helpful. The best defense is to trap the dust before it is inhaled.

Various compounds are used to produce smoke and fog effects on stage. Because they are inhaled, smoke materials can be hazardous to people with asthma and other lung and heart disorders.

Carbon dioxide (dry ice) fog is relatively safe, but in high concentrations in poorly ventilated areas it deprives the air of oxygen necessary for breathing. The majority of chemical fogs are water-glycol mixtures that pose few hazards when ingested but can be respiratory irritants.

Know the ingredients of these mixtures and the health condition of the actors and crew. It is wise to use fog materials only in safe concentrations in a well-ventilated stage and for a short period.

Welding hazards are numerous and complex, requiring those who weld to be familiar with safety regulations for each form of welding. Besides the obvious potential for burns, fires, explosions, and electrical hazards, there are a number of health dangers as well. These include the hazard of infrared and ultraviolet radiation that can cause severe burns and eye damage. Fumes, the release into the air of tiny oxide particles, are produced as metal melts. Gases come from the compressed gas cylinders, from different types of welding rods, or from coated metals when heated. Welding requires an isolated area with proper ventilation, protective clothing that covers the entire body, and hand, face, and eye protection.

The best defense is a knowledge of health hazards. Information about toxic materials can be found in OSHA publications. The Center for Safety in the Arts compiles data and research findings and publishes valuable information about health and safety hazards.

Storage and Disposal of Hazardous Materials

Toxic material must be stored in tightly sealed, nonbreakable metal or plastic containers. Labels on the containers should clearly identify the contents and its hazards. Solvents should never be left exposed to the air and should be covered to prevent contaminating the air. Stored chemicals should be separated to avoid any chance of chemical reactions of materials in the same area. Spills should be cleaned up immediately so vapors and dust do not become airborne. Soaked paper towels and rags used in the cleanup of flammable liquids need to be placed in an approved, self-closing waste can that is emptied daily. In case of accidental spills on the skin, use water to wash away the material. If eye contact occurs, the eyes should be rinsed for several minutes and medical assistance should be sought.

Flammable and combustible materials should be stored near an outside entrance of the shop. Approved safety cans or cabinets are necessary for proper storage. Keep these items away from flames, sparks, and smoking areas. A fire extinguisher located nearby is a sound precaution.

Disposal of hazardous wastes is another important need. Hazardous and toxic liquids should never be poured down drains or sewers. They should be collected in safety containers and disposed of by an authorized waste or pollution control agency. If there is some question, learn from the manufacturer the proper way to dispose of its products.

Personal Protective Equipment

In addition to proper clothing, gloves are frequently needed to protect the hands from chemicals, heat, radiation, and abrasion. Manufacturers of industrial gloves provide information on the proper gloves for various materials. Leather gloves are needed for welding, and woven fiberglass gloves are excellent for other heat-producing tasks. Avoid asbestos gloves. Working with manila rope or abrasive materials calls for the protection of regular cotton work gloves. Rubber and plastic gloves are needed to avoid skin contact with irritating chemicals.

In addition, special creams, known as "barrier creams," will protect the skin from occasional splashes or light exposure to chemicals. Choose the right cream for the job. Some provide protection from solvents,

FIGURE 4–4 Personal protective equipment.

SAFETY GOGGLES SAFETY GLASSES FACE SHIELD RESPIRATOR

EAR MUFFS HELMET WELDERS GLOVES WORK GLOVES LATEX GLOVES

others from acids and various oils. It is wise to apply a barrier cream as a special precaution.

Eye and face protection requires the use of safety glasses or goggles or face shields to guard against splashes of chemicals, the impact of flying chips and particles in wood and metal work, and radiation from welding and lasers. Special antiglare goggles are necessary for most welding, cutting, and brazing, and a complete welding helmet is needed for arc welding. The equipment used should meet the requirements of the American National Standards Institute for the appropriate hazard.

Any task that produces dusts, mists, fumes, or vapors requires respiratory protection. Even with adequate ventilation, face masks and respirators will provide better protection from hazardous airborne materials. Air-purifying respirators are either equipped with filters to trap particles, dusts, or metal fumes or with cartridges to trap gases and vapors from solvents. The correct filter or cartridge must be selected for the specific contaminant and replaced frequently. The respirator must fit the face tightly. Under high levels of contaminants, respirators cease to be effective; thus, effective ventilation is needed. If dusts and mists are highly concentrated, only an airline respirator, which provides a flow of air to the face, is effective.

Generally, with well-oiled machinery on vibration mounts, noise levels of shops are not excessive, but the nature of tools and the shop environment may indicate the need for ear muffs or plugs for hearing protection. Some common protective equipment is illustrated in Figure 4–4.

PRODUCTION PRACTICES

Rehearsal and Performance. Safety procedures are necessary during rehearsals and performances. Some concern the use of properties and special effects. Security is vital in caring for firearms used to fire blank cartridges. Swords, daggers, and other weapons require special care. Well-rehearsed and choreographed action is demanded. Offstage, such items should be in the special care of a trained crew member for cleaning, loading, and appropriate security.

Open flame onstage is another concern. In some locations, a special fire permit may be necessary. But, in any case, the use and location of fire must be well planned and rehearsed, a specific crew member assigned to the task, and a fire extinguisher held by a stagehand in the wings ready for any emergency.

Food and drink to be consumed by the cast must be properly prepared. Is there a refrigerator to preserve perishables? Are dishes, pans, and utensils washed thoroughly? These practices are important to the actors' health.

The physical condition of the stage should not be neglected. The stage must be made safe for cast and crew to move about without hazard. Low-intensity work lights are needed in crossovers and egresses. During blackouts, obstacles, stair steps, and paths of movement may require phosphorescent paint or tape that glows in the dark, or the assistance of a stagehand with a flashlight, to guide crew and cast members. Do not forget handrails on escape stairways and platforms for safe exiting from the playing area. Antislip tape may be necessary on ramps and slippery surfaces.

Personal habits. Personal health and hygiene practices are important for your protection. Eating while wearing work clothing may result in ingesting of hazardous substances. Leave the hazards behind when you leave the shop by removing work clothing after work and washing hands thoroughly with soap and water.

Working long, extended hours in the shop is foolhardy. When you become tired, personal caution and alertness are de-

FIGURE 4–5 Special safety precautions must be taken when lighted candles are used on stage. Scene from *The Glass Menagerie* at Northern Illinois University, with setting designed by Kenneth Bunne. (Photo by George Tarbay)

creased, and the potential for accidents becomes much greater.

A first aid kit should be well stocked and its location known to all. In case of injury, know how to administer first aid and how to contact the nearest hospital, emergency room, or paramedics. If there was exposure to toxic substances, try to determine the identity of the material and length of exposure so medical authorities can apply the proper treatment or contact the nearest poison control center.

Finally, do not work alone. In an emergency, another person's help can be valuable.

Good Housekeeping. A clean and organized shop and stage promote physical safety and health. Keep the stage and shop free of unnecessary items and debris, because a cluttered area hinders movement of workers and increases risks when working with power tools and scenic materials. A shop needs a thorough cleaning and the removal of trash each day. Take care to avoid raising dust. The finest dust is the most dangerous and can remain in the air for a considerable time. If sweeping is the practice, use sweeping compound to reduce the dust level. Vacuuming is better, particularly if the vacuum tank has a proper filter to keep the fine dust from returning to the room. Wet mopping is the safest cleaning method of all.

Because safety and health are so dependent on concern and practice, no list of rules and regulations is ever complete. Even with the employment of all safety devices and proper maintenance, human error can create unsafe conditions. An individual must learn safety procedures, adopt a cautionary attitude, and report all conditions that may be unsafe.

SELECTED READINGS

Art Hazards News. Center for Safety in the Arts, 5 Beekman Street, New York, NY 10038.

Best's Safety Directory, 2 volumes. Oldwick, NJ: A. M. Best Co., 1989.

BURGESS, WILLIAM A., *Recognition of Health Hazards in Industry*. New York: John Wiley, 1981.

DAVIDSON, DR. RANDALL W. A., and PAUL VIERRA, *The Pocket Guide to Theatre Safety*. Campbell, CA: Risk International, 1990.

DEREAMER, RUSSELL, *Modern Safety and Health Technology*. New York: John Wiley, 1980.

Direct Safety Company, *Catalog Q 1991*, P.O. Box 50050, Phoenix, AZ 85076-0050.

General Scientific Equipment Company, *Catalog and OSHA Safety Guide*, Catalog GS-274. Philadelphia, 1974.

PETERSON, DAN, *The OSHA Compliance Manual* (rev. ed.). New York: McGraw-Hill, 1979.

Power Tool "Safety Is Specific." Power Tool Institute, Inc., 5105 Tollview Drive, Rolling Meadows, IL.

ROSSOL, MONONA, *Stage Fright: Health and Safety in the Theatre*. New York: Center for Occupational Hazards, 1986.

SITTIG, MARSHALL, *Hazardous and Toxic Effects of Industrial Chemicals*. Park Ridge, NJ: Noyes Data Corporation, 1979.

Standard First Aid and Personal Safety (2nd ed.). Prepared by the American Red Cross. Garden City, NY: Doubleday, 1979.

5

The Scene Shop

The shop is the major center for the scene technician. It is the location for the production of all scenic components between the preparation of technical drawings and the actual transportation of the setting to the stage. Quite naturally, the arrangement and working conditions of the shop play a vital role in the scenery manufacturing process. As with any productive operation, a successful workplace demands efficient layout and organization. The immense diversity of craft operations in a scene shop demands careful planning for the needed array of space and tool requirements. Shop organization must be sufficiently logical that all workers can quickly familiarize themselves with the location of items and the overall operation of the facility. Further, a shop must be structured and maintained as a safe environment for its personnel. This requires the conscious effort of everyone who works in the shop.

THE SHOP FACILITY

It is probably safe to say that the majority of shops have some inadequacies. Stage and auditorium areas usually have priority in planning and financial resources. Technical production areas tend not to receive this same attention. If production areas are provided at all within the performance facility, they are often only casually designed to meet functional needs. It is not unusual for shops to occupy peripheral areas of the facility or to be located in another building planned for another purpose. The result is something short of the ideal, with the single most common shortcoming being lack of space, sheer unencumbered space for construction. An analysis of shop needs must consider the type of producing agency, the amount and size of scenery produced, and the number of shop employees. Commercial scene shops and shops of large production centers are involved with several productions at the same time and perform several different kinds of construction activity simultaneously. Educational theatres need expanded shop space to serve their teaching functions in addition to building regular productions.

The overall size, shape, and height of the shop should be tailored to the most-demanding production circumstances anticipated, and should, in fact, include expected growth of the program in the future. The physical shape of the space should not be restrictive for any of the craft functions. Shop height should permit trial setup and painting of the setting. Walls of the shop should be of durable material that is fire resistant and capable of withstanding the abuse of construction. A wood floor, except in the welding area where fire is a danger, has advantages over a hard and potentially slippery concrete floor.

One Shop or Several?

There are two different types of shop facilities. One is separate shops for different crafts, such as a scene construction shop, a property shop, a paint shop, and a metal shop. This is appropriate in large production centers for the efficient division of work and personnel. Sometimes multiple shops are just the result of the lack of a single space large enough for all operations.

For instance, painting and trial setup might be located in a high-ceilinged area on the stage level, while carpentry, metalwork, and properties are assigned rooms at another location. Of course, there must be access from shop to shop to move the largest items constructed to the final assembly area and painting.

The second type of operation is a single shop of sufficient size to accommodate all of the crafts. The advantages of this plan include the proximity of all scenic functions and the opportunity to share common space, tools, and materials. Whichever plan is adopted, shops should be spacious enough and adequately equipped to serve the needs of the production program.

Accessibility

A shop must have sufficient provision for bringing in construction supplies and for moving the scenery from the shop to the stage. The outside entrance must be sizable enough to permit lumber and other materials to be conveniently unloaded into the shop. If the theatre or theatres are located in other buildings, a large loading door and a truck ramp have additional use. If the shop is in the same building as the stage, large doorways and ample passageways between the two rooms are essential. A shop on the same level and adjacent to the stage is the most convenient situation, provided adequate sound isolation exists. In this situation, the height and width of the doors should permit assembled sets to roll directly onto the stage.

Acoustical Needs

Acoustical considerations need to be carefully studied when a shop is constructed. There are several matters of sound control to be resolved. One of these is providing some absorption of sound from power tools to reduce a potentially hazardous noise level and to permit easy verbal communication in the room. Usually the shape of the room and absorbent acoustical materials on the walls and ceiling can be of considerable assistance. More difficult is keeping shop noise out of adjacent rooms. This becomes a serious problem when the shop is right next to the stage or studio. Work hours in the shop could be severely limited when rehearsals and performances are in progress unless shop sounds are fully isolated. Airborne sounds are best reduced by walls of weighty materials; concrete is fairly effective. An alternative is double-wall construction with an intervening air space. However, proper walls will not be effective unless doors and other openings in the wall approximate the transmission loss of the wall structure. Heavy, insulated doors that close with very tight seals along the threshold, top, and sides are essential. The best solution is a sound lock: a room and two sets of acoustical doors separating the shop from the stage. More difficult to isolate are impact sounds, that is, sounds carried by the floor and structure of the building to other rooms. A wooden floor is somewhat more absorptive than concrete, and vibration insulators on power tools are of some help. More effective for impact

sounds is an isolated concrete-slab subfloor or a floating floor carried on resilient mounts.

Lighting the Shop

Shop lighting should provide evenly distributed general illumination at bench, tool, and floor level and along the painting wall of the shop. A minimum 150 footcandles is generally recommended. Of course, individual equipment lights on major power tools and other more localized lighting sources are valuable to supplement the light level in the machine areas of the shop. Fluorescent tube lighting provides a very even and efficient light source. While these are accepted

FIGURE 5–1 The property and scene shop at the Theatre and Interpretation Center of Northwestern University. The shop serves four theatres in the center. This well-planned shop has an arrangement of individual craft areas and common service facilities that provide for maximum efficiency. (Based on a drawing courtesy of Northwestern University)

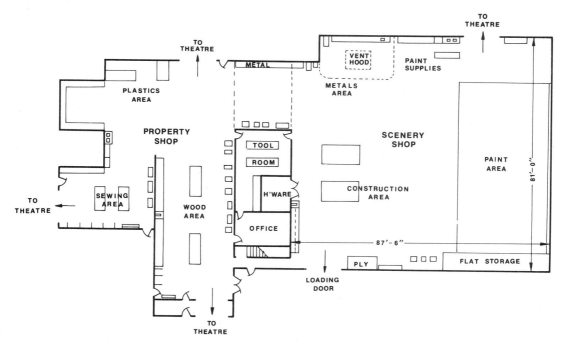

for construction areas, some technicians prefer a bank of incandescent theatre-type floodlights in the paint area so that painting can be tested under the colors that will be used in the production. Some shops have large window areas, especially on the north, to permit natural light for daytime work.

The Air Environment

Effective ventilation is necessary for good health and housekeeping. A general ventilation and makeup air system is needed for the entire area to remove the air particles generated by scene construction and to aid in drying paint and adhesives. In addition, high-capacity local exhaust systems should be provided for the welding area and for areas where toxic plastics and solvents are used (Figure 5-2). Dust-collection systems should be considered for safely removing sawdust generated by power tools. Dusts can be placed overhead or in floor locations. A shop that can be kept reasonably clean will benefit both in health protection and in physical safety. Provide for easy cleaning behind and under tools and benches, and employ grillwork or open-bracket racks instead of dust-collecting solid shelving and other dust-trap surfaces.

FIGURE 5–2 Local fume exhaust systems terminate in hoods over the working area or in movable "elephant trunk" tubes that can be located close to the work.

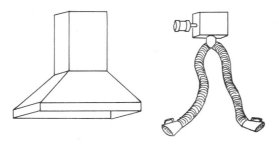

Fire Protection

A scene shop should be made as fire resistant as possible, and fire-protection equipment should be well planned. Sprinkler systems, fire doors, fire extinguishers, and fire alarm boxes should be installed and always kept free from obstructions. Tools and supplies should be placed in safe locations, and all combustible solvents stored in appropriate safety containers.

SHOP LAYOUT AND ORGANIZATION

The specific arrangement and use of space in a shop is based on several factors. While some of this relates to the nature and shape of the space and the particular needs of the productions constructed, much will depend on the individual approach to the shop operation. However, several general considerations should be addressed in determining the layout of a shop to maximize efficiency in constructing scenery.

Providing for Special Craft Needs

Whether there is one central shop or several, the individual craft areas need a degree of isolation to perform certain functions effectively. In a single facility, this often means designating certain portions of the shop for centralizing the equipment and work activities of these special operations. The most common are the crafts associated with wood, metal, fabrics, properties, plastics, and painting. Each has unique needs. Specific tools and supplies should be in close proximity to each area.

The Woodworking Area. The marking, cutting, and framing of long lengths of lumber and composition board require considerable space. For this reason, band saws and table saws are best placed in an open area.

A radial saw can be located along a wall with adequate lateral space for cutting lumber. A jointer must also take long lengths of lumber. Lathes, sanders, scroll saws, drill presses, and power miter-saws usually require less space. Template and workup benches need access from all sides. A sawdust collector system can be installed to remove dust from the tools. The lumber racks should be located conveniently near the power tools.

The Plastics Area. A vacuum-form machine and benches and tools for working with plastic foams, fiberglass, and other plastics need accommodation. Exhaust venting with a hood should be provided to remove toxic odors, fumes, dusts, and smoke.

The Metals Area. For metalwork, a fire-protected area is needed. Welding requires adequate ventilation through an exhaust system capable of removing fumes. Welding equipment, an anvil, heavy-duty vises, a grinder, sturdy benches, and other power and hand tools are needed. A drill press can be shared with the woodworking area. A storage rack for metal stock and cabinets for other supplies must be provided.

The Fabrics Area. The chief activity in this area is the sewing and grommeting of drops, draperies, curtains, and floor cloths. Heavy-duty sewing machines, cutting tables, and work tables are required. A large amount of space is generally needed because of the size of the items fabricated.

The Property Area. Property construction involves all the crafts of scenery and all areas of the shop could serve its needs. However, it is a matter of centralized convenience and of avoiding interference with regular scene construction to provide a sepa-

FIGURE 5–3 Dance Scenery. Scene from *Sleeping Beauty* at Northern Illinois University. Dance requires considerable floor space for movement. Scene design by Scott Marr. (Photo by George Tarbav)

rate locale for the space demands of upholstering, furniture making and repair, sewing, sculpting, and numerous other kinds of craft work. The acquisition of some hand tools and small power tools for props relieves the heavy use of tools in other areas of the shop.

The Paint Area. Usually both horizontal and vertical space is needed for painting. The floor area should be adequate enough to paint the largest set or drop laid in a flat position. Vertical painting requires a wall expanse of the same size. Horizontal and vertical strips of wood permanently secured to the wall will permit stretching a drop or lightly tacking flats to the wall in a full upright position for painting. A boomerang, a section of scaffolding, or a powered platform lift can be used to paint the upper portions of the scenery (Figure 5-4). A better solution is a paint frame that can be lowered into a pit in the floor as illustrated in Figure 10-10. A large industrial-type sink with hot and cold water and with an oversized trap for cleaning is a necessity for paint. Other equipment includes a mixing table, a fireproof locker for flammables and solvents, paint-storage bins and shelves, an applicator and tool-storage cabinet, paint-container racks, and portable palettes and mixing tables (Figure 5-5).

Providing for the Construction Sequence

The layout of the shop must also provide for the sequence of construction. The diagram in Figure 5-6 shows a graphic view of the flow of work from the time scene supplies are received and stored until the setting is finished and moved onto the stage or load-

FIGURE 5–4 Telescoping work platform powered by CO_2 gas tanks. Lifts of this type operated by hand winch, air, electricity, or hydraulics have many shop and stage uses. (Photo courtesy of Up-Right Scaffolds)

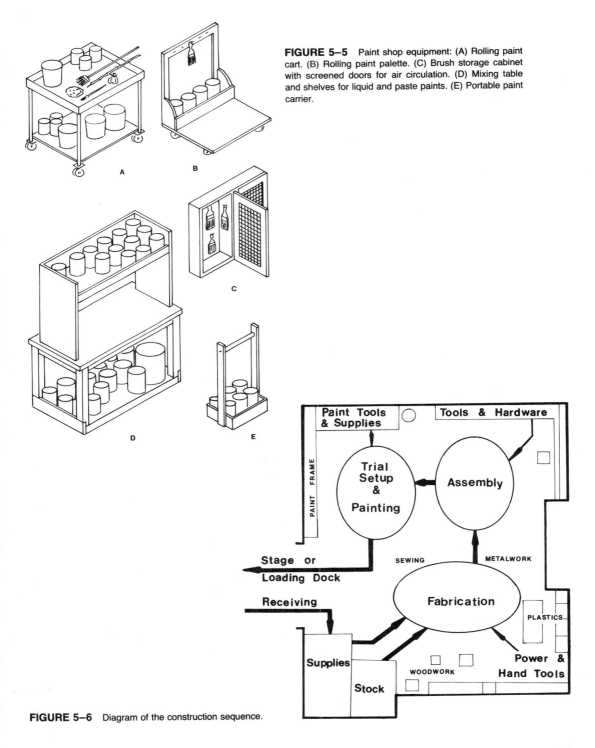

FIGURE 5–5 Paint shop equipment: (A) Rolling paint cart. (B) Rolling paint palette. (C) Brush storage cabinet with screened doors for air circulation. (D) Mixing table and shelves for liquid and paste paints. (E) Portable paint carrier.

FIGURE 5–6 Diagram of the construction sequence.

ing dock. Fabrication, assembly, and trial setup/painting describe the general steps in the construction sequence.

Fabrication. This process is centered in the individual craft areas. Lumber is marked and cut, wood joints are fashioned, and framing is completed. Fabrics are cut and sewn for drops, flats, and floor cloths. Metal is cut, bent, riveted, and welded into components and frames. Plastics are cast, shaped, cut, and formed into scenic structures.

Assembly. Individual elements of the set are brought together for assembly into modular units. Flats are covered and hardware is attached. Flats are joined together; hinges, stiffeners, and dutchmen (cloth masking over joints between flats) are added. Sill irons are installed; door and window units are fitted to openings; moldings, relief work, and textured surfaces are applied. Platforms, steps and irregular structures are legged, braced, padded, and covered and joining hardware is installed. Wagons and jacks are castered, joined, and fitted to units. A somewhat larger space is required for the assembly process than for fabrication.

Trial Setup and Painting. With the completion of the setting into units, an area equivalent to the size of the stage is needed for a trial setup. The constructed units are brought together, walls are placed on platforms and wagons, bracing is added, and projected trim and moldings are fitted for alignment at corners. Methods for joining, bracing, shifting, and securing units together receive a final examination. After the trial setup, the setting is painted. This often results in separating the setting for placement on the floor or paint frame.

This sequence is common practice in many shops. The stage is frequently not available until a few days before final rehearsals. The setting must be fully ready to be set up on the stage in a very short time. However, it is not unusual in film and television for the setting to be assembled and painted on the location site or soundstage.

Assemble-in-place settings are sometimes possible and desirable to live theatre situations particularly if the scenery is predominantly platforms, ramps, and large three-dimensional structures. Because rehearsals are difficult without the actual playing elevations, platforms become a top priority in the construction sequence.

Providing for Shop Flexibility

Contemporary scenic practice includes many different types of settings and design approaches and considerable diversity of construction materials. Some settings are predominantly metal structures. Others rely chiefly on see-through skeletal panels, a series of multilevel platforms, two-dimensional painted units, intricate kinetic moving constructions, or reflective plastic surfaces in unusual shapes and patterns. A shop should be capable of some reorganization to the special construction needs of each setting. Space flexibility permits a shop to adapt to meet the needs of the mode of scenery and the predominant materials and techniques employed.

A shop encumbered with immovable equipment and fixed centers of activity inhibits adaptation and rearrangement. Heavy and space-consuming workbenches, supply cabinets, and hardware racks can be made mobile or can be constructed as separable units. Casters on sewing machines, fabric dispensers, and certain power tools allow them to be relocated to another area of the shop. Portable tool cases, paint containers, and hardware cabinets can be moved to the site of construction. A flexibly organized shop can be rearranged to the unique scenic requirements of each production. This will result in better use of the total space and greater construction efficiency (Figure 5-7).

Providing for Shop Tools and Supplies

Convenience and unnecessary travel across the shop are important reasons for

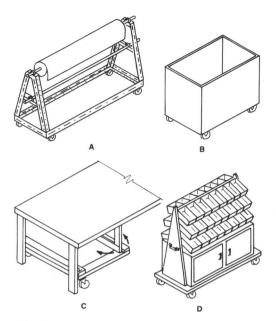

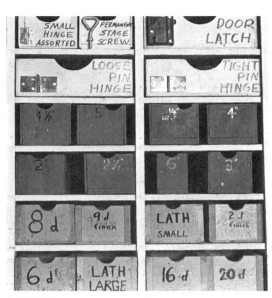

FIGURE 5–7 Mobilizing shop equipment: (A) Mobile dispenser for rolled fabrics and plastic sheeting. (B) Rolling box for fabrics, draperies, and large hardware items. (C) Casters on a heavy workbench. (D) Mobile hardware- and tool-storage.

FIGURE 5–8 Arranging tools and supplies for easy location, organization, and inventory. Methods include labeled and color-coded boxes, slanted and removable bins, and tool racks that allow tools to be found and returned easily. (Photo by Renata S. Jasinski)

locating tools and supplies as near as possible to the work areas. Grouping tools and materials at different points in the shop is one answer to this need. Another solution is a centralized tool room or tool and supply room. For tools, this also provides for security, by issuing tools to workers and checking them in at the end of the working session. The inventory is fully maintained and re-placement costs are minimized. Other shops are more concerned with the speed and ease of locating and returning tools. Tool racks can be carefully organized by tool type and purpose. Special identifying positions and mounts can be built to assure the return of tools to the right place. They permit the identification of missing tools by a quick glance at the rack. The same convenience in finding hardware and scenic materials is desirable. Transparent, open-front, or an-gled-bin units are especially helpful in visu-

FIGURE 5–8 *(continued)*

ally locating supplies. Color-coded boxes and graphic labels are usually superior to printed tags. Boxes and bins that can be removed and carried to the construction area are particularly handy (Figure 5-8).

Storage racks and shelving (Figure 5-9) that allow flexible organization of items will permit the logical regrouping of items as new tools and construction materials are added in the future. Pegboard racks for tools serve this goal. Flexible shelving can be constructed of Unistrut channels, slotted steel angle, or pipe and slip-on pipe fittings. These can also serve for storage racks for lumber, plywood, and other supplies.

Each major power tool has its own minimum working space requirement. Ample space around power saws and other machines is essential to protect operators from hazards. Warning signs hung overhead or a painted safety zone on the floor may serve

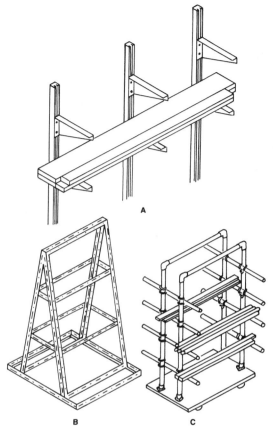

FIGURE 5–9 Adjustable storage racks: (A) Lumber rack of Unistrut channel. (B) Sheet lumber rack of slotted angle. (C) Metal storage rack of pipe and slip-on fittings.

to identify needed safety in the area and to discourage people from distracting the tool operators.

POWER NEEDS

Electrical Power

A shop must have ample electrical outlets for tools and equipment. More and more, electrical tools are replacing hand-powered tools for most kinds of work in our shops. It is ideal to have many electrical outlets throughout the shop, on the walls, along permanent workbenches, from drop lines overhead, and from roll-up retractable-cord reels. A sufficient number of well-placed outlets is advantageous because it reduces the lengthy runs of extension cords that clutter up the construction space. Floor outlets are not advisable in most areas of a scene shop. The largest power tools often require 220-volt, three-phase service for the motors to operate effectively. All plugs and receptacles should provide for proper grounding.

Tool safety is obviously most essential. Tool guards should always be used with power tools. It is also important that adequate space be provided around bench- and floor-mounted equipment, that built-in work lights are provided, and that all tools have appropriate safety switches.

Both repair and maintenance of tools demand regular attention. Vibrations and unusual noises are often warnings resulting from inadequate service checks. Maintenance manuals are helpful in making repairs and in checking motors, belts and pulleys, tool alignment, and loose or worn setscrews and bolts. More basic is providing proper lubrication and keeping blades and other cutting components properly sharpened and secured.

Air Power

Pneumatic tools have become increasingly important in the shop. Air is used to power spray guns and pneumatic tools such as staplers, nailers, drills, saws, sanders, impact wrenches, and grinders.

Pneumatic tools are generally small and compact. They contain few moving parts to wear out. They are economical to operate and, with care, have a long life. The source of power is compressed air. Air pressure is measured in pounds of pressure per square inch, called psi. Pressures below 65 psi, such as needed for spray painting and air casters, are considered low pressure. Many air tools

and actuators require a minimum of 90 psi. This means that the compressed air supply in a shop must provide a gauge pressure of 120–200 psi to power several tools simultaneously. Volume of air, determined by cubic feet per minute (cfm), is another factor in considering pneumatic equipment. All tools and other pneumatic devices have minimum volume requirements. For instance, while an air drill might require 90 psi (pressure) and 4 cfm (volume), an air caster (12″ diameter) may require only 25 psi of pressure but up to 15 cfm in air flow.

A compressor is a machine that takes in air at regular atmospheric pressure and increases it to a higher pressure. The most useful are those that include a tank to store compressed air. This increases the volume capacity needed for devices that require high air volume, and it builds up an adequate volume of air ready for immediate use by air tools. A gauge and regulator on the storage tank controls the psi in the tank and turns on the motor and compressor when the pressure drops to a predetermined level. A separate output gauge and regulator regulates the pressure needed to power a specific air tool or activator. A relatively modest compressor system is a portable paint spraying unit (Figure 5-10). This consists of a motor (1 to 2 HP), a compressor, and a storage tank (12- to 30-gallon capacity). The most complete and expensive system is a central, built-in air supply piped throughout the shop and stage with air outlets at convenient locations. This requires a large compressor and tank (perhaps 60- to 200-gallon capacity) located in another room to isolate the motor noise.

Pneumatic system accessories include filters and lubricators. The purpose of a filter is to remove moisture and air contaminants that accumulate in the air lines and storage tanks of compressed air systems. Moisture results from condensation of the humidity in the air. Removing this moisture and dirt and rust particles is vital to protect pneumatic tools. The lubricator keeps the moving

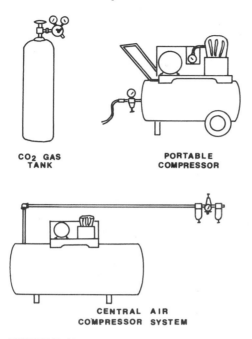

CO₂ GAS
TANK

PORTABLE
COMPRESSOR

CENTRAL AIR
COMPRESSOR SYSTEM

FIGURE 5–10 Compressed-air systems.

components of pneumatic tools running smoothly, prevents rust, and keeps seals from drying out.

Compressed air is distributed to working areas by pipes and hoses. Pipes are permanent conduits used in built-in systems to distribute air to outlet stations throughout a shop. All pipe fittings must have good seals to prevent leakage. An outlet station needs fittings for connecting tool hoses, a filter, a lubricator, a regulator, and an outlet pressure gauge (Figure 5-11). Regular air hose should be used for most pneumatic equipment because it is rated for up to 250 psi of working pressure. The inside diameter of the hose determines the volume of the air flow. Each pneumatic device has its own requirement. Most pneumatic tools require $5/16''$ or $1/2''$ inside diameter (ID) hose. Connections to air lines and tools are made conveniently with quick air couplers which do not require tools. Installed on all hoses, tools, and outlets, connections and disconnections are made by pulling back on the locking collar of the coupler.

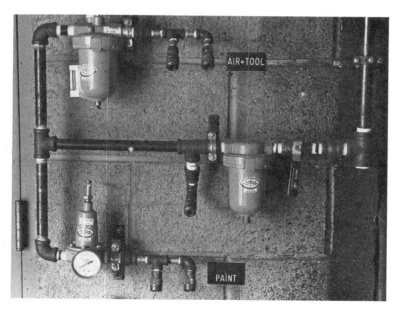

FIGURE 5–11 Air outlets in the shop. Compressed air passes through a filter to remove contaminants and moisture, and a lubricator to protect the moving parts of pneumatic tools. A regulator (and gauge) controls the air pressure. Note the quick couplers for rapid hookups to air hoses.

Besides air tools, other devices can translate air power into mechanical action (Figure 5-12). These have considerable potential for performing tasks needed in the shop or in a stage setting. They can fly scenery, move objects, power lifts, mobilize wagons, and perform numerous special-effects actions. Many of these functions can operate with the ease and portability of CO_2 gas canisters as the pneumatic power source.[1] A regulator and two pressure gauges are necessary on the canister. Rod cylinders are probably the most commonly used. They can be either single-acting or double-acting rods. Cable cylinders contain a loop of plastic-coated cable attached to each side of a piston in the cylinder. The cable passes around a sheave at each end of the cylinder and terminates in a bracket. Air casters are plastic "doughnuts" that provide a cushion of air to lift objects for moving. Rotary actuators, which rotate in arcs up to 360°, are available. All air devices require special valves to control the air flow appropriately, and those used on stage

during a performance may also have silencers to reduce the noise. Pneumatics is a "soft" power source, with considerable elasticity in its volume of air and, therefore, often requires a lock or brake to hold a load at a particular position.

Hydraulic Power

Hydraulic systems are familiar to us as compact power cylinders on truck end gates and on the basket lifts used to trim trees and repair overhead electric cables. These are found increasingly on lighting towers, hoists, and platform lifts useful as paint and construction scaffolds. Wood and metalworking tools are appearing with hydraulic power. Hydraulics is also being employed on stage to power elevators, flying systems, wagons, and scissor lifts. Because hydraulics is a rigid system, that is, its fluid compresses very little under load, it is widely used for lifts and platforms in the theatre. Besides powering tools and moving equipment, available fluid power sources with assorted fittings and accessories can perform numerous other work tasks.

GLUES AND ADHESIVES

Because the construction of scenery has long relied on glues and adhesives, a stock of these materials is standard in any scene shop. Hundreds of new adhesives are marketed today that have almost entirely replaced the traditional animal glues and pastes so common in scene technology of the past. These new adhesives meet many different structural and lamination needs and therefore are extremely valuable for both time-honored as well as new scenic materials. The task is to become familiar with adhesive products, their trade names, and their applications and functions. Many of the synthetic glues are limited to certain materials, often require tight-fitting joints, and may or may not be effective at filling gaps.

FIGURE 5-12 Some air devices.

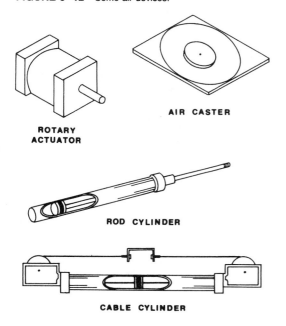

ROTARY ACTUATOR

AIR CASTER

ROD CYLINDER

CABLE CYLINDER

Does the project require an adhesive that has a specific curing time, that is flexible or rigid, that is waterproof, that is nonstaining, or that can be easily cleaned from a surface? How safe is it to use the product? Does it emit toxic vapors, does it require ventilation, does it need a specific solvent during cleanup? These and other questions are important in selecting an adhesive. Because of the wide choice available, it is often desirable to test an adhesive before adopting it for a project.

A brief listing of the most common types of adhesives is provided in Figure 5-13. This list will help answer some of the questions about their uses and characteristics. The following are some adhesives employed frequently in scene construction.

White glue: Popular in the shop, this is an all-purpose adhesive for porous surfaces such as wood joints, as a paste for fabric, or thinned for sizing. Requiring air to dry, it will not dry

FIGURE 5-13 Some common types of adhesives.

TYPE	USES	CHARACTERISTICS
White glue (polyvinyl acetate)	Wood, furniture, cloth, paper, leather, and other porous materials.	Common popular wood glue, relatively inexpensive, medium in strength and in moisture resistance.
Yellow glue (aliphatic resin)	Wood, furniture, and other porous materials.	Stronger than white glue, good in heat resistance and moisture resistance, but not waterproof.
Hide or animal glue	Wood; useful for indoor furniture, cabinets, and other porous materials.	Some (carpenters and gelatin glue) come in ground or flake form and must be soaked in water and heated in a double boiler or glue pot. Inexpensive. A good gap filler. Not waterproof.
Casein glue	Wood, paneling, fiberboard.	Available in powder form and mixed with water. Good gap filler. Moderate moisture resistance.
Plastic resin glue (urea-formaldehyde)	Wood, panels, and fiberboard.	A water-mixed adhesive, strong bonding power, water resistant, must be worked at temperatures of 70°F or above.
Resorcinol glue	Wood, panels, and fiberboard.	A two-part glue that must be mixed together. High strength, slow drying, and waterproof. Expensive. Withstands extreme temperatures. Good gap filler. Must be used at 70°F or above. Requires a long curing time.
Acrylic resin adhesive	Wood, panels, metal, glass, but not plastic.	A two-part adhesive (liquid and powder). Has a strong bond and is waterproof. Good gap and crack filler.
Hot-melt glue (thermoplastic polyamide or polyethylene base)	Wood, fabric, leather, metal, and plastic.	Uses an electric glue gun. Must work fast as glue dries in 10 to 60 seconds. Nontoxic, odorless, and nonflammable. Avoid contact with glue and heating chamber when hot.

FIGURE 5–13   Some common types of adhesives.   *(continued)*

TYPE	USES	CHARACTERISTICS
Contact adhesive (solvent-based, chlorinated-based and water-based types)	Panel and sheet plastic laminates, metal, wood, fiberboard, ceramics and similar materials. Water-based adhesives are effective for plastic foams.	Both surfaces must be coated; when tacky they are joined together. Alignment must be accurate. Solvent-based types are highly flammable and sometimes toxic. Water-based types are slow drying—up to an hour is needed before joining the two surfaces.
Epoxy adhesive	Rigid materials: metal, tile, glass, masonry, ceramics, wood, and some plastics. Not for polyethylene, polypropylene, and Teflon.	A two-part adhesive (resin and catalyst) that must be mixed. Strong, water resistant, and expensive. A good gap filler. Use where high strength is needed.
Construction and panel adhesive	Paneling, ceiling and floor tile, ceramics, fiberboard, metals. Check label for the material it will secure. Certain solvent-based adhesives damage plastic foams.	Paste-like material. Some are applied with a caulking gun or squeeze tube. Check to see whether particular adhesive is flammable.
Floor adhesives	Wood, carpet, concrete, tile. Some are subfloor adhesives (meeting standards of the American Plywood Assn.), which hold plywood to framing members to act as a one-sided stressed skin panel.	Sometimes available in caulking tube form. Note appropriate solvent for cleaning up spills and tools.
"Instant" or "super" adhesive (cyanoacrylates)	Fast bonds for nonporous surfaces: metal, china, glass, jewelry, rubber, ceramics, leather, and most plastics.	So-called one drop glue. Dries rapidly. Caution: it will bond to skin. Keep away from eyes and face. Very expensive.

in a tight joint of nonporous material. It is not waterproof and needs overnight to fully cure.

Yellow glue: This is a somewhat stronger glue and is valuable for wood and other porous surfaces. It is moisture resistant but not waterproof.

Phlexglu: This is a commercial name for a flexible vinyl-acrylic white glue that dries to transparency. It is especially useful for fabric and soft materials that must move, flex, or fold. It can be layered for buildups, thickened for texture, mixed with dyes or paints for colored glass, or thinned for spraying and applying protective coats on surfaces.

Hot-melt glue: Heated by an electric glue gun, hot-melt glue dries as quickly as it cools. The fast-drying feature of this adhesive makes it very attractive to use. However, it is not a strong glue and is usually limited to small prop and decorative details. It is often useful for making small relief ornamentations.

Contact cement: This adhesive must be applied to both surfaces and allowed to dry for a specified period of time before the surfaces are joined. Once joined, the surfaces cannot be repositioned. The water-based types, such as 3M Fastbond 30-NF, are excellent for bonding layers of rigid or flexible foams. As a paint undercoating, it gives a protective coat to low-density foam and permits the surfaces of etha-foam to hold paint without flaking.

Epoxy adhesive: Epoxies are excellent where high strength is a must and particularly for nonporous materials. This two-part adhesive must be mixed together in the exact amount needed for the job. It is waterproof, limited to rigid materials, and a good gap filler. Cleanup is difficult for spills.

Instant or super adhesive: Cyanoacrylates are fast-bonding adhesives for rigid materials. Because of its cost, it is usually limited to small objects. Extreme care is needed to avoid skin contact.

Spray adhesives: Aerosol adhesives are convenient to apply and are available for many different surfaces and applications. An extensive range of industrial-quality spray adhesives are manufactured by the 3M Company. These include adhesives for instantly bonding foams; pressure-sensitive adhesives for objects that can be repositioned without leaving residue on surfaces; high-tack contact cements; rubber and vinyl adhesives; and high-strength adhesives for porous and nonporous surfaces. The 3M Company also has a citrus-based aerosol cleaner that is an excellent and safe nonsolvent liquid for cleaning the skin or other surfaces of grease, oil, dirt, and most adhesive and tape residues.

Labels should be read carefully in selecting the proper adhesive for the task at hand.

Directions for applications often must be followed very precisely. Most important, be aware of the toxic and physical hazards of the material and follow all safety and health procedures. Copies of the Material Safety Data Sheets for each product should be studied.

SELECTED READINGS

BOWMAN, NED A., *Handbook of Technical Practice for the Performing Arts*. Wilkinsburg, PA: Scenographic Media, 1976.

BURRIS-MEYER, HAROLD, and EDWARD C. COLE, *Scenery for the Theatre* (rev. ed.). Boston: Little, Brown, 1971.

BURRIS-MEYER, HAROLD, and EDWARD C. COLE, *Theatres and Auditoriums* (2nd ed.). New York: Reinhold, 1964.

HEDGES, CHARLES S., *Industrial Fluid Power*, 2 vols. (2nd ed.). Dallas, TX: Womack Educational Publications, 1970.

MILLER, ROBERT S., *Adhesives and Glues*. Columbus, OH: Franklin Chemical Industries, 1980.

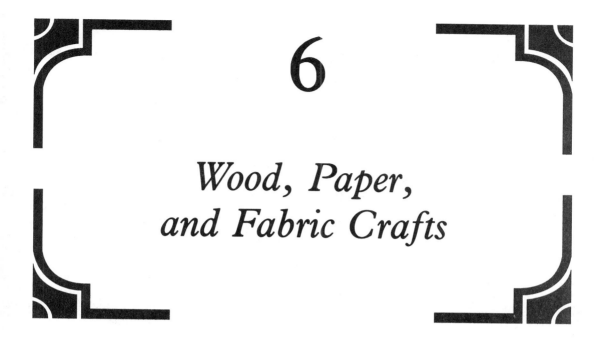

6

Wood, Paper, and Fabric Crafts

While scene technology is a special construction endeavor with its own unique requirements, specific purposes, and technical precision, it nonetheless is rooted in a number of basic crafts. Wood, paper, and fabric are the most traditional technologies used for scenery. The acquisition of knowledge and development of skill in these foundation crafts is essential. Tools are dangerous items until their functions are known; learn all safety practices and attain personal skill in their use. Building materials have limited value to us without an understanding of their functional and structural properties. Additionally, methods exist for constructing objects to meet an endless number of circumstances and demands. It is the application of these tools, materials, and practices that permits the finding of solutions to production challenges and situations. Both extensive study and the acquisition of skills help advance a technician's proficiency and judgment. As a foundation for acquiring

knowledge and developing skills in wood, paper, and fabric, some of the basic tools and materials will be analyzed and discussed.

WOODWORKING

The working of wood is probably the oldest craft known to humanity; wood is a highly workable material, and supplies are replenished as forests continue to exist. With the cooperation of modern forestry and the lumbering industry in improved reforestation, harvesting practices, and tree genetics, an ample supply of this natural resource may let woodworking continue to be a viable craft in the foreseeable future.

Wood Products

Wood products clearly meet the requirements of scenery, and, therefore, they are valuable scene construction materials. Such softwoods as pine, redwood, spruce, cedar, and Douglas fir are suitable for scenery. Of these, the white pines are generally preferred for most scene construction. White pine is reasonably strong, lightweight, and relatively soft. It is easily worked with hand tools and resists splitting and splintering. Douglas fir is a heavier and stronger wood and is particularly useful for weight-bearing structures. It is available in 2″ thicknesses for this purpose and is also employed in the construction of plywood.

Lumber Grades. Lumber must be carefully selected for scene construction. The frame of a flat, for instance, must be straight and true to retain its shape and to fit tightly to an adjacent unit. Wood with twist or warp, with knots that cause points of weakness, or with other defects and blemishes is not satisfactory. As lumber is cut at the mill, it is classified and graded for quality by a uniform set of national standards. It is then cured or seasoned by drying in the open air or in a large kiln. This lowers the moisture content to reduce warping, twisting, and cracking of boards.

Yard lumber, the classification of lumber used for general building purposes, is usually divided into two grade categories, Select and Common. The **Select grades** identify lumber of good appearance and finishing qualities. Select lumber ranges from A to D, with A Select practically clear and D Select having a few tight knots and other blemishes. The high cost and scarcity of the top select grades usually means that C Select is the best available. D Select can be used sometimes if the bad portions are removed. **Common grades** are classified in numbers from 1 to 5. They are suitable for construction and utility purposes where the wood is not visible. Number 1 Common is generally free of structural defects and contains large tight knots. Larger knots and defects in the grain are found in number 2 Common lumber. Subsequent grades are progressively poorer in quality. For scenery, Common lumber is mostly limited to bracing, flooring, or supports for structural units.

Lumber Sizes. At the sawmill, lumber is cut into rough-surfaced boards. After it is air or kiln dried, it is processed through a planer or surfacer to smooth its surfaces. Finish lumber is generally surfaced on four sides (S4S). The actual (dressed) size is less than the rough (nominal) size as cut at the mill. Despite the dressed measurements of lumber, we refer to lumber by its original dimensions. Thus, 1″ thick lumber is actually nearer ¾″, and 2″ stock is approximately 1½″. Actual thicknesses and widths are generally uniform, although slight variations occur between batches of lumber owing to differences in shrinkage and the drying process. Each piece of lumber must be measured before it is used. Lumber of 1″ and 2″ nominal thickness is the most common for scenery, although occasionally 1¼″ lumber is useful.

In identifying lumber, the first number is always the thickness, the second the width, and the third the length. Length is always listed in feet. A 1 × 6 × 12 is a board 1″ thick, 6″ wide, and 12′ long. The standard lengths of yard lumber range from 8′ to 16′ in intervals of 2′.

Because the dimensions of scenery to be constructed are usually known in advance, lumber is usually ordered by specifying the number of pieces of a particular length (such as 14 pieces of 1 × 4 of a designated lumber grade). The cost of the purchase is then determined by the price per piece. If specific lengths are not important, lumber can be purchased by the *board foot* and, in fact, random lengths may be provided. Large quantities of both softwood and hardwood lumber are priced and sold by the board foot. A board foot is the equivalent of a 1″ × 12″ × 1′ board. Should you need to know, the simplest way to determine the board feet in a given piece of lumber is to multply its dimensions and divide by 12 as expressed in the following formula:

$$BF = \frac{T \text{ (in inches)} \times W \text{ (in inches)} \times L \text{ (in feet)}}{12}$$

As an example, compute the number of board feet in a $1'' \times 3'' \times 14'$.

$$BF = \frac{1 \times 3 \times 14}{12} = \frac{42}{12} = 3\frac{1}{2} \text{ board feet}$$

Once you determine the board feet in a single piece, this figure may be multiplied by the number of pieces desired and then multiplied by the cost per board foot of the wood grade ordered.

Moldings and Worked Lumber. A variety of trim work and decorative lumber is a definite asset for scenic detail. Chief among these are readily available standard **moldings** (Figure 6-1). Lumber dealers stock ponderosa pine molding in select grades for house construction. Moldings come in a range of patterns identified as quarter round, half round, picture molding, nosing, chair rail, base, crown molding, and many others. These are invaluable for enriching architectural paneling, cornices, and trim for a setting. Doors, fireplaces, and similar items often require decorative treatment. Embossed and machine-carved moldings are more costly but are particularly useful for decorating furniture, picture frames, and cabinetry. Moldings are sold by the *linear foot*. Turned posts, balusters, newel posts, and other decorative lumber can also be obtained in standard shapes, but the cost of these is generally high.

Other types of worked lumber (specially shaped, matched, or patterned) include forms of siding and flooring lumber. These have been finished to join together by overlapping, by tongue and groove joints, or by shiplapped edges. They can serve scenery either for decorative functions or for regular construction purposes.

Plywood. Plywood is a special processed wood product consisting generally of three or five thin layers of wood glued together.

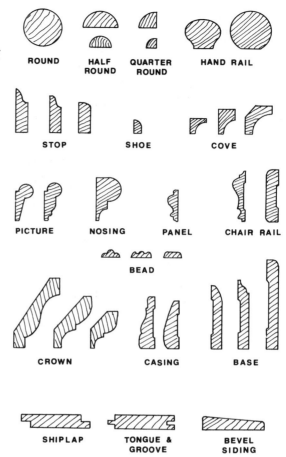

FIGURE 6–1 Moldings and worked lumber.

The grain of each layer or ply is at right angles to adjacent layers. This provides greater strength and stability than regular lumber of comparative dimensions. Plywood is produced in standard panels of $4' \times 8'$ and even larger by special order. It is most commonly available in thicknesses of $\frac{1}{8}''$, $\frac{1}{4}''$, $\frac{3}{8}''$, $\frac{1}{2}''$, $\frac{5}{8}''$, and $\frac{3}{4}''$. It is manufactured for the construction industry in many grades and surfaces ranging from "natural finish" veneer face ply for furniture, cabinets, or wall paneling to structural panels for sheathing and floor underlayments.

FIGURE 6–2 Moldings and decorative lumber contribute in a major way to a setting. A scene from *Tartuffe* produced at Northern Illinois University. Scene designer, Alan Donahue. (Photo by Barry Stark)

Plywood is available in two types, interior and exterior, differing in the moisture resistance of the glue used in the laminations. Interior panels are adequate for scenery except, perhaps, in outdoor productions. In each type, there are several grades of plywood. They are identified generally by letters (such as A–B or C–D), which define the face and back veneers, respectively. The letter A stands for a smooth, sanded, and paintable ply; B for a solid surface with tight knots and repair plugs; and C and D with surface splits, flaws, and imperfections not suitable for a finished surface. A–A plywood has a clear surface on both sides but is expensive. A–D grade has one smooth surface and is usually satisfactory for most scenery construction. Grade C–D is cheaper, and not inferior in strength, but lacks a face veneer appropriate for an appearance surface. This grade is usable only where it will be covered or unseen.

Many scene shops purchase less expensive ³⁄₁₆″ lauan panelboard for scenic surfaces where the strength of regular ¼″ plywood (for corner-blocks, for instance) is not needed. Plywood panels are priced by the *square foot.*

Hardboard. Hardboard, sometimes better known by the trade name *Masonite*, is a medium- to hard-density material manufactured from wood fibers. Formed into a mat, it is compressed and bonded into a hard, durable panel. Hardboard is a dense and brittle material more water resistant than wood. It is made with one smooth surface (S1S) or both surfaces finished (S2S). **Standard hardboard** is light brown in color. **Tempered hardboard** is dark brown in color and has an extremely hard and durable surface. It is coated with oil and baked to increase hardness, strength, and water resistance. Carbide-tipped saw blades are necessary to cut tempered hardboard.

Hardboard is most commonly available in ⅛″, 3⁄16″, and ¼″ thicknesses and in 4′ × 8′ sheets or larger. It is sold by the square foot. Perforated with holes, it is sold as "pegboard" for storage racks. It is also available with prefinished surfaces of wood, tile, brick, and textured patterns.

Particleboard. Particleboard is a panel product formed by compressing wood chips and particles together with an adhesive. Similar composition boards are known as waferboard (compressed wafer-like particles or flakes), composite (a particle core with veneer face and back plies), and oriented strand board (compressed strand-like particles arranged in layers oriented at right angles to each other). These composition boards are not as strong as plywood and have inferior properties. The edges must be protected from chipping or flaking. They are useful for furniture, cabinetry, and underlayments. Particleboard is usually less expensive than plywood. Thicknesses available include ⅜″ and ¾″, and it is sold in 4′ × 8′ panels.

Common Wood Joints

The construction of wood-framed scenery relies heavily on the knowledge of lumber strength and the selection of wood joints. A 1″ × 3″ will support minimal weight through its thickness but has enormous structural strength end to end (see Figure 6-3). Similarly, a joint must be strong enough to resist the stress and the directions of force put upon it. The examples in Figure 6-4 demonstrate the increased strength of a dado joint and a butt joint in compression when a downward force is applied.

The limited amount of time to build scenery (and to rebuild stock scenery) is an-

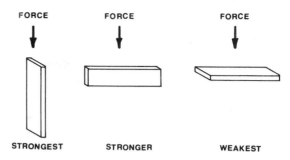

FIGURE 6–3 Comparative strength through the end, side, and thickness of a 1″ × 3″.

other factor influencing the selection of joints. Some joints need more time and skill to construct than is available. Others become permanent joints not suitable for scenery that is to be altered and reused again. In addition to these factors, joints must be constructed with care and precision. Some of the most common joints used in scenery are pictured in Figure 6-5.

The **butt joint** is widely employed in many scenery structures. The lumber must be cut square and true for a tight fit. Generally easy to construct, butt joints are often strengthened with reinforcements. An end-to-edge butt joint is reinforced with plywood or metal plates in many forms of two-dimensional framed scenery. In assembling the corner of a flat frame, for instance, 10″ × 10″ cornerblocks are placed ¾″ from each edge and secured with a minimum of nine to

FIGURE 6–4 Comparative strengths of wood joints.

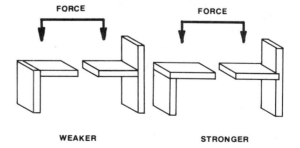

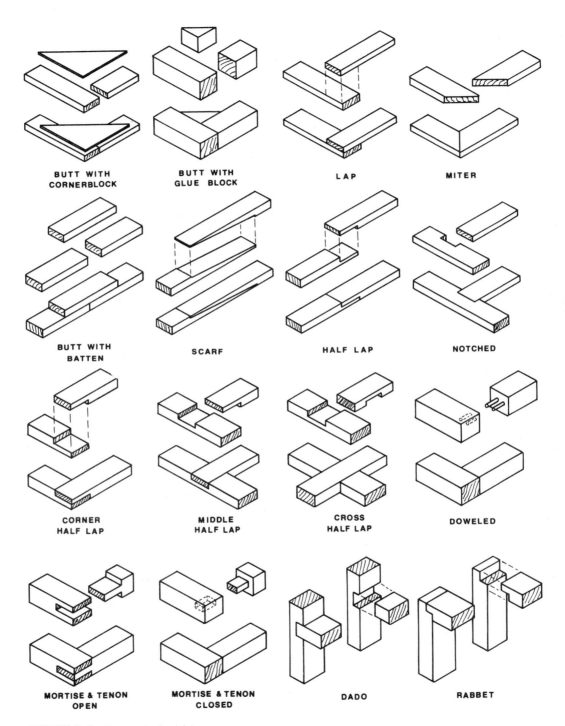

BUTT WITH
CORNERBLOCK

BUTT WITH
GLUE BLOCK

LAP

MITER

BUTT WITH
BATTEN

SCARF

HALF LAP

NOTCHED

CORNER
HALF LAP

MIDDLE
HALF LAP

CROSS
HALF LAP

DOWELED

MORTISE & TENON
OPEN

MORTISE & TENON
CLOSED

DADO

RABBET

FIGURE 6–5 Common lumber joints.

eleven fasteners. Sometimes butt joints are reinforced with angled glue blocks. Battens, attached with nails, air staples, or screws, are used to give support to end-to-end joints.

The **lap joint** is a form of butt joint in which lumber pieces overlap and are joined with standard fasteners. This is frequently used for supporting frames. A **half-lap joint** is a face-to-face join of two pieces of lumber by the removal of half the thickness of each. The result is a flush surface connection that resists rotational stress. Regular fasteners and sometimes glue are needed to hold the joint.

The **scarf joint** is an end-to-end joint to create a batten longer than regular board stock. Each board is given a tapered cut 1'–6" long with a ⅛" straight cut at each end. The cuts must be planed smooth to eliminate high and low points that will prevent a tight fit. The joint is held with glue and screws.

A **miter joint** results from a 45° cut on one or both pieces of lumber. It is sometimes used for diagonal bracing for structural frames. For paneling and picture frames it serves a decorative purpose: to match the design of the molding and give a continuous surface without exposing the end grain.

The **mortise and tenon** is one of the strongest joints and can withstand stress in several directions. The closed mortise and tenon is time-consuming and difficult to make without specialized power equipment. A smooth tight fit is needed. Glue is often sufficient to hold the joint securely.

A **doweled joint** is a method of strengthening a butt joint. Holes are drilled in both boards by careful marking with a try square and a marking gauge. Hardwood dowel is the most preferred. All joining surfaces are glued and held in clamps until dry.

A **notched joint** involves cutting a slot in one piece of lumber the width of the other piece of lumber. It has the strength characteristics of a dado joint. The **dado** and **rabbet joints** are similar. The dado is a groove in lumber to fit the end of the other member. Commonly used on shelving, this joint resists

shear forces. The rabbet is a groove joint at a corner.

Woodworking Tools

Tools are precision items designed for specific functions. When they are used properly, they are safe and effective. When used improperly, tools can be damaged and the worker injured.

Quality power tools are expensive but are worth the investment. Lightweight home-shop versions are seldom a bargain. They rarely hold up to the needs of a scene shop.

Learn how to use tools, know their safety precautions, and have a supervisor assist you in your first experience with them. Some of the more common tools are identified in the following functional classifications.

Measuring and Marking Tools (Figure 6-6). Measurements are commonly made with spring-loaded **steel tapes**. Those with locks to hold the tape when extended are especially handy. The most convenient lengths are 8', 10', 12', 16', and 25'. For longer measurements, 50' and 100' **windup tapes** are available.

Squares and levels assist in the accuracy of angles. The **try square** is used to make right angle lines for saw cuts. The **combination square** can mark lumber for both 90° and 45° angles. The adjustable head of the **bevel protractor** permits this tool to mark any angle. The **T bevel** has an adjustable blade for checking or marking all angles. The **framing square** (carpenter's steel square) is essential to confirm the accuracy of 90° angles at the joints of framed lumber. True horizontals and verticals are determined by a **level**.

Among marking tools, the **marking gauge** is used to mark a line parallel to the edge of a piece of lumber. **Trammel points** attached to a rod or strip of wood are used to scribe arcs and circles. A **scratch awl** is valuable in locating positions for starting screws and drill bits. Guide lines needed for construc-

tion and painting layouts can be snapped with a **chalk line**.

Calipers and dividers are special measuring tools. **Outside calipers** are used to measure outside thicknesses such as cuts in a lathe-turned baluster. **Dividers** are used to transfer measurements, to step off divisions of a line, and to draw arcs and circles in the manner of a compass. A divider or **pencil compass** also is useful in scribing a line to match an irregular surface.

Clamping tools (Figure 6-7). These tools hold wood securely for sawing and other work processes or while glue is drying. The

FIGURE 6–7 Clamping tools.

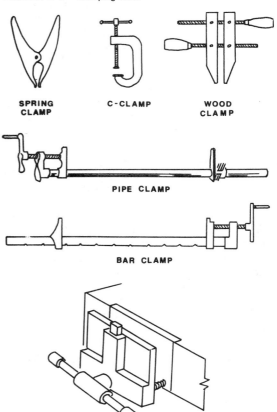

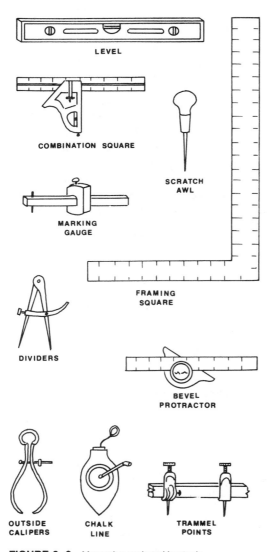

FIGURE 6–6 Measuring and marking tools.

spring clamp works well on small projects where light pressure is adequate. Available in a range of sizes, **C clamps** provide a tight grip on lumber. **Wood clamps** provide a secure hold on flat as well as angled work. Large boards or frames that are glued can be held together with a **bar clamp** or a **pipe clamp** (clamps attached to a length of ¾″ pipe). Long pipe clamps are very handy at times and can be achieved by two shorter lengths of pipe threaded at the ends and joined with a coupler. A **woodworking vise** mounts on the end of a workbench to clamp lumber firmly while shaping, drilling, or other woodworking.

Driving Tools (Figure 6-8). Hammers and mallets are familiar driving implements. The **claw hammer** is a common carpentry tool and nail driver. Its curved claws are used for pulling nails. A block of wood placed under the head is needed for leverage in pulling long nails. The straight claws of the **rip hammer** equip it for separating joined lumber. Hammer sizes range from 10 oz (small), 13 oz and 16 oz (medium), to 20 oz (large), indicating the weight of the head. The **wooden mallet** is the proper tool to drive wood chisels. This and other soft-faced mallets (rubber, rawhide, and plastic) are used where steel-headed hammers would damage the work. A **nail set** is used to countersink finish nails.

Staple drivers are a quick and efficient means of attaching materials to wood. With a squeeze of the lever a **compression stapler** drives staples as small as ⁵⁄₃₂″ up to ⁹⁄₁₆″ by a spring-actuated mechanism. In the manner of a hammer, the **hammer tacker** discharges a staple with each blow to a surface. **Electric staplers** drive staples from ⅜″ to ⁹⁄₁₆″ with a minimum of physical fatigue. Air power makes possible the use of large staples capable of joining flat frames and other wood structures rapidly and securely. An **air stapler** can handle several staple lengths (⅝″, 1″, and 1 ½″ are common) with the ease of a trigger action. It uses heavy wire staples with staple legs, which are pointed to spread

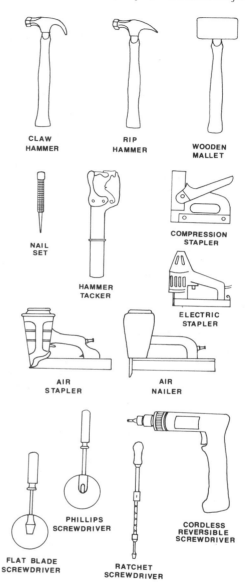

CLAW HAMMER

RIP HAMMER

WOODEN MALLET

NAIL SET

HAMMER TACKER

COMPRESSION STAPLER

ELECTRIC STAPLER

AIR STAPLER

AIR NAILER

PHILLIPS SCREWDRIVER

FLAT BLADE SCREWDRIVER

RATCHET SCREWDRIVER

CORDLESS REVERSIBLE SCREWDRIVER

FIGURE 6–8 Driving tools.

when entering wood and adhesive coated for better holding power. For safety purposes, a worker must press the safety yoke against the work and pull the trigger simultaneously before a staple is discharged. In a shop where several different staple drivers are used, it is important to prevent the jamming and damaging of tools that occurs by loading the wrong staples in a stapling tool. **Air nailers**, which drive special nails and brads, are also available and convenient to use. Pneumatic power systems for air tools are described later in this chapter.

Another set of tools is designed for driving screws. Several sizes of **screwdrivers** are needed in order to have blade tips appropriate to fit the variety of screws used. A **Phillips screwdriver** is necessary for cross-slotted screws. The automatic action of **ratchet screwdrivers** is particularly handy in a scene shop. Some experience is needed to learn to drive and remove screws by direct pressure of this spiral-action tool.

Be careful not to bend the spiral shaft or leave the tool extended on the shop floor where it can be stepped on. Also avoid releasing the spring-held shaft from its retracted position in the direction of another person. **Variable-speed electric drills** and speed reducers for single-speed power drills can be fitted with screwdriver bits to drive and extract screws with a minimum of physical effort and time. More useful are **cordless reversible screwdrivers**, which avoid the nuisance of extensive cords especially when working on a ladder and in other difficult situations.

Air-powered screwdrivers offer the same convenience and are ideal for construction projects requiring numerous screws. A pilot hole is usually needed to start a small screw, and most large screws require a predrilled hole. Screwdriver tips should be kept sharpened to reduce damage to screw heads.

Drilling Tools (Figure 6-9). The **brace and auger bit** is the historic tool for boring holes in wood. The turning force is generated by rotating the frame. A ratchet brace permits partial sweeps necessary in confined spaces. The bits range in diameter from ¼″ to 1″. Countersink bits and screwdriver bits are also available. Expansion bits can bore

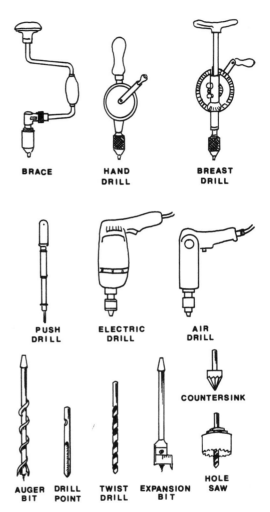

FIGURE 6–9   Drilling tools.

holes up to 3″ in diameter by extending the cutter blade to the proper radius. The **hand drill and twist drill bit** bores holes up to ¼″ in diameter by turning a crank and gear wheel in "eggbeater" fashion. A larger version of the hand drill, the **breast drill**, has a chuck to take up to ½″ bits. By leaning against the breast plate more pressure can be applied. For drilling small holes in wood, the **push drill and drill point** rotates by a spring-loaded shaft when pressure is applied to the handle. Drill points are stored in the handle.

Power drills have become essential tools in scene construction. **Portable electric drills** with ¼″, ⅜″, or ½″ chuck capacity are the most convenient. Variable speed and reversible controls are additional desirable features. High-speed twist drill bits are effective for both wood and metal. In addition, countersink bits, screwdriver bits, and wide-tipped spade bits (for wood only) are available for use in electric drills. **Expansion bits** and **hole saws** can be employed to cut circles in a range of sizes.

Other electric drill accessories include disk sanders, wire brushes, and buffers. **Cordless electric drills** are valuable where power is not available or when lengthy cords would be impractical. The largest electric drill is the **drill press**, permanently mounted on a floor stand or bench. It can be used for wood, although its chief value is for drilling in metal. Attachments can adapt it for mortising, routing, shaping, and planing. **Air drills** are excellent power boring tools, especially in driving and removing self-tapping bugle screws.

Shaping, Planing, and Sanding Tools (Figure 6-10). Struck with a wooden mallet, or with hand pressure alone, **wood chisels** are designed to remove wood. Grooves, slots, and mortises can be cut out of lumber. Snugly fit into wooden handles, the steel blades range from ¼″ to 1½″ in width.

Shaving tools are employed to shape and smooth lumber edges. The **draw knife** provides rough shaping or planing for straight or curved edges. A slightly smaller tool, the **spokeshave**, is intended to smooth the surface of a curved edge of wood. A **block plane** shaves and smooths the end grain of lumber. The blade is adjustable from 12° to 20° in angle and in depth of cut. Another plane, the **smoothing plane**, is a longer and heavier tool. It is used to smooth the surface of lumber in the direction of the grain. The blades

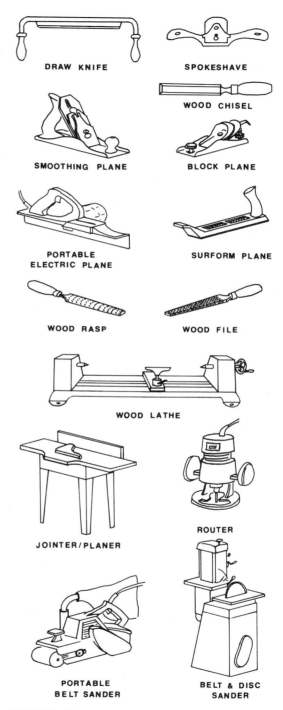

FIGURE 6–10 Shaping, planing, and sanding tools.

are adjustable in depth of cut. The blades of these tools must be kept sharp to be effective shaving instruments. If planing becomes a regular necessity in a scene shop **portable electric planes** are available to increase the speed of the work. Floor-mounted **electric jointers** and **wood shapers** have circular cutting heads for producing a smooth surface on lumber. They can cut bevels, chamfers, and tapered and decorative edges.

Rasps and files remove particles of wood with rows of sharp teeth. The **wood rasp**, either flat on both sides or with one half-round side, has coarse teeth for the rough shaping of wood. The unique **Surform tools**—the plane, the round file, and the file—utilize perforated steel blades with sharp-edged holes that remove wood particles rapidly. They also can be used on light aluminum, copper, and plastic surfaces. **Wood files** may be flat, round, or half-round. They provide a smoother surface than rasps and Surform tools. Files must be cleaned frequently with a file brush.

Two power shaping tools have special significance in building scenery. The **portable electric router** is useful in cutting grooves and decorative edges on lumber. A large number of router bits are available for various groove shapes and molded edges. It is a hand-held, compact unit. "Turned" carvings are produced on the **wood lathe**. Balusters, furniture legs, and other turned ornaments are made from a block of wood placed in a lathe and shaped with wood turning chisels and gouges. After cutting grooves, beads, and coves on the stock, sanding and finishing can also be performed while the work is spinning in the lathe.

A smooth-sanded finish is often required on a woodwork project. The simplest tool is a **sanding block** wrapped in coarse, medium, or fine grade sandpaper. An inexpensive **disk sander** attachment can be acquired to fit a standard portable electric drill. Special abrasive disks 4″ to 9″ in diameter are backed by a rubber pad. More powerful is the **portable electric belt sander**, which re-

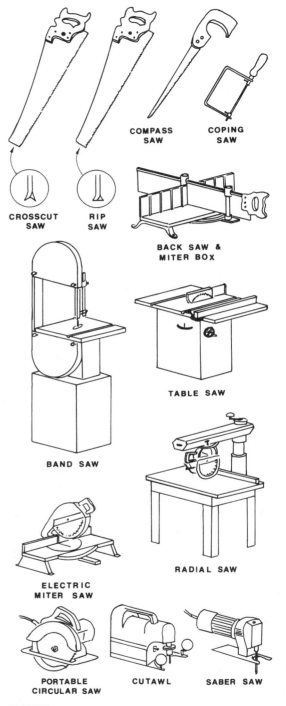

FIGURE 6–11 Saws.

moves a considerable amount of material. Those with dust-collecting bags reduce dust particles in the air. Be sure to wear a particle respirator or filter mask. Floor model **belt and disk sanders** are highly effective for finishing wood.

Saws (Figure 6-11). Hand saws are designed to cut lumber in lengths, widths, and shapes. The number of points per inch indicates the fineness or coarseness of the cut. More points will produce a finer cut. The teeth are set (bent outward alternately) to permit the blade to move easily through the kerf (the path of the cut) without binding. The **crosscut saw** is designed to cut across the grain of the wood. Crosscut teeth have sharp outer points to cut the wood like knives. Eight- to ten-point saws are standard for crosscutting. The **rip saw** is intended to cut with the grain of the wood. Six to eight points per inch is standard. Rip teeth are filed flat to remove the wood like chisels. The **compass saw** has a narrow, tapered blade. After a small hole is drilled, it is used to cut holes or openings in wood or to saw in tight spaces where other hand saws will not fit. Scroll work, irregular shapes, and curves in thin stock are cut with a **coping saw**. The **backsaw and miter box** is used to make accurate angular cuts. The blade is stiffened at the top by a metal rib and its crosscut teeth (with 12 or more points per inch) are designed for fine and precision cuts. The miter box is adjustable for the angle of cut.

Power saws are valuable additions in the scene shop for increasing the efficiency of construction. Know their principles of operation and their safety precautions.

The **circular table saw** is a bench- or floor-mounted machine typically using an 8" or 10" diameter circular blade projecting through a slot in the table. Essential accessories include an adjustable rip fence and a miter gauge for crosscutting that is adjustable for angled cuts. The blade is adjustable in height to suit the work, and a tilting arbor feature permits the blade to be tilted for bev-

eled cuts. This saw is useful especially in ripping lumber and panel stock. Dado cuts also can be made. Long lengths of lumber must be supported after passing through the blade. A push stick is necessary when feeding lumber close to the spinning blade. Good quality blades are made of milled tool steel. Cheaper versions use stamped cold-rolled steel. Choose the right blade for ripping, crosscutting, and cutting plywood. Carbide-tipped blades stay sharp much longer than regular blades, but they will cost more when teeth need sharpening.

The **radial arm saw** positions the circular blade and motor on an armature above the table. It is somewhat safer to use than the table saw. In crosscut sawing, the lumber remains stationary and the blade is pulled across the work. Since the blade is above the work, the sawing action is clearly visible. It is a highly versatile power tool. It can be used for ripping, dadoing, rabbeting, and many other types of sawing. The blade can be raised and lowered, and it can be tilted at any angle in both vertical and horizontal planes. The saw can be placed along a wall with adjacent workbench tops to support long lengths of lumber.

The **band saw** is designed to make circular and irregular cuts in lumber. The blade is a thin steel band welded into a continuous loop. The depth of the throat (governed by the diameter of the wheels) determines the width of the material that can be fed through the saw. Throat sizes of 14" to 24" are the most common. The band saw can also make straight cuts. A rip fence and a miter gauge are accessories for this purpose. The table can also tilt for angular cutting.

An **electric miter saw** is a time-saving power saw for cutting miters and square cuts on architectural trim. The table is easily and accurately adjustable for degrees of angle.

Portable power saws often have distinct advantages over the large, fixed machines. The **portable circular saw** is lightweight and convenient for ripping and crosscutting at the site of construction. The 7½" blade is common. This saw is particularly useful when, because of size or location, the stock cannot be sawed on a table or radial saw. The blade can be adjusted for depth of cut and tilted for bevel cuts. Special safety precautions should be followed in using this tool. The **saber saw** is a useful tool in the scene shop; it is ideal for cutting irregular sweeps and curves in plywood and other sheet material that could not be handled through the band saw. It can start its own hole and cut out openings inside the stock. The pneumatic saber saw is a small, compact tool that is powerful and highly versatile. The **Cutawl** is an excellent tool for cutting clean intricate patterns in plywood, Upson board, stencil board, and other materials. It can be fitted with saw, knife, or chisel blades appropriate to the stock. The blade is adjustable in depth. Soft fiberboard must be placed beneath the work while cutting.

Dismantling Tools (Figure 6-12). The **nail puller** is invaluable in removing nails and air-driven staples from lumber. The jaws are driven into the wood beneath a nail or staple head and, with the leverage of the handle, are easily pulled from the material. The **wrecking bar** and the **ripping chisel** are used to separate joined lumber with lever action. Both have tapered ends for prying and claws to pull nails.

Other Tools. The **utility knife** and the **linoleum knife** are useful tools for cutting and trimming wood, cloth, fiberboards, and many other materials. The **putty knife** can be used to apply wood putty and paste fillers in holes and dents in wood before finishing. The **electric glue gun** provides hot liquid glue with the squeeze of a trigger and dries in 60 seconds. It is excellent as an adhesive for many materials.

Basic Construction Hardware

In constructing scenery, many items of hardware serve as fastening, attachment, and reinforcement devices. While a few are special or unusual items, the majority are standard woodworking hardware available in regular hardware stores. They are essential items in scene building. Types of hardware for the assembly, bracing, rigging, and shifting of scenery are presented in a later chapter.

Nails and Tacks (Figure 6-13). Nails are standard fastening devices. The length of the majority of nails is described in the ancient penny system. Those generally used for scenery range from two penny (2d), which is 1″ long, to sixteen penny (16d), which is 3½″ long. **Common nails** are made of the thickest wire and are used for heavy construction. This includes platform construction and structures using 2″ stock. **Box nails** are of thinner wire stock. Because of this, they are less likely to split lumber. Box nails, therefore, are used extensively for

FIGURE 6–12 Dismantling tools, and others.

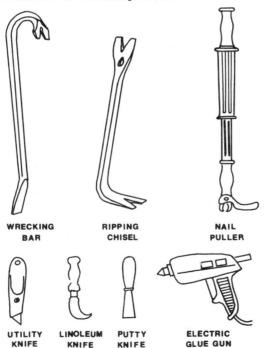

| WRECKING BAR | RIPPING CHISEL | NAIL PULLER |

| UTILITY KNIFE | LINOLEUM KNIFE | PUTTY KNIFE | ELECTRIC GLUE GUN |

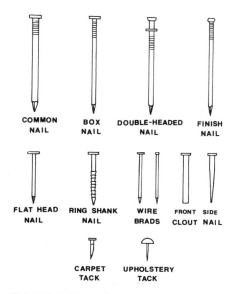

COMMON
NAIL

BOX
NAIL

DOUBLE-HEADED
NAIL

FINISH
NAIL

FLAT HEAD
NAIL

RING SHANK
NAIL

WIRE
BRADS

FRONT SIDE
CLOUT NAIL

CARPET
TACK

UPHOLSTERY
TACK

FIGURE 6–13 Nails and tacks.

scene construction. **Finish nails** are used where nail heads must be hidden. These are thin-shaft nails with very small heads that are countersunk into wood with a nail set. The hole is then filled with wood putty or paste to conceal the nail. The **double-headed nail** has the diameter of the common nail and two heads. It is used for scaffolding and other temporary structures. These nails protrude from the surface to permit easy removal with a hammer or a wrecking bar. **Flat-headed wire nails** with large flat heads are used to secure soft materials such as fiber boards that cannot be held securely by small-headed nails. **Ring shank nails** (drywall nails) have specially designed shanks with increased holding power for securing hardboards. Nails should be long enough to penetrate ¾″ into the framing. **Wire brads** are thin fasteners and range from ½″ to 1½″ in length. They are valuable for nailing thin moldings and trim work without splitting the wood.

The **clout nail** is now outdated and rarely used, but it was once very common in scenic practice as a fastener for plywood-rein-

forced wood joints. Exceeding the combined thickness of the wood by ¼″, the flat tapered shafts of the nails could be bent over on the opposite side, thus providing a firm fastening, and only a nail puller could remove them. This was accomplished by placing a steel plate, called a **clinch plate**, under the material, which clinched the end of the nail when driven into the lumber.

Carpet tacks are available in a number of sizes. They are used to hold fabric and upholstery materials to wood. **Upholstery tacks** have ornamental heads and are used as a decorative feature as they secure fabric to the frames of furniture.

Staples (Figure 6-14). Strands of wire, wire screening, and other materials are commonly held to wood by staples. Among hammer-driven staples, the galvanized **fence staples** are the largest. Smaller, flat-crowned **screen staples** are bluish in color. Both of these have been largely replaced by the convenience of mechanical and power-driven staples. There are hand-driven compression staplers, hammer tackers, electric staplers, and air-driven staplers. Not only does each require a different kind and size of staple but each manufacturer of a given type requires its own staples. You will need to stock the proper staples for each machine. If the wrong staples are used, the machine can be jammed. One-inch air staples are used on plywood-reinforced joints on flat frames, and 1½″ staples can replace nails in many scenic structures.

Wood Screws (Figure 6-15). Screws provide greater strength than either nails or sta-

FIGURE 6–14 Staples.

FENCE
STAPLE

SCREEN
STAPLE

STAPLES FOR
STAPLERS

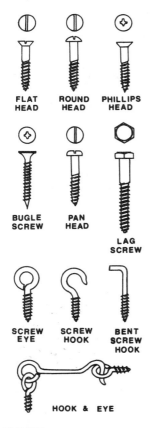

FIGURE 6–15 Wood screws.

ples. They are also easier to remove and are reusable. They range in length from ½″ to 3½″ generally, and a shop needs to stock several lengths for most scene construction. The diameter of screws is identified by number. Number 2 screws are ³⁄₃₂″ in diameter and #12 screws are ⁷⁄₃₂″ in diameter. **Flat-head screws** are designed to countersink into wood and hardware so the head is flush with the surface. Stage hardware is pre-drilled for #8 or #9 screws. **Round-head screws** have heads that protrude above the work. **Phillips screws** are available with a variety of head styles. The X-shaped slot requires the use of a Phillips screwdriver. **Pan-**

head screws are usually intended for metal, but the larger head is an advantage in securing hardware with overly large screw holes. For rapid insertion and removal **bugle-head screws** (drywall screws) are excellent for general scenic use. They do not require pre-drilled holes, are self-tapping and self-countersinking, and will not split wood. They are small in diameter and have sharp drilling points which easily penetrate soft wood and thin metal. Having Phillips heads they are easy to drive and remove with electric or air-powered screwdrivers. Because there is less chance of slot damage, Phillips-head screws have greater reusability. **Lag screws,** sometimes called lag bolts, have screw threads and square or hex heads for driving with a wrench. They are used for heavy fastening. Screws are sold in boxes of 100.

Specialized screws are used to attach a variety of objects to wood. They include the **screw eye,** which has a looped head for connecting to rope, wire, hooks, or other items. The **screw hook** has an open loop for the hanging or suspending of attachments with easy removal. The **bent screw hook** is another open type of connection. The **hook and eye** is a combination attachment. Commonly used on doors and gates, it is useful for a variety of quick connections of scenic units.

Bolts, Washers, and Nuts (Figure 6-16). Bolts are the strongest of all fasteners. They are inserted into holes drilled the diameter of their shafts and tightened firmly with washers and nuts. The **carriage bolt** has a slightly rounded head and a square shank below. The shank wedges into the bolt hole to keep the bolt from turning as a wrench tightens the nut. The need for only one wrench gives the carriage bolt considerable advantage, but it must be inserted carefully to avoid chewing out the hole that secures the square shank. Sizes range from ¼″ to ¾″ in diameter and from 1″ to 24″ in length. The **machine bolt** has a square or hexagonal head and requires two wrenches to install and remove. Washers are needed at both

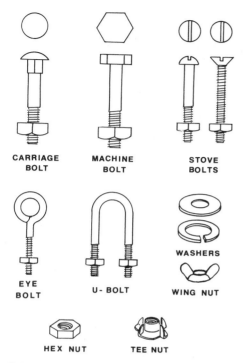

FIGURE 6–16 Bolts, washers, and nuts.

Hinges (Figure 6-17). Hinges are used in scenery not only as movable joints for doors and gates but also as convenient fastening devices. Hinges vary in purpose and hinging action. Dimensions refer to the height and total open width. There are a wide variety of **butt hinges** for cabinet and regular doors. Some are intended to be mortised into the wood, others are full surface. **Strap hinges** are long and narrow with tapered leaves. They are made of light, medium, or heavy metal with up to 8″ leaves. **T-hinges** have one regular and one strap leaf.

Back-flap hinges have special uses for scenery and are usually only obtainable from theatre suppliers. **Tight-pin back-flap hinges** are used to join scenic units for a setting, such as two flats placed edge to edge

FIGURE 6–17 Hinges.

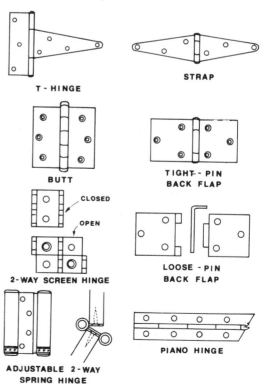

ends for wood. Diameters vary from ¼″ to 1″ and lengths extend from 1″ to 30″. **Stove bolts** have either flat or rounded heads which are slotted for a screwdriver. Bolts under 2″ in length are threaded up to the head. They are available in diameters of ⅛″ to ⅜″ and in lengths up to 6″. **Eye bolts** are useful when it is desirable to make secure attachments to scenic units. **U-bolts** are available in diameters from ¾″ to 2″ and are used to hold pipe or other round stock to a surface. **Flat washers** and **spring-tension lock washers** are available for all bolt sizes. **Nuts** are hexagonal in shape to fit wrenches. **Wing nuts** are used for hand tightening, desirable particularly for rapid fastening and removal. Another type of nut, the **tee nut,** is also useful for quick and easy disassembly. After the bolt hole is drilled, the nut is hammered into the hole where it is held by projecting prongs.

to form a straight wall. This provides a somewhat permanent joint and allows the scenery to be folded compactly like a book for striking and transporting. Tight-pin hinges are available in sizes suitable for scenic framing: 1½" × 3⁷⁄₁₆" and 2" × 4⅜". **Loose-pin backflap hinges** provide temporary attachments of scenic units. The pin can be removed, separating the two leaves. Special pin wire is also available to replace the standard pins. This is an easy, quick way of joining and separating scenery for a scene shift, storage, or travel. **Two-way screen hinges** can be mounted on the edges of frames to fold in a full 360°. They are most common in ¾" and 1" wood thicknesses. The **adjustable two-way spring hinge** is used on swinging doors. The spring tension can be adjusted for the weight of the specific door shutter. **Piano hinges** are used where a continuous hinge is appropriate. They are narrow in width and are obtained in lengths up to 6'-0". The hinge is cut to the length required.

Plates and Irons (Figure 6-18). Plates are metal reinforcements for wood joints. They are especially necessary for door casings and skeletal framing. While narrow plates ⅜" and ½" wide are available locally from hardware dealers, wider ones more suitable for the width of the lumber commonly used in scenery must be acquired from theatrical hardware suppliers. The **flat corner plate** and the **T-plate** are 1¾" wide and 7" × 7". The **mending plate** can be obtained in three sizes: 2" × 6", 2½" × 12", or 3" × 18". **Sill irons** are used to securely hold the bottom of a door opening. They are made of ³⁄₁₆" × ¾" strap steel and extend to each side of an opening a minimum of 6". A sill iron is notched into the wood and is secured by countersunk screws. Large door openings formed with two flats require a **hinged sill iron,** drilled and riveted to hinge in the center. A **saddle iron** has short vertical straps riveted to the base iron to provide greater support.

Angles and Corners (Figure 6-19). The corners of framed structures can be rein-

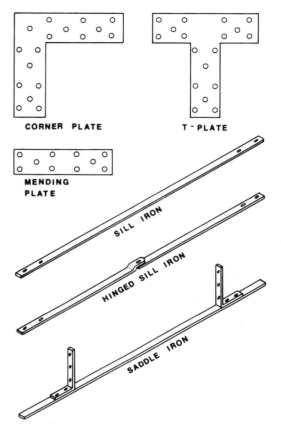

FIGURE 6-18   Plates and irons.

forced with special hardware. **Corner angles** are ½" to ¾" wide steel straps bent and pre-drilled for screws. These are designed for inside corner support. **Crate corners** are wider (2½" wide) by 3" × 3" and are intended to reinforce outside corners. The **crate corner and shoe** provides a support for all surfaces of a corner. Crate corners are useful to strengthen platform edges where nails tend to loosen. **Joist and beam hangers,** which are versatile corner hardware items, are available in a variety of joint forms.

Locks, Bolts, and Catches (Figure 6-20). Doors are held in a closed position by a variety of hardware. Standard catches serve similar functions in stage settings. Cabinet door

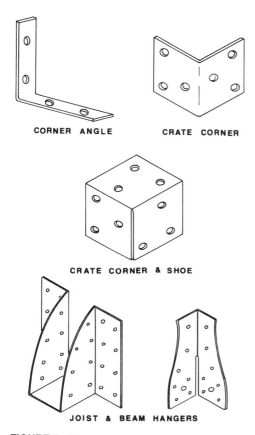

FIGURE 6–19 Angles and corners.

CORNER ANGLE

CRATE CORNER

CRATE CORNER & SHOE

JOIST & BEAM HANGERS

many types of door bolts. Common among them is the **barrel bolt,** which has a sliding rod and a slot to secure the rod handle. Another valuable lock mechanism is the **casket lock.** This is a butt-joint fastener that can be concealed and locked by a setscrew wrench. It is ideal for securing two surfaces together, such as two walls or two platform units.

PAPER AND FIBER CRAFT

Paper has long played a role in the decorative and building crafts in many diverse ways. Although historically as a molded compound called papier-mâché it was fashioned into table tops, trays, boxes, and other objects, the structural properties of paper were not fully exploited until fairly recent times. Modern technology has produced paper and fiber materials that are used for roofing, wall and display panels, soffits, sheathing, house siding, and core material for stress-

FIGURE 6–20 Locks, bolts, and catches.

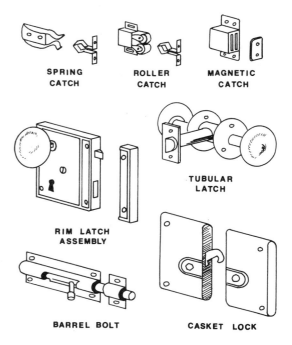

SPRING CATCH

ROLLER CATCH

MAGNETIC CATCH

TUBULAR LATCH

RIM LATCH ASSEMBLY

BARREL BOLT

CASKET LOCK

catches are the simplest. In addition to their use on cabinet and cupboard doors, catches are also used on regular and French window sashes and full-sized stage doors door. The **magnetic catch** contains a small magnet and a metal striker plate. Spring or roller action is used for other types of catches.

The most authentic door latch for doors that hinge *offstage* (made of 1″ stock) is the **rim latch assembly.** It mounts on the back of the door shutter and has the same action and sound as a standard mortise lock. For the door shutter that hinges *onstage* (1¼″ or thicker), a standard **tubular latch** is relatively simple to install. It is inserted in a hole drilled in the edge of the shutter. There are

bearing structures. Recent laminations of resin-impregnated paper for the tops of desks, cabinets, and counters suggest that paper technology has even more to offer in the future.

Paper and Fiber Products

Today, paper materials are made almost entirely from wood. Sawdust, chips, bark, and other sawmill by-products, along with an increasing amount of recycled paper materials, are processed into paper products. The raw materials are cooked, washed, and beaten in mechanical and chemical processes to produce the fiber structure for a particular paper. The coarse, strong paper familiar to us as brown kraft paper is made from ʋ.ood pulp in a special sulfate pulping process. Paperboard and fiberboard are the heaviest paper products. They are produced in various ways by heat, glue, compression, and lamination. Many are lightweight, strong, low cost, and highly workable materials.

Soft Fiberboard. More commonly known by the trade names *Celotex* and *Homasote*, this is a soft, low-density, porous panel material made of wood and vegetable fibers. Untreated it is brownish in color; with one white side, it is popular for inexpensive bulletin boards. This product is sold in 4' × 8' sheets and in common thicknesses of ½" and ²⁵⁄₃₂". Unframed, the softness of the material causes it to break and crumble at the edges. It may be cut easily with regular saws and knives.

Upson Board. Manufactured by the Upson Company, this product is a laminated fiberboard made of virgin and recycled wood fibers. It is available in several combinations of pebbled and smooth surfaces in thicknesses of ⅛", ¼", ³⁄₁₆", and ⅜". It is produced in 4' × 8' sheets. The thinnest (⅛") is called *Easy-Curve* board because it can be bent easily into curved shapes. The ³⁄₁₆" and

¼" Upson board is stronger, more rigid, and suitable as a covering or cutout material. The ⅜" board, named *All Weather*, is a rugged waterproofed material. Upson board can be cut with any type of saw, but a knife or a Cutawl produces a cleaner edge.

Fiberboard Tubes. Round rubes and cans, as well as other tube shapes, are formed of laminations of paperboard, often spirally wound to form thick-walled structures. Carpet and vinyl flooring tubes are among the smallest in diameter. Cylindrical tubes used in construction for forming concrete columns are available with inside diameters from 8" to 48" with wall thicknesses ranging from ⅛" to ½". Frequently it is necessary to cover tubes with cheesecloth to conceal the spiral rib lines. Tubes are normally available in 8' lengths and longer lengths in the smaller diameters. Tubes with ½" walls are also available in oval, triangular, elliptical, hexagonal, square, and other shapes. The walls are tough and can be used as weight-bearing structures (Figure 6-21).

FIGURE 6–21 Fiberboard tubes with walls up to ½" thick are available in different shapes and sizes.

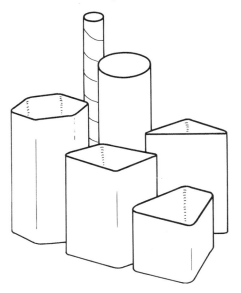

Corrugated Board. Familiar to us in corrugated boxes, corrugated board has been used for building furniture, walls, and properties. Single-faced corrugated board consists of heavy kraft paper fluted in a corrugation machine and pasted to a smooth sheet called a liner. This is easily bent into curves of all types. Double-faced corrugation is a layer of fluted paper between two liners. Double-walled corrugated board is even thicker and stronger, with two corrugations separating three liners. This material can be obtained in sheets up to 4' × 8' depending upon the supplier. It is easily cut and shaped with a knife (Figure 6-22). Painting tends to warp corrugated board, but thin coats applied by spray gun reduce the water action. It is best if flameproofing is applied by the manufacturer.

Foam Board. Foam board is a product made of two sheets of heavy brown kraft paper separated by a layer of rigid plastic foam. It is available in 4' × 8' sheets in ⅛",

¼", ³⁄₁₆", and ½" thicknesses. It also can be obtained with a dull-white mottled paper surface or with a white clay-coated surface for drawing, lettering, and art work. Foam board is extremely light in weight, rigid, and easy to cut.

Honeycomb Board. This is an extremely durable panel board of heavy kraft paper glued to an inner honeycomb core (Figure 6-23). It is sold in ½", 1", and 2" thicknesses. The ½" board is available in 4' × 8' sheets; the 1" and 2" board comes in sheets 4' × 8', 4' × 10', and 4' × 12'. It is suitable for vertical structures or for platforms and other weight-bearing objects. It can be cut

FIGURE 6–23 Honeycomb board: (A) Slit-scoring with a table saw. (B) Cutting 45° angles for a miter joint.

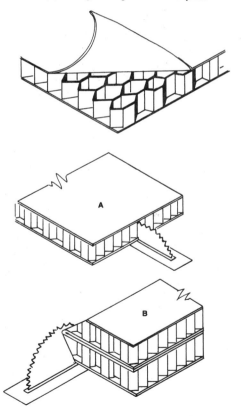

FIGURE 6–22 Corrugated board: (A) Scoring and folding to form a corner. (B) Scoring one liner to form curves when reinforced. (C) Laminating with alternate layers.

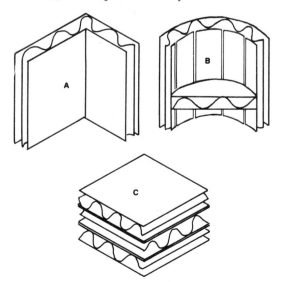

and shaped by regular saws. The inner core material can be purchased separately up to 6″ thick for bonding into sandwich panels of plywood or other sheet products.

Other Paper Products. Numerous other paper products have use in scenery and properties. Wallpaper, flocked paper, metallic coated paper, crepe paper, shredded paper, colored papers, resin-impregnated paper, and gummed or adhesive papers are only a few for which direct applications are recognized.

Sometimes certain textures have special uses. Reinforced papers or paper that substitutes for cloth, as used in disposable uniforms, have considerable potential for scenic purposes.

Constructing with Paper

The sheet materials that have been described can be cut and shaped without difficulty with saws and knives. The Cutawl with the knife blade is the best solution for clean cuts in paper products, especially for intricate pierced designs. A sheet of soft fiberboard should be placed below the work to be cut. A Cutawl can cut patterns in several sheets of Upson board at the same time. A knife is valuable for slit-scoring one liner of corrugated and honeycomb board so you can bend the material into curves or angles. A 45° cut with a saw in honeycomb board is necessary for creating inside corners. Large flat-headed nails are necessary to adequately secure Celotex and Upson board to a frame. Water-base adhesives and hot melt glue are best for fastening materials to paper boards or for paper laminations.

Paper is also a useful modeling material. Known as **papier-mâché,** this process utilizes absorbent paper soaked in a water-based adhesive. The *strip technique* is used to build up a "skin" over a wire mesh form. Paper is cut into strips, soaked in paste, and applied in an overlapping fashion over the wire. Three or four layers are necessary, and a final layer of cloth strips gives a tough surface. Newspaper is adequate for general purposes. For very fine detail, soft facial tissues are useful. Sculpted and modeled objects can be created with papier-mâché *mash technique.* Confetti and shredded paper are soaked in water to break down the fibers, then mixed with paste. It can be molded into relief ornaments on scenery or modeled over a wire armature or a frame. In the manner of soft clay it is shaped with the fingers. Commercially prepared papier-mâché mash, under such names as *Instant Papier-Mâché* and *Shreddi Mix,* can be purchased. Just add water and the material is ready for use. Papier-mâché will take a number of hours to dry, but heat and fans can hasten the process.

FABRIC CRAFTS

In a setting, fabric is most conspicuously used for flat coverings, scenic backgrounds, window treatments, floor coverings, and upholstery. Because of this range of usage, the many different attributes of fabrics must be considered in selecting one for a given scenic purpose. The technician needs a knowledge of fabrics and such qualities as drapability, visual appearance, texture, opacity or translucency, strength, and serviceability. This awareness, an understanding of fabric practices, and acquired skills are necessary to scene technology.

Scenic Fabrics

Fabrics of all kinds have a purpose in scenery. Many are available in local yard goods departments and drapery or upholstery fabric stores. More unusual cloth must be obtained from companies specializing in theatrical fabrics. Some are special materials needed to serve a function somewhat unique to scenery or to provide an aesthetic characteristic such as a weave, a texture, or a boldness of pattern of a particular theatrical value. The fabrics listed here are some of the principal ones used.

Canvas and Muslin. **Linen canvas** is a superior covering for scenic frames and as a floor cloth material. It is strong, resistant to tears, and has a long life. Its natural color is tan. It is an expensive fabric. **Cotton canvas** is nearly as strong as linen and less expensive. Canvas is rated by weight (ounces per square yard). For covering flats, 8 oz canvas is sufficient. Heavier canvas is sometimes preferred for floor cloths and platform covers. **Unbleached muslin** is a popular fabric for covering scenic frames and for drops. It is inexpensive; and while it lacks the strength of canvas (it is relatively easy to tear), it can be patched easily and, with care, is highly serviceable. The most common scenic grades of muslin are medium weight (128 threads per inch) and heavy weight (140 threads per inch).

Canvas and muslin expressly marketed for scenery are available in widths of 69″ or more. They normally are sold in bolts of 50–60 yards. The cost per running yard is often higher for quantities less than a bolt. There is an extra charge for flameproofing. Muslin is also loomed in widths of 14′ and 19′ and 30′ widths for seamless drops. Cotton canvas and muslin can be obtained dyed light blue for sky drops or cycloramas.

Pile and Napped Fabrics. Pile fabrics are materials that have yarns projecting from the surface to form a fuzzy finish. The projecting loops of terry cloth are an example of uncut-pile threads, and velvet is a cut-pile fabric. **Velour** is a heavy cut-pile fabric often used for stage draperies because of its durability and rich appearance. Made of cotton or mostly cotton, velour is a tough and long-lasting material. It is available in several grades depending on the tightness of the weave and the length of the pile. **Velveteen** is a low-pile fabric; it is less expensive than velour and widely used for upholstery and window draperies. Another pile fabric, **corduroy,** is sometimes used as a substitute for

velvet and velveteen in upholstery and draperies.

Napped fabrics have a hairy or downy surface created by raising the fibers. **Duvetyn** has one or more sides napped, sheared, and brushed to create a suede-like finish. It is sometimes used as a substitute for pile fabrics for stage draperies, maskings, or as a cyclorama material.

An improvement to duvetyn, **commando cloth** is a lightly napped but unbrushed fabric. When sewing panels of any of these fabrics, the direction of the nap or pile must be consistent. Pile or nap running up makes the fabric appear darker, and running down looks lighter and shinier.

Jute Fabrics. **Burlap** is a coarse fabric made of jute. It is useful for textured scenic draperies, platform coverings, tree and rock form coverings, and as an underlayer in upholstered furniture. **Erosion cloth** is a loose netting of heavy jute threads known for its very textural quality. Other open-weave jute nettings are also available. **Jute webbing** is used to secure springs in upholstered units and as a reinforcement for the supporting hems of stage draperies and drops.

Nettings and Scrims (Figure 6-24). Open-mesh fabrics are used in framed and unframed scenery for transparencies and translucent effects. One of the most transparent materials is **theatrical gauze.** It is a thin fabric and not very durable. It is available in 6′ widths and wider through some suppliers. **Sharkstooth scrim** is heavier and stronger with diagonal threads like a row of shark's teeth. It is commonly used for transparencies. Similar to sharkstooth, but less dense, is **opera net.** Both are available in special 30′ widths for seamless drops. **Bobinette** is another open-weave fabric in wide widths. It is a heavy netting with hexagon-shaped openings. It can be obtained from ⅛″ to ³⁄₁₆″ mesh. **Marquisette** is a lightweight netting and somewhat tighter in weave than bobinette.

Netting with larger openings is sometimes

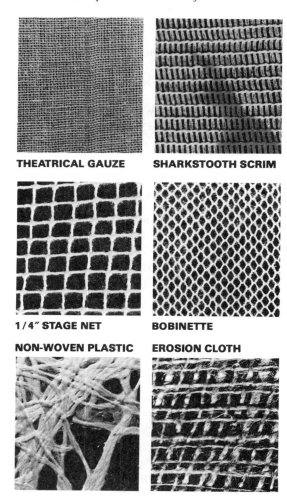

THEATRICAL GAUZE   SHARKSTOOTH SCRIM

1/4" STAGE NET   BOBINETTE

NON-WOVEN PLASTIC   EROSION CLOTH

FIGURE 6–24 Nettings and scrims. (Photos by Renata S. Jasinski)

desired for highly textured transparencies and other effects. **Stage net,** made frequently of cotton cord, is available with ¼", ⅜", ¾", and 1" square mesh. **Fishnet** has larger openings. An unusual nonwoven textured netting has been widely used in Europe. Made of rayon-like threads with a polyvinylidene resin binder, the material has a random curved pattern. It is sold by the name of *Texture or Contra-H* and is made in three densities and two colors.

Other netting materials are available in local yard goods stores. **Nylon netting** is a common veiling fabric. Nylon netting, marquisette, bobinette, and plastic or galvanized screen wire is often used as a glass substitute in scene windows. Inexpensive **cheesecloth** is a loose and stretchy gauze. The woven, not the knitted, variety is very useful to give a hardened surface to soft plastic foam objects and for textured surfaces.

Textured Fabrics. Fabrics with coarse textures that absorb light and offer rich effects are highly appropriate for stage settings. **Cotton rep** has a ribbed or herringbone weave and is unusually durable and opaque. It is sometimes used for background draperies. **Monk's cloth** is woven in a pronounced basket weave. It is soft, drapes well, and can be dyed without difficulty. Because of its loose weave, it is not as strong as rep. **Waffle cloth** is a heavy, deep-textured fabric with a waffle or honeycomb weave. It is a cotton fabric that can be dyed or painted as desired.

Shiny Fabrics. Fabrics with lustrous surfaces or sheens are used for decorative draperies, window curtains, and upholstery. **Satin** has a single lustrous surface and may be light or heavy in weight. There are a wide selection of satin fabrics in plain weaves or prints. **Sateen** is a lightweight cotton fabric with a pronounced sheen surface. It is inexpensive and has a variety of scenic uses. **Taffeta** fabrics often have a rich, silky luster. They are available in plain or ribbed weaves or woven in a way that the colors seem changeable. There is a good selection of colors and weights. **Damask** is a heavy glossy fabric. Patterns are woven in high luster with a duller background that reverses on the back side. It is useful for curtains, draperies, and upholstery.

Window and Upholstery Fabrics. There are many other fabrics in addition to those already listed for window coverings and furniture upholstery. Window treatment includes the sheer curtain materials of organdy, lace, voile, and nettings; medium-weight fabrics such as chintz and cretonne, and heavy-weight drapery materials including brocades, velvets, and suede cloth. Drapery departments in local stores feature a variety of these fabrics. Brocades and other heavy fabrics are common upholstery materials. Other furniture fabrics are stiff, highly durable materials, often with rubberized backings.

Sewing Tools and Materials

Stage draperies, drops, borders, and cycloramas are finished goods of considerable size. Flown or hung above the scene, top edges are reinforced with cotton or jute webbing to support grommets and tie lines or snap hooks for attachment to pipe battens or drapery tracks. Large bottom hems are necessary for the inclusion of weights. The edges of framed drops and floor cloths also require grommets so they may be stretched tautly. Many technical directors prefer to have large draperies, drops, and cycloramas fabricated by professional scenic studios where large tables and equipment will assure accurate, straight seams and true, wrinkle-free curtains.

The sewing of furniture upholstery and curtains and draperies for windows requires sufficient work space. Accuracy in measuring, cutting, and sewing is certainly assisted by proper equipment. It is useful to have a large flat surface in working with curtains and draperies. A 4′ × 8′ sheet of plywood padded with cotton or wool blankets and covered with canvas makes an excellent table for measuring, cutting, and ironing. The sewing machine should be equipped with needles compatible with various fabric weights. Special machine attachments may be helpful. Learn to experiment with stitch length and thread tension to suit the needs of a given fabric.

Basic Sewing Tools (Figure 6-25). The **sewing machine** should be reliable and capable of sewing a variety of fabrics. A heavy-duty machine is often desirable for heavy velour, canvas, and upholstery material. Measuring tools include a **steel tape** for long measurements, a **yardstick** for marking cutting lines, and a **framing square** for squaring off the ends of yardage. **Tailor's chalk** is used for marking lines. A **hem gauge** is valuable for measuring seam allowances and hems. **Bent-handled shears** are the easiest to use for fabric lying flat. A **steam iron** or **hand steamer** serves to remove wrinkles or folds in the fabric before marking and cutting.

The top edges of stage draperies and soft drops are reinforced with 3½″ cotton or jute **webbing. Brass grommets,** size 2 (⅜″), are inserted into holes made by a **grommet hole**

FIGURE 6–25 Basic sewing tools.

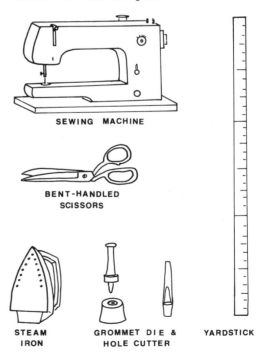

SEWING MACHINE

BENT-HANDLED SCISSORS

STEAM IRON   GROMMET DIE & HOLE CUTTER   YARDSTICK

cutter, and the two halves are driven together with a **grommet setting die.** Lightweight **jack chain** or **lead weights** in a cloth tube are used to add weight to the bottom of draperies. While pleats are often sewn in the top hem of draperies to provide appropriate fullness, **pleater tape** is sometimes used in sewing window curtains. Regular **drapery hooks, pleater hooks,** and **rings** made of metal, wood, or plastic are hanging hardware for window curtains and drapes.

Curtain rods are mounted on windows for curtains and draperies. Adjustable **flat curtain rods** attach to small brackets on the wall or window frame. **Cafe rods** hang from extended brackets. For a more traditional look, **wood poles** and decorative brackets are available. The **traverse rod** permits a drapery to be opened and closed by ⅛″ cord pulls.

Upholstery Tools and Materials

Whether upholstering a new piece of furniture or repairing and reupholstering an old one, certain basic materials and tools are needed. Measuring tapes, scissors, staplers, and a sewing machine are essential for this work and already have been listed. Many materials are satisfactory for cushioning material. **Cotton felt** and **rubberized hair** are common padding materials. However, **flexible urethane foam,** which is available in many thicknesses, is convenient and widespread in usage. Work on springs, padding, and upholstering is best accomplished when the furniture is at a comfortable height on a table or a sheet of plywood on trestles.

Special Upholstery Needs (Figure 6-26). The **upholsterer's tack hammer** has a magnetic end to hold the head of a tack to be driven. Small tacks, 4 oz to 8 oz, are used to hold fabric to the frame, while larger sizes, 12 oz to 14 oz, are needed to secure webbing. Tacks are pulled with a **tack lifter** and a **ripping chisel** is needed to strip the frame and remove deep-set tacks. A **webbing**

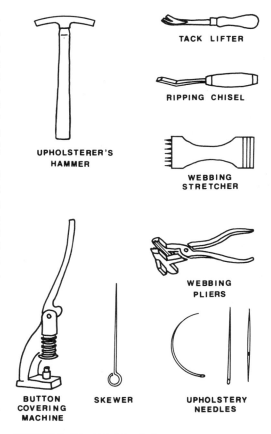

FIGURE 6–26 Upholstery tools.

stretcher or **webbing pliers** is helpful in pulling webbing tight before tacking it to the frames.

Two types of upholstery needles are needed. **Curved needles** in 3″ and 4″ sizes are needed for hand stitching. **Straight needles** with single points are used for outside edges and for securing the springs to burlap. Six- to eight-inch needles are adequate. Double-point needles are for sewing in both directions. **Upholsterer's skewers** hold upholstery covers temporarily in place while they are being fitted. A **button machine** covers buttons with fabric. **Spring twine** is used to tie springs in place. Used extensively in upholstery trim, **welt cord** serves as the dec-

FIGURE 6–27 Fabric yardage chart.

ITEM	UPHOLSTERY	SLIPCOVER	
	48"/50"/54"	*Narrow 34"/36"*	*Wide 48"/50"*
Sofa, 4 seat	13 yds	24 yds	17 yds
Sofa, 3 seat	11 yds	22 yds	15 yds
Sofa, 2 seat	8 yds	16 yds	11 yds
Basic armchair	6 yds	10 yds	8 yds
Open armchair	3 yds	6 yds	4 yds
Wing chair	6 yds	12 yds	8½ yds
Barrel or fan-back chair	6½ yds	12 yds	9 yds
Boudoir chair	3½ yds	7½ yds	5 yds
Ottoman	1½ yds	4½ yds	3 yds

orative edging on the sewn corners of the fabrics. A **cording foot** is a valuable accessory for the sewing machine.

Several fabrics are used in the upholstering process. Burlap covers the webbing and springs to provide a foundation for the padding. The cushions and padding are covered in muslin before the upholstery cover is tacked and sewn in place. The final fabric must be carefully and accurately cut and sewn. Corded edges and other trim are included. Slipcovers are temporary, loose-fitting furniture coverings. The accompanying chart (Figure 6-27) indicates approximate yardages of upholstery and slipcover fabric needed for different types of furniture. When using a patterned fabric, an additional amount should be purchased in order to match up the pattern in the design when laying out the cover.

SELECTED READINGS

BAKER, G. E., and L. DAYLE YEAGER, *Wood Technology* (2nd ed.). Indianapolis: Howard W. Sams and Co., 1976.

CARTER, PAUL, *Backstage Handbook*. New York: Broadway Press, 1988.

CLANCY, J. R., *Theatrical Hardware Catalogue No. 59-A*. Syracuse, NY: February 1982.

Curtains, Draperies and Shades. Prepared by the editors of Sunset Books and Sunset Magazines. Menlo Park, CA: Lane Publishing, 1979.

DURBAHN, WALTER E., and ROBERT E. PUTNAM, *Fundamentals of Carpentry* (5th ed.). Chicago: American Technical Society, 1977.

JACKSON, ALBERT, and DAVID DAY, *Tools and How to Use Them*. New York: Knopf, 1979.

LEE, BRIANT HAMOR, and DARYL M. WEDWICK, *Corrugated Scenery*. Baton Rouge, LA: Oracle Press, 1982.

7

Metal and Plastic Crafts

More and more, metal and plastics are becoming important crafts in scene technology. This has become increasingly evident over the years as the cost of traditional scenic materials has risen and tool and technique advances have improved metal and plastics fabrication. In addition, the contemporary interest in three-dimensional scenery practically assures the place of these crafts in today's scene shop. The unique properties and moldability of these materials give them distinct advantages for three-dimensional structures. It can be argued that many scenic objects can be created more effectively with metal or plastics and sometimes they are the only solution to a problem. At the same time, these crafts pose new and different health and safety hazards requiring special precautions in the workplace.

METALWORKING

Metal has qualities and functions that make it a superior material for scenery. Its strength per volume surpasses that of other materials, and mechanical or welded joints enhance its solidity. Besides its structural advantage, metal can provide light and delicate forms for grillwork, furniture, decorative properties, and ornamentation. The qualities of strength, thinness, and light weight give metalworking the versatility to serve the practical and aesthetic needs of contemporary scenery from three-dimensional structures to light, decorative framing. The malleability and fusibility of metal permit it to be formed into many irregular and unusual shapes. While the cost of metal is higher than the cost of other materials, its reusability is a major economic factor. In addition, metal is entirely flameproof. The scene technician needs a knowledge of metal and training in metalworking skills.

Metals

Many kinds of metals and metal alloys have properties suitable for numerous structural needs. However, for the general needs of scenery, we can limit our attention to only a few.

The common form of steel, called **mild steel**, has the greatest use. Steel is easy to cut, shape, bend, and drill. It can be forged or fused by welding. Its strength and hardness are sufficient for most scenic requirements.

Despite its high cost, **aluminum** is becoming a more common metal in scene shops. In its softest forms it can be cut, drilled, and worked with standard wood tools. Heavier-strength aluminum alloy is excellent for structural beams, yet it is unusually light in weight. Similar to steel, aluminum is available in a range of forms at local metal suppliers. Many household and decorative forms are also available in hardware and home supply stores. Other useful metals include copper, brass, and ordinary wrought iron. Soft copper tubing is particularly valuable for bending and soldering into fanciful ornamental designs.

Metal is available in a number of shapes by casting, rolling, forging, or extruding. Some of the most common steel and alumi-

FIGURE 7–1 Scenery often benefits by metal and plastic materials. *West Side Story* as produced at Northern Illinois University. Scene designer: Alexander F. Adducci. (Photo by George Tarbay)

num forms, named for the shape of their cross sections, are listed in Figure 7-2. All forms, including bar, wire, conduit, mesh, even concrete reinforcing rod, have potential service for scenery and properties. While the initial cost of metal is often high, it does not wear out, and each purchase is another addition to the shop stock. Furthermore, economical treasures can often be discovered at scrap metal yards.

A number of ready-to-assemble metal products provide rapid and easy fabrication of an infinite variety of structures (Figure 7-3). *Unistrut* is a trade name for a special steel channel with grooves to hold spring-held nuts for bolting to fittings. The channels can be cut to length and assembled with special corner angles, flanges, and other hardware. *Telespar* is another trademarked product of the Unistrut Corporation. It is square tubing, in graduated sizes, each fitting inside a larger size. The sides of the tubing are

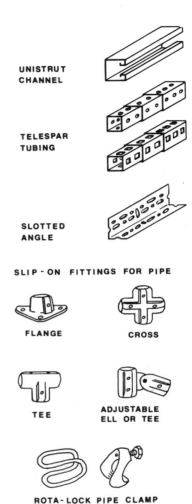

UNISTRUT CHANNEL

TELESPAR TUBING

SLOTTED ANGLE

SLIP-ON FITTINGS FOR PIPE

FLANGE   CROSS

TEE   ADJUSTABLE ELL OR TEE

ROTA-LOCK PIPE CLAMP

FIGURE 7–3 Ready-to-assemble metal.

FIGURE 7–2 Forms of metal.

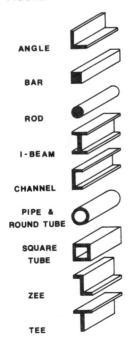

ANGLE

BAR

ROD

I-BEAM

CHANNEL

PIPE & ROUND TUBE

SQUARE TUBE

ZEE

TEE

perforated with holes for bolting to other sections. It permits sections of different widths to be telescoped within each other and secured by bolts in aligned holes. **Slotted angle** is steel angle perforated with round holes and elongated slots. Two pieces can be joined by bolting through matching holes. Slotted angle can be easily cut with a special angle cutter. **Slip-on pipe fittings** are designed to attach easily to standard pipe. Flanges, ells, tees, crosses, and other fittings can be slipped on lengths of pipe and secured with a setscrew wrench. **Rota-lock pipe clamps** are available for joining pipe together at 90° angles.

Metalworking Tools

Although some woodworking tools are also used to work metal, there are specific metalworking tools and machines. The acquisition of these tools should grow with the expansion of the metal shop and the increase in metal crafts for scene construction. Be sure the metalworking area is a properly ventilated and fireproofed space.

Measuring and Marking Tools (Figure 7-4). Regular steel tapes and squares are used to measure and mark metal. In addition to dividers and calipers already listed, **inside calipers** are particularly useful for metalworking because they are used to measure the inside dimensions of metal structures (pipes and similar structures) where other measuring tools would be inaccurate. The **Vernier caliper** is valuable for the fine mea-

surements required in working with metal. The **scriber** is a sharpened steel tool for scratching marking lines on metal. A **center punch** is helpful to start holes for drill bits, to make small indentations for laying out lines, and to locate centers for circles and arcs.

Bending Tools (Figure 7-5). An **anvil** is necessary for bending metal either cold or

FIGURE 7–5 Metal-bending tools.

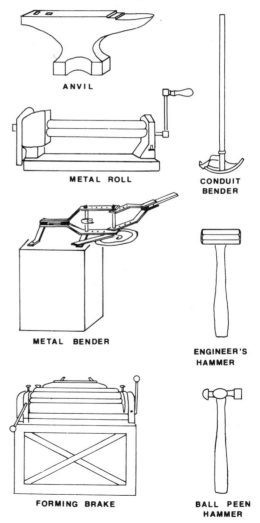

FIGURE 7–4 Measuring and marking tools for metal.

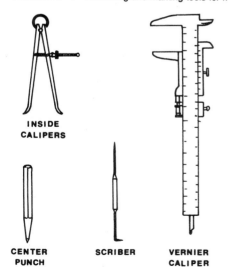

by softening first with a torch or a forge. An **engineer's hammer** is a heavy-duty hammer for metal. A **ball peen hammer** is also used for forming metal and heading rivets. Thin-wall conduit is curved easily with a **conduit bender**. More expensive machinery includes the hand-operated **slip roll** for curved bends in sheet and bar stock. The Hossfeld **metal bender** is equipped with a variety of attachments and dies for bending several different types of metal. With a variety of accessories and dies, simple hand-operated benders can bend rods, angles, tubing, and bar stock from simple wrought iron up to 1¼" standard pipe. The **brake** makes precise bends in sheet metal. Instructions with these special tools should be followed carefully.

Clamping Tools (Figure 7-6). A **machinist's vise** holds metal while it is being worked. It is heavy duty to withstand the work and often includes a small anvil for light bending. A **drill press vise** secures metal while it is being machined in a drill press. A **pipe vise** grips pipe with grooved jaws or an encircled chain for a firm hold. A *Vise-Grip* **wrench** is particularly helpful to

clamp round stock and sheet metal; it has many other uses as well.

Wrenches and Fastening Tools (Figure 7-7). Several sizes of **open-end wrenches** and **box wrenches** are valuable in a shop. The **adjustable-end wrench**, commonly called a *Crescent wrench*, can be altered to fit several bolt and nut sizes. A **socket wrench set and ratchet** handles bolts and nuts with the convenience of rachet control. When bolts are heavily used, an **air wrench** may be desirable. A **nut driver**, which drives nuts like a screwdriver, is ideal for small nuts and in tight areas where regular wrenches would be awkward.

A **setscrew wrench**, sometimes called an Allen key or hex wrench, fits into the hexag-

FIGURE 7–7 Wrenches and fastening tools.

FIGURE 7–6 Metal-clamping tools.

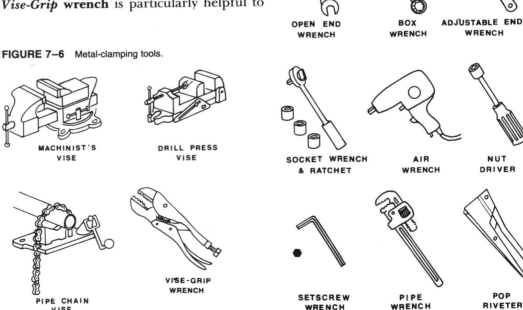

OPEN END WRENCH   BOX WRENCH   ADJUSTABLE END WRENCH

MACHINIST'S VISE   DRILL PRESS VISE

SOCKET WRENCH & RATCHET   AIR WRENCH   NUT DRIVER

PIPE CHAIN VISE   VISE-GRIP WRENCH

SETSCREW WRENCH   PIPE WRENCH   POP RIVETER

onal hole at the end of recessed setscrews. A **pipe wrench** is an adjustable wrench with serrated jaws for gripping pipe and other round stock. A **pop riveter** is used to join thin sheet material together with rivets.

Cutting Tools (Figure 7-8). The **hacksaw** is the regular hand saw used to cut metal. The **power hacksaw**, if affordable, saves energy. The **metal cutting band saw** is another excellent cutting tool for metal. **Abrasive cut-off saws** have the capacity for cutting 1½″ solid and 2½″ pipe stock. Abrasive cut-off discs can also be obtained to fit portable and fixed circular saws used for wood. But, remember, to prevent a fire, remove all sawdust from the machine before cutting metal. As with other metal operations, goggles and flameproofed clothing must be worn.

Tin shears make straight cuts in sheet metal, and **aviation snips** are valuable for curved or straight cuts with improved leverage. Wire can be cut with **end-cutting nippers** or **side cutting pliers**. A **bolt cutter** is useful for cutting bolts or rod stock. Light angle stock, such as slotted angle, can be easily severed with an **angle cutter**. A **pipe cutter** makes a clean and square cut through pipe. The **cold chisel** will cut metal, such as rivets and bolt heads, where saws and shears are unsuitable.

The **drill press** is the heaviest tool for drilling holes in metal, although the ½″ portable drill is also suitable for many forms of metal. Only high-speed steel twist drills will cut metal. Be sure to have a metal countersink bit when screw or bolt heads must be flush or recessed into the surface. When drilling, hold the work firmly with clamps or a vise. Oil must be applied to keep the drill sharp and to avoid unnecessary heat.

Metal files are used to remove metal, eliminate rough metal edges, and provide smooth surfaces. Several are needed in rough, medium, and smooth grades. **Bench grinders** have abrasive wheels for grinding metal to shape and for sharpening cutting tools. A grinder usually has two wheels, one

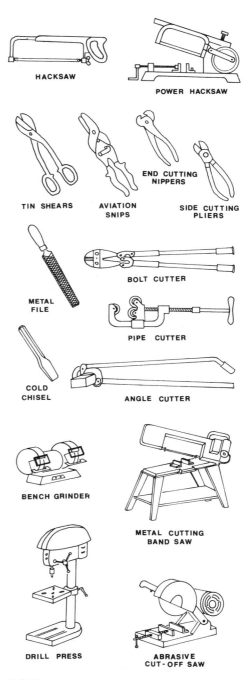

HACKSAW

POWER HACKSAW

TIN SHEARS

AVIATION SNIPS

END CUTTING NIPPERS

SIDE CUTTING PLIERS

METAL FILE

BOLT CUTTER

PIPE CUTTER

COLD CHISEL

ANGLE CUTTER

BENCH GRINDER

METAL CUTTING BAND SAW

DRILL PRESS

ABRASIVE CUT-OFF SAW

FIGURE 7–8 Metal-cutting tools.

coarse and one fine. Wear goggles when using a grinder.

Taps and Dies (Figure 7-9). A **tap** is used to cut internal screw threads in metal so it will serve as a nut. Placed in a **tap wrench**, the tap is turned gradually clockwise and counterclockwise in a predrilled hole until threads are cut. **Dies** form threads on rod stock. Taps and dies are generally sold in sets of various sizes. A **pipe die** is used to thread the end of pipes. Metal must always be well lubricated when cutting threads.

Metal Fasteners

Several standard devices are used to hold metal together. The material and nature of the join usually determine the appropriate fastener.

Bolts. Types of bolts have been examined in an earlier section. A hole is drilled for the bolt and it is secured either by a threaded hole in one of the joining pieces or by a nut and lock washer.

FIGURE 7–9 Taps and dies.

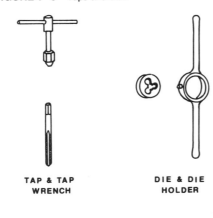

TAP & TAP
WRENCH

DIE & DIE
HOLDER

PIPE DIE

Sheet Metal Screws. Pieces of sheet metal can be joined easily with sheet metal screws. They are self-threading or, if preferred, can be started with a small hole. They are available with pan, round, flat, or countersink heads.

Rivets. A more permanent join is made with rivets. Holes are drilled, rivets are inserted, and the end of the shaft is rounded into a head with a ball peen hammer.

Pop Rivets. A pop rivet is a hollow-tube rivet inserted and self-headed by a pop riveter. It is an easy, quick procedure. These rivets can be applied in the blind, when the underside is inaccessible. A hole is first drilled or punched into the metal. After the riveter is properly loaded, the body of the rivet is pushed into the hole as far as it will go. With a squeeze or two of the handles, serrated jaws on the inside compress the rivet body, and the metal is firmly clinched together.

Soldering and Welding

Metal can also be joined by metallic bonding, which penetrates the metal. Techniques of soldering and welding require actual experience in order to develop skills for achieving successful adhesion. Major equipment is illustrated in Figure 7-10.

Soldering. If applied properly and to a joint of sufficient area, soldering can be an effective way of joining metal. Soldering is the process of heating a metal joint until a low-temperature alloy of tin and lead melts and forms a good bond with the metal. Solder is not particularly strong as a material. The secret of its effectiveness is achieving sufficient penetration into a joint to provide a good bond when cooled. Metal surfaces must be cleaned of paint, oil, oxidation, and scale by the application of abrasives. **Soldering flux** is then applied to cleanse the metal and prevent oxidation when the metal is heated so the solder penetrates the material

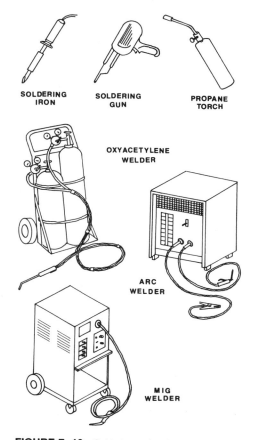

SOLDERING IRON

SOLDERING GUN

PROPANE TORCH

OXYACETYLENE WELDER

ARC WELDER

MIG WELDER

FIGURE 7–10 Soldering and welding equipment.

heating, "tinned" with solder to keep the tip from oxidizing. When the tip of the iron heats the joint sufficiently, solder applied to the iron will flow into the joint. The solder is shaped as the iron is moved along the joint. The joint must be held rigid until the solder cools. A propane torch can also be used in soldering. After the joint is cleaned and flux is applied, the torch is used to heat the metal. Be careful not to burn away the flux in the area of the joint. Solder, dipped in flux, is applied when the temperature is adequate.

Oxyacetylene Welding. Welding is the permanent joining of metal by complete fusion. This requires heating the material to the melting point. One method of welding is by **oxyacetylene** flame. This is achieved by mixing pure oxygen and acetylene, which burns at approximately 6000° F, sufficient to melt most metals (oxyacetylene cutting torches are also available to cut metal). The gases are stored in steel tanks under considerable pressure. Regulators on the top of these cylinders control the pressure of the gas necessary for the welding process. Special flexible hoses carry the gas to the **welding torch**. The gases are mixed in the torch and adjusted by valves for the proper flame. In the welding process, the torch is held in one hand and a length of welding rod in the other. The flame is placed a slight distance from the metal. As the material begins to melt, the torch is directed along the edge and the welding rod is melted, adding a bead along the joint.

Before welding, the metal must be properly cleaned; all grease, oil, paint, rust, and dirt is removed by grinding, sanding, or chemical removers. A slight gap, 1/8″ or less, is left between the pieces to be welded. To allow the heat of the flame to penetrate adequately, a vee (approximately 60°) must be ground on the edge of steel 3/16″ to 1/2″ thick. Welding is done on the beveled side. A double vee is needed on 1/2″ or thicker steel. For effective fusion of the metal, the weld should be slightly convex and fill up the entire

effectively. Flux is available in liquid, paste, and solid forms. It is in the core of some solder wire and mixed in solder powder. **Rosin flux** is noncorrosive and is used for electrical connections. Various **acid fluxes** are used for other metals and must be washed off in warm water after the joint is finished to prevent corrosion.

Soldering is most commonly accomplished with an **electric soldering iron** or **soldering gun**. Soldering tools are available in several wattages. Relatively heavy materials require an iron or gun with a minimum of 200 watts. The copper tips of either must be cleaned first, dipped into flux, and after

depth of the joint as well as all holes and cracks. The **butt weld** is simple and economical (Figure 7-11). The two pieces are aligned on a flat surface and joined with one weld. In some situations it may be necessary to join metal with a **lap weld** when two plates must overlap. Both sides must be welded to give this type of joint adequate strength.

A **flange weld** is used for joining sheet metal. Bent flanges on the edge of each sheet are butted together. The torch melts the flanges into a weld nearly flush with the surface. Little, if any, filler rod is needed. Pieces

of steel that meet at an angle are joined with a **fillet weld**. If complete penetration cannot be achieved on one side only, welding is necessary on both sides. **Plug welds** are made through holes drilled in overlapping pieces when only moderate strength and a smooth surface are needed.

Welding should never be attempted without proper safety equipment. **Welding goggles** must be worn to protect the eyes from the intense glare of the welding flame and flying metal. **Leather gloves**, preferably with protective gauntlets, are necessary to protect the hands from the heat, sparks, and molten metal. The body should be fully covered with protective clothing. When using the cutting torch, a **leather welder's apron** should be worn for protection from splashes of hot metal. For protection from radiation, a **barrier cream** (sunblock lotion) is a standard safety item for welders. Work in a fireproof and well-ventilated area and remove all flammable materials.

Before lighting the torch, make sure all valves on the torch are off and all connections tight. Then, (1) open the acetylene torch valve one turn. Screw in the acetylene regulator screw until the gas escapes at the correct pressure on the gauge. Quickly shut off the acetylene torch valve. This process is repeated with the oxygen regulator and oxygen torch valve. (2) Open the acetylene torch valve slightly and use a friction striker to light the torch. (3) Open the acetylene torch valve until the flame no longer produces free carbon and makes a slight roaring sound. (4) Slowly open the oxygen valve until a neutral flame is formed. The equipment is ready for welding.

In forehand welding, the welding rod is held in front of the torch and moved in small arc motions to heat the metal evenly. As the edges of the joint are evenly heated, a puddle of molten metal from the rod will fuse to the metal. The puddle is built up to the top of the joint. The torch and rod are then moved forward ½″ to heat the next portion of the joint. With experience, an evenly rip-

FIGURE 7–11   Types of welds.

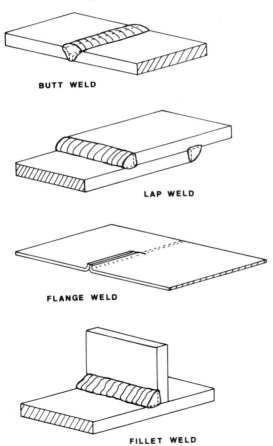

BUTT WELD

LAP WELD

FLANGE WELD

FILLET WELD

FIGURE 7–12 Welder at work at the PCPA Theaterfest. In some production companies, most scenic construction is done with metal framing. (Photo courtesy of the PCPA Theaterfest, Santa Maria, California)

pled bead can be produced. When finished, the oxygen torch valve is turned off followed by the acetylene valve. Both tanks are turned off. The oxygen torch valve is turned on until both oxygen gauges read zero. The oxygen regulator screw is opened and the oxygen torch valve is turned off. The process is repeated for the acetylene.

Arc Welding. Arc welding is a fusion technique that uses an intense electric arc of about 13,000° F for melting the metal. The electric power is generated by the **welding transformer**. A ground cable leading to the transformer is attached to the material. When an electrode connected by cable to the power source is brought in contact with the work, the circuit is completed and the resultant arc melts the metal. In the process the electrode rod also melts, which adds to the

molten metal filling up the gap and reinforcing the joint.

The outer coating of the electrode is made of flux that burns in the welding process, providing an atmosphere or screen to protect the molten metal from oxidation. The electrode is generally held laterally perpendicular to the metal for even distribution of filler material in the joint. However, the tip of the electrode should be angled down to the joint as you progress along the seam. A slight rotary action helps to fill the joint evenly. If the electrode sticks to the metal, a rapid twist will usually free it. The flux combined with impurities rises to the surface to form a coating of slag, which is chipped off when the weld cools. Experience teaches you how close to hold the electrode to the work and how to bounce it along the joint to produce an evenly rippled bead.

The shower of sparks and splatters of metal require a welder to wear flameproofed clothing, to leave no exposed skin, and to use leather gauntlet gloves. The intensity of the arc produces harmful ultraviolet rays. This requires wearing a **welding hood** to cover the entire head. A dark glass filter protects the eyes from the dangerous rays. Other people in the room must be cautioned not to look directly at the arc. **Welding curtains or screens** to surround the welding operation are advisable. Some of these are smoke or grey transparent curtains which filter out ultraviolet rays.

TIG and MIG Arc Welding. Two arc welding systems known as TIG (tungsten inert gas) and MIG (metal inert gas) improve the welding process by providing an inert gas shield to protect the molten metal from oxide formation. In TIG arc welding, a stream of the protective gas is emitted from the electrode holder. The electrode rod, which creates the arc, is nonconsumable tungsten. It is held in one hand, and a regular welding rod is held with the other. The welding process is similar to the two-handed oxyacetylene welding technique. MIG arc welding also directs a protective gaseous shield to the welding zone. The electrode is a roll of wire fed automatically through the electrode holder as it is consumed in the welding process. MIG welding is becoming the standard welding process in the scene shop. It is a one-handed welding process that produces clean welds rapidly. It is the most effective and versatile process for welding steel and aluminum with precision and speed. Unlike other systems, MIG welding is easy to use, and minimal skill and training are necessary. Costs for MIG systems have decreased considerably in recent years. Both of these gaseous shield systems are especially useful in welding aluminum.

PLASTIC CRAFTS

Plastics are synthetic materials rather than natural products such as wood and metal.

The first plastic substance was conceived in 1868, but the majority have been developed since the 1940s. Created primarily for industrial use, plastics and their processes have been steeped in highly scientific terminology. In addition, many plastics can be worked only with elaborate and costly equipment under controlled conditions. These and other factors have served as deterrents to the adoption of plastics in scene construction.

However, plastic technology is a remarkable field. As products of chemistry, the raw materials that produce plastics can be combined so as to provide nearly any property desired in the end product. Thus it was inevitable that they would be valuable in serving the special needs of scene technology. Plastics have become a major material in our lives. Each year new compounds and processes bring expanded usage. Besides their practical values such as lightness, strength, low cost, moldability, and rapid processing, plastics have also greatly extended the aesthetics of scenery in the form of new surfaces, transparencies, and textures.

Plastics are divided into two general categories: *thermosetting plastics* and *thermoplastics.* Thermosets are plastic materials that have been set into a permanent shape by the application of heat and pressure in the molding process. Enough heat will destroy the material but will not change its shape. Thermoplastics can be reshaped by heating them until they become soft, and they harden when cooled. The process is repeatable. If it is not reshaped, the melted plastic will return to its original shape after cooling. This is sometimes described as the thermoplastic's sense of "memory."

Plastics are chemically formed entirely or partially from various combinations of six elements: carbon, hydrogen, oxygen, nitrogen, chlorine, and fluorine. Carbon is the central element of almost all plastics. The combining of these elements produces a chemical compound or mixture of compounds. Chemically, this causes smaller molecules to form larger molecules, resulting in an identifiable polymer or resin. Essentially, each polymer is a special recipe created by a different mixture of ingredients. The polymerization process, the chemical reaction that produces this change in molecular structure, is produced by heat, pressure, and sometimes the addition of a catalyst (a chemical that assists or induces the chemical reaction). Each polymer is a unique material with a particular set of properties that differ from the properties of any of the original elements.

Plastics are produced in several forms, including sheet, liquid, powder, paste, and foam. The properties of any given resin remain the same in whatever form except as modified by additions. An additive may alter opacity, color, flame retardance, rigidity, or other properties. For instance, foams are expanded plastics produced by the addition of gas in the manufacturing process. After a general acquaintance with plastics, the scene technician needs to become familiar with the many properties of plastic resins and the techniques of working with them. Addi-

FIGURE 7–13   Classifications of plastics.

NAME	COMMON FORMS	CHARACTERISTICS	USES
Acrylics			
Plexiglas, Lucite, Acrylite	Rigid sheet, tube, rod, casting resin; clear, colored, opaque, and translucent	strong, rigid, light, weather resistant; abrasives and acids can damage; optical clarity in clear form; can be cast and molded	substitute for glass; floor and wall surfaces; decorative trim and ornaments
Cellulosics			
Most common of 5 types:	Sheets, film, rod; clear, translucent, opaque	can stand moderate heat, moisture, weather; abrasives can damage; CAB has greater stability and moisture resistance	glass substitute; jewelry; ornaments; projection slides; CN used in colloid-treated cloth for 3-D sculpting
Cellulose acetate (CA)			
Celanese, Vupak			
Cellulose acetate butrate (CAB)			
Tenite			
Cellulose nitrate (CN)			
Pyroxylin, Celastic			
Epoxies			
Resiweld, Devcon	Liquid, casting resin, molding compounds, foams, solids, coatings	durable; resists moisture, chemicals, weather	strong adhesives; auto body putty; castings; sealants; coatings
Fluorocarbons			
Teflon, Tetran, Fluon, Halon, Kel-F	Powder, sheet, coatings, tape	chemical resistance, hard, low friction, non-stick qualities, durable	smooth, low-friction surfaces for guides tracks, saw blades; lubricant, sealants
Polyamides			
Nylon	Rod, tube, sheet, filament	high resiliency and tensile strength, hard, glossy, low friction surface, resists chemicals and abrasions	fabrics, monofilament line, rope, low-friction glides, brushes

FIGURE 7–13 Classifications of plastics. *(continued)*

NAME	COMMON FORMS	CHARACTERISTICS	USES
Polyesters Unsaturated: Fiberglass Saturated: *Mylar, Dacron, Celanar, Melinex*	Unsaturated: casting resin Saturated: fiber, sheet, film	strong, rigid, hard surfaces; resists solvents, acids; good weathering qualities	Unsaturated: casting jewels, and clear objects; with glass fiber for molded surfaces Saturated: woven tapes and cloth; matte, metallized, mirrored or textured sheets
Polyethylenes *Dow, Dylan, Alathon* Foam: *Ethafoam*	Sheet, film, filament, rod, pipe, foam; rigid or flexible; clear, translucent or opaque	moisture proof, resists chemicals and breakage, slightly wax-like surface, strong and flexible	moisture barriers, paint cloths, cleaner bags, projection surfaces; flexible water pipe; Foam: decorative trim
Polypropylenes *Poly-Pro, Poly-Fax*	Film, solids, sheet, filament	hard surface, scratch resistant, good tensile and flex strength; moisture proof; resists chemicals	marine and outdoor rope
Polystyrenes *Dylene, Styron, Lustrex* Foam: *Styrofoam, Dorvon*	Sheet, casting resin, solids, foams	hard, rigid, somewhat brittle; poor weather resistance, high impact types have better strength and impact resistance; *Foam:* raspy to touch	glass simulations, vacuum-form sheet ornaments; castings; *Foam:* cut or cast for decorations
Silicones	Resins, molding compounds	resists heat and chemicals; water repellent; weather resistant	lubricants, coatings, sealants, castings, silicone rubber
Urethanes *Estane, Tuftane, Hylene,* *Polyfoam, Polyrubber*	Rigid and flexible foams, liquid castings, resins, solids	good adhesion quality; resists chemicals and water; resists tears and abrasions	sculpted rigid and flexible foamed objects for trim and decor; cushions
Vinyls Most common: Polyvinyl chloride (PVC) Polyvinyl acetate (PVA)	Sheet, pipe, film, resins	tough, strong; rigid forms have limited flexing; resists water, chemical, heat, cold; resists normal abrasions	sheets used for thermoforming for decor, props; PVA used for paint and adhesive bases; PVC pipe can be heat bent

tional study in the plastic crafts is highly desirable.

The Classifications of Plastics

Plastics generally belong to one of several major classifications or resin groups. A number of the principal groups are described briefly in Figure 7-13 to identify the range of plastics most useful in scenery. Some trade and common names are presented as well as the more technical terminology. The description includes some of the chief characteristics, uses, and manufactured forms.

The Use and Fabrication of Plastics

The numerous plastic materials and products available can often be found at home building dealers, hardware stores, craft or hobby shops, and specialized plastic retailers. Others are sold by theatre and display suppliers. Because of the seemingly infinite variety of properties and characteristics—type of surfaces, textures, moldability, range of transparency/translucency/opacity, and other qualities—plastics offer enormous potential for scene technology.

Becoming aware of their value and learning where they can be obtained will take continuing effort. New products and new applications of established polymers are discovered yearly. Be aware that some plastics require specific storage conditions, and many resins and chemicals have a limited shelf life. Know the safety precautions needed in working with plastic materials.

Plastic Pipes. Polyethylene pipe is a flexible black water pipe available in diameters

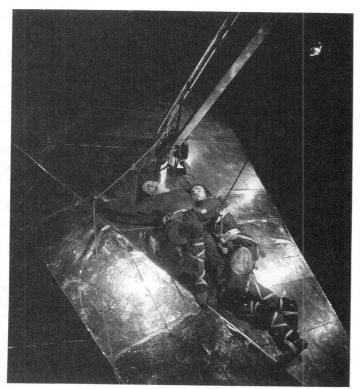

FIGURE 7–14 Plastic sheeting used in a production of *K-2* at Northern Illinois University. Scene design by Alexander F. Adducci. (Photo by George Tarbay)

of ½″ to 2″. It is sold in 50′ rolls or larger or in cut lengths. A rugged product, it can be fitted with a variety of fittings and clamps to carry water. It is also useful for curved components of stairway and iron railings and for other decorative work. Polyvinyl chloride (PVC) pipe is a rigid product but can be heat-shaped. Small-diameter PVC tubing is used for lawn sprinkler systems and some indoor plumbing. After being filled with wet sand to increase the density of the tube, it is placed in an oven or special heater using infrared heat lamps (Figure 7-15). After heating, the tubing is then shaped in a wood jig to the curved pattern. Gloves are necessary for this procedure. While in the jig, a cold water bath will restore the PVC to its natural rigidity. Localized bends in small pipe and rod stock can be achieved with an electric heat gun. Take precautions when heating and tooling PVC. Toxic hydrogen chloride gas and other vapors can be released in the process. Adequate ventilation is required.

Plastic Fabrics. For the multiple fabric needs of the stage, there are many woven fabrics made of acetates, polyesters, and other polymers. Nylon and Dacron are two better-known materials. These materials have attractive appearance and offer unique fabric advantages: easy washing, quick drying, wrinkle proof, self-extinguishing, and moth and mildew resistant. Soft sheet vinyls

FIGURE 7–15 Thermoplastic heaters.

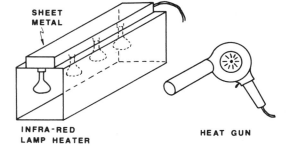

SHEET METAL

INFRA-RED LAMP HEATER

HEAT GUN

FIGURE 7–16 Plastic woven material (Glamé) for shimmering fabric effects. (Photo courtesy of Rosco Laboratories, Inc.)

simulating leather are valuable upholstery materials. Other products such as Rosco's *Shimmerscrim* and *Glamé* are drapable materials (Figure 7-16). They are often nonflammable or self-extinguishing and can be sewn or taped together. Special woven nylon is used for the convenient hook-and-loop fastener called *Velcro*. This is useful as a fabric and small-prop fastening device. Aircraft Dacron is also an unusually durable covering fabric for a flat frame, especially for outdoor productions or where the scenery receives exceptionally rough treatment.

Sheet, Roll, and Film Plastics. Sheet materials are available in polyethylenes, polyesters, acrylics, acetates, polystyrenes, and vinyls. They may be relatively rigid or flexible products. The thickest of the soft materials are designed for floor coverings (especially as dance surfaces), as cycloramas, and as rear screen surfaces. Stiff materials serve as covering and decorative trim for scenery and props. The thinnest materials are films and foils. Clear or transparent products are useful as glass substitutes or for see-through effects. Many materials have smooth, textured, or creped surfaces; some are metallized and mirrorized (including a shrink mirror plastic). Some of the foils have a pressure-sensitive adhesive for attaching to a surface. Rigid sheets can be secured to surfaces with polyvinyl glue, vinyl adhesives, or *Rosco-bond*. Seams in soft thermoplastics can be heat welded with an iron at a low temperature. Large shops and industrial firms use sonic sewing machines for sealing thermoplastic materials. More versatile and economical are plastic welders, which use a thermoplastic welding rod.

Vacuum Forming. To produce a line bend in thermoplastic sheet requires a strip or rod heater localized by insulation along the specific area to be bent. However, for complex and overall sheet thermoforming, the entire sheet must be heated uniformly. Vacuum forming is the most cost-efficient and convenient method of molding sheet plastics. Preformed sheets are available in a variety of bas-relief and three-dimensional ornamentation. Molded relief work such as stone and brick, molding, ornaments, and prop objects are available in small sheets (Figure 7-17). Even entire wall panels, doorways, and fireplaces as large as 4′ × 8′ or more can be obtained.

While commercial **vacuum-form machines** can be purchased, shop-made machines are relatively inexpensive and not difficult to assemble (Figure 7-18). Several methods of building a machine have been described in Nicholas Bryson's book, *Thermoplastic Scenery for the Theatre*, and in articles in *Theatre Design and Technology* over the years. A vacuum-form machine consists of (1) an oven where a plastic sheet is heated between 200° and 400°F and (2) a vacuum table where air is exhausted to pull the softened plastic tightly around a mold. The sheet of plastic is clamped in a metal frame to secure it firmly. The vacuum power is provided by a vacuum pressure in a large tank. This is connected by piping and a valve to the vacuum table. Pegboard with holes on 1″ centers forms the table surface. Objects placed on the vacuum table can be faithfully

FIGURE 7–17 Vacuum-formed scenic textures. (Photo courtesy of The Great American Market)

reproduced in plastic. A machine that forms 2′ × 3′ panels is often adequate. Large shops and studios have machines that thermoform 4′ × 8′ sheets. Complete and uniform heating of the plastic is essential. Hot spots will bubble or scorch the sheet at localized points, and spots not hot enough will result in malformed reproductions. Among thermoplastics, vinyl, cellulose acetate butyrate (CAB), acrylic, and high-impact polystyrene sheets adapt well to vacuum forming.

Celastic. *Celastic* is cloth, usually cotton flannel, that has been impregnated with pyroxylin (cellulose nitrate) plastic. When dipped into a solvent, it will soften, adhere to many materials, and dry to a very rigid state. Celastic often replaces papier-mâché as a surface skin over a shaped chicken-wire form. It also can be used to copy an object

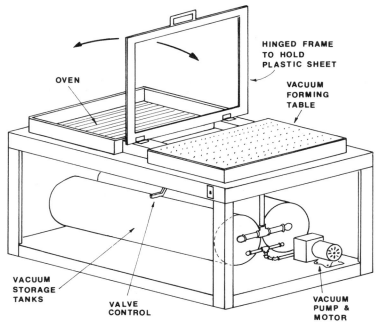

OVEN

HINGED FRAME
TO HOLD
PLASTIC SHEET

VACUUM
FORMING
TABLE

VACUUM
STORAGE
TANKS

VALVE
CONTROL

VACUUM
PUMP &
MOTOR

FIGURE 7–18 Vacuum-forming machine.

by shaping on a mold. Statuary, armor, set trim, and other set or prop objects can be fabricated in Celastic. The material is available in four different weights depending on the detail of the object to be molded. It is usually torn into strips before it is dipped into the solvent and applied to the work. Acetone (diluted with denatured alcohol) is the most common solvent used. Be sure to wear rubber gloves and provide adequate ventilation. While low in toxicity within its class of solvents, acetone is hazardous to skin, the nervous system, and the upper respiratory tract. It is also extremely flammable; beware of smoking and flames.

One layer of Celastic is usually adequate if strips are overlapped adequately. The final surface can be sanded, or puttied and then sanded, for a smooth surface. Because Celastic will adhere to most materials, a mold must be covered with aluminum foil or coated with vaseline or spray silicone before

applying the strips. It is not classified as a flammable material.

Fiberglass. The wide use of polyester resin reinforced with glass fiber assures that fiberglass materials are available in most communities. Its use in boat hulls, automobile bodies, furniture, and a host of other products attests to the great versatility and strength of fiberglass–reinforced plastics. The spun glass reinforcement material is available in several grades of cloth, matte, chopped strand, and powder. The choice of material for a specific project depends on the fineness of detail and the structural strength needed. All-purpose polyester resin is the most commonly used. Special resins can be obtained to provide a sticky surface for better adherence of subsequent layers or a finish resin that provides a smooth, extra-tough surface. Before the resin will work, an activator must be added.

This is a chemical catalyst, usually methylethyl ketone (MEK), which causes the resin to harden. The hardener seldom exceeds 2 percent of the total mixture. The catalyst frequently is obtained in a squeeze bottle so that the drops can be accurately measured. Read the instructions carefully for the proper proportions. The amount of hardener determines the setting time of the resin, usually between 20 and 40 minutes. Local conditions of temperature and humidity may require a change in proportions. Be aware that MEK is a very toxic and flammable solvent and many chemicals in the fiberglass process are hazardous. Wear appropriate gloves and have good ventilation.

The general procedure in using fiberglass is to cover a frame, buildup, or mold with the glass fiber material and then to brush on the resin mixture. A special framework or core can be constructed of any material: wood, chicken wire over a light frame, cardboard, or wads of paper. The glass cloth can be spot stapled or wired at edges or hollows or be simply placed loosely over the core as the resin is applied. The core can be removed after the fiberglass has set up sufficiently. An actual object or surface can be used as a mold. As the resin will bond to most materials, a parting agent is necessary. Polyethylene sheeting (such as dry cleaner's bags) or aluminum foil works well, as does petroleum jelly on nonporous surfaces. Owing to the amazing rigidity and strength of fiberglass, one layer on a small prop or tree stump is often sufficient. When more structural strength is needed, additional fiber and resin layers can be applied. Thin layers are transparent or translucent. Special colored dyes can be added into the resin mixture to give a stained glass appearance. Textured surfaces are also possible by the addition of almost any material including sawdust, rope, and shredded paper. The rough edges of the curved fiberglass can be trimmed with saws or snips. Beware of hardened glass threads; they become as sharp as knives and inflict painful cuts.

Acetone is the solvent for the resin before it sets up. Brushes, spray guns, and other equipment must be cleaned thoroughly before the resin hardens. Rubber gloves should be worn when working with polyester resin and acetone. Goggles and dust masks are needed to protect the eyes and mouth from the catalyst and glass powder. Smoking and flames should not be permitted in the working area.

Casting Resins. Casting resins are favorite hobby shop items and are ideal for small props, jewels, and simulated glass objects. Polyester resin is the most common, but acrylic and epoxy casting resins are also available. A special polystyrene resin is used for slush moldings of glass simulations, bottles, and other objects. Special molds or parting agents are needed. Negative molds are often ceramic, polypropylene, or silicone rubber. Molds can be made of almost any material and sprayed with a silicone or other parting agent. Flexible molds are best. The catalyst must be mixed with polyester resin as described for fiberglass. Throw-away waxed paper cups are the most convenient containers for mixing the resin. The resin must be poured into the mold within 20 minutes. Curing may require 12 or more hours.

Silicone and Other Synthetic Rubber Materials. *Hatamold* and *Weave Filler* are two flexible latex materials manufactured by Haussmann of West Germany. Weave Filler is an elastic material that will fill in the holes of scrims and nettings up to 1″ mesh or create ornamental designs when applied through a cake decorator syringe. Hatamold is a flexible casting material for pouring into plaster molds at normal room temperatures. It can provide medallions, relief designs, and applied decoration. Silicone rubber is useful in making flexible molds, especially for casting objects made of rigid urethane, polyester, and acrylic. A carefully measured catalyst must be added to the silicone base material and gently but thoroughly stirred with a stick or spatula. Air bubbles should be avoided in the mixture. The mold master may be of any material but will probably require coating with a special sealer. The silicone mixture is poured evenly over the master and allowed to dry for 24 to 48 hours. Bas-relief work uses an open mold, but a three-dimensional object requires a two-part mold held together by a wooden frame.

Polystyrene Foam. Commonly called by one of its trade names, *Styrofoam*, expanded polystyrene is available in 4′ × 8′ and 2′ × 8′ sheets from building suppliers. The most commonly available thicknesses are from ¾″ to 2″. For thicker buildups, sheets can be bonded together with polyvinyl glue, rubber cement, or panel adhesive. Dow's *Mastic #11* and 3M *Fastbond 30-NF* are strong immedi-

ate bonding adhesives for plastic foams. Polystyrene foam is relatively inexpensive, easy to work, and lightweight. Therefore, it is advantageous for creating moldings, columns, turned spindles, statuary, and other decorative items. If the created foam object must bear weight, a piece of wood can be built inside to give the structural support.

The type of foam appropriate for scenic uses should have sufficient density for the details required of carved, sculpted, and shaped ornamentation and contain a flame retardant. Common white foam (called "beadboard" because it is a molded sheet of little foam beads) does not meet this criteria. It is not treated for flame protection and it is a low-density foam that results in a rough and coarse surface when machined. Extruded polystyrene, usually light blue or

FIGURE 7–19 Polystyrene foam shaped by a drill press and special bits. (Courtesy of the Krannert Center for the Performing Arts, University of Illinois at Urbana–Champaign, Thomas V. Korder, Technical Director, and Ken Egan, Scene Shop Coordinator. Photo by Bernhard Works)

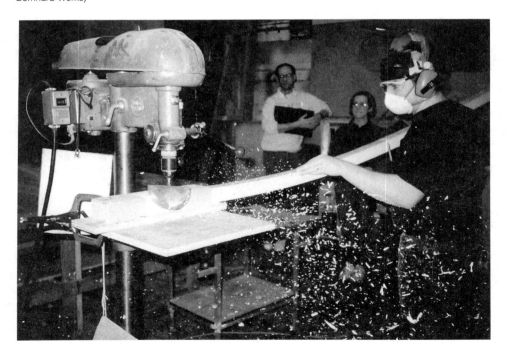

pink in color, is satisfactory for shaping and cutting distinct details and finishes in a smooth, paintable surface. It is fire resistant and does not require protective coatings to protect against accidental ignition.

Regular shop tools can be used to cut and shape polystyrene foam. Knives, especially those with serrated edges, are useful to carve the material. For a smooth cut with power saws, a slow feed rate is desirable. Similar to wood, shapers and routers will shape foam. A drill press using special bits and a guide jig is effective as a foam shaper for producing moldings (Figure 7-19).

The health risks involved in working with polystyrene foam include airborne dust particles and the release of gases from the material. It is essential to work in an open, well-ventilated area if a local ventilation system is not available. A dust collection system or a vacuum system at the bench or tool level is needed. After working, clean the tools and the shop thoroughly with a shop vacuum or a wet mop (not a broom) to avoid increasing dust levels in the air. A dust particle mask should be worn, or better, a respirator with a vapor cartridge. Eye protection should be provided by wearing goggles.

Another method of shaping polystyrene foam is the use of **hot-wire cutters.** A variety of hot-wire and hot-knife tools are available commercially for this purpose. Shop-built cutters can be constructed of resistance wire (*Nichrome* wire gauge 18–22). Sometimes coat hanger wire or low carbon steel is effective. A step-down transformer (filament transformer) is necessary to provide a low voltage to heat the wire. With the wire, cutter knives, table cutters, and molding jigs can be built to cut the foam (Figure 7-20). A hot-wire gun can be fashioned by replacing the soldering tip of a heavy-duty electric soldering gun with Nichrome wire. Have effective ventilation from the vapors and practice safety precautions against electrical shock, burns, and fire hazards from the heat of the wire.

Polystyrene foam can also be melted by the application of flame, heat, or solvents.

An electric soldering iron, for instance, which melts foam upon contact, can be a carving tool. Similarly, a propane torch or an electric hot-air gun waved across foam will melt the surface. Sculpted ornamentation can be created by painting high relief areas with water-base paint to protect them from melting when the torch or air gun is used. All areas around the painted portions will be recessed relief. Certain solvents, such as banana oil, mineral spirits, or lacquer thinner, will also corrode the surface. The fumes from melting foam require technicians to wear respirators and to work in a well-ventilated area or outdoors with fumes blowing away from the face.

A finished foam product can be painted with water-base paint. The surface of polystyrene foam is soft and easily dented. It

FIGURE 7–20 Hot-wire cutters for polystyrene foam.

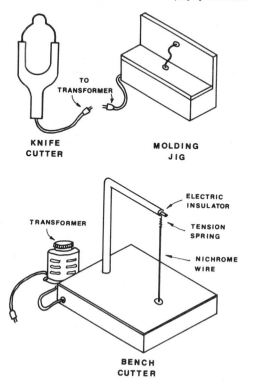

can be toughened with a sealer coat of 3M *Fastbond* 30-NF, or with the application of a layer of woven cheesecloth glued to the surface. For a tougher surface, Haussmann sells a water-soluble surface coating for foam. Called *Armor Putty*, this paste provides a rigid and flame-resistant surface.

Urethane Foam. Expanded polyurethane is available as flexible foam or rigid foam. Flexible foam is the most common cushion material for upholstered furniture. It is generally white and is sold in slabs, sheets, and billets in all sizes and thicknesses. It can be cut and shaped with knives, saws, and other cutters. Soaped saw blades will reduce the risk of snagging the foam. It is useful for creating curved moldings and "soft" decoration. Rigid urethane foam has a weight-to-strength advantage similar to polystyrene foam. Unlike polystyrene, it is a closed-cell foam made with a gas blowing agent. The release of these trapped gases when the foam is cut requires considerable caution. Adequate ventilation should be provided when cutting urethane foam with a power saw. *Never* use a hot-wire cutter on urethane foam. Heating and burning releases dangerous cyanide, carbon monoxide, and other gases. Preformed architectural trim, including moldings and false beams made of urethane foam, is available at lumber yards. Some of these are tough, high-density products that have distinct scenic uses.

Flexible and rigid urethane foams are especially suited for mixing and foaming in the scene shop at normal room temperatures. Urethane foams will adhere to any material except polyethylenes, waxed, and silicone sprayed surfaces. The final plastic can be coated with any paint materials. Foams can be prepared by the pour-in-place or spray-pack methods.

Pour-in-place foaming involves several ingredients which are combined conveniently into two components, A and B, which are poured together to produce the foaming action. The components must be measured accurately before they are combined. Throwaway mixing containers such as paper cups or food tins avoid the cost of regular containers and the time-consuming task of cleaning them with acetone or other urethane solvents. After measuring, the components are poured into the mixing container. Only about 30 seconds are available to stir the mixture before chemical action causes it to expand. Mixing must be thorough to achieve uniform density and foaming reaction. While small amounts may be mixed with a stirring stick, larger amounts usually require a **power mixer.** An electric drill with a wire beater works well. The mixed ingredients should be poured into the mold and spread thoroughly before foaming action begins so the foam will be distributed throughout the mold and with uniform density.

One-piece open molds are used for projected or relief objects, while a two-part closed mold is needed for three-dimensional structures. Mold materials must be strong enough to withstand the pressure caused by the rising foam, and you must consider the tendency of urethane to adhere to most surfaces. The temperature caused by the chemical reaction during the foaming process often penetrates through the usual oils and waxes used as parting agents. Therefore, urethane varnish or urethane **mold release** materials are the best release agents.

Any number of mold materials can be used for urethane objects; the choice often is determined by the nature of the project. However, rather than rigid plaster or fiberglass, preferred mold materials are flexible and elastic. Since foam expands to fill a mold tightly, a stretchable mold can more easily be removed by flexing and peeling it from the molded object. In addition, flexible molds will not crack from clamping and from foam pressures.

One standard mold material is **rubber compound.** A box is formed around the

FIGURE 7–21 Objects made of pour-in-place urethane foam in open and closed molds.

model and a release agent is applied on all inside surfaces. The compound is mixed and poured into the box. After curing, the resultant mold is firm, rubbery, and faithful to the detail of the model. Another mold solution is a combination of latex and flexible urethane foam. After applying the release agent, four coats of liquid latex are brushed on the model and the inside surfaces of the enclosing box. Flexible urethane foam is then prepared and poured into the box. Latex reproduces details of the model extremely well, and the foam bonds well to the latex skin and gives sturdy but flexible support to the mold. When making molded urethane objects, pressure is needed to contain the foam in the mold and to make to it fill all crannies and achieve density. When the foam begins to rise, pressure should be applied. With an open mold the top can be covered with a sheet of polyethylene film and covered by a board and some weights. Foam will not adhere to polyethylene, and a smooth, hard surface will be formed. On closed molds, clamps are necessary to hold the parts together during the foaming pro-

cess. A foamed object can be reinforced with strips of wood, metal, or wire inserted in the mold. Tiny air holes (up to $\frac{1}{16}''$) are sometimes necessary in deep molds to permit air and foam gases to escape. Special pigments are available to add to the pour-in-place mixture, and common dry scene paint also works effectively. The prepared foam mixture is also effective when spread on a surface for textural effects. Flexible foam, for instance, creates a foldable and sculpted floor surface on a ground cloth.

Spray-pack foaming is achieved with prepackaged frothed foam mixed as needed. The pack consists of two components in pressure bags, with hoses and a dispenser. One product is known as *Insta-Foam Froth Pak*. The components are mixed in proper proportions as the trigger is released. The nozzle unit must be replaced before each spraying, and the entire package is disposable when the components are consumed. A spray pack can be used for filling molds, but it is more effective in producing interesting textures—stucco, plaster, rock, or tree bark—when sprayed onto a scenic surface.

A local ventilation system and an air-supplied respirator are both required to spray foam safely.

Polyethylene Foam. Expanded polyethylene is a flexible foam material known most commonly by one of its trade names, *Ethafoam*. It is a lightweight closed-cell foam with a waxy or slippery surface. The material is available in extruded rod, sheets, and planks. The sheet form, sold as *Bubble Board*, has a translucency useful for rear lighting and projection. Ethafoam flexible rod is widely used for moldings on columns, curved frames, and decorative railings. It can be worked easily with knives and saws. It can be split or quartered on a band saw. The 3M Fastbond adhesive, for one, is effective in securing ethylene foam rod to surfaces and coating the visible sides to accept most paints without flaking and peeling. It is available in diameters of ¼″ to 2″.

SELECTED READINGS

ALTHOUSE, ANDREW D., CARL H. TURNQUIST, WILLIAM A. BOWDITCH, and DEVIN E. BOWDITCH, *Modern Welding*. South Holland, IL: The Goodheart-Wilcox Co., 1980.

BAIRD, RONALD J., *Industrial Plastics*. South Holland, IL: The Goodheart-Wilcox Co., 1971.

BOWMAN, NED A., *Handbook of Technical Practice for the Performing Arts*. Wilkinsburg, PA: Scenographic Media, 1975.

BRYSON, NICHOLAS L., *Thermoplastic Scenery for the Theatre. Vol. I: Vacuum Forming*. New York: Drama Book Specialists, 1972.

NEWMAN, THELMA R., *Plastics as an Art Form* (rev. ed.). Philadelphia: Chilton, 1969.

TAYLOR, DOUGLAS C., *Metalworking for the Designer and Technician*. New York: Drama Book Specialists, 1979.

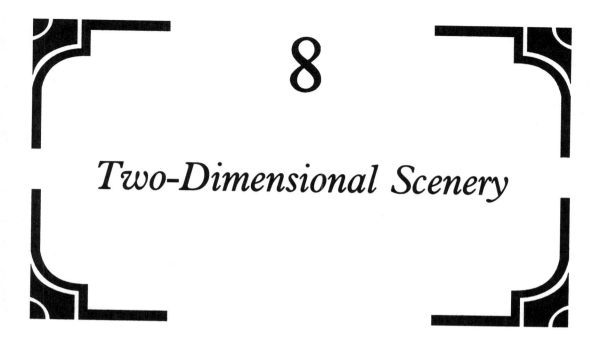

8

Two-Dimensional Scenery

Two-dimensional scenery is one of the oldest and simplest scenic elements found in the history of scene technology. Two-dimensional structures can be defined as scenery with only one side or surface visible to the audience; that is, to be seen in length and width but not in depth. Probably no physical elements are more allied with theatrical performance than draperies, drops, and flats. Although associated most often with 19th-century practice—when this scenic form reached perfection—two-dimensional construction remains a necessary and valuable form of scenery today. The cloth-covered wooden frame called the **flat** has reached an engineered perfection of structure over the many centuries of its use and refinement. This is not to say, of course, that the flat may not someday undergo considerable change or be almost totally replaced with structures using more contemporary materials, tools, and techniques. Several new materials and

technologies have already been adopted in scene shops recently. However, fabric and lumber remain standard materials in scene construction.

DRAPERIES

Draperies, fabric or material hung in folds, serve a variety of functions in theatrical performance. One of these is the concealment of the entire scene from the audience. In this situation draperies hide the setup and shifting of scenery used in the performance, opening to reveal the scene and closing at the end of the scene. In the proscenium theatre, this function is made possible by the front curtain and the grand drapery border.

Another set of draperies is sometimes used to surround the performance space. These draperies serve to delineate the area reserved for the performers and to conceal behind-the-scene functions and visual elements that would tend to distract attention from the scene. This masking is one of the most fundamental purposes of scenery. Many multipurpose stages have one or more sets of enclosing draperies. The most common forms of these are (1) a rear drapery plus a series of drapery panels forming the sides of the playing space and (2) a series of legs and borders masking the sides of the stage and backed by a rear drapery (Fig. 8–1). It is common practice for "no scenery" or "suggested scenery" productions to be backed by a set of enclosing draperies or a cyclorama. The cyclorama is often used for light projections or lighted for sky or mood effects. However, enclosing draperies are treated most often as masking—generally dark so the performer and scenery will take focus—giving a "plucked out of the void" effect. A neutral background is a frequent convention in theatrical production.

The third major type of drapery is used directly as decorative background for the performer. This practice is most evident in certain stage musicals, television variety shows, and night club and revue entertainment of all kinds.

Fabrics

Many materials have potential value for theatrical draperies, depending on the function to be served or the specific scenic effect desired. Durability is required of most fabrics selected because of the abuse draperies take in the course of a production. Traveling-production drapes and the enclosing draperies of a multipurpose theatre receive such unusual punishment that economy generally demands fabrics have long life. Opacity is another generally desired quality for draperies unless the special requirement of translucency or transparency is the effect to be achieved. Of course, drapes are lined when necessary. Fabric that tends to absorb rather than reflect light is most often pre-

FIGURE 8–1 Draperies enclosing the playing space.

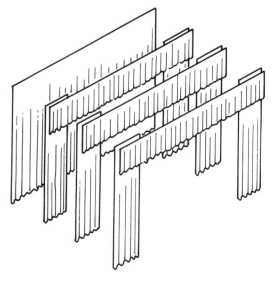

Legs & Borders

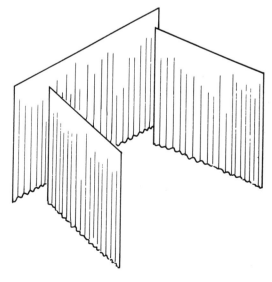

Side Panels

ferred for background draperies. Such material competes less with the performer and scenery for attention.

Similarly, light-absorbent fabric that provides a rich, luxurious quality of soft highlights and shadows is frequently desired for a front curtain and grand drapery border. Cut-pile fabric is among the most effective in absorbing light. Napped, looped pile or highly textured materials are economical substitutes. Velour, a cotton fabric with heavy pile, is the most common cut-pile material in use. Good quality velour is a tough fabric, dense, thick, and rich in texture. Other cut-pile fabrics include plush, a form of velvet with pile more than ⅛" in height, and *Ultralure II*, a nylontriacetate blend fabric. Duvetyne and *Commando Cloth* are names of fabrics with a napped surface on one side similar to flannel and relatively inexpensive. Rep and monk's cloth are textural materials that can be effective for draperies. Lightweight fabrics are easily subject to air movement and often must be heavily weighted.

The fabric for the front or show curtain requires special consideration. Frequently desired is a rich, decorative curtain, one appropriate to the style and mood of the performance. Ideally, the front curtain should enhance the qualities of the specific production. If a theatre or a performing group cannot afford to change its front curtain for a given production, a front curtain should be provided that will best satisfy the range of theatrical genres produced. Certainly, a splashy satin curtain would be out of place for a classical tragedy.

Designers and technicians must be acquainted with the variety of fabrics available for draperies. Draperies used purely as decorative backgrounds for the performance offer the greatest range of opportunity. Almost any fabric or material that takes folds well is worthy of consideration. A particular satin, damask, or patterned fabric may be appropriate for a specific scenic statement. Muslin or other hard-surface material may be used if a painted or dyed scene or decor

is wanted. Gloss fabrics, synthetic fabrics, and the growing variety of nonwovens and plastic and metallic sheet materials provide interesting possibilities.

Generally, the enclosing draperies on a stage should be dark and neutral in color. Black, charcoal, or dark blue are ideal. This permits the performers, the setting, and the costumes to "take the stage," and avoids conflicts in color harmony.

Construction

In sewing drapery panels, 50 to 100 percent fullness is often added to the finished width. A minimum of 75 percent fullness is usually required for the richness of folds of a front or show curtain. To achieve a 20' wide drapery panel, an additional 15' of fabric width is necessary for 75 percent fullness. This fullness must be evenly distributed and shirred into the top in box or plain pleats double stitched to 3 ½" wide cotton, nylon, or jute webbing (Figure 8-2).

Since the entire drapery is hung or suspended from the top, proper and secure attachment of the reinforcing webbing and associated hanging devices is critical. Jute webbing is less desirable because it seldom lasts the life of the drapery fabric. Draperies

FIGURE 8–2 Draperies pleated at the top and double-stitched to webbing.

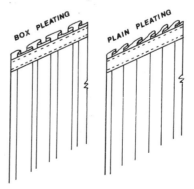

extending to the floor should have a 6″ bottom hem. A chain weight in a continuous canvas pocket is sewn inside the hem. The canvas pocket prevents the chain from wearing holes in the bottom of the hem. All other drapes have 3″ bottom hems. Side hems of 3″ are usually adequate, while the leading edges of draperies on curtain tracks require hems a minimum of 18″ owing to the flapping of the fabric during use.

Draperies are normally designed either to tie to pipe battens or to be attached to curtain tracks commonly called travelers. Tie-on draperies are constructed with #2 grommets (⅜″ diameter) installed on 1′ centers in the top webbing. First, holes are made through the fabric and webbing with a grommet hole cutter and a few strokes of the hammer. A block of wood is placed under the fabric to protect the cutting edge of the cutter. Grommets are then installed with a grommet die (see Figure 6-25). Three-foot lengths of ⅛″ diameter braided cotton rope are secured through the grommets with ring hitch knots. These tie lines serve to secure the drapery to pipe battens (Figure 8-3). Bow knots are used to attach tie lines of all draperies to the pipe battens to assure their easy and quick removal. Merely pulling on the loose end of each tie line releases the knot. One-inch twill tape sometimes replaces cotton rope, but it is more difficult to untie.

Draperies designed for hanging exclusively on curtain tracks are often constructed with a different type of attachment. In place of grommets and tie lines, snap hooks are secured to the top of the drapery by a loop of heavy (1″ wide) cotton belting. The belting straddles the drapery and is best riveted rather than sewn to the webbing (Figure 8-4). The snap hooks are positioned 1″ to 2″ above the top of the drapery and can be hooked easily to the chain links on the curtain track carriers.

Additional refinements may be included in the construction of draperies. For instance, a petticoat or apron (a double thick-

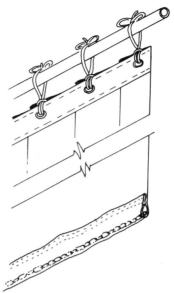

FIGURE 8–3 Draperies are hung to pipe battens by installing grommets on 1′ centers and tie lines secured through them with ring hitch knots. The bottom hem contains a chain weight in a canvas pocket.

ness of fabric) hanging 2″ below the bottom hem will act as a dust ruffle and light seal at the floor level. The opening and closing of a drapery on a curtain track often results in considerable flapping of fabric on the lead-

FIGURE 8–4 Snap hooks are used on draperies primarily intended for curtain tracks.

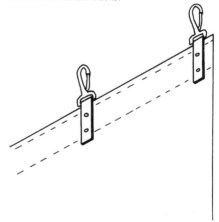

ing edges. This can be corrected by a weight consisting of lead shot in a 1″ diameter canvas tube several feet in length hung by a chain inside the hem of the leading edge. The chain and weight should be suspended directly from the master carrier on the track. Inexpensive cotton material may be used as lining for draperies if additional opacity is desired. The lining should be open and hung free at the bottom to accommodate the difference in shrinkage of the two materials. A catch stitch every few feet will prevent the fabric from ballooning outward when operated on a track. Reversible or double-faced drapes, two different draperies sewn together back to back, are sometimes useful in theatres and studios with extensive I-track systems. A change of color in the background is provided by simply reversing the drapery on its tracks.

The fabrication of draperies requires care and sufficient work space to avoid wrinkles and sags in the sewing process. All seams must be vertical; cross seams should not be allowed. The material must be fed evenly and with equal stretching through the sewing machine. Selvage edges are usually clipped to allow the fabric to hang properly. To assure proper draping of the fabric, all drapes over 10′ in height should be hung for a day before hems are sewn. All the fabric for a drapery must be from the same dye lot and matched in nap direction before sewing. All draperies should meet local code requirements in flame-resistance standards.

When not in use, draperies can be folded and stored in rolling hampers, trunks, or canvas bags. When folding, draperies should be spread out evenly on the floor. The front surface is folded to the inside to keep this side clean and protected during handling and storage. If the top edge of the drape is exposed in the final folding, the drapery may be rehung with a minimum of handling. Draperies occasionally need brushing to remove lint, steaming to remove wrinkles, and dry cleaning.

DROPS

A drop is a flat expanse of fabric without folds. Full-sized drops are often extremely large. Backdrops exceeding 20′ in height and 40′ in width are quite common. The actual size of a drop will depend on the demands of the total set design and the audience sight lines in a particular theatre or the camera view in a TV or film studio. Because rectangular-shaped drops tend to sag at extreme sides, some technicians prefer to construct trapezoidal shaped drops with the top 3′ to 4′ wider than the bottom.

Drops are usually painted or dyed for particular scenic effects. Landscapes, cityscapes, interior scenes, and foliage borders are some examples of representational or symbolic scenes. Highly decorative or mood designs are used for many types of performances. Muslin, canvas duck, velour, and linen are probably the most frequently used materials for drops. However, any number of fabrics are employed for particular effects. The availability of a wide variety of new materials in recent years has stimulated an interest in the visual effects of materials. New plastic materials now offer a wide range of textures, glittering metallic surfaces, mirrored reflective surfaces, and translucent or transparent qualities. They have considerably extended our concern for material, texture, and the range of effects that can be achieved in two-dimensional surfaces.

Seams are usually sewn horizontally on drops so they hang taut and are as invisible as possible. Taking exception to this, some technicians prefer vertical seams, especially on large drops and cycloramas, arguing that the weight of the stretched fabric places unusual stress on the single row of stitching of each horizontal seam. Several seams are usually necessary. Velour is obtained in 54″ widths, regular scenic canvas and muslin in 69″ to 72″ widths and wider, and most other fabrics in widths less than 6′. Special scenic fabrics loomed in 30′ widths permit the construction of seamless drops. Welded seams on vinyl projection screens and cycloramas must be vertical to avoid separation when stretched for long periods.

Because drops are entirely two-dimensional units, any illusion of depth must be achieved by perspective painting or light projection. Further illusion of depth can be effected by combining several types of drops together (and lighting them separately). For example, three-dimensional illusion is enhanced if leg drops are hung in the foreground, a cut drop inset in the middle ground, and a regular drop (backdrop) located in the background. Several common types of drops are shown in Figure 8-5.

Battened Drop

The top and bottom edges of this drop are attached to a pair of 1″ × 4″ battens (Figure 8-6). The fabric is tacked and glued to one batten, and a second batten is secured on top with screws to form a "sandwich" batten for added strength. Because the batten length frequently exceeds available lumber lengths, scarf joints or reinforced butt joints must be provided for each sandwich batten. The battened drop historically precedes contemporary counter-weight rigging systems, and therefore was designed to be flown on a rope-line rigging system. The rope lines may be attached directly to the top batten, generally at 10′ intervals.

On a contemporary pipe-batten system, the top of the drop may be hung by short lengths of rope, batten clamps, or trim chains so adjustments can be made to remove sags. The bottom batten is secured to the floor so the fabric is stretched taut. When the drop is taken down, the bottom batten rolls up the drop, face side inward, into a long compact roll for traveling or removal

FIGURE 8–5 Types of drops.

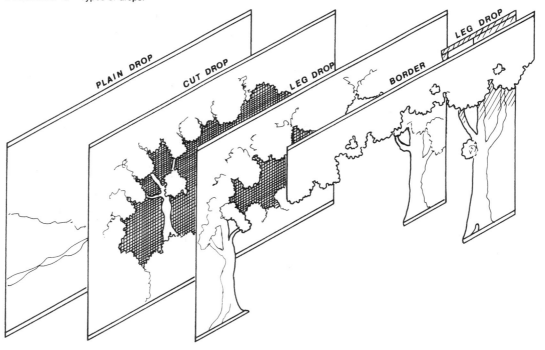

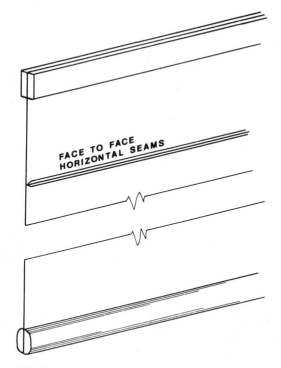

FACE TO FACE HORIZONTAL SEAMS.

FIGURE 8–6 Battened drop.

to storage. The length of the roll requires that the design of the stage and associated facility permit easy access of the drop to the drop storage area.

Framed Drop

Occasionally, a drop with a more rigid structure is required. (A door or window included in the drop would indicate this need.) On a framed drop, the top and bottom 1″ × 4″ battens are permanent; that is, they are tacked and glued to the back side of the fabric. This permits the drop to be rolled up for transportation and storage in the same manner as the battened drop. The remaining members of the frame are removable. They are assembled to the top and bottom battens when the drop is laid out on

the floor face down. Ceiling plates are used to join members of the frame. One end of the ceiling plate is fastened to the ends of the removable battens with screws. The other end is joined to the permanent battens with carriage bolts and wing nuts through predrilled holes. The loose edges of the drop are several inches wider than the frame. They are reinforced with webbing. On these edges ⅜″ grommets and cotton rope are provided to lace the cloth to the frame. The rope is laced around a row of protruding roundheaded screws (Figure 8-7).

FIGURE 8–7 Framed drop.

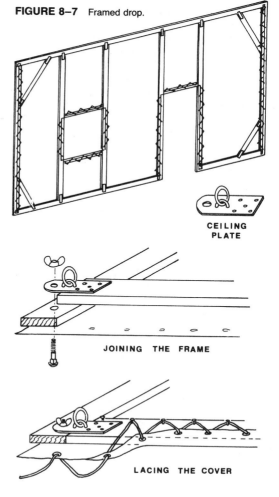

CEILING PLATE

JOINING THE FRAME

LACING THE COVER

Soft Drop

This drop is constructed without any framing battens. It relies on a pipe batten of the stage rigging system for top support, and on a weighted stiffener inserted in the bottom hem to maintain stretch and tautness (Figure 8-8). Therefore, it is fully "soft" and can be folded up and placed in a canvas bag, trunk, or hamper for travel and storage. A 3 ½"-wide webbing is sewn to the top of the drop with grommets on 12" centers for tie lines. A double hem is provided at the bottom edge to insert a ¾" ID pipe batten. It is common practice to identify the center of the drop with a mark on the back of the webbing or by a colored center tie line. The drop is then folded in a specific manner so the webbing edge and center mark are exposed (Figure 8-9). This saves considerable time and effort in rehanging the drop. Soft drops are tied to pipe battens (with bow

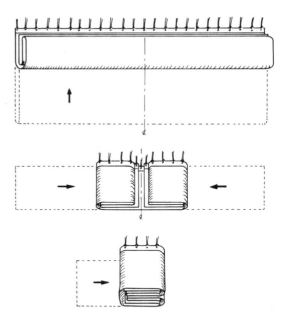

FIGURE 8–9   For convenience of rehanging, a soft drop is folded repeatedly from the bottom to the top to a convenient width, then from the sides to the middle.

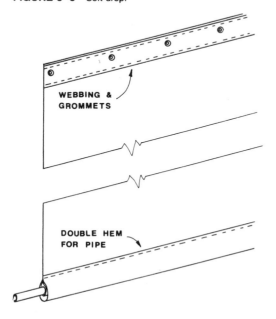

FIGURE 8–8   Soft drop.

WEBBING & GROMMETS

DOUBLE HEM FOR PIPE

knots, of course) from the center outward, keeping the fabric as taut as possible.

Cut Drop

Constructed in any of the forms already listed, the cut drop contains cut-out openings in the fabric. A forest scene of trees and foliage is a typical cut drop. The portions of the fabric are cut out after painting to avoid curled edges caused by the drying paint. Black bobinette or netting is secured to the back of the fabric over the openings with flexible glue so the drop will hang straight (Figure 8-10). The drop must be placed face down on the floor, the netting stretched out squarely on top, and the paste applied without wrinkling the netting. The bobinette or netting will be invisible to the viewer. Vision

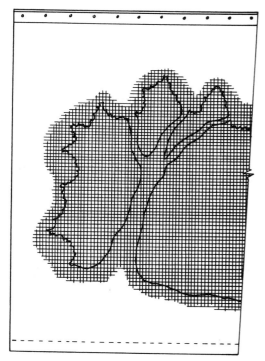

FIGURE 8–10 Flexible glue holds black netting around the openings of a cut drop to keep the fabric from sagging when hung.

through the openings in the drop enhances the illusion of depth.

Translucent Drop

Both the front and rear of this drop are used for scenic effects. When front lighting is darkened and rear lighting provided, images painted, dyed, or projected on the rear side are visible to the audience. Thus, the scene on the back side replaces the image on the front. The control and proper location of lighting is the key to this change of scene. After the cloth has been sealed with size, dye or paint thin enough not to fill the openings of the fabric is applied. Areas may be made opaque if desired. Muslin is one of the most-used fabrics for translucent drops, but numerous screen and plastic materials are also available. To be translucent, the drop must be free of seams and framing. Muslin may be purchased in 30′ widths, so a seamless drop is possible. Interest in scenic light projection (both front and rear) has increased the use of translucent drops and screens for both background and multiscreen scenic effects. A variety of plastic rear-screen materials is available which provide unusually high luminosity for projection images. They may be obtained in black, gray, or white materials. Seams can be ultrasonically welded or may be specially taped to reduce visibility. A translucent drop is constructed in any of the forms already discussed.

Transparent Drop

Theatrical gauze, sharkstooth scrim, opera net, bobinette, certain transparent plastics, and cotton and nylon net are among the varieties of materials useful for transparent drops. When lighted from the front in extremely steep angles, with reduced lighting from behind, the drop appears opaque or nearly opaque. When the front lights are removed and objects are lighted behind the drop, the material becomes nearly transparent. Scrim, bobinette, and opera net can be obtained in 30′ width for seamless drops. All other fabrics are loomed in 6′ width or less and will require seams. Sharkstooth scrim, one of the strongest materials, is also one of the least transparent. Theatrical gauze will stretch with the application of pigment or dyes and therefore must be painted before it is sewn into a finished drop or attached to a frame. Heavy coats of paint, or cloth appliqued to the drop, will opaque desired portions for the design. These same fabrics also may be applied to regular flats when a transparency or see-through quality is needed.

Border

A border is an overhead, horizontal strip of cloth hung at the top of the scene. While it is essentially an element of the setting, it also serves as a masking unit to conceal overhead staging equipment. It may be constructed in the manner of either a battened or a soft drop. More than one border is frequently necessary. Borders are often cut and colored to represent a ceiling, foliage, or clouds. Portions may be cut out similar to the cut drop.

Leg Drop

Although this unit may be simply one or two cloth wings (or legs) at the sides of the scene, it is often an arch-shaped drop serving as a border, and attached legs. It can be devised in any of the drop construction methods.

Sky Drop

This is a drop used for sky or background effects created by lights and light projectors. When fabric is employed, it is left a natural off-white color or tinted light blue-grey. If it is constructed of plastic screen material, the drop can double as a rear projection screen as well.

Cyclorama

The cyclorama is a sky drop that curves around the performance area. It frequently extends to the full height of the stage or studio for maximum sight lines and camera long-shot views. It is often made of canvas or muslin dyed light blue-grey and faced with another drop of sharkstooth scrim. The scrim masks the seams in the canvas or muslin and gives a textural quality that enhances the blending of cyc lighting. Filled scrim is sometimes used as a single-fabric cyclorama.

In recent years, plastic screen material with welded seams has been replacing traditional cyc fabrics. A cyclorama of black fabric can be hung for scenes requiring dark backgrounds. Specially curved pipe battens or curved tracks are usually required for cycloramas.

Other Types of Drops

A ribbon curtain is another special form of drop. This type of drop permits the performer to enter or exit at any slit in the fabric. It may consist of ribbons several inches wide, objects hung on strings (similar to a beaded curtain), or regular material cut into strips to a height of 8′ to 10′, high enough to permit entrances (Figure 8-11). The top of the drop must be sewn onto webbing or secured to a wooden batten. Another variation includes the use of wider strips of material—banners or shutter-like widths—that can be attached to controlled frames at the top, bottom, or both to rotate open and closed or to twist vertically. Stretched cords and louvres of cloth have been employed by

FIGURE 8–11 A ribbon curtain formed of two layers of fabric sewn together at the top. Slits provide for entrances at any location.

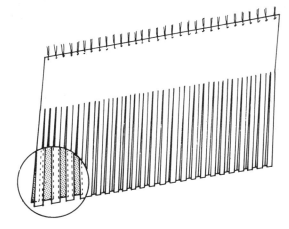

a number of designers as drops or projection screens.

Other types of drops or variations are subject only to the imagination of designers and technicians and to the unique scenic effect to be achieved.

FRAMED UNITS

It is the thesis of this book that scene technology requires precision and accuracy. Nowhere is this more necessary than in the construction of the most basic element of scenery, the two-dimensional framed unit. Poor construction inevitably results in flapping canvas on a frame, protruding tacks or staples, discolored paint from improper adhesives, and units that will not fit together tightly. These and other examples of poor handiwork shatter the total illusion being created. Stage carpenters, as all scene technicians, are illusion artisans. When the illusion is broken, they have failed in their efforts.

The methods of construction presented here have been found effective in creating framed scenery. This is not to say, of course, that there are not other acceptable methods, variations of techniques, or even short cuts in construction. Every practicing technician develops personal methods of construction that have proven effective through experience and application. Furthermore, construction systems vary slightly from one theatre group to another according to (1) the types of performances produced, (2) the needs of the particular production media, (3) the skills of the construction personnel, (4) the nature of the scenery stock, and (5) the shop facilities and equipment. A good technician discovers different approaches and techniques and adapts the best to his or her particular endeavor.

The selection of lumber for the construction of framed units can be as critical as for any other construction craft. The strength and lightness of good lumber is not enough. The stile of a flat requires lumber that is straight and true without warp or twist, well seasoned, and as free of knots and imperfections as possible. A warped, bent, or bowed flat is of little use. Lumber for other constructed units, particularly in shorter lengths, may not pose such exacting demands. Therefore, before proceeding to build framed scenery, appropriate lumber is selected for the specific project. This may be done at the lumber yard, or an inspection should be conducted on delivery, and those pieces not suitable should be returned to the dealer.

The Flat

Essentially, a flat is a frame of lumber designed to hold cloth flat and taut. Its strength is calculated expressly for this purpose, which determines structure, lumber, and joining methods. A flat is conceived to be light in weight so that even the largest may be handled with ease by a skillful crew member. Adding more strength to the structure than is required by the cloth cover unnecessarily increases the weight and complicates maneuverability.

Conventional flat construction—in fact, the entire canvas-and-paste-craft—is of another era and may seem out of place in modern technology. There are many contemporary variations of flat construction including stiff and lightweight Upson board, foam board, and other paper boards to replace the often insubstantial covering of stretched cloth. Where weight is not a problem, plywood is used as a surface material. Further, the high cost of lumber and dwindling supplies of high-quality soft wood have encouraged entirely different two-dimensional structures of honeycomb board, plastics, and metals in many state-of-the-art settings.

Flat Sizes. Up through the 1950s, when the box set was the rage, flats were often built as part of "sets." A set was a collection of flats of the same height. A producing group that maintained a stock of scenery might have several standard sets of flats. A 10'-high set might be used for small interiors or cabins; another set, 14' perhaps, would be for average interiors; and a tall set, 18', would become the throne rooms and two-story exteriors. Current emphasis on more suggestive settings has placed less importance on a limited range of standard heights in live theatre. Television and film scenery is governed by the height of the studios and soundstages and by the camera position.

When it is necessary to maintain a reusable stock, it is wise to restrict the height of most flats to multiples of even feet. On the other hand, considerable variation is desirable in the width of flats. For commercial productions, where scenery is constructed for one show only without concern of reuse, there is seldom any standardization of width. However, for theatres that maintain a stock of scenery, an attempt is frequently made to limit the widths of flats to multiples of 6". Flats seldom exceed 5'-9" or 6', which is the normal width of scenic muslin and canvas. Wider flats require seams in the fabric; are more difficult to handle; are awkward, if not impossible, to transport and carry through doorways; and are problems to store. When a special or extra-wide unit is constructed, it is usually destroyed after the production unless it has unusual potential for reuse and there is adequate storage space available.

The Flat Frame. Similar to terms used in paneling, the top and bottom horizontal members of the flat frame are called **rails.** **Stiles** are the vertical members that stretch between them to form the sides of the frame (Figure 8-12). Rails extend to the full width of the flat. The bottom rail acts as a skid that permits the flat to be pulled across the floor without splitting the lumber. **Toggle bars** are horizontal, interior members of the structure that keep the stiles the proper distance apart. The number of toggle bars should follow the general rule that the flat covering should not be unsupported for more than 5'. Therefore, a 10'-flat requires

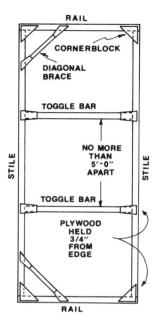

FIGURE 8–12   The frame of a flat.

only one toggle bar, a 12'-flat needs two, and so on. Additional toggle bars are added where pictures or other objects are attached to the flat in a given scene. Two diagonal braces along one side of the structure complete the frame.

Stock 1" × 3" lumber is used for frame construction. The actual dimensions of this lumber, of course, are nearer ¾" × 2½". The extra strength needed for oversized flats (over 16') requires 1" × 4" lumber. Some shops build stiles and rails of ⁵⁄₄" stock (1¼" lumber) for greater durability. Toggle bars are 1" × 3"s, and the two diagonal braces are cut from 1" × 2" stock.

Lumber Joints. The mortise-and-tenon joint is by far the strongest joint. Shoe-mortise joints can be provided on toggle bars to permit them to be readjusted within the frame if necessary. However, cutting mortise-and-tenon joints requires proper equipment, extreme skill, and considerable time. They are used sometimes for productions scheduled for long runs or for the rigors scenery takes on tour.

The reinforced butt joint is more commonly used. It is relatively strong and easy to construct with simple tools. In addition, butt joints make it possible for flats to be altered and rebuilt later for other productions. One-quarter inch (three-ply) plywood is employed to reinforce the butt joints. Plywood **cornerblocks** are cut as right isosceles triangles 10″ on each of the right angle sides. **Keystones** are often not the familiar tapered shape but rectangles approximately 3″ wide and 8″ long. For maximum strength, the size and placement of these plywood pieces are critical. The maximum strength of three-ply lies in the direction of the wood grain on its outer two layers of veneer. Cornerblocks and keystones must be placed so the outer grain is perpendicular to the lumber joint that is being reinforced. Special keystones must be cut for the diagonal braces.

Constructing the Frame. The rails are marked to be cut to the actual width of the flat, the stiles are measured to the length of the flat *minus* the actual width of the two rails, and the toggle bars are marked to the width of the flat *minus* the actual width of the two stiles (Figure 8-13). Remember, 1″ × 3″ stock lumber is not really 3″ wide and must be measured when used. Once marked, lumber may be cut on a radial arm saw or table saw. This will assure accurate 90° cuts. If the sawing is to be done by hand tools, the lumber must be marked by a try square for true right angles.

Cornerblocks and keystones are placed ¾″ from the outer edges of the frame and ¾″

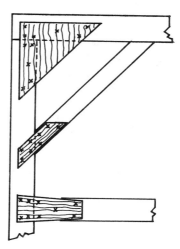

FIGURE 8–14 Cornerblocks and keystones shown with wood grain running perpendicular to the joints and ¾″ from the edge of the frame.

from any door, window, or other opening in the flat (Figure 8-14). This is done to permit the addition of a thickness piece or return flat that must fit flush to the back of the flat. A scrap piece of 1″ stock lumber can be used to be sure the cornerblocks and keystones are positioned properly. The reinforcing plywood is secured by one of several types of fasteners. The most common are ¾″ wood screws or 1″ pneumatic staples. Screws provide the strongest hold but require the most time and effort to install. Starter holes help to drive the screws more easily. Fortunately, modern power screwdrivers can drive and remove screws with little effort.

Pneumatic-driven staples are the fastest to install of all fasteners. They are heavy-duty staples. The legs of the staple are coated to resist loosening and are pointed at the ends to spread as they are driven into the wood. Thus, they have more holding power than standard nails. Air pressure must be adjusted to drive them fully into the lumber but not so far that they stick out on the front side. They are strong fasteners and will withstand normal amounts of stress on the flat frame. A nail puller is necessary to remove

FIGURE 8–13 Measuring the lumber for the flat frame.

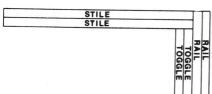

them. Owing to the power of compressed air, staples can be driven into wood whether it is placed on a hard surface or not. This makes it convenient when adding a forgotten toggle bar when the flat is upright in an assembled position.

Uncoated staples can be used if the cornerblocks and keystones are glued to the frame; however, the flats are more difficult to alter in the future.

In the older practice, 1¼" clout nails were used for plywood-reinforced wood joints. Having a flat shaft and being ¼" longer than necessary, the clout nail could be clinched over on the back side of the lumber. A clinch plate (a plate of iron or steel) under the joint is all that is necessary to clinch the nails over when driven by a hammer. Unlike regular nails, they will not loosen and work out of the wood. A nail puller is necessary to remove them. However, clout nails can split the wood and must be placed in a staggered arrangement to prevent the alignment of two or more from acting as wedges. Further, the flat edge of the blade must be positioned perpendicular to the grain of the 1" × 3"s.

Cornerblocks require no less than nine fasteners. Eleven is the general practice. Fasteners must be distributed (see fastener patterns in Figure 8-14) the full width and length of the cornerblock and keystone for adequate strength. For odd-shaped cornerblocks and keystones, a cluster of three fasteners in triangle patterns is a good rule-of-thumb. Corrugated fasteners often are avoided because they split lumber and provide little strength.

Assembling the Frame. Extreme care in the assembly of a flat frame is essential. The slightest inaccuracy in the angle of a corner joint will destroy the rectilinearity of the frame, and it will not fit squarely with others in a set.

To the novice, the frame assembly process may seem to require four hands instead of two. A framing square must be placed firmly against the corner joint of rail and stile to assure a 90° angle. While this is held, the cornerblock is positioned ¾" in from each outer edge, and the fasteners are applied. The process is easier if a couple of fasteners are driven on one side to hold the cornerblock in place. Then more attention can be given to the accuracy of the angle while driving in the remaining fasteners. Measuring the diagonals is another way of squaring the frame before applying the fasteners. The location of toggle bars must be marked before they are attached. Some shops prefer to use a template bench for building flats. This bench has a raised frame around the outer edge, which eliminates the need to use a framing square at each corner. On a narrow frame or frame section, such as the side of a door flat, the tips of overlapping cornerblocks may be cut off. For a very narrow frame section (16" or less), a single plywood piece should be used to reinforce both corners (Figure 8-15).

Fabric Covering. The most common covering materials for flats are lightweight canvas (8 oz) and medium- or heavyweight muslin. Standard scenic quality of these materials is available through theatre supply companies and wholesalers. They are available already flameproofed to satisfy fire code requirements. Canvas is tougher than muslin, and its texture makes it slightly more desirable for painting. Cotton velour, although costly, is even more preferred as a rich textured surface for paint. Burlap and terry cloth are among many other fabrics that could be used for covering a flat. An inexpensive substitute for scenic-grade mus-

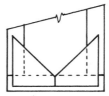

FIGURE 8–15 On narrow frame sections, tips of cornerblocks are cut off or replaced with a single plywood piece.

lin is lightweight muslin sheeting available in local stores.

Fabric Adhesives. Fabrics require the continuous holding quality of an adhesive to secure them to a frame. Point fasteners such as tacks and staples cannot prevent wrinkles and looseness of the cloth. The adhesive must be strong, to hold the material to the frame; thick-bodied, to absorb well into the threads and weave of the fabric; and non-bleeding, so it will not discolor or darken scene paint applied over it. These criteria usually result in special formulas. Animal glues and polyvinyl liquid glue are common bases for these formulas. Animal glue (known mostly as ground carpenter's glue and gelatin glue) is a very strong adhesive. This type of glue is in solid form; it must be covered with water and heated in a double boiler or in a thermostatically controlled glue pot to be dissolved into a liquid. Used full strength it will bleed through layers of scene paint, discoloring the finished appearance. One formula uses one-third hot ground glue mixed with two-thirds wheat paste. The wheat paste is prepared by pouring dry wheat paste gradually into a container of water while stirring it to remove lumps. Then the hot ground glue is added to it.

Another paste formula uses one-half hot ground glue to one-half whiting. Whiting is used in scene painting. It is mixed to a thick paste by adding water to it slowly while mixing to achieve a smooth consistency. An equal amount of hot ground glue is then added. Both of these adhesive mixtures will cool and congeal overnight but can be reheated for use the next day.

Polyvinyl liquid glue is the common white glue available at most hardware and paint dealers. In full strength it also tends to discolor paint and give a glossy appearance on a flat. However, when thinned by a third with water, it becomes a suitable fabric adhesive. Dry pigment may be added for more body.

Covering the Frame. The covering fabric must be unrolled and placed across the frame with a minimum of an inch or two excess on all sides. The first task is to hold the cloth reasonably taut across the frame while the fabric adhesive is applied and dries. This is done by tacking the fabric to the outer members of the frame with small tacks or ¼″ staples about 1′ apart. The tacks or staples are placed on the inner edges of the rails and stiles so the fabric can be folded back to allow the adhesive to be applied to the exposed framing (Figure 8-16). While tacking, the cloth must be pulled reasonably tight, but not so tight that semicircular wrinkles, which cannot be removed with the hand, form around the tacks or staples. If

FIGURE 8–16 Covering the flat.

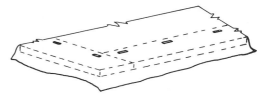

STAPLES TO HOLD FABRIC TAUT

APPLYING THE PASTE

TRIMMING THE EDGES

only one person is doing the covering, it would be best to tack along one rail, then the opposite rail, then along one stile, and finish along the opposite stile by working from the middle outward to the ends. This will help avoid improper stretching and bunching of the fabric. A final check should make certain the cloth is stretched evenly and tightly across the frame.

By folding back the edges of the cloth, you can brush the adhesive directly on the lumber. The cloth is flipped back over the lumber and firmly pressed down into the adhesive with the hand or small piece of wood so it will soak into the fabric. Use a generous coat of paste. An extra application of adhesive on top of the fabric along the outer edges of the frame will keep the edges well glued when the final trimming occurs. Adhesive is not applied to the toggle bars or other inner members of the frame.

The adhesive must be thoroughly dry before the covering can be trimmed around the frame. This usually requires 10 to 14 hours. A sharp knife is used to cut the cloth along the outer edges of the frame, although many shops prefer to trim the fabric ⅛″ in from the edge to avoid overhanging threads. All loose portions of fabric should be repasted. When the adhesive is dry, some technicians prefer to remove the tacks or staples. If they are left, be sure they are flush and not protruding from the surface. The flat is now ready for sizing.

Sizing. The final tightening of the cloth is achieved by sizing, or size water. The covering must acquire a drum tightness or it will be too flabby for use in a setting. Sizing is a thin coat of glue intended to shrink the fabric, hold it taut, and fill the threads so paint may be more easily applied. Normal strength size can be prepared by mixing one part hot ground glue with 16 parts hot water or one part polyvinyl liquid glue to five parts water. Sizing should be brushed or sprayed on the front of the newly covered flat. Avoid brushing size on the pasted edges of the flat for it will tend to loosen the bond. Many prefer to add pigment into the size mixture to see more easily where it has been applied. If the fabric is not already flame-treated, the appropriate chemicals should be applied separately or in the size solution.

Other Covering Materials. There are occasions when a stiffer covering surface is desired on a flat. This may be necessary when a more rugged use is contemplated. An extremely tough covering can be achieved with aircraft-grade Dacron. It can be attached to the frame loosely with regular carpenter's glue or aircraft super seam cement, allowing 10 percent for shrinkage. When the glue is dry, the fabric is shrunk tight by heating it with a household iron set for wool (200°–300°F). Keep the iron moving slowly, because the fabric will pull tight in seconds. If some wrinkles remain, the heat can be increased slightly but must not exceed 400°F, the temperature that melts the cloth. The surface is then given two coats of aircraft *Poly-Dope*, which gives the cloth added strength, better paint adhesion, better weather protection, and flameproofing. The surface will take all paints except very thin scenic pigment. The fabric can also be sewn as an envelope to cover both sides of the frame. An aircraft Dacron covering is exceptionally durable and strong and is ideal for outdoor productions.

Sometimes sheet materials are appropriate as coverings for flats, for strength or when a particular surface texture is difficult to achieve on cloth. These materials include ¼″ plywood, ½″ soft fiberboard, ⅛″ and ³⁄₁₆″ Upson board, corrugated or honeycombed fiberboard, hardboard, and foam board. They can be nailed or stapled to the frame. The more fragile materials will require large-head nails to hold them to the frame securely. Many of them will bow or warp when painted and will require additional toggle bars or internal stiles for support. Care must be taken in handling these flats because the edges of the materials are susceptible to breaking or tearing by rough usage.

Window Flats

A window flat is a variation of the plain flat. Toggle bars form the top and bottom of the window opening, and internal stiles form the sides (Figure 8-17). The size and location of the opening is determined by the scene design. A round window can be constructed by cutting sweeps from 1″ stock lumber or ¾″ plywood and joining them to the toggles and stiles with cornerblocks and keystones. The cornerblocks and keystones must be held ¾″ from the edge of the opening for the addition of thickness pieces. In

FIGURE 8–17 Common types of flat frames.

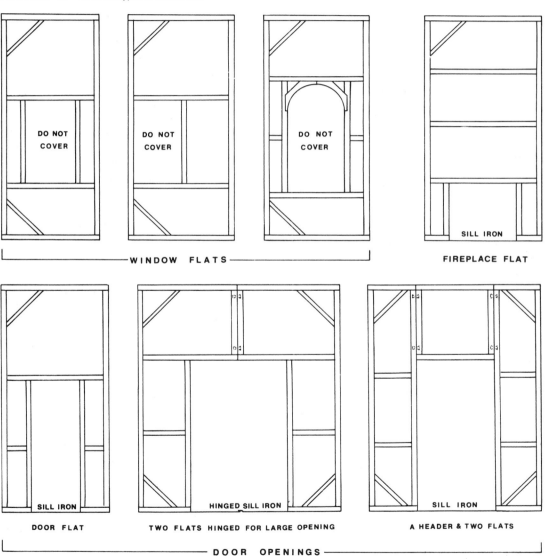

WINDOW FLATS   FIREPLACE FLAT

DOOR FLAT   TWO FLATS HINGED FOR LARGE OPENING   A HEADER & TWO FLATS

DOOR OPENINGS

cutting sweeps, pointed edges of lumber are avoided when possible because they break easily. The covering process is the same as for a plain flat. After the fabric has been stretched and tacked on all four sides, it is tacked around the window opening. These staples or tacks are placed along the face of the lumber farthest from the window opening. The fabric is then cut within the opening so it may be folded back for applying adhesive on the inner framing.

Door and Fireplace Flats

Openings in these flats generally extend to the bottom of the unit (see types of these units in Figure 8-17). Therefore, a sill iron notched into the frame is necessary to secure the bottom of the flat. Without a sill iron the framed sections on the sides of the opening will bow, break, or destroy the accurate shape of the opening. Malleable strap iron or steel, ⅛″ × ¾″, is used for this purpose (Figure 8-18). A sill iron must extend a minimum of 6″ to each side of the opening. Holes drilled into the sill iron allow screws to be driven into the bottom rail (at least two screws on each side). The screws must be countersunk into the sill iron to prevent protruding screw heads from damaging the floor. Openings for double doors or large

FIGURE 8–18   The flat frame is notched for placement of the sill iron, which is secured with countersunk screws.

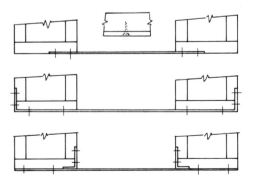

archways usually must be constructed of two flats. These flats are joined together on the front by hinging and at the bottom with a hinged sill iron (overlapping ends of the sill iron are joined with a rivet). This will allow the flats to be folded for convenient transport. Door and fireplace flats are covered in the manner described for window flats.

Repair and Alteration of Stock Flats

Many production groups maintain a scenery stock to effect savings in labor and materials by the reuse of standard units. Flats can be easily altered if constructed in ways that have been described. The frame of a flat can be reduced in size by loosening and folding the fabric cover, removing cornerblocks and keystones, recutting lumber, and rebuilding the frames. Door and window openings can be altered in size or converted into plain flats with minimal reconstruction and recovering. Fabric covers will tolerate up to thirty coats of paint before cracking and chipping requires replacing the cloth. In repairing flats, broken framing members must be replaced, loose edges of the cloth covering reglued, and the entire fabric tightened by sizing the unpainted side. A tear or hole can be repaired with a dutchman patch applied on the back side. An inventory file of stock scenery containing information on size and condition of each unit will aid the economy of using scenery stock.

The Profile

An irregular-shaped flat or a flat with irregular pieces added to it is often called a **profile** (Figure 8-19). It may be a two-dimensional silhouette of a tree, a building, or other object, with the illusion of the third dimension created by paint. If the unit is a wing, a piece located at the side of the scene, only one edge may be irregular. Profile set pieces located in the center of the scene will have several irregular edges. A standard flat sometimes becomes the central portion of the profile with additional framing of $1'' \times 3''$s and $1'' \times 2''$s attached to the flat frame. Cornerblocks and keystones reinforce all joints. Lengthy additions may require short stiffening battens. The additional framing may be cut to precisely conform to the outline of the design. In this case, regular scenic fabric can be pasted to the framing or the irregular edges may be cut from sheet stock (such as plywood, Upson board, or foam board). If this choice is made, the support framing need not duplicate the outline precisely as long as it is within a few inches of the edges at all points. The sheet material is nailed to the frame. A beveled edge should be provided where the sheet material overlaps on the flat so a dutchman can be applied to conceal the edge and change of surface thickness. The unit must be handled in a way that does not damage the unsupported edges of the sheet stock.

Sometimes it is best to construct the entire profile from sheet stock instead of building onto the edges of a flat. If this is decided, it is usually easier to mark and cut the sheet stock first, and to construct a frame to fit the final shape. One standard means of transferring a design to the actual materials is by squaring the sketch (illustrated in Figure 3-18). The outline can also be projected onto the material by making a transparency of the scaled elevation for use in an overhead projector. Once the sheet material has been cut, a frame can be constructed to support it. Staples or large-head nails should be used to hold the material to the frame. Because paint tends to curl composition materials, and their edges can be easily broken, the frame should extend as close as possible to the outer edges of the profile.

A long horizontal profile along the floor is identified as a **ground row**. It often is devised to mask the bottom of a cyclorama and intended to represent a horizon effect (a city skyline, a hillside terrain). Ground rows are

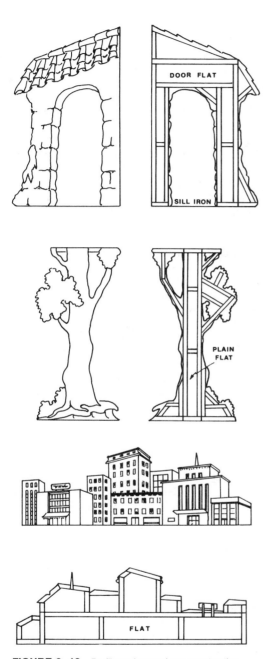

FIGURE 8–19 Profile and ground row construction.

constructed in the same manner as other profiles.

Curved Units

Curved units must be constructed of sheet material that can be bent easily to the desired radius. One-eighth-inch Upson board, known as *Easy-Curve* board, is one of the easiest materials to form curves with. One-eighth-inch plywood can be curved if the outer layer of veneer is scored regularly with saw cuts. Single-corrugated fiberboard will bend easily, and double-corrugated or honeycomb board can be knife-scored to curve. The rails and toggle bars of the curved frame must be cut as flat sweeps from wide strips of stock lumber or from 3/4" plywood (Figure 8-20). Regular 1" × 3"s are used for stiles and are attached to the rails and toggles

FIGURE 8–20 Curved wall construction.

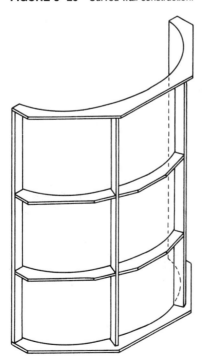

by nails or screws without cornerblocks and keystones. The covering material is nailed to the frame with wide-head nails. Dutchmen are needed to cover surface joints.

The Hard Flat

Another type of framed scenery distinctly different from the cloth-covered flat is the rigid, hard unit. This type of structure is frequently required where the audience has a close view of the setting. Hard scenery is used extensively for settings of motion picture and TV dramas and for situation comedies. The closeness of the camera reveals the instability of standard flats. Door slams and other physical actions cause shaking and vibrations easily discerned by the viewer. Similarly, theatre-in-the-round and other intimate theatre forms frequently rely on hard-wall scenery. The strength of the structure and materials also makes this form of scenery the best choice for outdoor performances.

The most workable surface material is 1/4" plywood or 1/8" or 3/16" lauan. Hardboard is a possible substitute but is harder and more brittle, and most other panel materials lack strength and rigidity. Edges can be beveled slightly with a router to prevent the plies from splintering.

The frame of hard flats is constructed of 1" × 3" lumber. But similar to the frame for curved units, the plywood is nailed to the edges of the lumber (Figure 8-21). Toggle bars and other internal framing should provide support every 2' to 4'. The frame is best joined together with countersunk screws rather than nails. The plywood covering, of course, acts as one large cornerblock to assure the squareness of the unit and reinforce the frame joints. Adjacent hard flats can be held together with carriage bolts and wing nuts or clamps.

Settings made of hard scenery are among the strongest and most durable of two-dimensional scenery. When properly con-

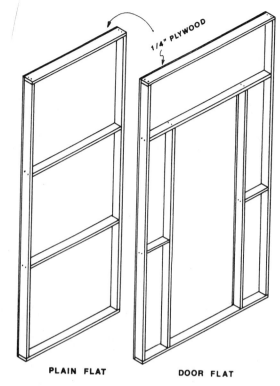

PLAIN FLAT   DOOR FLAT

FIGURE 8–21   Hard flat.

structed, assembled, and braced they will take rough use. For this reason, they are the best choice for permanent or unit sets, which are built to last a long time and are frequently assembled and disassembled. Further, the hard surface of these units makes possible the greatest variety of surface textures. This includes the creation of realistic textures, such as brick or rock, through buildups of plastic molding materials or preformed sheets. (Texture techniques are detailed in Chapter 9.) Motion picture studios still use real plaster, although this practice is waning due to its high cost. Lightweight and relatively inexpensive foams, latex formulas, adhesive mixtures, and vacuum-formed plastics are readily available for applying to hard scenery. Plywood increases the cost of

this type of scenery, and it is heavier and more difficult to move and transport than other units.

Variants

There are numerous variants to the list of two-dimensional scenery described in this chapter. Modern practice includes many types of outline, pierced, skeletonized, and see-through scene units of unusual construction. Scenic units are constructed of metal, plastic, and other materials with different qualities of texture, strength, and surface. Welded structures of square steel tubing are becoming more popular, and for lightness, frames can be made of the many forms of extruded aluminum. Metal surface materials include expanded metal sheeting and wire mesh. Among the plastics, interesting two-dimensional units can be devised of foam or fiberglass. Honeycomb board and other paper or fiber products offer another range of flat scenic units. The construction methods must meet the requirements of the material and the effect to be achieved.

CEILINGS

In the days when the complete box set was the standard for interiors in the theatre, a ceiling was essential for the final illusion. Today, the emphasis away from realism has led to more limited use of ceilings. One practical problem in their use has always existed; that is, the ability to adequately light the performer and the scenery with the obstruction of a masking overhead. When full ceilings are employed, lighting designers beg for beams, niches, or other openings that can provide mounting positions for lighting equipment. Contemporary practice relies on multiangled light sources. This need is equally critical in film studios, where catwalks overhead faithfully mirror the outline of the settings below to provide the maximum of positions for lighting the action. Despite its limitation, the partial, if not the full, ceiling remains in present-day scene practice, although with increasing rarity. Ceiling pieces are effective in enhancing the illusion and character of a setting. They add stability to the walls of the set, and they may aid the acoustics by amplification of actors' voices.

Partial Ceilings

Small sections of ceilings, suggested or abbreviated pieces, and partial beamed or sloped ceilings are frequent components of settings. They are often easily achieved by use of standard or large flats. Stiffening battens may be necessary to prevent sagging of the flat in a horizontal position. In film studios, a sheet of canvas is unrolled across a beamed ceiling for long or establishing shots and rolled back again for the rest of the filming so lights can penetrate the scene from overhead.

Full Ceilings

A full-size ceiling for a set can be of enormous size. For a stage setting in a theatre, it is not unusual for a ceiling to be 36' long and 12' wide. Any framed unit of this dimension will pose a challenge to shift, to transport, and to store. There are two construction solutions that resolve these problems (Figure 8-22).

The **roll ceiling** is similar to the framed drop. The long sides of the ceiling fabric are glued to 1″ × 4″ battens. This permits the ceiling to be rolled up into a long narrow roll for storing. It is assembled by unrolling it face side down on the stage floor and attaching crosswise battens by means of ceiling plates. The loose cloth at the ends of the ceiling are secured to the end cross battens by a row of temporary staples or by lacing. The rings of the ceiling plates permit ready attachment to overhead pipe battens for raising and suspending the ceiling above the setting. The **book ceiling** is essentially two oversized flats front hinged together. It is hung from three adjacent pipe battens. When the middle line is raised, the ceiling will fold up book fashion as it rises. Reverse control of the lines will flatten the ceiling as it lowers onto the setting. This rigging allows the ceiling to be flown and conveniently stored overhead when not in use. When the ceiling is stored in this manner, all other battens of the counterweight system are available for use.

FLOOR TREATMENT

Achieving appropriate floor treatment for a setting can be one of the most difficult tasks for the technician. Furthermore, the floor has become increasingly more important in contemporary scene design. For one thing, with the trend toward more suggestive settings, the floor is often the largest visible expanse in the scene. This is particularly true in arena and open stages. The stage floor has become far more visible in new theatres built with stadium or steep-sloped auditoriums. Second, interest in realistic rather than painted texture in intimate theatres challenges our search for effective floor treatment. Ideally, materials and techniques to treat the floor of the scene must withstand physical action far more rigorous than a wall surface, must lay flat on the floor and not be scuffed by actors' feet, must be relatively inexpensive, and must often be changed quickly between scenes. Needless to say, these criteria, though incomplete, are difficult to satisfy. Failure to provide or afford successful floor treatment has led some theatre groups to regard the floor as a convention, without specific scenic detail. The floors of many theatres are painted or stained black for this purpose. One of the most interesting contemporary approaches is the projection pattern (gobo): ellipsoidal spotlight lighting projection casting a pattern on the floor.

FIGURE 8–22 Ceilings.

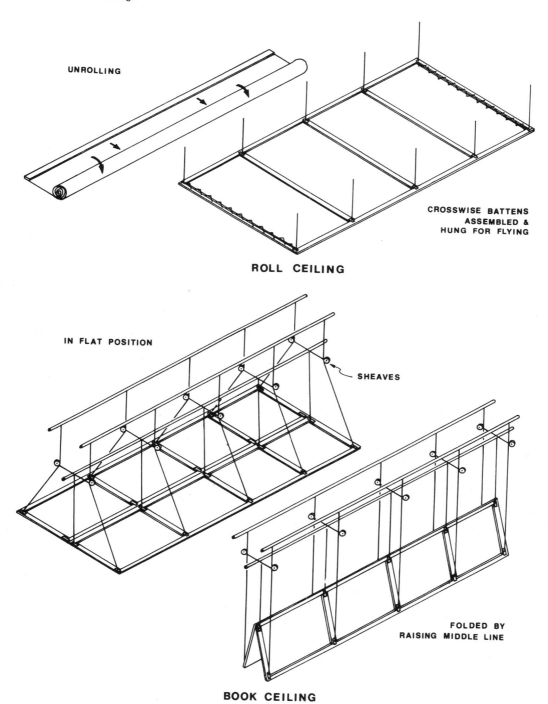

UNROLLING

CROSSWISE BATTENS
ASSEMBLED &
HUNG FOR FLYING

ROLL CEILING

IN FLAT POSITION

SHEAVES

FOLDED BY
RAISING MIDDLE LINE

BOOK CEILING

Perhaps the most traditional stage floor covering is the floor cloth. This is a large cloth of heavy canvas duck (10–12 oz) sewn with double-stitched flat seams and hemmed on all sides. Painted to represent the floor or ground effect required in the scene, the floor cloth must be tightly stretched and tacked to the floor every few inches on all sides. Rug padding is often laid beneath the floor cloth to help deaden footfalls on the wooden stage. Felt, heavy fabric, corrugated fiberboard, or thin sheets of foam are padding alternatives. Canvas over padding is commonly used to cover platforms as well. As a floor treatment, the floor cloth is relatively permanent and cannot be removed easily between scenes.

Rugs and carpeting are frequently required for a scene. Soft rugs easily kicked up must be held to the floor with tacks or double-faced carpet tape. Indoor/outdoor carpeting offers several advantages. It is usually thin, and its stiffness allows it to lay flat on the floor with minimal attachment. Not only is it available in wide widths but it also can be obtained in square tile form. It is usually among the least expensive of carpet materials. Carpets with a rubber backing tend to be the most satisfactory. Nonwovens without this backing can stretch in bulges, which are difficult to remove.

Vinyl flooring (linoleum is rarely available now) makes an ideal floor covering for a setting. Some of the printed or colored patterns may be appropriate, although this is not likely; but, placing the back or felt side up will provide a surface that can be painted or textured. The cheapest vinyl flooring is sufficient and may be purchased in widths up to 12′ wide or sometimes in precut rugs (9′ × 12′ or 12′ × 14′). It is easy to paint the back side with latex, vinyl, or acrylic paint and then a coat of gloss or matte finish to withstand mopping. It usually lies flat on the floor with a minimum of taping or vinyl adhesive around the outer edges. Vinyl flooring needs to be stored by rolling it in long compact rolls to avoid tearing and creasing. It is fully reusable for other productions.

Flooring is a special concern for television and film studios. If the floor of the scene is

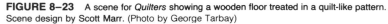

FIGURE 8–23   A scene for *Quilters* showing a wooden floor treated in a quilt-like pattern. Scene design by Scott Marr. (Photo by George Tarbay)

shared with the camera, it must be smooth and even. One of the solutions that has been found satisfactory involves large vinyl tiles, approximately ⅛″ thick and up to 3′ square. They are thick enough to lay flat and remain in place without adhesive. A floor of most any size and shape can be achieved without waste of material. Tiles of this type are reusable numerous times. The floor is easily cleaned and polished for each performance.

A smooth floor surface is also a fundamental requirement for dance performances. Rough and pitted stage floors are a special problem for dancers. A variety of special dance floor surfaces is available, such as vinyl flooring material with nonslip surfaces. Some are intended for permanent installation and will tolerate the movement and rolling of scenery and heavy equipment. Some are also foam backed to provide some cushioning of footfalls, but will not replace the essential resiliency which floors should have for most forms of dance. A portable vinyl floor surface is widely used by dance and opera companies. Available 63″ wide, it can be purchased in any length. It rolls out flat and lays in place well. It is a flexible material and highly resistant to cracking or breaking from movement or temperature changes. Slight bulges caused by stretching usually flatten out soon after relaying. Vinyl tape can be used to hold down edges if they tend to curl. Touring groups find this floor surface lightweight and easily transportable. It is double-faced in two color combinations (black on one side/white or gray on the other).

Tempered hardboard (⅛″ or ¼″ thick) is another useful flooring surface. While it generally lies flat, ring shank nails will be necessary to keep the edges from lifting up. The tempered service will take rugged use and can be painted or textured. Left as a smooth surface, hardboard and vinyl are suitable for scenery shifted on air casters or furniture glides. Canvas or thin foam under

it helps to deaden footfalls. An extra-rugged hardboard, such as *Benelex* made by the Masonite Corporation, is a valuable floor material for exceptionally heavy usage. The floor surface in the Broadway production of *42nd Street* was constructed of ¼″ Benelex mounted on ¾″ plywood to withstand the wear of the company of dancers and the rolling of heavy scenery units. Nails will not penetrate this material. It must be cut with tungsten-carbide-tipped saw blades and high-speed or tungsten-carbide-tipped drill bits.

A variety of materials can be obtained for special textural qualities. Molded rubber panels simulating flagstone, herringbone brick patterns, and other effects are available from specialty suppliers. Soft fiberboard can be grooved or cut for stone or brick floor patterns. Grass effects are achieved by artificial grass mats woven on a jute fabric or by tightly woven outdoor grass carpeting on a rubber backing. Various forms of wood flooring are best created by wood itself. The pronounced grain in plywood makes it ideal for cutting into strips and staining for a simulated planked floor.

SELECTED READINGS

BRETZ, RUDY, *Techniques of Television Production* (2nd ed.). New York: McGraw-Hill, 1962.

BURRIS-MEYER, HAROLD, and EDWARD C. COLE, *Scenery for the Theatre* (rev. ed.). Boston: Little Brown, 1971.

GILLETTE, A. S., and J. MICHAEL GILLETTE, *Stage Scenery: Its Construction and Rigging* (3rd ed.). New York: Harper and Row, 1981.

MILLERSON, GERALD, *Basic TV Staging*. New York: Hastings House, 1974.

WADE, ROBERT J., *Staging TV Programs and Commercials*. New York: Hastings House, 1954.

WOLFE, WELBY B., *Materials of the Scene*. New York: Harper and Row, 1977.

9

Three-Dimensional Scenery

Three-dimensional scenery is relied on for the ultimate of reality in modern settings. Visually, sculptural form is more satisfying to the aesthetic senses, as is shown by appreciation for dramatic lighting that expresses plastic form in ranges of light and shade. While two-dimensional scenery can provide a background, it cannot create the real depth and solidity that complements the three-dimensionality of the actor. In addition, three-dimensional structure is functional scenery. It permits the actor to move and act directly in association with the spatial environment. The actor may physically relate to the environment, using it through moving in it, on it, and under it.

Scenery with dimensional form and mass has unique construction requirements. Materials and techniques employed must be analyzed for specific and valid structural characteristics such as weight-bearing potential. For example, technicians need to develop a functional knowledge of how to achieve strength in construction without undue sacrifice in weight and portability.

DOORS AND WINDOWS

Doors and windows can be constructed two dimensionally and the illusion of depth achieved by paint. A door, for instance, can be simply a covered frame hinged within the opening of a door flat, and the opening of a window can be fitted with strips of wood or tape to suggest the bars between window panes. However, doors and windows are more commonly created as three-dimensional units. A variety of architectural forms give authenticity and style to the setting.

Doors

There are three major components of a doorway. The **casing** is the decorative trim framing the door opening. It is generally

146

created of special molding or molding build-ups in appropriate style. The casing at the top of the door is often of special architectural interest and treated with a cornice or a pediment. In scene construction, the casing is frequently constructed of 1″ stock lumber and built up with standard moldings. The **thickness piece**, sometimes called the reveal or depth piece, is the framed depth of the doorway suggesting the wall thickness. The **door shutter** is the component hinged to the thickness and opens and closes as one enters. Shutters can be flush (solid surface) or can be paneled with recessed fields and decorative moldings in a variety of patterns. Real-life shutters fit within the thickness pieces of the doorway. A strip of molding is attached to the thickness to stop the shutter from swinging beyond the limit of the hinges. A shutter placed within the thickness requires accuracy in construction and extremely rigid bracing. Any slight tilt to the door can wedge the shutter in its frame. For this reason, one construction method for a door that opens offstage places the shutter outside the thickness frame.

Door Built to the Flat: Opening Off-stage. A door that swings offstage offers several advantages. The door shutter is seen only on one side and therefore can be thinner and lighter in weight. It swings over its own braces for maximum support, and when hinged on the upstage side partially masks the offstage area. Further, by swinging offstage, the shutter does not interfere with the playing space and furniture placement in the scene.

CONSTRUCTION. (1) Cut and join together lumber for the thickness pieces. Side members should be the height of the door opening, and the top member 1½″ longer to overlap the side pieces at the top. (2) Nail or screw the thickness frame to the back of the stiles and toggle of the door opening. (3) Cut and attach the casing to the front of the door opening, using nails or screws. (4) Cut and assemble the door shutter. To fit behind the thickness frame, the width of the shutter

must be 1½″ wider than the door opening. (5) Join the door shutter to the thickness frame with two strap hinges. One flap of the hinge will need to be bent so the hinge pin is aligned with the joint. Before joining, place a ¾″ block of wood under the bottom of the shutter so it will clear the floor easily and raise the shutter to butt against the top of the thickness frame. (6) A rim latch assembly is attached to the back of the shutter with a hole drilled for the knob bar. The bolt catch is attached to a short length of lumber which is secured by screws to the outside edge of the thickness frame. (See Figure 9-1).

FIGURE 9–1 Door built to the flat.

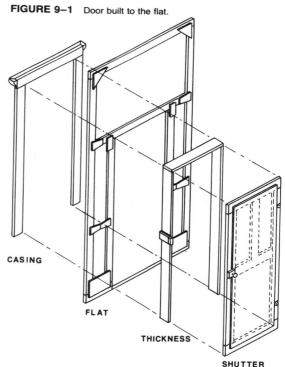

CASING

FLAT

THICKNESS

SHUTTER

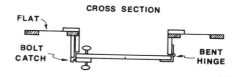

CROSS SECTION

FLAT

BOLT CATCH

BENT HINGE

DOOR SHUTTER CONSTRUCTION. For a door shutter with only one visible side, the frame is constructed of 1″ stock lumber (Figure 9-2). If it is a flush door, the face of the frame can be covered, similar to a flat, with cloth, Upson board, or ¼″ plywood. While fabric can be stapled and pasted, Upson board requires large-headed nails and the plywood is best attached with ¾″ screws. The plywood will act as a large cornerblock to reinforce the joints of the frame. If cloth or Upson board is used, regular cornerblocks and keystones will be needed on the backside of the frame. For a panel door, the frame is exposed on the front in the dimensions and panel design appropriate to the door style. The fabric, Upson board, or plywood is attached to the backside to represent the recessed panel fields. Appropriate decorative molding is added to edge the panels.

A door built to the flat is relatively simple and quick to construct. It has one major disadvantage. The additional weight added to the flat makes the unit difficult to transport and store. It is, therefore, largely limited to a single-set production or when the setting is mounted on a wagon for scene shifts.

Detachable Door Unit: Opening Off-stage. A door can be constructed as a completely separate unit to be attached and removed from the door flat. Easy removal makes it possible to transport and shift the scenery without difficulty.

CONSTRUCTION. For this type of door the casing is attached directly to the thickness frame with flat-head screws (see Figure 9-3). Flat corner plates are useful to reinforce the joints of the casing. The bottom of the doorway must be held together securely to sup-

FIGURE 9–3 Detachable door unit.

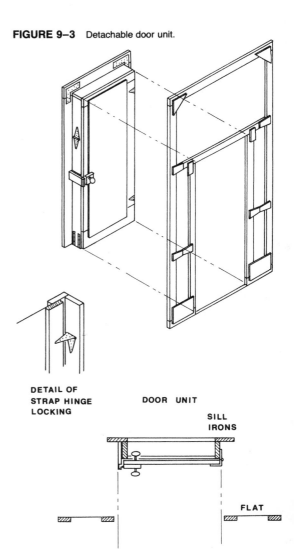

DETAIL OF
STRAP HINGE
LOCKING

DOOR UNIT

SILL
IRONS

FLAT

FIGURE 9–2 Two-dimensional door shutters.

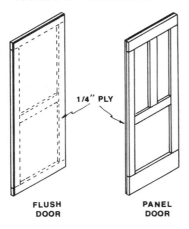

1/4″ PLY

FLUSH
DOOR

PANEL
DOOR

port the rectangular frame. This can be achieved with a threshold piece of 1″ lumber joining the bottom of the thickness pieces or by two sill irons of strap steel. The opening in the door unit must be at least 4″ less in width and 1½″ less in height than the opening in the door flat. This is necessary to permit the door unit to be inserted easily into the flat opening. A detachable door unit is commonly held to the flat by strap hinges on each side of the thickness frame. The lower flap of the hinge is secured to the thickness at a slight angle. The free flap is dropped downward to lock tightly against the stile of the flat. Carriage bolts and wing nuts will provide a stronger attachment if the doorway receives rough usage.

Door Opening Onstage. A door that must swing onstage is usually required for a specific purpose: to permit a particular action by the actors or to represent an exterior door. When this is determined, the additional construction is usually warranted. A door shutter that swings onstage can be fitted into either a detachable door unit or a door built to the flat.

CONSTRUCTION. The door shutter is inserted into the onstage edge of the thickness frame (see Figure 9-4). It is held by butt hinges with the hinge pin protruding forward sufficiently for the shutter to clear the casing when opened. Usually the hinge should be mortised into the thickness piece and the edge of the door shutter. A strip of lumber serving as stop molding should be placed inside the thickness frame to prevent the shutter from swinging too far when closed. Because the shutter swings away from its support, brace jacks must be well secured to the back of the flat and held firmly to the floor. It helps if the door flat is recessed in the setting so that adjacent flats counteract the tendency of the wall and door unit to lean forward as the shutter is opened.

DOOR SHUTTER CONSTRUCTION. For a three-dimensional flush door shutter, a framework can be constructed of 1¼″ lum-

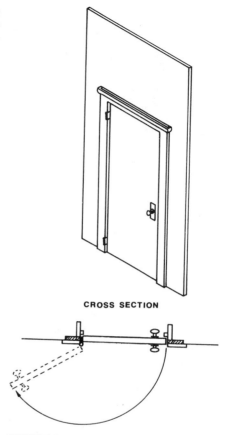

CROSS SECTION

FIGURE 9–4 Door opening onstage.

ber or 1″ lumber on edge to provide the thickness of a real door. It can be covered on both sides with thin Upson board or plywood. Several toggles will be needed in the frame to support the covering material. It will be necessary to include a solid block in the frame to install a standard tubular latch unit. A panel door can be constructed of 1½″ thick lumber. Panel fields can be cut from ⅛″ plywood or Upson board and held into the openings of the door shutter with narrow strips of molding (see Figure 9-5). The shutter should be raised about ¾″ off the floor to provide ample clearance and should have a slight tolerance in fit at the top and sides.

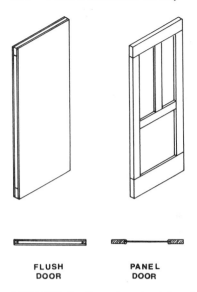

FLUSH
DOOR

PANEL
DOOR

FIGURE 9–5 Three-dimensional door shutters.

Swinging Doors. Two-way swinging doors are sometimes found as kitchen doors, saloon doors, and gates. The door shutters must be constructed to be visible on both sides. The hinging action is critical. Most two-way spring hinges are too powerful for lightweight scenery. However, an adjustable two-way hinge permits the spring tension to be adjusted to the weight of the shutter. The hinges are attached to the edge of the shutter and in the center of the thickness piece. Because vigorous action in using the door generally causes the swing to exceed 180°, it is best to attach the hinge to a batten projecting from the thickness so the shutter will not bang against the edges of the door opening (see Figure 9-6).

Sliding Doors. In house construction, sliding doors are suspended from a C-shaped track mounted above the top thickness. This works well in scene construction if the doors are not large and the wall is well braced. Tracks and carriers are available from building suppliers. However, because the weight of the doors is transferred to the scenery at a point where solid bracing is dif-

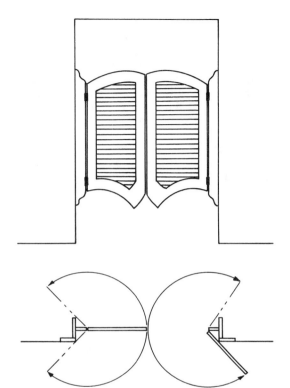

FIGURE 9–6 Swinging doors.

ficult, the walls may move visibly when large doors are operated. Therefore, in many situations, the best solution is to support the weight of sliding doors directly on the floor (Figure 9-7). This is accomplished by mounting two rigid casters on each sliding door. The casters are mounted on a 1″ × 6″ plate held at right angles to the back of the door by triangular blocks. The door shutter is raised off the floor by a ¾″ clearance. A **guide track** at the top prevents the doors from falling over or rubbing against the back of the thickness frame. The guide track is formed of a strip of lumber and angle iron, providing a groove for the top of the shutters. A **floor track** is also necessary to keep the casters in the prescribed path of movement. This is constructed of ¼″ plywood and strips of thin lumber or molding. It is se-

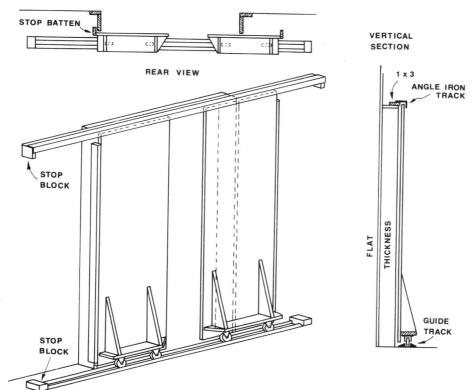

FIGURE 9–7 Sliding doors supported on the floor.

cured to the floor. Both guide tracks must be double the width of the door opening. At each end of the guide tracks are stop blocks to keep the doors from rolling out of the tracks when opened. Stop battens are also placed at the outer sides of each door shutter. These butt against the back of the thickness piece, preventing the door from moving past its position in the door opening when pulled closed.

Curved Archway. An archway is simply a doorway without shutters. It consists of a thickness frame and casing or sometimes the thickness frame only. A curved archway requires a different method of construction. Door shutters can be added if an arched doorway is required.

CONSTRUCTION OF AN ARCHWAY BUILT TO THE FLAT. A standard method is to duplicate the shape of the archway by constructing a framework of 1″ × 3″s and curved sweeps mimicking the stiles and arch curve on the flat (Figure 9-8). This frame must be secured at the bottom by a sill iron. The frame is joined to the flat by short lengths of 1″ × 3″s cut for the appropriate depth of the thickness. One-eighth-inch plywood or Upson board is curved and nailed to the inside of the two frames. A dutchman is usually necessary to mask the onstage joint of the plywood or Upson board. A casing, if needed, is attached to the flat.

CONSTRUCTION OF A DETACHABLE ARCHWAY. The thickness frame of the arch can

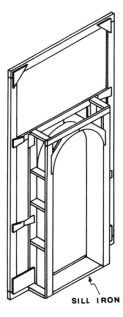

SILL IRON

FIGURE 9–8 Thickness frame for a curved archway.

be a detachable unit. In this case, two 1″ × 3″ frames and curved sweeps are constructed and joined together by short lengths of lumber. Two sill irons or a threshold is needed at the bottom. The joined frames are covered with the plywood or Upson board, creating an independent thickness frame that can be attached to be back of flat with loose pin hinges.

Windows

A window has three major components: the casing, the thickness, and the frame for glass, called the **sash**. The sash is mounted inside the thickness frame. Because of its weight, its highly reflective surface, and the hazards resulting from breakage, glass is not advisable in scene windows. In fact, glass simulation is often unnecessary, either because its absence is accepted as a convention or because it is not visible to an audience. Where simulation is necessary, clear plastic

sheeting can be effective as a glass substitute if its rigidity does not cause a bothersome wobble in the frame. Even more effective is stretchable material such as cloth netting in a colored tint or the galvanized or plastic-coated screening commonly used for screen doors. Translucent plastic or filled screening can suggest etched or frosted glass. Dye-painted lightweight muslin or plastic sheeting lighted from offstage is effective for stained glass simulations.

Window Built to the Flat. Window components can be joined to the flat in the same manner described for building a door to a flat. The casing and thickness frame for a window are four-sided structures. The sash is nailed either at the back or inside the thickness frame. The sash frame is usually made of 1″ lumber 1½″ or 2″ wide. Interior **muntins** (small bars between panes) of ¾″ or 1″ width are notched into the outer frame. This type of window construction is desirable only if the additional weight does not complicate shifting the wall.

Detachable Window Unit. This unit is built in the manner described for the detachable door unit (Figure 9-9). The casing is joined with flat-head screws to the thickness frame. The sash frame is attached to the back or inside the thickness frame. Adequate clearance must be provided for the unit to slip into the window opening easily. The inside dimensions of the window unit must be at least 3″ less in width and 2¼″ less in height than the opening in the flat. Strap hinges are used to secure the unit to the flat.

Special Windows. Windows sometimes must be constructed to be practical, that is, to be used in a particular way. If an actor must enter or exit through a window, the window sill, or perhaps a window seat, must be built as a platform. This will necessitate separate structural support directly to the floor and adequate framing for the entire window and wall. Practical sashes must be made to be opened. Most windows are either the **casement** type, which are hinged to

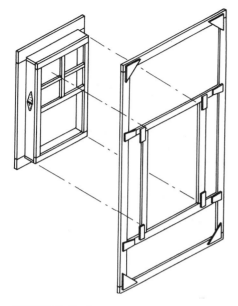

FIGURE 9–9 Detachable window unit.

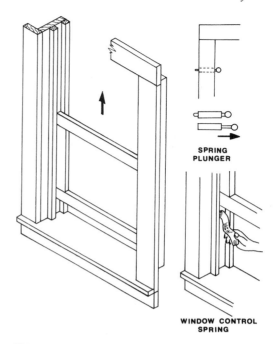

SPRING
PLUNGER

WINDOW CONTROL
SPRING

FIGURE 9–10 Double-hung window showing movable lower sash.

swing outward, or **double hung**, which are raised and lowered. Practical casement windows are easy to construct. Double-hung window sashes require guide tracks consisting of strips of ½″ × ½″ lumber. The sashes can be made to stay up when raised by tapering the guide strips slightly at the top to wedge the sash frames when lifted, by commercial metal plungers fitting into holes drilled into the thickness piece, or by window control springs. Designed for real windows when the sash cord is broken, these spring steel strips are held in the window tracks with nails and press against the window sash to hold it up at any position (Figure 9-10).

There are several other types of windows. Each type requires a different construction approach. Sliding windows are built similar to sliding doors. A French window is really a door frame with hinged sashes rather than typical door shutters. The reader will also recognize that built-in bookcases, cabinets, niches, and similar architectural units are constructed in the manner of windows or doors, with casings and thickness pieces. A flat attached by hooks and eyes to the back of an archway, often referred to as a **plug**, can convert an archway into a recessed niche.

WEIGHT-BEARING STRUCTURES

Platforms, ramps, and steps are the kinds of weight-bearing structures we associate with a setting. There are, of course, other scenic units which in the course of the action of a drama may be used as elevations for actors and must be built as platforms. A practical rock, a window sill, a barroom counter may require such special construction for a given production. There are many ways to construct weight-bearing structures and a relatively few principles to understand. Knowing the variety of construction methods, it is advantageous for the scene techni-

FIGURE 9–11 Motion Picture Scenery. A scene from the United Artist release *Octopussy*, © 1983 Danjaq S.A. An interior setting with spiral staircase in the luxurious Monsoon Palace. Production designer: Peter Lamont. (Photo courtesy of MGM/UA Entertainment Company)

cian to select the one most appropriate for the specific load-bearing object and the production circumstances. At the same time, a production organization with an ongoing season also may find it economical in time and cost to adopt a particular construction system for the majority of conventional scenic elevations. In selecting this system, such factors as cost, strength, portability, assembly (and reassembly) time, skills of construction, and storage requirements need to be considered.

The hard, thin surface of a platform top often produces a disturbing drumlike sound from actors' footfalls. A layer of padding such as old carpet, carpet padding, or corrugated paperboard covered by canvas that is stretched and fastened around the edges will generally reduce this noise. Sometimes a layer of insulation such as acoustical fiberglass batting under the platform top is equally effective.

Commercial Platforms

A number of commercial platform units are available. The most common have fold-out metal legs designed as risers for music and choral groups, theatre seating, and portable stages. They are often equipped with clamps to secure adjacent units and with devices for safety railings. Generally, they are limited to certain standard sizes and heights. At least one system on the market, however, has a special foldable leg structure that can lock in place at five different heights on 8″ increments, including several ramp configurations (Figure 9-12).

Platforms with 2″ Lumber Framing

One standard construction method is sometimes referred to as the **rigid platform**. It commonly consists of a framework and

FIGURE 9–12   *Nivoflex* platform. A commercial platform that locks in place at five different heights. (Photo courtesy of Rosco Laboratories, Inc.)

legs of 2″ lumber in post-and-beam construction supporting a ¾″ plywood top (see Figure 9-13). Small platforms are built with 2″ × 4″s with structural support no more than 4′ apart. While there are legging alternatives, one method attaches each leg to the inside of the frame with two staggered carriage bolts. Legs over 1′ in length require diagonal bracing with scrap lumber. In some kinds of construction, the legs are placed

FIGURE 9–13   Two-inch lumber platform construction.

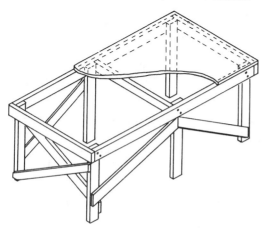

under the 2″ × 4″ frame to keep the joints in compression. This also provides a flush surface for the addition of facing material. These structures are strong and heavy, and because of their weight they are not easily moved in a scene shift. However, by the addition of casters, rigid platforms are easily converted to rolling wagons and revolving units for shifting. It is a distinct advantage that they can be constructed in any height, size, or shape to meet the specific needs of the setting. They are difficult to store because of their weight and bulk.

Platforms with 1″ Lumber Framing

Generally, there are two kinds of weight-bearing structures that can be built with 1″ lumber stock. One of these is the kind of platform described above, but with 1″ × 6″s instead of 2″ stock. The width of a 1″ × 6″ has nearly the strength of a 2″ × 4″. Legs can be reinforced by two 1″ pieces at right angles in an L-shape. The resultant unit is somewhat lighter in weight than a 2″ × 4″ unit.

A second system consists of the construction of weight-bearing frames of 1″ × 3″

lumber with rails, stiles, and diagonal supports not unlike flat frames (Figure 9-14). The frames are assembled with mortise-and-tenon joints, halved joints, or butt joints reinforced with cornerblocks and keystones. Each frame is a combination of beam and post and is strong because of the way the lumber is used. Many three-dimensional objects that will support actors and yet be lightweight can be constructed of these frames. The most common application is the construction of collapsible platforms and ramps known as **parallels**. A parallel consists of an understructure of these supporting frames and a separate, removable top or lid. The supporting frames are joined together with hinges to fold compactly for transporting and storing.

Three-quarter-inch plywood is commonly used for the platform tops, although oversized tops are sometimes built of flooring lumber (tongue and groove or shiplap).

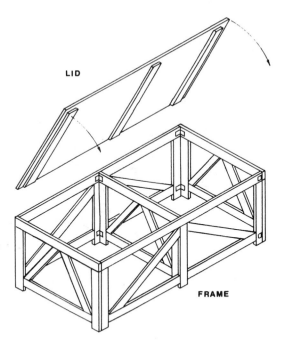

FIGURE 9–14   One-inch lumber supporting frames.

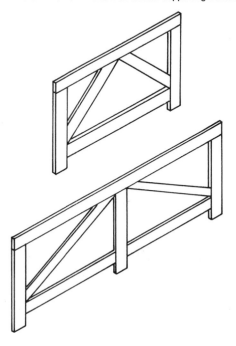

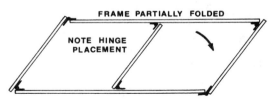

FIGURE 9–15   Parallel platform.

Cross battens of 1″ × 4″s are secured with screws to the underside of the lids about 1″ from each end and near the center. These battens sink within the understructure, butting against the supporting frames to hold the top in place and to prevent the frames from folding.

Small parallels (if the length is twice the width) have a single center supporting frame hinged to the side frames (Figure 9-15). The support structure folds to a combined length equal to the width and length of the platform. Larger parallels require several inner supporting frames. For effective folding action and compactness, these frames must be removable.

They slide into grooves formed by 1″ × 2″ cleats secured with screws to the side frames (Figure 9-16). Bent hooks on the outer edges of the inner frames hold the side frames in position. The end frames fold in the middle so the folded length is no longer than the platform itself. Parallels have several advantages. They are lightweight, easy to carry and handle, and easy to store. But they are time-consuming to build, require considerable accuracy in construction, and are difficult to alter. They become permanent equipment, fixed in height and size in contrast to the flexibility of other platform systems. However, due to the combined virtues

of strength and lightness, the 1″ supporting frame is widely used for many weight-bearing structures in a setting. Among these are window seats, curved stairways, counters, and similar three-dimensional units.

Metal Component Parts Systems

Component parts systems consist of standard structural parts and fittings that can be assembled quickly with a minimum of tools and effort. The flexibility of these standard parts permits the assembly of structures in a great variety of shapes and heights. All parts are reusable, and when dismantled, the components are compact and easy to store. Systems have been advocated for constructing 2″ lumber platforms of component parts (reusable predrilled legs and beams). However, wood eventually splits, bolt holes enlarge, and the life of components is limited. In contrast, metal components are nearly indestructible; they can be used indefinitely and seldom need replacing. For this reason, while metal component parts for platform construction are initially higher in cost, they are cheaper in the long run than wood structures. (See Figure 9-17.)

Unistrut Construction. *Unistrut Channel* is well adapted for a component-parts system. It consists of special channel steel with grooves to hold spring-held nuts for bolting to fittings. The channels can be cut to length and assembled with special corner angles, flanges, and other fittings in post-and-beam construction. It becomes a flexible system permitting the construction of platforms in a variety of sizes and shapes. Final structures are sturdy and quite heavy.

Slotted Angle Construction. Slotted angle is another flexible building system for post-and-beam construction. It is steel angle (usually 1½″ × 2¼″ and 1½ × 3″), which is perforated with round holes and elongated slots. When joining two pieces together, two holes line up for attachment with standard bolts.

FIGURE 9–16 Supporting frame for a large parallel.

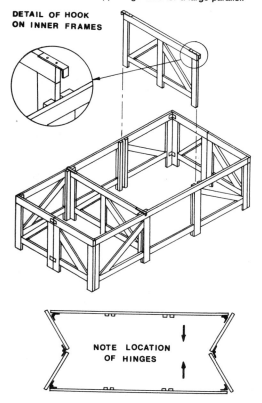

DETAIL OF HOOK
ON INNER FRAMES

NOTE LOCATION
OF HINGES

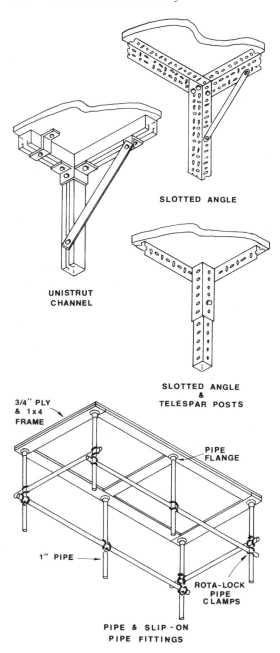

SLOTTED ANGLE

UNISTRUT
CHANNEL

SLOTTED ANGLE
&
TELESPAR POSTS

3/4" PLY
& 1 x 4
FRAME

PIPE
FLANGE

1" PIPE

ROTA-LOCK
PIPE
CLAMPS

PIPE & SLIP-ON
PIPE FITTINGS

FIGURE 9–17 Component-parts platform systems using ready-to-assemble components.

A special angle cutter is available to cut the angle easily and quickly. Beams, posts, and diagonal braces can be cut and assembled in many configurations. Plywood tops can be bolted to the beams with flat-head stove bolts. A structure is easily converted to a wagon by the addition of a frame joined beneath the posts to which casters are bolted. Angle sections stack conveniently for storage. Slotted angle creates strong structures that are lighter in weight than Unistrut platforms.

Telespar Tubing. *Telespar* is another trademarked product of the Unistrut Corporation. It is square tubing, in graduated sizes, each fitting inside a larger size. The sides of the tubing are perforated with holes, which permits lengths of different sizes to be telescoped to a given dimension and secured in place by bolts through matching holes. It can provide flexible legging for platforms. Telespar posts normally must be joined to slotted angle beams for the construction of an entire weight-bearing frame.

Pipe and Slip-on Pipe-Fitting System. With the development of slip-on pipe fittings, metal pipe has become an increasingly versatile and convenient structural material. Fittings (flanges, tees, crosses, ells) slip on the pipe and are secured by setscrews, thus eliminating threading or welding. Fittings are available for ¾" to 2" standard pipe. Based on a study and extensive experience with numerous scenic structures,[1] a method for constructing weight-bearing units of pipe has been adopted as a stock system by some producing organizations. The system eliminates the standard structural beam by reinforcing ¾" plywood platform tops with 1" × 4" battens. Slip-on pipe flanges are secured to the 1" × 4"s with 1½" screws. Legs of black steel pipe, cut by a hack saw or pipe cutter, are inserted into the flanges and secured by a setscrew wrench (sometimes called an Allen or hex wrench). Cross bracing is provided by lengths of pipe and *Rota-Lock* pipe clamps (a special hardware manufactured by Upright Scaffolds). One-inch pipe and pipe fittings are adequate for necessary strength. Legs are placed 3 to 4 feet apart. Unlike other platforms, the top is constructed first and the supporting structure added last. Most platform systems, since they are post-and-beam structures, are more suited to rectilinear shaped platforms. The pipe system is more versatile—easily capable of providing curved and irregular shaped platforms.

In addition, the thinness of the top and leg supports makes this method appropriate for open, light, and "floating" elevations which many other platform systems cannot achieve. If this system is adopted as a stock platform system, it is best to establish a module or incremented height standard. This will reduce the number of lengths of pipe to store. With a 6″ module plan, pipe can be cut in lengths of 4½″, 10½″, 16½″, and so on (allowing for the thickness of the top) and can be stored in appropriate bins for easy access.

Commercial Scaffolding. Metal scaffolding used in construction and maintenance fields is another structural system of reusable parts. Made of steel or aluminum alloy tubing, scaffolding usually consists of welded vertical end sections joined together by diagonal side braces, and can be capped with plywood or plank platform tops. The units are generally standardized in approximately 4′ widths and 6′ lengths, although some units approximately 2′ wide and 6′, 8′, or 10′ in length are designed to move through regular doorways fully assembled. They can be assembled together in many combinations, mostly above 4′ in height. Some have adjustable legs for slight height variations and locking casters for mobility. They are rapidly assembled, sometimes with attachment hardware requiring no tools whatever. Scaffolding is less rigid and more wobbly than other component parts systems. And because it is limited to standard sizes, scaffolding is less flexible in achieving a variety of configurations.

Welded Platforms

Welded steel structures are ideal for platforms and other weight-bearing units. Metal is unusually strong and thin. Welded joints do not loosen or creak. A welded platform frame is an integral unit of considerable durability. Relatively thin stock, such as square tubing and angle and channel steel with appropriate bracing, is excellent for platform frames. Square tubing of 1″ or 2″ thickness is commonly used for thin, lightweight frames. Longer spans are fabricated with shop-made or commercial steel trusses. Small-diameter rod and bar stock can be used for other weight-bearing structures. When welding frames, the pieces must be clamped together in a jig so they will remain square and true. Plywood tops can be attached to the frame with bolts (see Figure 9-18).

Truss Construction

There are occasions when settings require an upper floor with an open room below, a bridge, or some other type of elevation that must span some distance without post support. When the span exceeds the capacity of standard beams, a **truss beam** may be the

FIGURE 9–18 Platform of welded steel tubing.

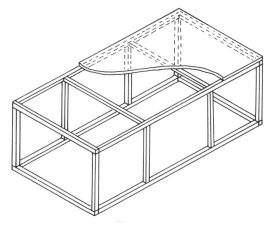

proper solution. A truss is a framework consisting of top and bottom beams called **chords** reinforced and separated by vertical and inclined bracing called **web members.** Wooden trusses can be constructed of 1″ × 4″ or 2″ × 4″ chords and web members (Figure 9-19). Trusses can bear a considerable load while remaining relatively lightweight. The ends must be supported securely by posts and diagonal bracing in all directions. Offstage platforms and stair units can assist in bracing. The trusses can be covered with

¾″ plywood sheets well secured to the trusses with screws. Lighter and less bulky steel and aluminum trusses can often be obtained or welded.

Cantilever Construction

Balconies, overhanging platforms, stairways, and other structures that project into the scene without post support or suspended cables are developed by the cantilever principle. Essentially, a structure behind the scene is designed to more than counterbalance the anticipated load on the overhanging level. The balcony or projection is achieved by a series of continuous beams that are part of the offstage structure and extend forward to form the overhanging platform (Figure 9-20). Each beam is constructed as part of a frame with two or more posts and with

FIGURE 9–19 Truss construction.

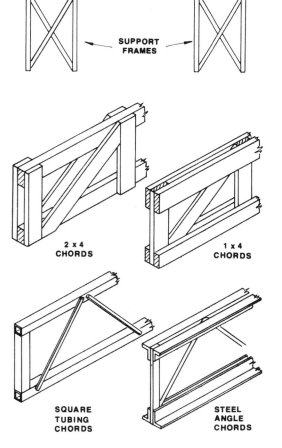

2 x 4
CHORDS

1 x 4
CHORDS

SQUARE
TUBING
CHORDS

STEEL
ANGLE
CHORDS

FIGURE 9–20 Cantilever construction.

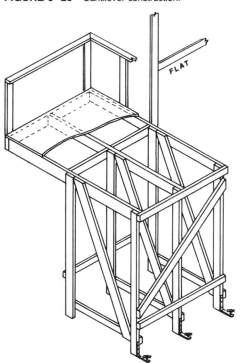

horizontal and diagonal bracing. The frames are joined together to form an off-stage platform that provides access to the projecting level. The size of the offstage structure—with the addition of weights or foot irons and stage screws—is calculated to balance the load on the onstage overhang. The structure can be built of either metal or wood.

Stressed-Skin Platforms

Sheets of plywood securely glue-bonded to an inner structural framework of lumber results in a lightweight and strong panel. Known as stressed-skin construction, this structure acts as a single unit in which the load or stress is distributed by the internal framing. The inner framework consists of stringers and cross framing securely nailed and glued together. The top and bottom surfaces consist of plywood sheets firmly screwed and glued to the frame. Splice plates are needed at joints in the plywood. With an ordinary beam, the top compression surface and bottom tension surface carry the load in two directions, that is, the length of the beam. In contrast, a stressed-skin structure spreads the load in all directions from the load point. Unusually long spans or fewer leg supports are possible with this type of platform. The result is a structure that can be thin, has amazing strength, and is lightweight.

A standard 4″ × 8″ stressed skin platform can be constructed with a 2″ × 4″ or 2″ × 3″ frame or a combination of 1″ and 2″ thick lumber. Either lengthwise or crosswise members should be on a minimum of 16″ centers. The top skin can be ⁵⁄₁₆″ plywood and the bottom skin ³⁄₈″ plywood. Weights are placed on the unit to compress the joints until the glue dries. In the process of construction and lamination, curved platforms can be made. By using a curved frame, thinner, bendable ¼″ plywood can be warped into freeform compound curves [2] (Figure 9-21).

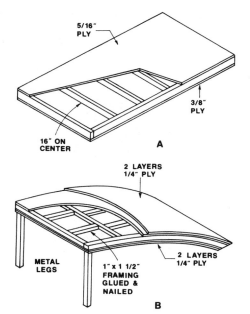

FIGURE 9–21 Stressed-skin platforms. (A) Straight 4″ × 8″ platform. (B) A thin curved ramp. The bottom two layers of ¼″ plywood are bent to shape and glue-bonded. The inner framing of thin lumber strips is glued, nailed together, and laminated to the bottom skin. The top layers of plywood are laminated and screwed to the frame. In each step glue is generously applied and weights are used to secure elements as the glue dries.

Paper Construction

One kind of ready-to-use material for weight-bearing objects is fiberboard tube. We are most familiar with cylindrical tubes in a variety of diameters used as forms for pouring concrete pillars. However, tubes are also available in oval, elliptical, hexagonal, square, triangular, and other shapes and are sold for the display industry. With walls up to ½″ thick, they have considerable weight-bearing strength (Figure 9-22).

Small platforms and step units can be constructed by laminating several layers of corrugated board with polyvinyl glue up to 1″ or more in thickness (Figure 9-23). For greater strength, the fluting should alternate perpendicularly on each successive layer.

FIGURE 9–22   A weight-bearing structure made of fiberboard tube with 1/2″ walls and a plywood top.

Weights are necessary to hold the layers while the glue dries. Both support frames and platform tops can be created and assembled with glue. Cross-support frames can be slotted to fit together for interior support. A top of ¼″ plywood adds strength to the weight-bearing surface.

Honeycomb board has brought increased possibilities for lightweight platform struc-tures. As with corrugated board, it can be cut with regular saws and knives. Curves can be formed by scoring an outer surface at regular intervals. It can be laminated, braced, and bonded with any water-based adhesive or hot-melt glue. Any number of weight-bearing structures can be achieved with 1″ thick board if sufficient cross bracing is provided (Figure 9-24). A thin plywood sheet laminated to the top will make the sur-face puncture resistant.

Sandwich Panel Laminations. Lamin-ations with honeycomb core material are commonly employed for roof and canopy construction. It makes possible a structure of great lightness, thinness, and load-bearing capacity far exceeding traditional construc-tion. Similar to stressed-skin construction, a sandwich panel consists of two outer panels thoroughly bonded to an inner core so that it acts structurally as an integral unit. Kraft-paper honeycomb core material can be pur-chased and laminated to outer layers of ply-wood with polyvinyl or urethane glue (Figure 9-25). This has proven to provide remarkable weight-bearing structures.[3] Long spans can be constructed of ½″ ply-wood skins and 6″ thick honeycomb paper. The open edges of these platforms are en-closed with hardboard or plywood to

FIGURE 9–23   A step unit made of laminated layers of corru-gated board.

FIGURE 9–24   A weight-bearing unit of honeycomb board.

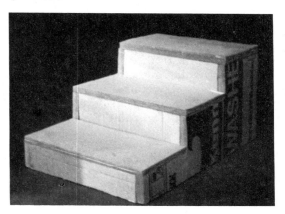

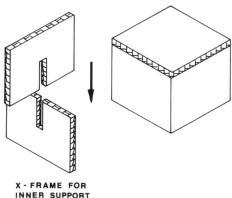

X - FRAME FOR
INNER SUPPORT

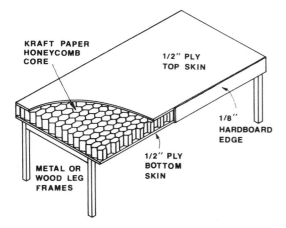

FIGURE 9–25 Sandwich panel construction. Kraft-paper honeycomb core is thoroughly laminated to outer layers of plywood.

strengthen the edges. Sandwich structures of this type are acoustically quiet to actors' footsteps. The highly flexible honeycomb material permits freeform and compound curved platforms. Hill-like structures can be shaped with ⅛" plywood skin and honeycomb laminations or created with paper skins and later fiberglassed for tougher surfaces. The application of glue must be generous and cover the entire surface. During the glue drying process, weights must be distributed over the entire area to assure tight and firm adhesion. This pressure can also be provided by covering the unit with heavy plastic sheeting taped to the shop floor, and exhausting the air with a vacuum pump.

Foam Construction

Rigid polyurethane foam can also be used for small pour-in-place platform structures. A breakaway box mold is employed. As the foam rises, the lid is closed and the mold is tightly clamped. Lining the box with ethylene sheeting will harden the outer surface of the foam structure. Small escape holes are needed in the top of the mold to ensure foam consistency throughout the structure.

Steps and Stairs

A stairway consists of three basic parts: **treads,** on which we walk; **risers,** the vertical faces between the treads; and **carriages,** the supports to which the risers and treads are attached. The height of the risers and depth of the treads of a stairway usually depend on the type of stairs represented and the nature of the action. There are several standard stair structures, although all the weight-bearing systems already outlined are suitable for stair construction.

Stairs of 1″ Lumber. Carriages should not be more than 1′-6″ apart if they are the only support for the treads. In this type of structure, risers can be simply a rigid masking material such as ¼″ plywood (Figure 9-26).

FIGURE 9–26 Stair construction.

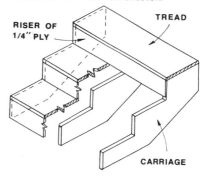

RISERS AS MASKING

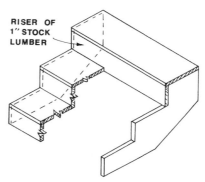

RISERS AS SUPPORT

However, if 1″ lumber is used for risers, thus providing bearing support to the front and back edge of each tread, carriages can be 3′ or more apart.

Carriages are cut from 1″ × 12″ lumber. A framing square is used to make the lumber for each riser/tread cut (Figure 9-27). For the first step, the carriage must be cut ¾″ less in height to allow for the thickness of the first tread. Treads can be made of 1″ stock lumber or ¾″ plywood and must be wide enough to lap over the front riser. On interior stairs, treads usually extend beyond the face of each riser with a rounded edge. However, some technicians prefer to build them flush to the riser and add a decorative molding for this protrusion. Carriages, treads, and risers can be joined together by nails, although screws are recommended for better securement.

Open-riser stairs is a construction form useful in emulating the style of open stairs or as an offstage escape from a platform. Escape stairs can be narrow, usually 2′ wide or less, with a 1″ × 8″ on each side acting as a carriage. Treads are 1″ × 8″s placed

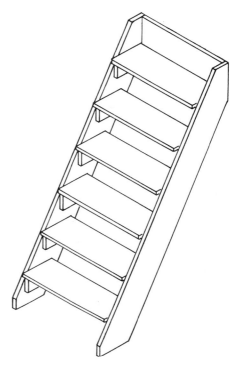

FIGURE 9–28 Open-riser stairs.

between the two carriages and reinforced with 1″ × 4″ cleats (Figure 9-28).

Stair Support. Some type of structural leg support is necessary for a flight of stairs to remain upright. One method is to transfer the support of the stair unit to an adjacent platform. This is particularly desirable to reduce the size of a long flight of stairs. A 2″ × 4″ batten can be attached under the top tread of a set of stairs to be set upon another 2″ × 4″ bolted to the platform legs (Figure 9-29). Steel cleats projecting downward from the stair batten will secure this attachment but allow the stairs to be removed when lifted upward. Self-supported stairs require the construction of a leg structure for each of the carriages. The simplest is a 1″ × 3″ lumber framework with diagonals and toggles held together with plywood cornerblocks in the manner of the support

FIGURE 9–27 Making stair carriages.

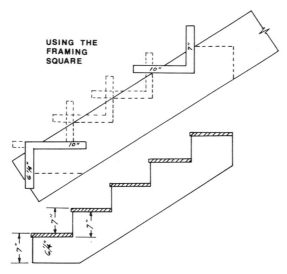

USING THE
FRAMING
SQUARE

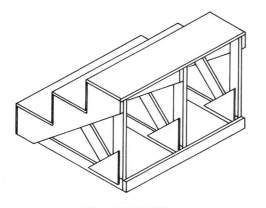

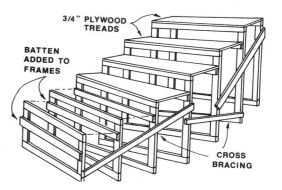

FIGURE 9–30 A curved flight of stairs using 1″ lumber support frames.

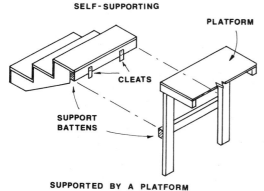

FIGURE 9–29 Stair supports.

frames of parallel platforms. These are attached with screws to each carriage, and the frames are securely cross-braced.

Circular stairs can be constructed with a series of 1″ × 3″ support frames. A separate frame is built to support the front of each tread. A 1″ × 3″ batten is then added to the front of each frame at the height of the next smaller frame. The stairway is developed by attaching a tread between the top of one frame and the projecting batten of the next frame (Figure 9-30).

In assembling the unit, the frames must be positioned upright in the shop as determined by curved lines drawn on the floor. The frames are braced together both horizontally and diagonally with lengths of lumber. The treads of ¾″ plywood are indi-

vidually cut and fitted. Similar to a curved flat, Upson board can be bent around the curved face of the stairway and secured to the frames and treads.

Hand Rails and Balustrades. Balustrades are architectural features of interior stairways, landings, and balconies. They usually consist of large posts, called **newel posts,** located on the lowest and highest steps and at each corner or turn of the stairway. The **hand rail** extends between these posts, and **balusters** are the smaller vertical posts. Normally, a balustrade must be reasonably sturdy, and this will take careful construction. One method is to build the balustrade directly to the stair unit. The newel posts can provide the major strength by extending below the treads for attachment to the carriages. Individual balusters can be butt jointed to the treads and secured by screws from below. The hand rail must be firmly attached to all posts. A balustrade can also be constructed as a separate unit with the masking piece of the stairway. This is not as strong, but it breaks an otherwise massive unit into segments more compatible for shifting and touring. The masking face of the stair unit can be constructed as a flat or as a more solid structure. The newel posts should be well secured to the frame and extend to the floor for greatest rigidity. The final masking and balustrade unit can be secured to the stairway by loose-pin hinges located on several treads (see Figure 9-31).

Metal Stairs. All of the metal component-parts systems are adaptable for stairway construction. They result in heavy structures and may require casters to move them conveniently. Metal is especially desirable for open, riserless stairs. With the pipe and slip-on fitting system, the back legs of one tread can project upward to support the front of

FIGURE 9–31   Stair balustrades.

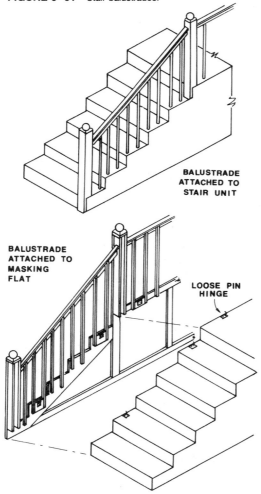

BALUSTRADE ATTACHED TO STAIR UNIT

BALUSTRADE ATTACHED TO MASKING FLAT

LOOSE PIN HINGE

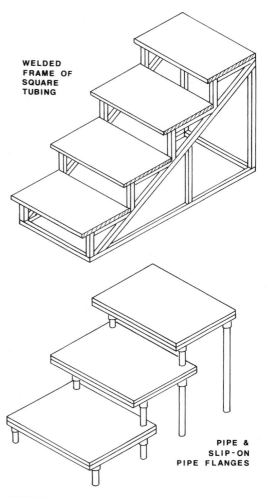

WELDED FRAME OF SQUARE TUBING

PIPE & SLIP-ON PIPE FLANGES

FIGURE 9–32   Metal stairs.

the next tread as well. Welded stair frames are also effective. Brackets supporting treads can be welded to thin structural steel placed at the inclined angle of the stairway (see Figure 9-32).

NONWEIGHT-BEARING STRUCTURES

Many three-dimensional objects do not bear loads of any appreciable weight. They are required only to support themselves and to withstand the rigors of shifting and transporting. They are usually made as lightweight as possible, especially if they are large, for easy handling. This governs the materials used and the construction techniques. Large, awkward pieces can be constructed with concealed hand holds, grips, or straps to aid in transporting. Fireplaces, pillars, mounds, hills, rocks, trees, logs, beams, and fountains are examples of scenic elements that are often nonweight-bearing.

Geometric Objects

Fireplaces, pilasters, and similar objects are generally rectilinear in shape. They are easily created with lumber framing similar to a flat frame with added side frames or thicknesses. They may be fabric covered, although more rigid material is often preferred for greater solidity and for ease of adding applied ornamentation. Counter tops and fireplace mantels usually only need to be strong enough to support hand properties. Objects that have geometric curves are formed with a framing of curved sweeps held together with strips of lumber. One-eighth-inch plywood or Upson board can be bent to form the curved surface.

Freeform Objects

Irregular, odd-shaped scenic structures depend on different construction techniques. Three-dimensional trees, rocks, mounds, and logs are examples of these objects. In general, items of this nature are created by a lightweight structure to provide body and shape, over which a contour is formed and a final surface skin is applied (Figure 9-33).

Building the Frame. The designer's model or perspective view of freeform objects must be translated into a series of sectional drawings. With these as a guide, the technician is able to begin the framing. It is

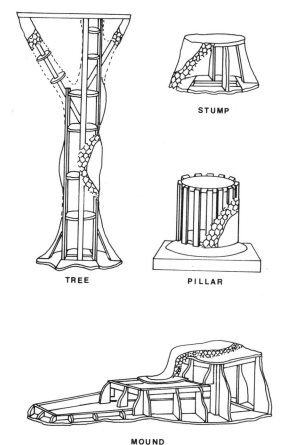

FIGURE 9–33 Freeform three-dimensional objects.

usually helpful to use an outline of the object on kraft paper or on the shop floor to build a foundation frame of lumber. The upright framing and surface material can be fastened to this foundation frame. Scrap lumber is cut and fitted together in accordance with the dimensions of the sectional views. The measuring, cutting, and fitting of lengths and angles is a custom process. Nails, screws, and pneumatic staples are used to attach members of the frame together. If preferred, the frame can also be constructed with metal. Rod, bar, or light-conduit stock can be cut, bent, and welded together. Be sure to anticipate the method of carrying and shifting the unit before it is constructed. It may be best to build a very large or heavy object on a wagon or as a tip-over caster unit. This must be decided before a proper frame can be constructed.

In many cases, parts of an object, such as a multilevel rock or embankment, are used for actor elevations. The framing for these levels must be constructed as platforms, and the remaining portions developed in light framework for freeform modeling.

Sculpting the Contour. At best, the frame is but a rough approximation of the final structure. It defines the location of selected points of the object to which a contour material can be secured. The most common material for this is 1″ mesh chicken wire, which is highly pliable and moldable. Fingers placed in the holes of the mesh can bend, crush and stretch the wire into many configurations. The wire is sculpted for the appropriate contour as it is placed over the frame. It is stapled to the frame (welded or wired if the frame is metal) to retain the shape. Tin shears are used to cut the wire and overlapping pieces must be wired together. All sharp wire ends must be twisted inward to avoid injuries and to prevent punctures to the final surface skin. Smaller mesh wire such as window screening would be a better contour material if the final surface is to be sprayed polyurethane foam. Sometimes, corrugated board, thin strips of wood, or other material may be useful in modeling the contour.

Applying the Surface

There are a variety of surface materials. A few standard ones will be examined. The choice of covering may depend on the nature of the object and the textural effect desired.

Papier-Mâché: Strip Technique. Absorbent paper dipped into a paste is a strong and proven surface material. Old newspaper or paper toweling is appropriate. Wheat paste is the standard adhesive with the addition of polyvinyl glue or heated gelatin glue not exceeding 33 percent of the mixture. Cut into strips, the paper is immersed in the paste and the excess paste removed with the fingers. The strips are applied over the chicken wire, overlapping each other on all sides. In concave areas, it is necessary to punch portions of the paper through the holes in the mesh to adhere to the other side of the strip. Otherwise, the paper will tend to pull away from the wire when drying. Usually two to four layers of paper are needed. A final layer of muslin or cheesecloth strips will give a tougher surface. It often takes several days for papier-mâché to dry, but heaters, heat lamps, or fans will speed the process.

Celastic. Similar to papier-mâché, Celastic is cut into strips, dipped into a softening agent, and applied over the chicken wire. Acetone thinned with alcohol is an effective softening liquid. Rubber gloves should be worn when working with Celastic to protect the hands from the acetone. Be cautious. Acetone is a toxic solvent and extremely flammable. Allow no smoking or flames in the area.

Overlapping strips should be pressed tightly. Poor adhesion will cause the edges to curl revealing individual strips. Remoisten with the softener if necessary to achieve tight adhesion. One layer of Celastic strips is sufficient for a strong surface. The material dries in a short time and can be sanded lightly for a smoother surface. Celastic can also be used to make copies of three-dimensional objects. The mold must be covered with aluminum foil or petroleum jelly because Celastic will adhere to most substances. When the Celastic is dry, it can be slit on one side and removed.

Fiberglass. A very strong surface for three-dimensional objects is fiberglass. In fact, it adds considerable structural strength to an object. Where its own draping and folds are appropriate for contour, as for a tree stump, a chicken wire base is unnecessary. Fiberglass cloth is laid over a contour and is stapled to hold it temporarily in place. Then the resin and hardener mixture is brushed on the fabric. Acetone is necessary to clean brushes. Rubber gloves should be worn to avoid skin contact. A face mask should be used when sanding hardened surfaces because particles can be injurious when inhaled. After fiberglass dries, be sure to trim off all razor-sharp threads, which can produce cuts.

Fabric-and-Glue Sizing. This is a solution that works well when a tough surface is not essential. Fabric can be stapled and pasted to a framework and then coated with double-strength size, or it can be dipped into the size solution and then draped and shaped on the frame while wet (Figure 9-34). A statue can be created, for instance, by fitting a glue soaked dress over a mannequin. Pins, wires, and clothespins can help to hold the folds of the draping until the glue dries. Muslin is a common fabric, although felt is more stretchable. A variation of this technique is the use of a solution of plaster and water instead of glue.

Spray-on Polyurethane Foam. Spray foam will easily adhere to screen wire or other contour materials. It has a rough, mottled texture for simulation of bark, plaster, rock, and stucco. While it is still wet, some sculpting of the surface can be achieved with a stick.

Spray foam casting should only be performed when extreme precautions are taken. This includes using a local exhaust system to enclose the work and using an air-supplied respirator.

ARCHITECTURAL TRIM, SCULPTURE, AND TEXTURE

A setting is given enriching depth and three-dimensional solidity in several subtle ways. In fact, it is often through architectural details, set trim, relief work, and texture that scenery gets its greatest interest and character. Architectural trim includes cornices, picture moldings, paneling, chair rails or dados, fireplace mantels and overmantels, door pediments, and base boards. High-relief and sculptured ornaments are needed for capitals of pillars, statuary, and terminating motives. Besides giving a feeling of substance to such materials as brick, stone, and plaster, surface texture enhances emotional action. Several applicable techniques have already been mentioned in this chapter. Figure 9-35 shows the sculptural potential of corrugated board. The following are additional means of achieving three-dimensional texture, relief, and ornamentation.

Lumber Buildups

Regular lumber and moldings are used to create architectural trim and relief for a setting (Figure 9-36). High-relief cornices can be built up with a combination of strips of lumber and molding attached to profile

FIGURE 9–34 A fountain made of muslin attached to a frame and tightened with double-strength size.

FIGURE 9–35 Corrugated board used for a sculptured figure. Created by Brian Lorbiecki for *Henry IV, Part 1* at the Great Lakes Shakespeare Festival.

frames. Curved surfaces can be formed by knive-scored corrugated board or moistened Upson board. Cornices can be attached to the top of flats by loose-pin hinges, specially bent hooks, or carriage bolts and wing nuts. Other architectural trim will need additional toggle bars or stiles on the flats for attachment with nails, screws, or picture hooks. Building up architectural trim with lumber requires careful measurements and the use of a miter box for appropriate saw cuts. Additional decoration can be provided by the appliqué of ornaments made of wood, fiber, or plastic available from building suppliers. They are useful to decorate fireplaces, overmantels, doors, and other trim.

Upholstery

The projection of stones, logs, brick, and other materials from a surface can be created by an upholstery technique (Figure 9-37). Shaped pieces of flexible foam, cotton batting, rug padding, wadded burlap or newspaper is pasted to the scenery surface in appropriate patterns. Muslin or woven cheesecloth dipped into double-strength size is used to cover the padding material. Flameproofing should be applied if the material is

FIGURE 9–36 Lumber buildups for a cornice and a pediment. (Photo by Renata S. Jasinski)

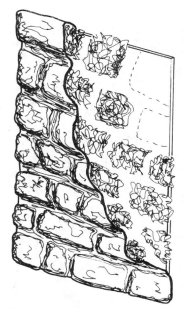

FIGURE 9–37 Upholstery for three-dimensional stones. Stone areas are first marked, padded material is then pasted to the surface and covered with cheesecloth soaked in glue size.

not fire resistant. When dry, the surface is ready to paint.

Plastic Foams

Foamed plastics are excellent for three-dimensional details and textures because they are light in weight and easy to shape. Polystyrene foam is useful for architectural trim and relief work. It can be cut with knives, saws, or routers or carved with a hot wire, a soldering iron, or a propane torch (Figure 9-38). Pieces of polystyrene are easily bonded together and held to frames with adhesives. Surface protection can be provided if necessary with woven cheesecloth or *Armor Putty*. Rigid polyurethane foam can be acquired in spray-on packs for freeforming and textural effects. Pour-in-place polyurethane is useful for creating objects in molds, such as balusters for a stairway and similar

items. Some stock moldings and ceiling beams are available at low cost from home supply dealers. Flexible polyurethane is effective as trim and molding on pillars and other round surfaces. Similarly, the flexible polyethylene foam rod is useful to decorate curved surfaces. It can be cut in half rounds or quarter rounds with a band saw and secured to a surface with hot-melt glue or other adhesives. Health and safety practices should be employed at all times when working with plastic foams.

Vacuum-Formed Plastics

Many types of molded patterns, ornaments, and moldings are available commercially in vacuum-formed sheets. Sheets of molded bricks and stone can be found in local home decorating stores. Other reproductions are sold primarily by theatre and display suppliers. A shop-built vacuum-form machine can reproduce three-dimensional relief and ornaments without difficulty. These can be cut from the plastic sheet and stapled, glued, or taped to scenery.

Papier-Mâché: Mash Technique

The strip technique of papier-mâché already described is also useful for texture and dimensional relief. The mash method, however, is generally more satisfactory for detail work. Mash can be prepared by cutting soft unsized paper into confetti and small bits. It must be soaked overnight in water before the paste is added to it. It is usually more convenient to purchase ready-made material which is sold in art and craft shops under such trade names as *Instant Papier-Mâché* or *Celluclay*. This is fully prepared, requiring only the addition of water. It can be applied and sculpted like clay. Ornaments and raised details can be applied directly to scenic objects and molded into shape with the fingers. Small statuary usually requires a foundation armature of wire to hold the papier-mâché

FIGURE 9–38   A pilaster and a low-relief figure from polystyrene foam.

while the shape is molded. It may be necessary to allow several days for the material to dry.

Liquid Latex

Latex and other flexible mold materials are valuable for producing applied ornaments. Some, such as *Hatomold*, can be poured into a mold for casting flame retardant ornaments. Regular liquid latex re-

quires from six to fifteen coats over a mold for a thick-skinned reproduction. Sawdust added to the wet latex helps to build up areas.

Scenic Textures

Texture on scenic surfaces is often a necessity or the final touch of illusion. Interesting effects can be achieved with auto body repair putty. This is a thick compound that can be applied with a putty knife or similar tool. A number of products are a mixture of metallic powder and an epoxy base. *Model-Metal* is one trade name, and others are sold as radiator repair material. These can be spread with tools or thinned to be brushed on a surface. When rubbed with a piece of metal or steel wool, a metallic luster is produced. Sometimes, graphite or bronzing powder in a medium of contact cement, lacquer, or latex will provide a similar effect.

A surface texture can be achieved by double-strength size and sawdust. The size is applied to the scenery, and, while it is wet, sawdust is sprinkled over the area. When the size dries, the loose sawdust is brushed off, and the scenery is ready for painting. The texture is appropriate for the roughness of rock, stucco, plaster, or old pitted metal.

An excellent texture material can be produced by a mixture of joint compound and carpet adhesive. The adhesive provides elasticity to the material. More compound in the mix will result in a stiffer substance and more adhesive will make it thinner and more flexible. The material can be thickened with the addition of sand, sawdust, kitty litter, or foam chips. It can be applied with a brush or trowel. A day may be necessary for it to dry. Additional layers may be applied until the appropriate texture is obtained. The dried surface is durable to walk on.

Flexible glue and paper can be another useful texture substance. After being water-thinned, flexible glue is brushed onto a surface, and various paper products (tissue paper, wrapping, or other papers) can be wrinkled and applied to the surface. A final coat of adhesive and layer of paint, without collapsing the wrinkles, completes the process.

Ground rubber obtained from a local tire recapper can also provide a textural surface. It can be mixed with a binder such as polyvinyl glue thinned with water up to 50 percent. The mixture can be spread onto scenery or floor covering with a trowel or other tool. Paint and additional thickening materials can be added to the mixture. It provides a coarse texture that will also support physical movement.

Some textured effects, such as clinging snow, can be produced by flocking. Special flocking spray guns and machines can often be rented. However, it is usually easier to contract the work to regular Christmas tree decorators. Be sure fire-retardant materials are used.

SELECTED READINGS

Bowman, Ned, *Handbook of Technical Practices for the Performing Arts.* Wilkinsburg, Penn.: Scenographic Media, 1972.

Burris-Meyer, Harold, and Edward C. Cole, *Scenery for the Theatre* (rev. ed.). Boston: Little, Brown, 1971.

Corbett, Tom, "Laminating Stage Platforms Using Honeycomb Paper," *Theatre Design and Technology*, Vol. 16, No. 4 (Winter 1980), 11–16.

Gillette, A. S., and J. Michael Gilette, *Stage Scenery: Its Construction and Rigging* (3rd ed.). New York: Harper and Row, 1981.

Jackson, Robert C., "Stressed-Skin Scenery for the Theatre," *Theatre Crafts*, Vol. 12, No. 1 (January and February 1978), 24–25, 57–58.

Lee, Briant Hamor, and Daryl M. Wedwick, *Corrugated Scenery*. Baton Rouge, La.: Oracle Press, 1982.

Taylor, Douglas C., *Metalworking for the Designer and Technician*. New York: Drama Book Specialists, 1979.

10

Scene Painting

Perhaps no area of scene technology is more clouded in mystery than the art and practice of scene painting. In this very specialized field, knowledge and skill have generally been limited to those who are masters in the profession. Until recent times, little has been written about the practice. In fact, scenic artists in the 19th century—the heyday of painted scenery—generally guarded their techniques as secrets, to assure their own employment. Thus, study and experience are needed to dispel the mystery of scene painting for scene technicians. The ingredients required for such an exorcism are a knowledge of color and color mixing, an eye to the appearance of objects in life, an understanding of painting techniques and materials, and the development or personal skills through practice and experience. It should be noted that herein the term *paint* is used in its general sense to mean all types of decorative and protective coatings including dyes and varnishes.

PAINT COMPOSITION

First we must consider the basic components of paint.

Pigments or Dyes. These are the foundation substances of all paints. They give color, body, and opacity to paint. They originate from either natural sources or chemical processes and are of two types: organic (animal and vegetable) and inorganic (mineral).

Binder. This is the material that binds pigments together and makes paint adhere to a surface.

Vehicle. A vehicle is the liquid substance that carries the pigment and binder. Dyes are dissolved in solution; pigments are held in suspension. Generally, the vehicle evaporates in the drying process. Premixed paints contain a binder and a vehicle but can often be thinned with a **thinner** or **solvent** for a change in consistency or to aid in application.

174

Frequently other materials or chemicals are added to the paint mixture. These include **driers**, to control drying time; **extenders** or **fillers,** to reduce the cost (and sometimes the brilliance) of the paint or to provide surface texture in the applied finish; and **emulsifiers,** to aid in holding dissimilar materials (such as oil and water) together in a mixture.

CHARACTERISTICS OF PAINT MATERIALS

Painting and dyeing scenic elements is quite comprehensive. It includes a wide range of materials (cloth, wood, metal, plastics), a diversity of depth and illusion (extending from transparencies to opaque finishes) and a host of different effects and simulations. No single paint medium is sufficient to satisfy all of these needs. In fact, many factors are critical in selecting the appropriate media for a given task. It is wise to explore carefully the characteristics of paint, varnish, and dye formulas and products, considering the following points:

Toxicity and Flammability. Hazardous materials continue to be used in painting. This includes certain specific pigments and solvents. When possible, avoid their use or substitute less hazardous materials. Precautions should be taken to combat toxic dusts, toxic vapors, and skin contact with irritating chemicals. Combustible and flammable materials require special precautions and maintenance. Protective equipment and proper ventilation, storage of materials, and cleanup are necessary (see Chapter 4). In recent years, extensive changes in paint chemistry have been imposed on manufacturers of premixed paints owing to increasing OSHA requirements for reducing the dangers of fire hazards and toxicity.

Water and/or Weather Resistance. Some paints are water resistant after drying; others, often labeled "exterior" paints, are resistant to extreme weather, sun fading, and so forth. A water-resistant finish may be necessary for maintenance of scene units handled frequently or under close scrutiny by an audience. Resistance to weather would be important for outdoor productions.

Finish. Matte finish meets the most common requirements of scene painting. However, the shine or hardness of a semigloss or gloss finish is frequently desirable for certain effects and techniques.

Hiding Power. This is the power of a paint material to obscure the surface to which it is applied. Some paints may require several coats.

Adherence to Materials. Some paints do not adhere well to all materials. Paints that effectively cover porous surfaces (canvas or wood, for instance) may not adhere adequately to nonporous material (metal, plastics) without an additional binder.

Dilutability. Since many paint techniques require transparent or translucent mixtures, the ability to dilute the paint without loss of binding strength is often a valuable characteristic.

Saturation of Colors. It is usually desirable for a paint medium to be available in a range of vivid colors of high quality pigments. Intermixing of colors should not create muddy hues, tints, and shades. Sometimes the intensity of aniline dyes is the only suitable choice for transparent or translucent washes.

Compatibility with Other Paints or Materials. Some paints and binder systems are compatible for intermixtures with other paints or allow the addition of other pigments. Some allow the addition of fillers for surface textures.

Cleanability. The ease of cleaning brushes, clothing, and containers is frequently a major factor in selecting a paint. This gives water-thinned paints a decided edge. For other paints, appropriate solvents and suitable precautions in cleaning must be used.

Spoilage and Storage. Some paints (with animal glue or protein binders) will spoil or putrefy eventually once the vehicle is added. These paints must be mixed only when needed. For most paints, original containers must be sealed properly in storage to prevent spoilage or the hardening of the paint material.

Cost. Cost is obviously a factor in the selection of paint because of the large quantities consumed for scenic units. As a general rule, premixed paints are the most expensive.

PAINT FOR SCENERY

Scene painting is so diverse, nearly every paint or paint formula has potential for solving some scenery or property need. Scenic artists and technicians must be aware of a wide range of media. Some of the major types of paint and decorative coatings will be explored under the three general categories which follow. Figure 10-1 lists some representative scene paints to illustrate the range of colors and finishes available.

Traditional Scene Paint

The long-time standard paint for scenery is entirely prepared and mixed by the painter. It consists of pure finely-ground pigment to which a binder and a vehicle are added. Obtained from scenic supply houses, the majority of the pigments are in a dry powdered form. A few, used less frequently, are available only as wet or pulp colors. The pigments are highly saturated and intermix well for a variety of hues, tints, and shades.

Size. Size (also called size water) is the traditional binder/vehicle used in preparing this type of paint. The preparation of animal-glue size is described in Chapter 8. One part hot ground glue with 16 parts of warm water results in a relatively flexible binder and causes the least discoloration to the paint. Sizing must be carefully prepared and tested. Too little glue in the paint will cause it to rub off, and with too much glue the paint will check and start to flake off. The paint is most easily prepared as follows:

1. The dry pigments are mixed together for the particular hue desired. This is approximately the color of the paint when it dries on the scenery. The addition of size will darken the mixture several shades.

2. Size is added to the prepared pigment to the desired consistency. The consistency will vary according to the paint technique to be employed, but normal consistency is that of heavy milk. Because this paint will deteriorate in time, only the amount needed should be mixed at a given time. Some of the mixed dry pigment should be saved for later color matching if necessary. Since some pigments tend to float on top of the liquid, a little denatured alcohol or detergent may be necessary to force them into suspension.

3. The paint must be stirred frequently during the painting process.

Dry pigment is the most economical paint available. It is not without serious limitations, however. The paint is not water resistant when dry. This is normally of little concern for painting a backdrop, but it can be a problem for scenic units handled frequently by actors or crew members, and closely seen by an audience. Since the liquid of the paint tends to loosen previous coats, overpainting must be done with light and rapid brush strokes. Further, certain intense colors tend to bleed through successive coats of paint. Scenery can be charged with only about twelve coats of this paint before the accumulated layers begin to chip off. The scenery then must be washed to remove the paint, or the fabric must be replaced.

Premixed Scene Paint

Any number of premixed paints may be useful for scenery. However, several products are specifically marketed for theatre, film, and TV scenery and for display work.

FIGURE 10–1 A representative listing of scene paints.

DRY PIGMENTS	PROTEIN PAINTS		LATEX, ACRYLIC, AND VINYL PAINTS		
*Gothic Scenic Colors**	*Iddings Deep Colors*	*Gothic Casein Fresco Paints*	*Flo-Paint Scenic-Decorator Colors (vinyl)*	*Cal-Western Show and Display Colors (acrylic)*	*Rosco Paint Super Saturated (vinyl acrylic)*
Whites					
Permanent White 171 Danish Whiting	Priming White 5550 White 5551	White	White Gloss 5055 White Flat 5033	White 520 Blockout White 565 Texture White 568 Hi Gloss White 5119	White Base 6002
Black					
Ivory Black 169 Hercules Black 170	Black 5552	Black	Black Gloss 5079 Black Flat 5034	Black 519 Hi Gloss Black 5120	Velour Black 6003
Yellows					
Lt. Chrome Yellow 103 Med. Chrome Yellow 104	Lemon Yellow 5566 Golden Yellow 5567	Lemon Yellow Golden Yellow	Lemon Yellow Flat 5050 Lt. Yellow Gloss 5075 Golden Yellow Flat 5051 Med. Yellow Gloss 5069	Acacia 506	Chrome Yellow 5981
Oranges					
French Orange Mineral 110	Orange 5563	Orange	Orange Flat 5052 Orange Gloss 5068	Orange 507	Moly Orange 5984
Reds					
Turkey Red Lake 121	Bright Red 5562	Bright Red	Bright Red Flat 5044 Gloss 5076	Phthalo Red 533	Red 5965
American Vermillion Red 113	Red 5560	Red	Deep Red Flat 5054 Gloss 5077	Fire Red 503	Spectrum Red 5977
Solferino Red 126	Dark Red 5561	Dark Red	Magenta Flat 5048 Gloss 5065	Magenta 502	Magenta 5975
Lt. Maroon 127 Dk. Maroon 124	Magenta 5569	Magenta			
Violets					
Purple Lake 130 Royal Purple 132	Purple 5568	Purple		Violet 505	
Blues					
American Ultramarine Blue 141 French Cobalt Blue 142 Italian Blue 143 Prussian Blue 144 Celestial Blue 146	Turquoise Blue 5570 Cerulean Blue 5572 Ultramarine Blue 5559 Navy Blue 5573	Turquoise Blue Cerulean Blue Ultramarine Blue Navy Blue	Cerulean Blue Flat 5049 Medium Blue Gloss 5067 Ultramarine Blue Flat 5045 Navy Blue Flat 5047 Dark Blue Gloss 5066	Ultramarine Blue 538 Phthalo Blue 508	Green Shade Blue 5968 Ultramarine Blue 5969

(continued)

FIGURE 10–1 *continued*

DRY PIGMENTS	PROTEIN PAINTS		LATEX, ACRYLIC, AND VINYL PAINTS		
Gothic Scenic Colors*	*Iddings Deep Colors*	*Gothic Casein Fresco Paints*	*Flo-Paint Scenic-Decorator Colors (vinyl)*	*Cal-Western Show and Display Colors (acrylic)*	*Rosco Paint Super Saturated (vinyl acrylic)*
Greens					
Lt. Chrome Green 150	Emerald Green 5564	Emerald Green Chrome Oxide Green Dark Green	Emerald Green Flat 5088	Phthalo Green 504	Chrome Green 5971
Med. Chrome Green 152	Chrome Oxide Green 5565		Light Green Gloss 5060	Green Oxide 501	Phthalo Green 5973
Dk. Chrome Green 153	Dark Green 5571		Chrome Oxide Green Flat 5037		
Emerald Green 151			Medium Green Gloss 5061		
Hanover Green 154			Dark Green Flat 5039		
			Deep Green Gloss 5063		
Earth Colors					
French Yellow Ochre 160	Yellow Ochre 5553	Yellow Ochre			Yellow Ochre 5982
Golden Ochre 161					
Italian Raw Sienna 165	Raw Sienna 5555	Raw Sienna	Raw Sienna Flat 5040 Gloss 5056	Raw Sienna 517	
Italian Burnt Sienna 164	Burnt Sienna 5556	Burnt Sienna	Burnt Sienna Flat 5041 Gloss 5057	Burnt Sienna 516	Burnt Sienna 5987
Raw Turkey Umber 163	Raw Umber 5557	Raw Umber	Raw Umber Flat 5042 Gloss 5058	Raw Umber 514	Raw Umber 5986
Burnt Turkey Umber 162	Burnt Umber 5554	Burnt Umber	Burnt Umber Flat 5043 Gloss 5059	Burnt Umber 515	Burnt Umber 5985
Van Dyke Brown 166	Van Dyke Brown 5558			Venetian Red 513	Iron Red 5980
Eng. Venetian Red 123					
Other					
	Acrylic/Latex Gloss 5580		Clear Gloss 5080	Clear Acrylic Glaze 574	Gloss Medium
	Acrylic/Latex Flat 5581		Clear Flat 5053	Acrylic Artist Paste 588	
			Krom-o-key Blue 5046	Acrylic Gel (Hi gloss) 539	
			Peel Paste 5083	5 Fluorescent Colors	
			Strip Coat 5084	4 Metallic Finishes	
			Heat Resistant Blue-White 5027		
			Battleship Gray Flat 5035 Gloss 5064		

*This is an incomplete listing of Gothic Dry Pigments but indicates the range of colors available.

Some are sophisticated chemical formulations that meet the special requirements of scene painting. Their characteristics should be examined and samples tested to learn the full potentials and limitations of each paint system. In general, they have several attributes in common. They are water thinnable, water resistant when dry, and available in a range of vivid colors, and they result in an appropriate matte finish. Most of them are prepared in concentrated paste form for thinning with an equal amount of water for opaque coats or reduced further for translucent or transparent mixtures. They can be divided into two general categories.

Protein Binder Systems. Chief among these are casein-base paints (casein is a protein substance precipitated from milk) and soya-protein-base paints manufactured under such names as *Iddings Deep Colors, Luminall Fresco Colors,* and *Gothic Casein Fresco Paints.* These paints are relatively economical and are purchased in paste form in quarts and gallons. The working range of Iddings is from two parts water/one part paint to six parts water/one part paint. Protein-base paints are available in a wide selection of brilliant colors, and they have high tinting strength. Colors intermix well for clean and vivid hues, shades, and tints.

Casein-type paints are uniquely compatible with other water-thinned paint systems. Casein colors can be used to tint latexes and vinyls, for instance. The paint will also accept additives including dry pigments, aniline dyes, latexes, acrylics, vinyls, and bronzing powders. Protein-base paint is effective for covering porous and semiporous materials. For nonporous materials such as metal and plastics, an additional binder must be mixed with the paint. Clear acrylic latex is appropriate for this additional binding strength and will also enhance the waterproof properties of the paint.

To prepare paint mixtures, some of the paint concentrate should be placed in a separate container. A small amount of water may then be added and mixed until smooth. This provides the proper consistency for mixing with other colors for specific hues, tints, and shades. Once this has been achieved, water may be added for the desired consistency for application. To prevent its drying out, the paint concentrate must be kept, without the addition of water, in the tightly closed original can when not in use. Mixed paint will last a few days if covered with a lid or a wet cloth.

Latex, Acrylic, and Vinyl Binder Systems. A Number of premixed paints are chemical formulations identified as latex, acrylic, acrylic latex, vinyl, or vinyl-acrylic binder systems. Manufacturers of these paints include Flo-Paint (vinyl), Cal-Western (acrylic), and Rosco Laboratories (vinyl acrylic). A range of vibrant colors is generally available in these paints. They have excellent tinting strength and hold up well in thin dilutions with water. Like protein systems, these paints are produced in paste form and are water thinnable. They provide excellent hiding power and dry to a deep matte finish.

Unlike protein paints, these systems will cover most porous and nonporous materials equally well. In some paints, binding strength is not affected by dilutions. For instance, Super Saturated Roscopaint may be reduced for washes and glazes with eight or more parts of water without affecting its binding strength. These let-down properties are possible with paints that have small kernel-size pigments.

Paints are mixed in much the same way as protein paints. Mechanical agitation is usually best for thorough mixing. These systems will not spoil or putrefy. Even after being mixed with water and left standing, these paints can be restirred and used for additional application. If a layer of water is added to the top, evaporation and drying out over a period of days is prevented.

Other Paints, Dyes, and Varnishes

There are a variety of other paint materials that have special purposes for scenery. Included among them are the following:

FIGURE 10–2   A comic cartoon style of painting. Scene from *A Thurber Carnival*. Designed by the author.

Dyes. Dyes are unusually brilliant and transparent colorants. They are valuable for painting drops and other fabrics that must remain soft and foldable. They are excellent for translucent muslin drops, scrims, cycloramas, and texture fabrics. Stained-glass window effects and other translucent or transparent illusions can be created. Dyes are invaluable for thin transparent glaze coats to enrich a painted effect and add depth. The dyes are in powder form and are water and/or alcohol soluble. A teaspoon of powdered dye dissolved in a quart of boiling water will make a concentrated solution. Dyes may then be intermixed for the appropriate color.

Special health precautions are necessary when working with dyes since most have toxic properties. The word *aniline* continues to be used by some manufacturers to mean *synthetic* dyes, but true aniline dyes, made from coal tar, are too toxic to be used safely. Be sure you know the dangers of the dye you use, and practice appropriate care. A binder may be added to the dye solution to prevent the color from spreading and from bleeding into succeeding coats. Common binders include

Clear vinyl (matte or gloss finish): Water thinnable; an excellent binder; especially desirable for nonporous surfaces such as plastics, glass, and metal.

Animal-glue size: Mixed as for traditional dry scene pigments.

Polyvinyl-glue size: Mixed with approximately six parts water.

Dextrine: A starch compound; soluble in warm water and heated in a double boiler before thinning to a size consistency.

Gum arabic or gum tragacanth: A flexible binder; soaked in water and cooked like dextrine.

Metallic Paints. Bronze powders are most commonly used to create metallic finishes on scenery. They are effective on soft or hard surfaces. A range of colors in golds, aluminum, brass, and copper is available. Regular bronzing liquid (a varnish-like material) can be used as a binder. Clear gloss latex and clear gloss vinyl are also excellent binders for bronze powders if thinned with water. Shellac thinned with alcohol is also appropriate, as is dextrine.

For properties and small scenic trim work, other metallic paints are effective. Though frequently limited in colors, aerosol can sprays are fast drying and will adhere to most materials. They are often best when applied over a dark prime color with a very light spraying. A textured surface makes their appearance more satisfactory. Another type of product, often called *Model-Metal*, is sold at craft and auto stores. This is a metallic powder in an epoxy binder. It can be applied in a thick paste form or thinned and brushed onto a surface. It gives wood and plastic objects the appearance of metal (a dagger made of wood, for example). When dry, rubbing with steel wool or a piece of metal will bring out a lifelike metallic shine. It is also useful for sculptured and relief constructions.

Gloss and Hard Finishes. Glossy, hard-finish paints have special purposes. A hard finish is invaluable as a foundation coat for many effects. Unlike matte finishes, glossy paints produce a hard, nonabsorbent surface so that subsequent coats will flow and puddle. The gloss paint should not be thinned excessively as this will reduce the hardness of the finish. Gloss vinyl paint is ideal, or a matte finish paint can be coated with water-thinned clear vinyl, clear shellac, or other sealer for a hard surface. Clear gloss varnishes are excellent for glaze coats, over-painted effects which require shiny or polished surfaces. Glazing enhances the illusion of finished woodwork, glass, marble, and other substances. Regular varnishes may be used on furniture and properties. Gloss clear vinyl and gloss clear acrylic latex (both water thinnable) are excellent glazing materials. The degree of reflective shine desired (gloss, semigloss, eggshell) is controlled by the amount of thinner added to the mixture. In addition, shellac thinned with alcohol, clear lacquer and lacquer thinner, and regular animal-glue size are often effective.

Other Paints. Occasional use is made of a variety of other paint materials. Spray paints in aerosol cans are convenient for small trims and properties. Upholstery dyes in spray cans are useful to liven up faded furniture fabrics.

Spray painting should be performed only in a spray booth or with good exhaust ventilation conditions and while wearing a proper respirator.

Fluorescent paints are activated to glow in the dark by black light (ultraviolet light) sources. Luminous (phosphorescent) paints glow after being exposed to a light source. These and other specialty paints should be viewed for the service they can provide for the painted scene.

PAINTING EQUIPMENT

Paint Applicators

Brushes and paint sprayers are the most common ways of applying paints. But some applications require special products.

Brushes. Brushes are among the most important applicators of paint. Basically, a brush is a set of **bristles** secured in rubber or plastic which is held to a **handle** by means of a metal **ferrule**. A brush works on the principle of adhesion. When it is dipped into paint, the paint adheres to the bristles. When the brush is then placed on a surface having greater adhesion, the paint leaves the bristles and coats the surface. The length and number of bristles on the brush will determine how much paint the brush can carry.

Because scene painting effects rely so often on brush technique, only high-quality brushes should be used. Good brushes are costly, but with proper care they will last for many years. The brush should have a full body of bristles (cheap brushes often scrimp on the number of bristles) and be high-quality natural or synthetic bristling material. The best is genuine hog bristle, European or Asian, which is strong and springy. Synthetic bristles, usually nylon, are a second choice. Horse hair is considerably inferior and will not hold up. The ferrule for scene painting should be designed to resist corrosion. Handles should be lightweight and well balanced. Brushes can also be acquired with 3'-long handles for painting scenery on the floor. Brushes are generally designed for a specific range of purposes and therefore have features unique from other brushes. Good scenic brushes are available from American and European sources. Figure 10-3 illustrates some standard scenic brushes.

FIGURE 10–3 Basic scenic brushes.

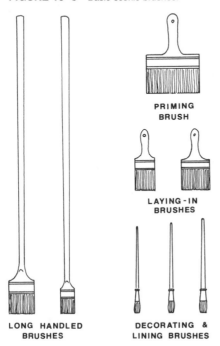

PRIMING BRUSH

LAYING-IN BRUSHES

LONG HANDLED BRUSHES

DECORATING & LINING BRUSHES

Priming brushes are large brushes 6″ to 8″ wide with bristles 4″ or more long. They hold a lot of paint and can cover large areas in a short time. **Dutch primers** have bristles that are 7″ long.

Laying-in brushes are from 3″ to 5″ wide and have bristles 4″ to 6″ long. They are large enough and hold sufficient paint to lay-in sizable areas, but are also able to cut sharp edges.

Decorating and lining brushes have longer handles for better control and range from ¼″ to 3″ wide. They are used for painting details in a variety of techniques or for lining with a straightedge.

A number of special-purpose brushes are also valuable to the scenic artist. **Graining brushes**, constructed of separated bundles of bristles, are used for wood-graining patterns or combing effects. **Lettering brushes** are valuable for lettering and other fine detail. They are available in all sizes in art supply stores. **Push brooms** are useful for priming as well as for smoothing or intermixing puddles of color on scenery. Special **stencil brushes** are best for applying stencil designs. A circular, pounding action prevents smears in painting through a stencil. **Badger blenders** are brushes with long, soft bristles of the badger family. Stroked lightly over wet spatter, graining, or veining lines, these brushes blend and feather out the paint. In addition, there are other brushes that have special use in scene painting.

Brush Care. Proper use and care of brushes is most important to maintain them as effective tools. When bristles curl, separate into clumps, fishtail, mat, or swell, you may be certain the brush was incorrectly used or improperly cleaned. Brushes in this condition will not perform effectively. A few precautions are important in brush usage:

Select the proper brush for the painting task. It is inappropriate, for instance, to use a fine-quality lining brush (designed to strike a sharp-edged line along a straightedge) for prime coating a chair leg. A small general-purpose brush will do the job.

Do not load the brush excessively. A brush should be dipped in the paint half way up to the ferrule and any drippings removed on the top edge of the paint container.

Stroke the brush lightly along the surface. A heavy scrubbing action is inappropriate. The paint flows from the tips of the bristles.

Do not stand the brush on its painting tip. This will cause the bristles to curl. Lay it on a flat surface or across the top of the paint container when not in use.

Never stir the paint with the brush. Use a stick or paddle for this purpose.

Brush Maintenance. Proper cleaning and storage of brushes is essential to assure long and successful service. The following rules are basic in brush care:

Clean the brush immediately and thoroughly after its use. Modern quick-drying paints will endanger the life of the brush. Water-thinned paints should be removed with warm water, or warm water and mild soap. The appropriate solvent must be used for other types of paint. Use your fingers to squeeze out the paint in the heel of the brush (the portion of bristles nearest the ferrule). Failure to do this will reduce the loading capacity of the bristles, decrease their elasticity, and ruin the shaping of the bristles. After the paint has been removed, the solvent should be squeezed out and the bristles shaped properly.

Hang up brushes vertically in a well-ventilated area to dry. This will cause the solvent to drip out and evaporate and help to keep the bristles straight and smoothly shaped. Lining brushes can be stored horizontally on open screen shelves to dry. Brushes should not be left to soak in water or paint and should never be left standing on the bristle tips.

Paint Sprayers. Sprayers offer several advantages over other paint applicators but they cannot duplicate many painting techniques achieved by other applicators. Spraying is well known as the fastest means of painting and perhaps the least tiring for the painter. This makes it ideal for priming, base coating, or glazing large areas of scenery. It is also useful for painting those awkward, multisurface objects (picket fences, louvered doors, wicker chairs) that otherwise require excessive hours with a small brush. More than this, spraying can provide several unique effects. The blending of multiple colors is smoother and subtler by spraying than by the usual wet blending with a brush. A sprayer produces a fine mist or light spatter that can be controlled to achieve subtle gradations of color when applied over coats that have dried. It can create variegated base coats and lightly spattered textured surfaces. Spraying can effectively alter or correct a colored hue. By careful matting, small areas can be sprayed, and stencil patterns can be painted in either solid or lightly spattered coats (see Figure 10-4).

The **Hudson tank sprayer** is one of the simplest and most useful spray units for scene paint. This sprayer is used for garden insecticides but is a commonly accepted sprayer in scene shops for paint, dye, and flameproofing. The 3- and 4-gallon capacity units are most common, although sprayers as small as 1 gallon are available. The sprayer is equipped with a hand pump to fill the tank with compressed air. The amount of air compression needed will depend on the consistency of the paint and the coarseness or fineness of the paint particles desired. Twenty-five to 35 pumps provide the normal pressure required. The sprayer is equipped with a short length of hose and a spray tube complete with valve control handle and nozzle. The nozzle is adjustable for a variety of cone-shaped sprays. The unit can be adapted with a tire valve fitting to be filled by an air compressor to about 30–40 lb. of air. Before filling the tank, the paint must be filtered through a screen wire strainer or through cheesecloth or fine cloth netting. This will prevent clogging in the nozzle. Immediately after use, the sprayer must be thoroughly cleaned and clear water or solvent sprayed through the unit to clean out the hose, spray tube, and nozzle.

Compressor spray-gun systems are the most sophisticated spray equipment. They

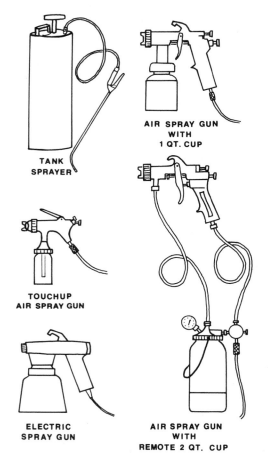

TANK
SPRAYER

AIR SPRAY GUN
WITH
1 QT. CUP

TOUCHUP
AIR SPRAY GUN

ELECTRIC
SPRAY GUN

AIR SPRAY GUN
WITH
REMOTE 2 QT. CUP

FIGURE 10–4 Spray-painting equipment.

provide a high degree of control and produce a smooth, even spray. A spray gun can achieve a finer spray than is common with the tank sprayer. This type of spray system consists of three units: the gun mechanism, the attached or remote paint container, and the air compressor. The gun mixes the paint and air pressure as controlled by a trigger and by adjustable screws which determine the width of the spray and regulate the flow of material. The most common paint container is a 1-quart cup that attaches directly to the gun. However, spray systems are available with remote 2-quart cups or 2- and 5-gallon remote containers for holding larger

quantities of paint and avoiding frequent stops to refill. Hoses for paint and air supply connect the remote container to the spray gun. Remote containers keep the gun light in weight for the convenience of applying paint.

A separate air compressor supplies the power for spraying paint. This may be either a small continuous running compressor or a compressor that stores air pressure in a tank regulated to a constant pressure. A built-in compressor system is ideal for spraying. Air outlets can be located conveniently near the painting area, and air hoses can be attached rapidly with quick couplers. The pressure gauge on the air line regulator must be adjusted to the appropriate air pressure. From 35 to 45 pounds per square inch (psi) is appropriate for the average paint material, although from 25 to 35 psi might be satisfactory for light-bodied solutions.

Professional spray equipment is available in several variations depending on intended use (Figure 10-5). These variations include

Air supply used: A **bleeder** type spray gun is designed to connect to a continuously running compressor. The air blows through the gun at all times, and the trigger controls the paint flow only. The **nonbleeder** type is used with a stored air supply. The trigger controls both air and paint. As the trigger is released, the flow of air stops.

Paint-feed method: The **pressure-feed** gun has an airtight paint container. Air pressure on the surface of the paint forces the paint up the tube and out of the gun. The **siphon-feed** gun works on the vacuum principle. The suction of air rushing past the lift tube forces paint to rise up through the gun. The vent hole in the top of the paint container identifies a siphon-feed gun.

Atomizing of the paint: Two different types of nozzles are used to form the paint spray. **Internal-mix** nozzles atomize the paint inside the nozzle and are better for heavy, slow-drying paint. **External-mix** nozzles combine the air and paint outside the nozzle. These are better for light, quick-drying paints that are more likely to clog an internal-mix nozzle. Siphon-feed guns use only the external-mix nozzles.

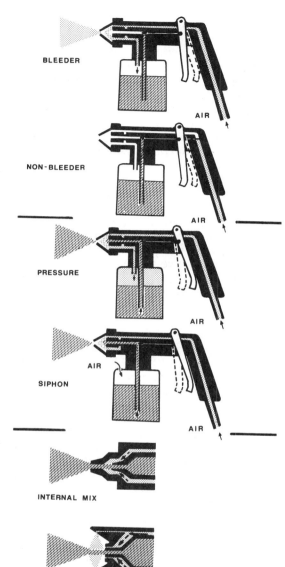

BLEEDER

AIR

NON-BLEEDER

AIR

PRESSURE

AIR

AIR

SIPHON

AIR

INTERNAL MIX

EXTERNAL MIX

FIGURE 10–5 Types of spray guns.

Major manufacturers of compressor spray paint equipment include Binks and DeVilbiss. Both have quality spray guns to serve any need. **Touchup guns** with 2-, 4-, and 6-ounce paint jars are handy for light production and touchup work where colors are changed frequently. Another spray unit used with an air compressor is the **air brush**. This is valuable for detail work and for creating shadows and soft edging.

Spray guns are precision tools that require proper use and maintenance. Paint must be mixed thin enough to spray effectively but not so thin that the paint will run when spraying in the proper manner. The paint must be mixed well, and it must be thoroughly filtered so large particles will not clog the gun. For a smooth, even application of paint, the painter must learn correct spray gun technique. The old painting adage that several thin light coats is better than one heavy coat applies especially to spray painting. Proper spraying will avoid errors in coverage, areas where coverage is too thin and areas where the paint is too thick, resulting in drips and runs. Before spraying, it is best to practice on another surface to adjust the spray pattern. Oval-shape spray patterns can be adjusted for vertical or horizontal strokes by loosening the nozzle cap and turning the nozzle. Normally the spray gun should be about 8″ to 10″ from the surface being painted. The secret of maintaining an even distribution of paint while spraying consists of

1. Keeping the gun aimed squarely at the surface.
2. Producing strokes that are parallel to the surface at all times (an arcing stroke will deposit a thick layer of paint in the center and only a mist on the edges). (See Figure 10-6.)
3. Keeping the gun constantly in motion when the trigger is open.

Flexible wrist motion is essential to achieve strokes that are parallel to the work. Each stroke should be triggered individually. Start the action of each stroke beyond the work area, then squeeze the trigger to start the flow of paint. At the end of the area being covered, release the trigger to stop the spray, but continue the stroke for a brief second after the flow of paint has ceased. Each stroke should follow this procedure

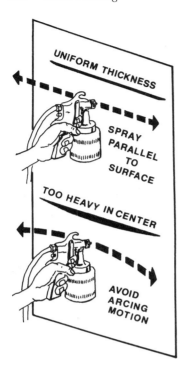

UNIFORM THICKNESS

SPRAY PARALLEL TO SURFACE

TOO HEAVY IN CENTER

AVOID ARCING MOTION

FIGURE 10–6   Spray strokes should be parallel to the surface.

and should overlap the previous stroke about one-third of its width for adequate coverage. Areas not to be covered should be well masked. Because of the mist caused by spray painting, the room should have an exhaust ventilation system and the painter should wear a respirator.

As with all good tools, spray equipment will last indefinitely if properly maintained. Nearly all problems with spray equipment are the result of inadequate cleaning. Immediately after use, the equipment should be thoroughly cleaned before the paint dries and endangers the gun. The paint container should be emptied and rinsed. The parts of the gun should be wiped with the paint solvent. Solvent (water in the case of water-thinned paints) should be sprayed through the gun until the spray is clear solvent. A final wiping of the gun parts and the threads

of the paint container is desirable. The gun should be stored with the fluid tube and the paint hose (in the case of remote paint containers) hanging downward. Instructions with the spray gun will indicate appropriate lubrication and other preventive maintenance procedures.

Other, more limited, spray systems may occasionally have a place in scene painting. One of these is a spray system based on the aerosol can **power pack.** An inexpensive sprayer, the can of compressed air powers the attached nozzle and paint jar. The power pack is disposable and replaced with a new aerosol can to continue painting. An **electric sprayer** works on centrifugal force to cause the material in the cup to spray onto a surface. At times, even a **fly sprayer,** a small spray unit with a pump handle, may be useful for small touchup painting. Although useful additions, owing to limited controls and features, none of these is a substitution for compressor spray-gun systems.

Paint Rollers. Rollers have a variety of uses in scene painting. They are excellent for creating textural effects or building up layers of glaze coats in painting landscapes and other illusions. They are also useful for painting floors and other large surfaces. Rollers are most commonly found in 7″ and 9″ widths although 1″, 2″, and 3″ rollers are convenient for detail work. Roller covers have various thicknesses and are available in lambs wool, mohair, *Dynel*, and foam. Extension poles in assorted lengths permit use of rollers in painting on the floor and for high or hard-to-reach areas. Special designs or patterns can be painted by a roller. Commercial pattern rollers are manufactured in a range of designs. Some are useful, for instance, for the background, if not for the final effect, of wallpaper. Pattern or texture rollers can also be made by cutting out portions of the roller cover or by wrapping or attaching wire, string, tape, or netting around the roller. A shop-made roller can be constructed by gluing (using waterproof glue) flexible foam around a piece of cardboard carpet roll. The foam can be sculpted or textured as desired. A metal yoke and handle will complete the roller. Roller accessories include paint trays, extension poles, and wire bucket screens for rolling off excess paint. All equipment must be cleaned thoroughly after use.

Other Paint Applicators and Application Aids. The immense range of effects to be achieved in scene painting is made possible by a variety of other paint applicators (Figure 10-7).

Large sponges (both natural and synthetic) are ideal for many effects. Sponges hold a lot of paint, and they can create a range of impressions by the manner in which they are pressed to the surface.

Foam stamps have a similar versatility. Foam rubber or flexible plastic foam can be shaped into specific patterns or textures. The foam patterns are securely bonded with waterproof adhesive to appropriately shaped pieces of ¼″ plywood to which a wooden handle is attached. The stamps are first dipped into a shallow pan of paint or dye, then applied to the scenic surface in a variety of ways.

Feather dusters made of turkey feathers are useful texture applicators. The large industrial dusters are the most desirable. Used primarily as stipplers, they create interesting patterned effects.

Fabric, especially burlap, terry cloth, or other textural material, is also a successful paint applicator.

Several tools are invaluable in removing or rearranging paint before it dries on the surface. Puddles of colors in coarse base coats or fine spatters for wood graining may be effectively over-brushed with a **push broom. Whisk brooms, rubber grainers, graining rollers,** and **graining combs** are used to remove paint or to create woodgrain patterns while the paint is still wet on the surface.

FIGURE 10–7   Other paint applicators.

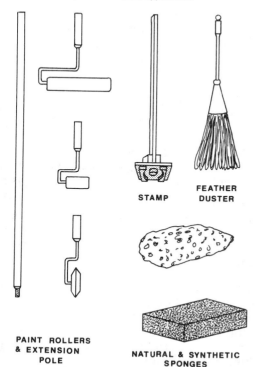

PAINT ROLLERS
& EXTENSION
POLE

STAMP

FEATHER
DUSTER

NATURAL & SYNTHETIC
SPONGES

Drawing and Layout Equipment

Charcoal. Charcoal sticks are preferable for reproducing designs for paint layouts. Charcoal is available in 6″ sticks up to ½″ in diameter. It can be used directly or inserted in the end of a short bamboo stick. The end of the stick is split by saw cuts so the charcoal can be wedged inside and held securely by a rubber washer or rubber band. Similarly, a large **compass** can be constructed so you can draw circles and arcs on scenery with charcoal sticks (Figure 10-8).

Snap Line. This is a cotton cord that is charged with charcoal or chalk to create lines on scenery to aid painting. The cord is stretched taut across the work and snapped to leave a powdered line on the scenery. A regular carpenter's chalk-line unit can be employed. This contains a metal container to hold the charcoal or chalk so the cord can

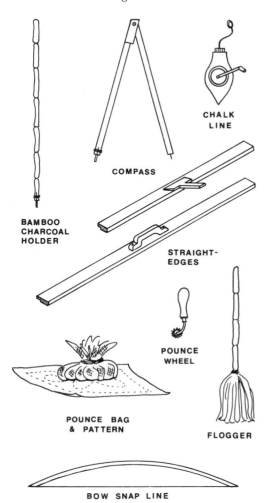

CHALK
LINE

COMPASS

BAMBOO
CHARCOAL
HOLDER

STRAIGHT-
EDGES

POUNCE
WHEEL

POUNCE BAG
& PATTERN

FLOGGER

BOW SNAP LINE

FIGURE 10–8   Drawing and layout equipment.

be retracted for recharging. Dry scene paint of the appropriate color can also be used in this container. A **bow line** is a short length of cord made taut by a bent wooden bow or stretched between two protruding ends of a narrow strip of lumber. One person can snap lines with a bow line.

Straightedges. Wooden straightedges are used to guide lining brushes in painting straight lines. Carefully selected, lightweight

lumber should be found. Lengths from 3′ to 6′ are the most convenient sizes. Edges are thoroughly sanded and beveled toward the scenery to prevent paint from running under the straightedge. Handles are attached in the center to be convenient for the painter. Warping can be prevented by a coat of varnish.

Flogger. Charcoal and chalk powders can be safely erased from scenery by a flogger. This is a stick to which narrow strips of muslin or other fabric are secured. The dusting action of a flogger prevents the powders from being rubbed into the painted surface.

Pounce Pattern. This is a design or pattern to be reproduced in paint on scenery. It is drawn out on brown kraft paper and perforated by a pounce wheel. The pattern is then transferred to the scenery by means of a pounce bag.

Pounce Wheel. Like a tracing wheel used in sewing, a pounce wheel has a wheel of sharp points. Rolled over paper placed over a soft underlayment, the points pierce a line of holes in the paper. The back of the paper is sanded lightly so the openings will be large enough.

Pounce Bag. A bag is created by several layers of cheesecloth filled with powdered charcoal or dry scene paint and tied into a bag. Rubbed lightly over a pounce pattern, the powder is forced through the holes in the paper, which reconstructs the pattern on the scenery.

Stencil. Repeated patterns and motifs can be painted directly through the use of a stencil. Stencils are usually made with oiled stencil paper that is carefully shellacked to reduce deterioration from liquids. However, plastic sheeting (polyethylene or even thin vinyls), which cannot be damaged by water, will outlast oiled stencil board. The designs are cut out with a stencil knife or a razor blade. A Cut-Awl is useful for cutting out multiple copies of a stencil at one time.

Templates. Paint applicator guides are sometimes necessary for painting certain effects. A template is created specially to assist in painting a particular pattern. It may consist of a cutout in Upson board to reproduce a border or molding detail, or two slats held apart a few inches to guide a brush in painting the illusion of raffia.

Paint-Preparation Equipment

Containers in various sizes are used to mix quantities of paint. **Plastic** and **galvanized pails** (from 1- to 3-gallon sizes) are needed for prime and base colors. Plastic containers are especially easy to clean and are light in weight. For smaller containers, empty gallon paint cans are useful, although the lip around the openings makes cleaning more difficult. Enamel buckets and pans are more durable for dyes. Large **fruit and vegetable cans** (size 10), which are available from restaurants, are ideal when mixing 2 to 3 quarts of paint and have lipless openings for easy cleaning. Plastic lids, which are sold with some canned products (such as 2-lb coffee cans) are excellent for sealing cans of prepared paint for later use (see Figure 10-9).

FIGURE 10–9 Paint preparation equipment.

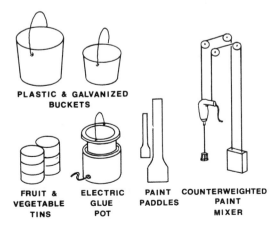

PLASTIC & GALVANIZED BUCKETS

FRUIT & VEGETABLE TINS

ELECTRIC GLUE POT

PAINT PADDLES

COUNTERWEIGHTED PAINT MIXER

A paint studio needs a number of **paint paddles** for mixing paint well. Shaped flat and broad at one end, a paddle will unify the ingredients more easily than a simple stick of wood. Electric or air-driven **paint mixers** will stir materials faster and with greater thoroughness. Commercial mixer blades that will not splash, scrape, or puncture buckets may be obtained to fit standard $\frac{1}{4}''$ drill chucks. Mechanical mixing is especially desirable for some of the contemporary plastic paints.

Paint **filters** of fine screen wire or cloth netting are necessary to strain out large particles that would not pass through sprayers. Other required items include **scrub brushes,** soap, and other cleaning aids for washing containers, paddles, and other paint preparation tools.

PREPARATION OF SURFACES FOR PAINTING

Scenery and properties for a given production may be newly constructed or pulled from stock. In either case, careful examination and preparation must be given to surfaces to be painted.

Check for Needed Repairs

All structural frames should be checked for needed replacement, and the strength and condition of reinforcing cornerblocks and keystones must be examined. Are there protruding nails, staples, or screws to cause future problems? The cloth covers on framed scenery must be replaced if the paint has begun to crack and flake off. New cloth covers on flats should be sized on the front side, and previously painted covers sized on the back side. Rips or holes in cloth should be repaired with a patch pasted on the back side. Repair loose edges of the cloth on framed scenery with paste. Are all dutchmen applied and are their edges firmly glued to the surface?

Flame Retardants

Most fire laws require that scenic materials be treated with a flame retardant. If muslin and canvas were not purchased already treated, these and other materials should be flame-treated in the shop. There is a family of flame-retardant solutions available commercially, each designed for different material (natural fabrics, synthetic fabrics, wood, etc.). The proper product must be selected to assure flame retardancy. Commercial products are preferred to shop-mixed, salt-based compounds because they are less likely to discolor the applied paint coat. Some of these products are premixed ready to use. Others are thinned with water before application. They should be applied liberally with a brush, roller, or sprayer. Many prefer to apply the flame retardant before painting or adding the compound in the size or prime coat. The coat should dry before applying other coats of paint. Some prefer to flame-treat scenery after painting by adding the flame retardant into the back paint mixture. Scrims, curtains, and drops can be immersed into the solution and stretched out to dry. An application of flame retardant only lasts a few years. Further, if curtains and draperies are washed or dry cleaned, the effectiveness of the flame retardant is considerably reduced. Testing and reapplication will be necessary.

Creating a Textured Surface

It is often desirable to provide actual three-dimensional texture to scenic pieces, to better simulate real-life materials. Many of the techniques for creating actual texture are reviewed in Chapter 9. However, some relate closely to the painting process. One technique covers the surface with heavy size, and while it is wet, sprinkles lightweight material (sawdust, ground cork, ground mica, paper confetti) over the surface. When the size dries, all of the loose bits of texturing material are lightly brushed away. Those particles held by the size provide a textured surface ready for painting.

Other techniques provide for a texturing powder in the first coat of paint. At least one of the manufacturers of premixed scenic paint (Cal-Western) has a special product for this purpose. Texture powders (coarse or smooth) are added to a special binder. This is applied and textured with a brush, a roller, a sponge, or a broom to achieve the desired surface appearance. Colored pigments may be added in the texture solution. On hard surfaces textured designs can be created by scenic paste. Paste can be prepared as a light or heavy mixture and can be sculpted on the surface with a variety of tools. Rubber latex is used in some formulas for creating textural surfaces on either soft or hard surfaces. It can be applied by squeeze bottle or with a trowel.

GENERAL PAINTING METHODS

Vertical and Horizontal Painting

The method of painting scenery laid out horizontally on the floor has had historical dominance. It requires a considerable amount of floor space and is limited to two-dimensional scenery: flats and drops. Floor painting offers several distinct advantages. First, all portions of the scene are easily accessible, and a number of painters can work on all portions simultaneously. The solidity of the floor gives rigid support for the painting of drops and other unframed fabrics.

Most of all, floor painting allows for a greater number of painting techniques that can be used. For instance, puddling and other wet-blending techniques are more difficult to apply to scenery in a vertical position because they often result in paint runs down the surface. Of course, painters walking on the scenery must be careful to keep it clean, and to avoid spilling paint or damaging the scenery. Special care must be taken with framed scenery. Stepping in the wrong places will press the fabric down around the frame. Likewise, excessive pressure with paint applicators can reveal an outline of the frame beneath the fabric. Before painting a drop, the floor of the shop must be thoroughly swept and wet mopped. Gray bogus paper or kraft paper is laid on the floor to absorb the water and paint applied on the drop. Then the drop is stretched on the paper and stapled every few inches. This must be done carefully to prevent wrinkles and an irregular shape. Guided by snapped chalk lines, staple the top of the drop first, from the middle outward, followed by the bottom edge, and, finally, the sides in the same manner. True vertical and horizontal lines must be accurately established on a drop before painting begins, to assure that the final design is positioned properly.

The vertical method of painting is best achieved with a wooden paint frame (Figure 10-10). The frame lowers into a slot in the floor to permit painters to reach easily any part of the scenery placed on the frame. Generally, the paint frame is constructed of

$2'' \times 6''$ lumber about $18'$ high or more and is wide enough for the largest drop or framed setting. Framed scenery rests on a protruding ledge at the bottom and is nailed lightly to the frame. Unframed scenery is tacked or stapled to the frame. A motor hoist controls the raising and lowering of the paint frame. This method of painting leaves the painter in a comfortable standing position on the shop floor and able to reach all portions of the scenery without ladders or platforms. It also saves considerable floor space. Furthermore, by stepping across the room from the paint frame, you can get a full view of the painted effect.

Certain wet-blending techniques of painting require more skill when scenery is in a vertical position; however, all other painting techniques are easily and completely achievable. It is an ideal position for spraying with a paint gun. Care must be taken in any form of paint application to avoid drips and runs on the scenery, but there is less danger from paint spills than with scenery in a horizontal position. An alternative to the paint frame is a series of wooden battens secured to a shop wall. Scenery can be temporarily attached to

FIGURE 10–10 The paint frame.

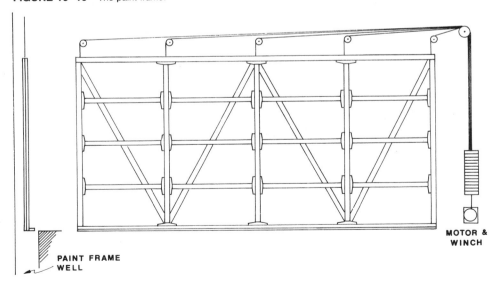

MOTOR &
WINCH

PAINT FRAME
WELL

these. However, the tops must be painted with the aid of **stepladders,** a rolling **scaffolding.** or a multileveled rolling platform called a **boomerang**.

Transferring the Design for Painting

The majority of designs to be painted can be measured on the designer's sketch and reconstructed in actual dimensions on the scenery. Similarly, small and detailed designs, especially those to be repeated, can be produced as pounce patterns for transfer. However, large, highly complicated and irregular designs, such as a street scene or a forest, require another means of transfer. **Gridding the design** for reproduction on scenery is one means of accomplishing this. This involves drawing a scaled grid of horizontal and vertical lines over the painter's elevations (Figure 10-11). A grid of 2′ is usually sufficient, but the broadness or intricacy of the design will determine the appropriate dimensions. This same grid in actual dimensions is drawn on the scenery with a charcoal

snap line. The outline of the design is then drawn on the scenery (cartooned) by reconstructing points that intersect with the lines of the grid. After painting the design, the charcoal grid is dusted off the scenery with a flogger. Sometimes stretched black thread is used to create the grid if it would be difficult to remove the charcoal. Highly detailed designs are cartooned in dye or felt pen to prevent erasure during broad lay-in painting.

Casting an image of the design onto the scenery by means of a light projector is another solution and a considerable time saver. With this transfer method, the design is cartooned (sometimes entirely painted) while the image is projected in a semidark room. Appropriate projection equipment and adequate space and distance from the scenery must be available to practice this transfer method. It functions most successfully when scenery is in a vertical position, as on a paint frame. An opaque projector or an overhead projector is the simplest equipment to use. All or part of the paint elevations can be placed in the projector for projecting on the

FIGURE 10–11   Gridding a design for transfer to a drop.

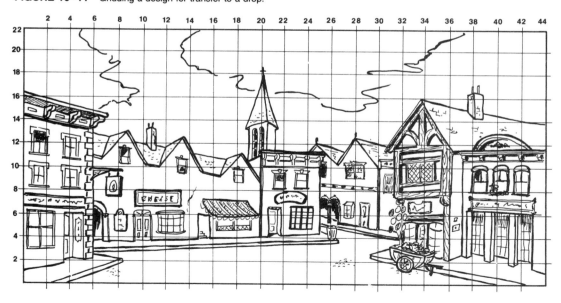

surface. A lens projector needs a special wide-angle lens system for casting large designs and also requires the preparation of the design on a slide. For designs of size, the projection method is a quick and effective way of transfer. It is also possible that a large design may be divided into sections for projection or that only the most complicated portions of an image are projected, with the rest reproduced by other means. Usually some preliminary lines should be placed on the surface to be certain the projected image is located accurately.

Application Methods

The painter is required to achieve many realistic, stylistic, and fantastic creations in paint. The effects include the simulation of substances (metal, wood, plastic), textures (plaster, raffia, foliage), and immense depth (landscapes, skies, cityscapes). In addition, these illusions may be small and highly refined for furniture or props or in vast and broad proportions for large scenic drops. Since the scenery is ultimately intended to be viewed by an audience, the painter must be aware of the location of the viewers (close to the scenery as in film, TV, and the intimate stage, or at a distance as in a large theatre). These factors result in techniques and methods that may exceed the demands of any other painting field. Permeating the catalog of techniques employed in scene painting are a variety of basic application methods including the following ones.

Wet Blending. This is the intermixing of paints in wet form while being applied to the scenery. The general purpose is to retain the individuality of a particular color while blending the edges into the adjacent colors. The intent may be to achieve a mottled effect for a rich foundation coat or the elongation or gradual fade-out of graining or veins in wood or marble. Separate brushes, textured cloth, or other tools may be used, or the blending may employ dribbles or splashes of paint or solvents on a painted area before it dries.

Shading or grading with set colors is also used to suggest rounded surfaces. Several values of the same hue are applied to achieve a smooth gradation. It is necessary to work a small area at a time with rapid strokes to blend colors while they are still moist.

When wet blending, the brush or other applicator requires special handling. The edges of painted areas must be cross blended while wet. The brush of each color can be stroked lightly into the adjacent paint area so it gradually feathers into the wet mixture. However, a separate blending brush or applicator is usually preferred to keep the brush of each mixture from intermixing with the other color. Painters must acquire the tilt and lifting strokes of the brush necessary in cross-blending wet colors. Once again, only the borders of the painted areas should be blended; the individuality of each color must be retained. If an area dries before it can be worked, it must be remoistened before blending is attempted. To avoid confusion, return each applicator to its own paint container when not in use.

Dry Blending. This is the blending of a color into another color that has already dried on the surface. Spattering, dry brushing, stippling, and spraying are a few of the techniques which can achieve dry blends. A graded color change will result if the wet color is applied with decreased density into the dried coat. For instance, a dry brush technique can feather a color into another, and spattering can fade into a color by gradually reducing the concentration of specks.

Glaze Buildups. A glaze is a thin, transparent layer of paint that alters but does not totally obliterate the previous coat of paint. It adds richness, depth, and variety to the effect. Many illusions can be created by buildups of a series of selectively applied glaze coats. This usually requires a base coat of the lightest color, with each successive glaze in a darker value. Glazes of gloss varnishes are used to create shiny or polished surfaces.

Removal of Paint. A number of techniques involve the removal of paint before it has dried on the surface. The richness of weathered or antiqued surfaces is enhanced by applying a dark glaze coat and then, while it is still wet, removing it from the raised or projecting portions of the surface by wiping lightly with a cloth. Wood graining can be achieved by the removal (or rearrangement) of paint with graining tools. In addition, sponges, cloth, wads of paper, and other materials are used to remove wet paint.

The Painting Process

The majority of scene painting effects require several applications of paint to fully complete the appropriate illusion. The number of applications depends upon the particular effect to be achieved, the nature of the material to be suggested or simulated, and the degree of reality to be achieved. In order of application, some effects may include the following painting coats:

1. Prime coat
2. Base or ground coat
3. Texturing and/or overpainting coats
4. Detail painting
5. A final glaze coat
6. Backpainting

Analyzing the Effect. To be successful in the final results, a scene painter must carefully study the design to be created on the scenery. This requires the examination of the designer's colored rendering and painter's elevations, conferences with the designer to ascertain the nature of the effect, and sometimes (in the case of the simulation of materials) the acquisition and examination of samples or photos of the particular marble or woodwork finish to be suggested. Examine total values and patterns of the sample that show highlights that catch the light, lowlights that do not, and cast shadows (the shadow cast by an object through its obstruction of the major light source). This study and preparation is essential for the painter to determine the painting techniques to be adopted, the color choices, and the painting process to be followed. The process includes the type of base coat to be applied and whether the base should be the lightest tone, the middle tone, or the darkest tone in the design. Subsequent texture and overpainting coats and specific colors are then decided.

Individuality of Painting. There are two ways individuality must be considered in the scene painting process. First, each painter is an individual; each absorbs painting procedures and techniques differently, elaborates on these fundamentals in an individual way, and develops unique skills and styles of painting. This is normal, and, assuming the painter is sufficiently competent, it generally does not prohibit his or her success in painting scenery to the specifications of the designer. Only occasionally, when there is a noticeable difference in the personal styles of two or more painters in highly detailed or advanced techniques, is it advisable to assign a given task to only one painter for the sake of consistency.

The second matter of individuality relates to the play and the production design. It would be rare if any two plays exhibited such similarity of plot, mood, and action as to necessitate identical visual environments. Furthermore, differences in interpretation and the production scheme lead to uniquely original visual expression even for two productions of the same play. The paint-by-numbers approach is just as inappropriate in scene painting as it is in any other art. There is not one, but numerous, ways of painting any given effect. In part, this relates to how realistic, suggestive, or abstract the illusion should be. The descriptions of specific techniques and formulas listed here or in other sources are only examples for the beginning painter. The individuality of each effect should be recognized, and an appropriate technique should be developed to achieve it.

SOME BASIC PAINTING TECHNIQUES

The Prime Coat

The prime coat, or priming, is the first and necessary undercoating for paint. The scenic pieces assembled for a setting frequently consist of a variety of substances and textures: canvas, muslin, plywood, lumber, metal, composition boards, and more. Some of the pieces may be of new materials, and others may have been taken from stock, resulting in a greater variety of textures and colors. It is the purpose of the prime coat to *reduce the porosity* of the varying surfaces and make them *more uniform*. Sometimes sizing and priming may be combined in one coat on a newly covered flat to simultaneously fill up the fabric and pull it tight across the frame. However, the painter should watch for any difference in texture between new fabric and previously painted fabric. A second prime coat may be necessary to increase textural uniformity.

Many painters prefer to prime with inexpensive pigments such as dry scene paint and glue size. The color may be white, a color close to the color of the base coat, or a tint of the base color. New lumber and plywood are sometimes primed in tinted shellac to seal the porous surface. A translucent muslin drop is usually primed in liquid starch, which gives it a transparent coating while filling the fabric appropriately. The prime coat can be applied in a rapid and even manner by a spray gun or a large priming brush with a cross-hatch brush action.

The Base or Ground Coat

The base coat is frequently the final coat to cover the entire surface of the scenery.

Texturing or overpainting coats may cover only portions of the surface. The base provides the background quality or foundation for the development of the completed effect.

Flat Base. A flat base coat is often desired when the total effect is a relatively smooth, flat, or posteresque surface. Applied by brush or sprayer in the manner of priming, an even application is the goal to be achieved.

Shaded Base. This is a two-color wet-blended base coat. It is used to show the variation of tones on a surface that should not appear to be freshly painted. Many locales should seem aged, faded, weathered, or viewed as lighted in a particular manner. Particularly effective for light-colored interiors, a shaded base accentuates the shadowing in the corners of a wall. In architectural paneling it increases the illusion of the recessed field of a panel. The middle of the panel or wall is painted the standard base color which is then blended into a slightly darker tone toward the outer edges (Figure 10-12).

Variegated Base. This base coat wet blends four colors together in a multicolored undertone (Figure 10-12). It can provide the foundation for the depth and variety of coloration found in shrubbery, foliage, a brick wall; the antiquated and weathered appearance of wood, plaster, or stone; or the rich variation of colors needed for a stylized or decorative treatment of a scene. Depending upon the effect to be achieved, the colors are usually related either in hue or in value. The pattern or shape of the pools of paint is determined by the effect desired. A plank fence, for instance, would have long, narrow pools extending in the direction of the planks.

Puddling. This technique is recommended as a base for extremely coarse effects with extreme variation of color, depth, and texture. It might serve as a foundation for a charred wall, shrubbery, or highly ab-

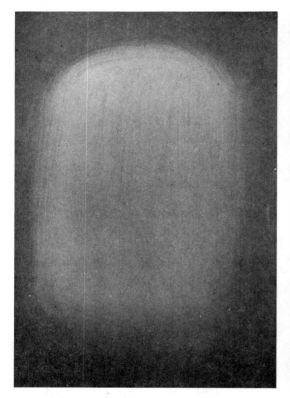 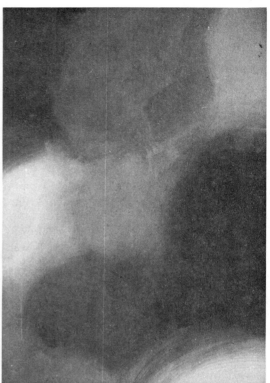

FIGURE 10–12 Base coats. A two-color shaded base (left), as might be used for a recessed panel, and a four-colored variegated base (right).

stract design. Three or four different paint colors are prepared. The scenery must be placed flat on the floor. Brushes are dipped into the paint and allowed to drip on the scenery. While the paint is wet, a straw broom or other applicator is used to lightly sweep the paint into patterns. Excessive sweeping must be avoided as this will only create a single composite color of the individual pigments.

Texturing and Overpainting Coats

Texturing and overpainting techniques are applied over the base coat of paint to provide a pattern, a dimension, or textural variety to the painted effect. They usually cover only portions of the total surface, allowing a large proportion of the base coat to be seen. Sometimes, within the unique pattern variation of each technique, an evenness of application across the area covered is desired. But often an uneven or random texture distribution is preferred. Considerable skill is required to execute successfully some of these techniques. It is advisable for a beginner to develop his or her ability in performing them. Experienced scene painters test and experiment with texturing on practice surfaces before applying them to the setting. The paint must often be of a specific consistency to be applied properly and of precise color value for effective contrast to the base coat. Applicators must function well before the desired effect can be achieved.

Many texturing techniques are a one-time application only and cannot be repainted. If they are improperly applied, the total effect is ruined and it is necessary to begin again with the application of a new base coat. There are many different kinds of texturing. A specific effect may require the invention of a new texturing method, a new kind of applicator, or a template. A combination of two or more techniques may be desired to produce a specific illusion. These techniques may be used only to suggest the reality of materials and scenes of life or to closely simulate them, or they may serve merely as interesting enrichments to the scenery.

It should be emphasized that within any listed formula for creating an effect, there is tremendous variety of emotional and stylistic qualities possible. As an example, wood graining can be made to appear harsh, dry, fluid, highly pronounced, gnarled, subtle, or playful. It is essential to determine the quality of effect that would be most visually appropriate for the particular play and the design style of the production. A listing of some common techniques follows. Effects which can be created by these techniques are suggested for illustrative purposes only. There is no rigid set of techniques for the creation of any specific effect. A few textures are illustrated in Figure 10-13.

Stenciling. Stenciling is used often for wallpaper pattern effects or whenever a specific pattern or ornamentation is to be repeated. Usually, patterns are connected in some way to give an overall effect rather than a pronounced visual emphasis upon the isolated patterns. Frequently, several colors are used in stenciled effects. In this case, each color normally requires a different stencil. A stencil is cut from a sheet of polyethylene plastic or heavy oil board (sometimes called stencil paper) shellacked to reduce damage from water soaking. It is stapled to a wooden frame for easy handling.

Special marks on the stencil are used to align the pattern to chalk lines placed on the scenery and to properly place adjoining patterns. The paint is applied by a light daubing with the brush. Spattering, sponging, dry brushing, or spraying may be used for a more subtle effect. After you wipe excess paint from the stencil, you can move it to the next location.

Stippling. This technique can produce a subtle or a relatively coarse texture. It is accomplished by touching the tips of a brush or feather duster to the scenery in an in-and-out motion. The applicator is dipped into the paint, the excess drips of paint are removed lightly on the edge of the container and the paint is applied in a daubing manner. The brush or duster is turned frequently to provide varying patterns. It is often advisable to stipple on two or more colors depending on the effect wanted. Other types of applicators may be used for variations in texture. As with other texturing techniques, the application may be either uniform or selectively uneven. It creates a decorative texture or can be used in the development of simulated objects such as shrubbery or foliage.

Dry Brushing. Dry brushing is effective in providing an unusual texture, in blending one painted area into another, or in creating the impression of particular substances such as wood grain, tree bark, brick, stone, and woven tapestries. Paint is usually applied by a brush with bristles that tend to bunch together or by a graining brush. The clustering of the bristles may be enhanced by cotton string passing through the bristles and tied around the brush handle. The technique creates a series of parallel lines with each brush stroke. The brush is charged with paint and the tips of the bristles lightly touch the surface. Great care and skill are necessary because dry brushing cannot be reworked. A practice surface should be available to test the brush before applying it to the scenery. When it is used for long

DRY BRUSHING

RAGGING

ROLLING

SPONGING

FIGURE 10–13 Each texturing technique has a unique quality and potential.

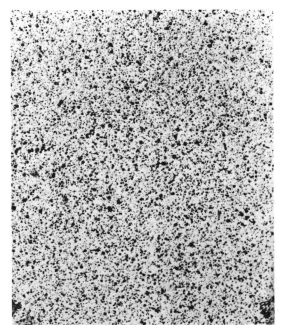

SPATTERING

STAMPING

STENCILING

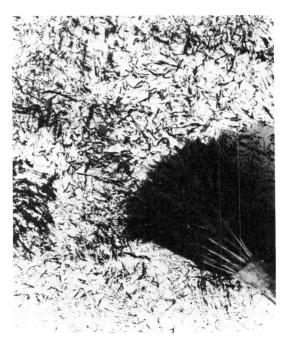

FIGURE 10–13 *continued*

continuous strokes, this technique is sometimes called **dragging** or **combing**. When authenticity is desired in duplicating the appearance of substances, the actual patterns of textures (such as wood graining) should be carefully studied. Alternately dry brushing top-to-bottom and left-to-right may be the effect needed for a tapestry or a woven material. Sometimes more than one color is appropriate. In wood graining, for instance, a dark color is often applied first in long strokes the length of the simulated board or wood surface. Then a lighter color is applied following the same pattern. Effective manipulation of the brush can duplicate many graining patterns. Tilting the brush slightly will leave a space for the later addition of a knothole.

Sponging. Sponge texturing is a standard method for creating interesting surface qualities. The technique capitalizes on the uneven surface and porosity of sponges. The best ones for scene painting are the large natural and synthetic sponges. A pattern in paint is transmitted to scenery by pressing the sponge to the surface in a flat or slightly rolling motion. As with all pressure texturing, care must be taken to avoid loosening the cloth cover on framed scenery or revealing in paint the outlines of the frame on the cloth surface. Usually the sponge impressions should overlap when seeking an overall textured effect to prevent the isolation and recognition of individual impressions. Applying the sponge in different positions coupled with varying amounts and direction of pressure can provide infinite variety. The sponge may be dipped partially into a shallow container of paint or may be completely immersed if the excess paint is squeezed out before application. The rectangular, sharp-edged impressions of large, synthetic sponges are useful in creating brick effects.

Stamping. Like sponges, paint stamps leave a textured impression when lightly pressed to a surface. Stamps are specially cut designs made of foam rubber or flexible plastic foam. The fineness of the texture of foam creates a nearly solid imprint of the design with a moderate amount of pressure, or the barest suggestion of the pattern with light pressure. The painter uses this to good advantage to gain variety in painting repeated impressions. Subtle tilting of the stamp varies the density within a single impression. Stamps may be made to paint repeated patterns in decorative tile, carpeting, or wallpaper. With an overlapping and clustering of impressions, stamping can produce a grove of trees, or boughs of leaves, or foliage. In these cases, several different colors of paint are usually necessary. The stamps can be dipped into a shallow pan of paint or into puddles of paint poured on a flat, nonabsorbent surface.

Rolling. While standard paint rollers are valuable for painting flat, even coats, they also have special use for texture and overpainting techniques. Variations in texture are achieved by the width of the roller, the thickness or type of roller cover, the amount of paint in the roller, the amount of pressure applied, the tilt of the roller, and the length of the strokes that are used. Unusual shapes, patterns, and jagged painted effects are possible. In addition, cotton rope or other materials may be wound around the roller for interlaced swirl effects, or wire, string, or coarse netting used to tie back portions of the cover material for another type of effect. Commercial pattern rollers are useful for creating final decorative patterns (as in wallpaper) or as foundation texture for a different final treatment. Shop-made rollers of cut or sculpted foam allow the painter to create an original roller pattern.

Ragging. Fabric has proven to be an effective applicator of paint. The most convenient size is a square of cloth 2′ or 3′ on each side. The edges are frayed to leave a fringe on all sides. Coarse or textured fabric such as burlap, monk's cloth, or terry cloth provide the most interesting effects. There are at least two ways to use fabric as a paint applicator. One method is to form the fabric into a roll, particularly with the fringe edges on the outside. The fabric is saturated in paint and the excess wrung out by hand. It is rolled onto the scenery with frequent changes in direction. The second technique uses the piece of fabric in an open, unrolled manner. The cloth is dropped on the scenery; the painted impression constantly changes with the manner and direction of the fall. The first few falls should be very lightly executed since the cloth is heavily charged with paint. Generally, the impressions should be overlapped for a consistent overall texture. Scenery in a vertical position can be ragged in this manner by pressing or swinging the fabric onto the surface, although it is more difficult to vary the painted impressions. The resultant texture is a composite of the raised nubs of the weave and the folds of the cloth.

Spattering. This is a texture technique capable of serving many purposes. It can provide a smooth, rich texture to break up an otherwise flat color or surface. It can shade or shadow portions of a setting (dry blending) with a single color or, by cross-spattering, with two colors. It can be used to correct, tone down, or change a hue slightly. It can suggest or simulate textures of substances such as plaster and stone. These are only a few of the services this versatile technique can provide.

Spattering is generally applied with a lay-in brush or a tank sprayer. Considerable brush skill is necessary in creating a spatter and in controlling the directional fall of paint. Only a small amount of paint is needed. The brush is dipped into the paint and the excess is removed. Spattering is achieved by hitting the ferrule of the brush gently against the heel of the thumb. Small specks of paint will fly from the brush onto the scenery. After several strokes, as the load of paint decreases, the brush may be struck harder. A newly charged brush should be tested on a sample surface to avoid large spots or possible runs caused by an overloaded brush. The scenery may be either in a vertical or a horizontal position. In either case, the brush should be 3' to 4' from the surface. The hand and brush must be *constantly moving* while spattering to prevent too many specks in one area. Clusters of dots at a distance may be seen as a shape or pattern. It is important to attain the type of distribution desired (an overall even application, a gradual blending out of dot density, or whatever the design requires). Practice is necessary to take aim and cover a specific area with relative accuracy. Be certain the density is appropriate along the edges of the scenery. Normally, spatters of two colors are necessary for most effects. In the simplest color scheme, this might be one shade lighter and one shade darker than the base coat. Sometimes coarse spatter—**splashes** and **dribbles**—is desired.

Glazing. Glazing is an overpainting process using a thin transparent color over other coats of paint. A glaze can cover the entire surface or be selectively placed. Glazing alters the tone already on the surface. Among other things, it can enrich or tone down painted effects, act as a blender of colors, aid in enhancing illusion through multiple layers of color, provide an antique appearance, become the final coat for finished woodwork or polished marble, or produce cast shadow effects. Most often a glaze is a darker tone applied over a lighter color. Several colors may be used in building the effect desired. As an antiquing medium, some of the glaze is removed with a wad of fabric or other material, retaining the color in recesses and low relief. Nearly any paint material can be used for glazing; however, aniline dyes and vinyls do not need an additional binder when thinned. Shellac and gloss finishes are particularly useful for polished surfaces.

Detail Painting

Lining. Lining is the process of painting narrow lines of various widths with a straight edge to guide the brush accurately. The most common effects created by lining are architectural paneling and moldings. These are accomplished by lining with the highlight, shade, and shadow lines. First, it is essential to study the style of architectural trim carefully to determine the correct way of representing it in paint. A cross-section view should be analyzed. The effect of light on the molding should be reviewed to assist in color mixing. The width of the lines and the placement of hard cutting edges and blended edges (on curves) must be determined.

Second, the location of the light source in the setting needs to be identified. Highlight is a shade lighter than the base color by the addition of white or yellow. Shade is correspondingly darker than the base. Shadow is a transparent glaze darker than the shade color and thinned with water. These colors must be mixed carefully and tested before the painting begins. Lining requires the utmost in skill to keep the lines uniform in width and parallel throughout the work. The straightedge is held firmly in one hand while a detail brush of the proper size is drawn along the edge lightly in long, even strokes. Gripping the end of the brush handle provides the best control of the brush. The brush must be in the best condition with bristles that maintain their shape in order to cut shape edges and accurate mitered corners.

Straightedge lining is also necessary for other line painting such as the overlaps in clapboard siding and mortar between rows of brick or cut stone. Line accuracy is still essential in most of these situations, but some variations may be appropriate for the purpose of reality or the nature of the substance. For instance, a broken line may best reveal the weathering of two tightfitting stones. Brick lining may include the mortar color in relief and the slight projection of the bricks. Templates are often used in place of the usual straightedge to guide the brush for special detail work. Figure 10-14 reveals some examples of detail painting.

Freehand Modeling. Several kinds of details require freehand painting without the help of aids to guide the brush strokes. Some are flat designs, but many must appear as three-dimensional elements. Projected ornaments, bas relief, and incised designs are common in this latter group. After the base coat has been laid in, the designs are realized through the application of highlight, shade, and shadow. The same considerations of light direction and color mixing discussed for lining must be followed. For the development of these detailed designs, it is essential that they have been drawn or pounced with considerable accuracy. Uniformity is sometimes improved if identical elements in repeated designs (all upper left highlights, for example) are painted at one time rather than changing colors or completing an entire design. Freehand painting requires the greatest brush control.

Back Painting

The back side of drops and flats must be painted if opacity is a necessity. Lights behind the scenery that can shine through the fabric make this essential. Sometimes back painting includes painting a thin layer of paint or dye on the back side of a translucent drop for projection through to the front side. (This effect is described in Chapter 8.) While most fabric used in scenery should already be treated with a flame retardant, lumber and plywood are usually not. Back painting with flame retardant in the paint is a desired precaution on the exposed wood of framed scenery and weight-bearing structures.

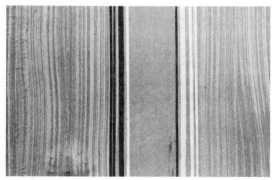

FIGURE 10–14 Detail painting showing straightedge lining for creating molding and the illusion of raffia aided by a template to guide the brush strokes.

SOME STANDARD ILLUSIONS

Not only is it impossible to present all methods of painting a specific illusion, it is presumptuous to identify any particular method as the most acceptable. There are many degrees of representation, from photographic realism to the simplest suggestion. Further, artistic individuality inspires endless stylizations and abstractions in decor. Scenic artists develop their own techniques of painting effects. The painter is bound only by the designer's intent and his or her own personal skills and abilities. Nevertheless, examples of painting methods can be useful for those who are developing abilities in scene painting. For this purpose, a few standard methods and general approaches to painting are presented here. It would be helpful for the beginner to study the conceptual process of building an illusion and to practice the various techniques to gain skills in painting. See Figure 10-15 for some examples of painting illusions.

Bricks

The painter needs to study bricks before attempting to create them in paint. Bricks may be smooth or rough textured; they may be glazed or flat in finish; they may be sharp-edged or old and rounded. Even within a single type and color of brick, there is a range of different tones and textures. The bricklaying pattern and type of mortar joints must also be determined.

One approach uses the mortar color as the base coat:

1. **Base coat.** Apply a flat base coat of the mortar color. Let it dry.
2. **Texturing.** Spatter a dark mortar color over the base coat with a slightly uneven distribution to suggest the roughness of mortar. A brick stencil is placed on the surface and the brick lay-in color is applied by spatter and dribble, tank sprayer, sponge, or roller. Varia-

BRICK

BRICK

WALLPAPER

TREES & FOLIAGE

FIGURE 10–15 Some painted effects.

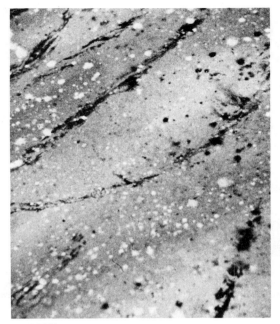

MARBLE

WOOD GRAINING

WOOD GRAINING

WOOD GRAINING

FIGURE 10–15 *continued*

tion of effects is desired. After this coat dries, some bricks may be treated with a dark glaze applied by a sponge, by a roller, or by a dry-brush technique. When this is dry, a light color is spattered through the stencil for further texture.

3. *Detailing.* Highlights and shadows are applied to the projecting bricks. Uneven and broken lines are used for old or round-edged bricks.

Landscapes and Cityscapes

Painted landscapes, cityscapes, and architectural scenes are among the most complicated tasks for scenic artists. They are frequently large and scaled in great depth, with many detailed objects. Thorough preparation is necessary before actual painting begins. Painting procedures and specific techniques must be selected for developing each object. In the designer's sketch, the direction and play of light on objects in the scene must be carefully studied. Further, analyze how color and scale help to differentiate between objects in the distance, middle ground, and foreground.

If a drop is to be painted, the cloth must be stretched on the floor or on a paint frame and stapled on all sides. it is then primed with paint, starch, or dye with a starch binder (starch is especially necessary for translucencies). The drop must be gridded and the design transferred, with all areas outlined in felt-tip pen.

The most distant background objects are painted first. The painter then works forward in distance, creating the foreground last. In preparing the paints to lay-in and model objects, color values must be determined and tested. Distant areas are often grayer in color, with more vivid tones reserved for foreground objects. Cool colors tend to recede and warm colors project forward. Sky is often the most distant background for a landscape. Generally, a sky should be highly blended. A dye coat is especially effective for long washes of color. Its long drying time is appropriate for wet blending. Paint may be applied by tank sprayers, with brushes or sponges used for overblending. Paint applied by a compressor spray gun can provide a dry-blended sky. Clouds must frequently be three-dimensional masses, and so require several colors. It is usually best to work from the darkest areas to the lightest areas.

In working forward in distance, the base coat of each object or area is usually a middle tone with lights and shades applied later. Care should be taken to achieve appropriate contrast and gradations of color. Generally, you should begin at the top of the drop and work downward. If the scenery is hung on a paint frame, drips of paint will not spoil the painted effects. Cast shadow, highlights, and architectural details complete the painting.

Marble

At hand should be the designer's rendering of marble or an actual sample or photograph to help in planning the painting process. There are many different types of marble, each with unique characteristics. Some have a pebble quality, some have a soft-blended quality, and others appear sharp and jagged. The painter must study the characteristics and coloring to be created with the awareness that there is infinite variety. The colors in marble are usually closely related in hue, but the final mottled appearance is usually a mixture of soft blending and sharp contrast within the given pattern. Awareness of this pattern and the direction and flow of the veining is important.

The process of painting marble is often achieved in the steps that follow. The type of marble to be created will suggest appropriate applicators and working techniques.

1. *Base coat.* Apply a base coat of the general tone of the marble. Apply smoothly and allow to dry. Later glaze coats and/or wet blending

often benefits by a hard and nonabsorbent base. Therefore, some painters prefer to apply two or more coats of a gloss finish paint, such as a gloss vinyl, or to cover a flat base with coats of thinned shellac or clear gloss vinyl.

2. ***Texturing.*** To achieve the mottled quality and veining, texturing can be accomplished in one of the following ways. It is usually necessary to work a small area at a time since the desired effect occurs while the pigment is still wet.

Wet blending. Clear water or lightly tinted water is sprinkled and dribbled onto the dried base coat. On this wet surface, darker tones suggesting the texture or veins of marble are applied allowing some spreading and blending to occur. Areas of excess water can be removed if spreading is too extensive, or more water can be sprinkled on where blending is not sufficient. Allow to dry. The process is repeated for the lighter (white is common) texture tones.

Glazing. Texturing also can be achieved by application of several transparent glazes. Several tones are usually necessary. The glazes are overlapped to build up the effect. Blending will occur where paints are wet, and intensities will increase by successive layering of glaze coats. After drying, further applications will create added depth. A light spatter of water here and there will add further to the texture.

In either approach, the paint can be applied by light, twisting strokes of a brush, light daubing of a sponge, or gentle turns and twists of a small roller. A sponge or soft wads of cheesecloth can be used to blot and remove paint and water. Blending can be enhanced by light strokes, or a badger blender, or stippling with a brush, sponge, or cloth. The painter should seek particular ways of achieving the unique fossil shapes and other markings in marble.

3. ***Detailing.*** After the texture has dried, some detail painting may be necessary to give greater depth or to reinforce light and dark tones. Hairline veins can be achieved with a feather, a fine brush, or a cord trailed lightly over the surface. For the polish of marble, give the surface a **final glaze** of dye, thinned shellac, clear gloss vinyl, or clear gloss vinyl tinted with dye.

Stones

There is enormous variety in stone, stonecutting, and stone-laying methods. The particular stone effect to be painted must be studied and a painting procedure worked out.

1. ***Base coat.*** Some painters may prefer to lay in the mortar areas before the stone work. However, it is usually easier to reserve the mortar for detail painting. Most stone effects benefit from a variegated base coat. Three or four colors may be wet blended either generally across the surface or within the boundaries of each individual stone. On rare occasions a flat base may be adequate for smooth-cut stone. Another variation is to prepare several closely related colors and paint the individual stones different flat base tones.

2. ***Texturing.*** Spattering in two colors is often appropriate for smooth-surfaced cut stone. For rounded fieldstone, rough stone blocks, or other types of stone, a coarser texture is more suitable. Sponging, stippling, splashes of paint, or ragging are all effective. Several colors are needed and should be applied to give three-dimensional modeling to each stone.

3. ***Detailing.*** Mortar lines should be painted unless they were laid in at the beginning. The stones should be given highlights and shadows. Other details may include cracks in the stone or other imperfections or unique features.

Trees and Foliage

Trees, shrubs, and foliage are among the most difficult objects to capture in paint owing to the enormous depth and infinite variety of color and pattern they exhibit. Frequently, the best that can be achieved is a reasonable suggestion or stylization. The painter needs an ample amount of source material for reference on types of trees and shrubbery and ways they have been painted. Above all, the painter must know what the designer wants. Before painting the tree,

FIGURE 10–16 **Opera Scenery.** A scene from *Don Carlos* at the Bavarian State Opera National Theatre, Munich, Germany. Scenic and costume designer: Rudolf Heinrich. (Photo by Alexander F. Adducci)

branches and foliage areas must be sketched out in charcoal. It must be drawn and conceived in depth with established foreground, middle ground, and background areas well defined. Foliage is best seen as clusters or patches of leaves at these various depths. Generally, the foreground is lightest in color, progressing into increasingly darker tones in the middle ground and background areas. An exception to this may occur if a well-lit clearing is to be suggested beyond the trees. Trees are best painted with a free and flexible, even casual, manner and without excessive brush strokes. The tree and foliage effect is greatly enhanced if we see through the branches and leaves frequently. This is achieved by showing portions of sky between the foliage on a drop, or by cutting out lace-like openings near the lower edge of a foliage border.

1. *Base coat.* Area colors should be laid-in starting with the most distance and moving to areas in the foreground. Generally, the color should be the middle value of the area. In the simplest order, this would be painting (1) the foliage clusters in the background, (2) the tree trunk and limbs, (3) the middle-ground foliage areas, and (4) the foreground foliage. While these are essentially flat coats of paint, any short, choppy, and overlapping strokes may help give it an uneven quality.

2. *Texturing.* The modeling of each foliage area, the shape of the tree trunk and limbs, is performed with strategic texturing. As in painting

the lay-in colors, you must begin with the background areas and work toward the foreground. This makes it possible for each successive area to overlap the previously painted areas and therefore appear nearer in distance. It is essential that the texture coats are applied very sparingly and selectively. They should be treated more as accents. Excessive texturing may destroy the depth and variety of the painted area. The dark tones should be applied first, followed by a frugal use of highlights. The direction of the light source gives insight to the placement of colors.

Foliage areas. Each color area of foliage must be textured with two colors: a dark tone or shaded portion of the foliage and a highlight tone where leaf clusters catch the light. Specific techniques for texturing foliage rely partially on the shape and clustering of the leaves (or needles) of the particular tree or shrubbery painted. Short daub-like brush strokes or a stippling brush may be appropriate. Specially constructed stamps are excellent for many foliage effects. A sponge or a feather duster is effective for small leaf plants. Leaf impressions must be applied with extensive variety and must be unevenly distributed to resemble natural leaf clusters. Some painters spatter/splash occasionally while painting foliage to intensify the texture of the surface.

Trunk and branches. These are modeled with a light and dark tone of the base color according to the location of the light source and the nature of the bark on the tree. An appropriate technique should be selected for this effect.

3. ***Detailing.*** Detail painting is usually limited to touches of highlights here and there caused by leaves which directly face the light source. Sometimes blossoms or flowers are required. Small detail brushes can be used for these.

Wallpaper

Effective wallpaper is not as easy to achieve by paint as it may first seem. Inadequate creations are frequently oversimplifications through use of limited texture techniques and very few coats of paint. An otherwise richly decorative wallpaper is reduced to a flat, excessively bold-patterned surface, a caricature of real life wall coverings. Worst of all is a painted wallpaper seen more as rows of identical and prominent motifs than as a whole, unified, richly textured surface. Obviously, careful planning is needed before painting begins.

Although it is not necessary to have in hand an actual sample to be duplicated, it is essential to follow the designer's rendering and intent and to know something about wallpaper. Some knowledge of wallpaper can be achieved by acquiring sample books from suppliers, especially discontinued wallpaper patterns. There is a wide range of wallpaper varying in patterns, textures, and finishes. Each is unique and will lead the painter to appropriate painting procedures. The following painting steps are suitable for general patterned wallpaper.

1. ***Base coat.*** The mottled background for wallpaper can be achieved with a variegated base. An alternative is an overall texture coat on top of the base which is applied before the stencil pattern. This texture may be created by long dry-brushing strokes, by a patterned roller, by spattering, or by a spatter/splash technique while the base is being wet blended.

2. ***Texturing.*** The first texturing coat is discussed above in relation to the base coat in providing an unusual background for wallpaper. The next step is reproducing the wallpaper pattern or motif. This is most often accomplished by a stencil process. The pattern effect is more interesting if it is painted in two or more colors, either for different parts of the pattern or one color partially over the other to enrich or give depth to the tone. Further, the stencil pattern can often be enhanced by painting it with a texture technique rather than with a solid coat of paint. Sponging, spattering, light spraying, dry brushing, and stippling can be successfully used with the stencil. A stamp or a patterned roller might sometimes replace the stencil method of reproducing wallpaper motifs; however, they are not as easy to align with accuracy as a stencil. Should a woven or tapestry effect be desired, a final texture coat by dry brushing can suggest threadlike lines over the entire surface.

3. *Detailing.* Any detail coats may be limited to the creation of lines that the wallpaper might require. A dye or thin paint glaze may enhance the total effect.

Wood Graining

Wood graining is used to re-create the finest interior woodwork and furniture woods as well as the roughest exterior wood surfaces. This represents an enormous range of effects and requires a variety of paint techniques and skills. The painter must learn the types of graining and texture patterns found in different woods. A clear plan precedes actual painting. Further, the appropriate direction of grain in various portions of paneling must be determined. The rest is skill in painting for the particular style required for the production, and this comes only with practice and experience.

Highly authentic wood graining is achievable with paint glazes. Because water paints (especially acrylic, latex, and vinyls) dry very rapidly, the painter must work the wet glazes very rapidly to create the appropriate graining effect.

1. *Base coat.* Using gloss vinyl for a hard surface, a two-color wet-blended base coat is applied. The colors are the lighter tones of the wood. The wet-blending patterns follow the direction of the grain. Lines between the boards are located and inked.
2. *Texturing.* A dark graining color is thinned to a nearly transparent glaze. For the most realistic effect, different texture techniques should be used for the different types of grain effects in wood. These include **straight grain,** which is the parallel grain lines running the length of lumber, **heart or cut grain,** which is the jagged, V-shaped and oval-shaped grain patterns, and the **short, broken grain** or specklelike pores in wood. The heart grain is applied with a detail brush, using the brush edge for painting the thin portion of the grain and the width of the brush to create the thick bends in the grain. While the graining is still wet, a badger blender or a whisk broom is used to feather blend the thick portions of the grain. Straight graining is applied with a graining brush or a brush with clustered bristles. The broken grain is achieved by a light spatter, and while wet, quick elongation of the speckles with a whisk broom, a badger blender, or a graining comb.
3. *Detailing.* Knotholes and the lining between individual boards are achieved in the usual manner. A final glaze of clear gloss vinyl would complete the effect of polished woodwork.

COLOR MIXING

To mix paint successfully, we must acquire an understanding of the phenomena of color and, through practice, develop skills of mixing pigments and dyes. Knowledge of the characteristics of color—its physical and psychological aspects, color theories, and color harmonies—is essential for scenic artists. A few basic concepts provide a foundation for color mixing.

Attributes of Color

Hue: Hue is the attribute that identifies and describes colors. There are thousands of hues with recognizable names, such as purple, chocolate, auburn, lilac, navy, rose, old gold, and beige.

Value: Value refers to the lightness or darkness of a color. White added to colors produces *tints* that are high in value. Darkened hues, called *shades,* are low in value.

Saturation: Saturation is the brilliance or purity of "chroma" in the color. A highly saturated color is undiluted. But when white, black, or other hues are added to a color, it becomes less saturated.

Subtractive and Additive Color Mixing

Scenery is colored with paints and dyes. Mixing paints is the **subtractive color–mixing** process. When colored pigments are mixed together, certain color wavelengths are blocked out; hence the term *subtractive mixing.* When true pigment primaries (red, blue, and yellow) are mixed together in equal portions they create black or dark gray. Dyes, inks, and color filters behave in the same way. On the other hand, **additive color–mixing** is the process that produces colored light. Just as pure white light can be dispersed (by a prism) into a rainbow spectrum of colors, the reverse is possible. The light primaries (red, blue, and green), when combined, "add" together to produce white light. Likewise, these three hues in various proportions can form intermediate hues on the color wheel. With scenery, we deal with a combination of colored surfaces and colored light. Known as **selective absorption**, a colored surface will **absorb** (subtract) certain wavelengths of color and **reflect** others. Thus, when a white light is cast on a blue wall, the green, yellow, red, orange, and violet rays in the spectrum will be absorbed and the blue rays reflected. Since most scenic paints are a mixture of hues, it is essential to understand the specific color components of both the light and the surface pigment and what will happen in the mixing process.

Color Theory

Various systems have been developed to communicate color identification and to explain the relationship of hue, value, and saturation. The **Munsell Color System** and the **Ostwald Color System** are two of these methods of color specification. Each is different but each adds to our understanding of color. Their explanations of color relationships are visually represented in diagrams or geometric forms.

The color wheel, representing the color spectrum in a circular form as a continuum of hues, is one of the most basic diagrams. The simplest wheel reveals the **hue families** of the primary and secondary colors of pigment (Figure 10-17). Red, blue, and yellow are the primary colors of the subtractive mixing process. They are separated on the wheel by the secondary colors: orange, violet, and green.

The color wheel illustrates color relation-

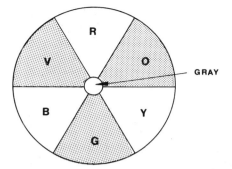

FIGURE 10–17 The color wheel showing the hue families of the primary and secondary colors of pigment.

ships and some of the phenomena of color mixing. The center or hub of the wheel is gray. Within each hue family, hues on the periphery of the circle are the most saturated; those near the gray hub are the most unsaturated. In the red hue family, firewagon red would be very saturated and such hues as brick and rose would be less saturated. Different hues are obtained by intermixing pigments. Mixing complementary colors (opposites on the color wheel) will create a less saturated hue in a hue family and mixed in equal proportions will create gray, a tone devoid of either color. Mixing adjacent colors will produce related hues or tertiary colors (Example: blue and violet mixed to obtain blue-violet or plum). Mixing together pigments that are too far apart on the color wheel will produce very unsaturated hues. For instance, a reddish-violet mixed with a greenish-blue will create a "muddy" or very low saturated blue-violet.

When the wheel is viewed as the center of two cones, a three-dimensional visualization of the interaction of hue, value, and saturation is seen (Figure 10-18). The gray hub is the center of an axis ranging from white at the top to black at the bottom. Each three-dimensional double wedge includes all the hues of that hue family. When white is added to a hue, the color is raised in value (becoming a tint) and it is reduced in saturation (drawn nearer to the gray axis). When

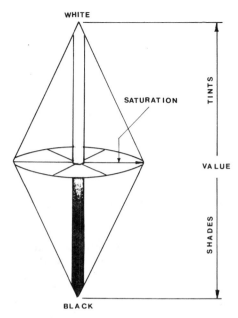

WHITE

SATURATION

TINTS

VALUE

SHADES

BLACK

FIGURE 10-18 Color diagram showing the relationship of hue, value, and saturation in color mixing.

black is added, the hue is lowered in value (becoming a shade) and it is reduced in saturation. A pigment can never become more saturated than in its original form.

The Paint Palette

Unfortunately, the color diagram describes the action of theoretically pure hues. While some pigments may approximate the primary and secondary colors, they are not exact. It is important to evaluate each pigment to note its particular composition before attempting to mix particular hues and intensities. For example, ultramarine blue is a reddish-blue and Italian blue is a greenish-blue. Thus, it is necessary to stock pigments that are close as possible to the primary and secondary colors, plus several variations of the six colors. Only then can the vast range of hues be obtained. Earth colors (yellow ocher, raw sienna, burnt sienna, raw umber, burnt umber, and brown) are necessary supplemental pigments in the scenic artist's pal-

ette. In addition to their use in creating wood and landscape colors, they are invaluable in modifying tints and creating deep tones.

With a good palette, a person, with experience, can create thousands of hues and shades. Paint mixtures can be lightened with white, brightened with yellow, warmed with red, cooled with the addition of blue, and dulled or neutralized with its complementary color. Use black sparingly in neutralizing colors since it darkens and reduces the chroma of pigments very rapidly. White paint often contains some blue that can alter tints inappropriately. First, mix a small quantity of paint, noting the exact proportions, before preparing the paint for a large job. Colors can be matched by placing samples on a piece of white paper for comparison during the mixing process. In mixing, start with the lighter tones and add the darker ones. This prevents preparing a greater quantity of paint than is needed for the task.

SELECTED READINGS

ASHWORTH, BRADFORD, *Notes on Scene Painting.* New Haven, Conn.: Whitlocks, Inc., 1952.

BOWMAN NED A., *Handbook of Technical Practice for the Performing Arts.* Wilkinsburg, Penn.: Scenographic Media, 1972.

BURRIS-MEYER, HAROLD, and EDWARD C. COLE, *Scenery for the Theatre* (rev. ed.). Boston: Little, Brown, 1971.

COLLINS, JOHN, *The Art of Scene Painting.* London: Harrap, 1985.

O'NEIL, ISABEL, *The Art of the Painted Finish for Furniture and Decoration.* New York: Morrow, 1971.

PECKTAL, LYNN, *Designing and Painting for the Theatre.* New York: Holt, Rinehart and Winston, 1975.

PINNEL, WILLIAM H., *Theatrical Scene Painting: A Lesson Guide.* Carbondale and Edwardsville: Southern Illinois University Press, 1987.

VEANER, DANIEL, *Scene Painting: Tools and Materials.* Englewood Cliffs, NJ: Prentice Hall, 1984.

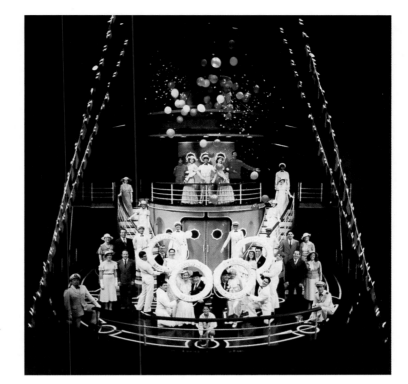

PLATE 1. Setting for *Anything Goes* at the Pacific Conservatory of the Performing Arts (PCPA) Theaterfest, Santa Maria, California. Scenic designer: Richard Seeger. A sparkling musical set for a thrust stage. (Photo courtesy of the PCPA Theaterfest)

PLATE 2. Setting for *An Enemy of the People* as produced at the Oregon Shakespeare Festival, Ashland, Oregon. Scenic designer: Richard L. Hay. Act I, Scene 3 set in the editorial office of the *Coastal Courier* in their 1920's Oregon version. Dramatic power through the spareness and starkness of sculptured space. (Photo courtesy of Richard L. Hay)

PLATE 3. Setting for *Misalliance* at Northern Illinois University, DeKalb, Illinois. Scenic designer: Richard Arnold. Color, line, and light used to enhance mood.

PLATE 4. Setting for *Second Sons* produced by the Cumberland County Playhouse, Crossville, Tennessee. Scenic designer: Leonard Harman. Suggestive see-through buildings before a backdrop capable of changing color with control of light. (Photo courtesy of Leonard Harman)

PLATE 5.   Setting for the *Emmy Awards*, 1981, for a live and television audience. Production designer: Roy Christopher. Plastic transparent surfaces enriched with colored lighting. (Photo courtesy of A. T. A. S.)

PLATE 6.   Stage design for the opera *Postcard From Morocco* by the Illinois Opera Theatre at the Krannert Center for the Performing Arts, University of Illinois, Urbana, Illinois. Scenic designer: Richard M. Isackes. A colorful, stylish setting in a contemporary romantic style. (Photo courtesy of Richard. M. Isackes)

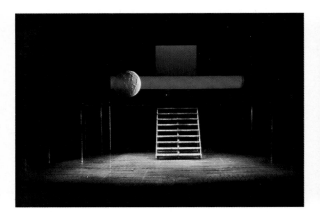

PLATE 7. Four settings for *A Midsummer Night's Dream* produced at the University of British Columbia, Vancouver, BC, Canada. Director: Claus Strassmann. Scenic and lighting designer: Robert A. Dahlstrom. A magical multi-setting using form and pencil-thin scaffolding enriched with light and color. (Photo courtesy of Robert A. Dahlstrom)

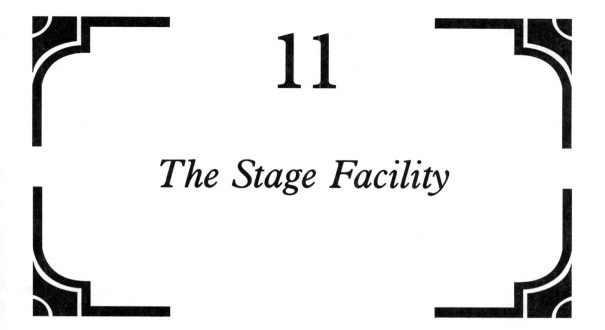

11

The Stage Facility

Early in the planning phase of a production, the producer, director, and designer face the reality that the performance and its scenery must be contained within a given production space. In addition to serving the needs of the performers and the script, the setting must be accommodated in the physical environment of the stage facility. Productions that tour have to face even greater accommodation problems, for they must be adaptable for setup and performances in a series of somewhat standardized facilities called *road houses*. The concern for the stage environment extends beyond a given amount of space and its surrounding envelope. A theatre or studio contains special accommodations and equipment to aid the technical staging of the production, for the mounting, operation, and control of sound, lighting, and scenic elements. Facilities may include a rigging system for scenery; electrical service, outlets, controlboard, and mounting positions for lighting fixtures; special floor

surfaces, traps, or lifts; curtain tracks and masking systems; cycloramas; power drives for flying; wagon systems and elevators; sound equipment, control consoles, and outlets; and control centers for operating the production. These elements extend even into the auditorium in facilities designed to accommodate live audiences. With the complexity of equipment and spatial arrangements, it is no wonder that the modern theatre plant or sound studio is so frequently described as a machine for performance. Learning about this machine and how it contributes directly to the performance is a necessity for the technicians who prepare the setting and run the production.

THE FORMS OF PERFORMANCE SPACES

With the growing interest in the performing arts in recent years, numerous production facilities have been constructed. These have included civic theatres, college and secondary school educational facilities, and theatres exclusively for professional performances in New York City or for specific regional professional companies. There has been a trend to restore old theatres and movie houses to serve the contemporary cultural needs of a community. Some new facilities are costly and elaborate constructions. These include the multifacility cultural centers such as the Kennedy Center in Washington, D.C. Other, more modest, structures have often been developed in "found" spaces such as old warehouses, churches, and garages. Some facilities have been designed for a single purpose (for instance, theatres planned primarily for drama, or dance, or grand opera). On the other hand, some theatres have been conceived as multipurpose facilities, programed to house several types of musical and dramatic entertainment. There are also outdoor performance facilities, dinner theatres, Las Vegas showrooms for elaborate spectacles, highly engineered theatres designed to be altered in acoustical and visual form, a wide range of television and film studios, and small experimental theatre forms with small audience capacities. This is indicative of the great diversity of contemporary performing arts facilities. The focus of this book does not permit a detailed study of the architecture of these production spaces. The nature of a performance facility, its architecture, and its functional requirements is a continuing controversy among architects, theatre consultants, and theatre practitioners. The immediate concern of the scene technician is the use of the stage, its spatial limitations, and its production machinery. For this purpose, several general forms of performance facilities will be examined.

The Proscenium Theatre

Ever since its inception in the Renaissance, the picture-frame stage has been the dominant form of theatre for live audiences.

It is a form that separates the performance area from the audience, providing both a physical and an aesthetic distance between them. The viewer is safely detached from the action, an observer of the scene. The typical proscenium theatre is two adjoining buildings, the auditorium and the stage house, separated by a framed opening. The performer is seen in a pictorial way, set against a background and surrounded by a frame not unlike a picture hung on a wall. The proscenium arch is closed off by a curtain to conceal scene shifts, and it is opened to reveal a new pictorial scene. To be sure, there has been some erosion of this concept of pictorial detachment over the years. Proscenium arches are seldomly enriched in ornate picture-frame style in modern theatres. They are most often minimized, subdued, or pushed into the walls and ceiling of the auditorium. The front curtain is sometimes left open during a production for a frank view of the mechanics and "magic" of the theatre. The aesthetic distance is often broken with direct address to the audience. The addition of an apron or forestage allows action to break through the arch. However, the audience/actor relationship of the proscenium stage remains essentially the same. This is true even in those theatres in which the stage is a platform at the end of a single room shared with an audience, sometimes called *end staging*.

The Stage. Few people outside the theatre realize the working space and equipment needed on the proscenium stage. Space for scenery, properties, lighting, performers, and operating crews requires a stage with considerable depth and wing space as well as provision to move objects high above the stage and through the floor. While opera, musical productions, and revue-type entertainments may have the largest casts and production requirements, a review of dramatic literature will demonstrate the extensive physical needs in the staging of regular plays. The **playing space** of a stage is an area beginning at the proscenium arch and extending upstage minimally 20' to 30' with slightly tapered sides as determined by the extreme sight lines of the auditorium (Figure 11-1). The **backstage area** includes the space behind the playing area, for scenery storage and crossovers, and the sides or wings, where waiting scenery, props, and performers are located during a performance. Large cast, multiset shows have an unusual need for this space. As a minimum, it is generally considered that the clear, unobstructed width of a stage should be twice the width of the proscenium arch, divided equally to each side. The stage depth should equal roughly one and one-half the width of the arch. This provides for a marginal amount of working space and storage for scenery. The stages in opera houses are near the ideal of three times the archway opening in width and two times in depth. This is necessary for storing large settings, often on wagons, for multiscene productions. A stage must have large loading doors and clear access to the loading dock or scene shop for moving scenery to and from the stage.

In addition to floor space, an extended area above the stage, called the **fly loft**, is needed to hang scenery, draperies, and lighting instruments. It should be high enough to raise scenery out of the audience sight lines when a full-size setting is placed in the playing space below. The floor of the

playing space is often provided with removable traps or lifts (elevators) for entrances, depressions, and scenery handling. In addition, the floor may contain a revolving stage and/or provisions for large wagons. These and other scene-moving equipment are examined later.

The Proscenium Arch. The size of the opening to the stage is not planned in isolation from the rest of the physical plant. First of all, the dimensions of the proscenium arch relate to the predominant type of productions to be staged in the facility. A proscenium width of 30' to 40' is standard for most dramatic productions. Musicals can afford slightly larger openings, and opera prosceniums may extend to 75' in width. The height of the arch is determined partially by the tallest scenery used. Second, the dimensions of the proscenium arch relate to the auditorium seating. A facility for live performances must maximize the audience's view of the playing area. Therefore, the location of the top and sides of the archway is considered in regard to sight lines from the uppermost seats in the balcony and from the extreme side and front seats to assure a good view of the stage for all spectators. In turn, these sight lines and the size of the proscenium arch influence the dimensions of the stage itself.

Because most proscenium arches are immovable and fixed in size, other means are employed to alter the frame to the desired dimensions of the stage picture (Figure 11-2). One method is the use of a **grand drapery border** (sometimes called the teaser) and **drapery legs** (tormentors). The grand border, often the same color and fabric as the front (act) curtain, masks the top of the proscenium opening. The tormentor legs are hung to narrow the opening to the appropriate width. Some technicians prefer **portals** as the adjustable frame for the stage opening. These are wood-framed units, sometimes hard-surfaced, covered with light-absorbing velour. The side frames may be designed to roll or slide on the floor or

FIGURE 11–1 The playing space and surrounding areas of the stage.

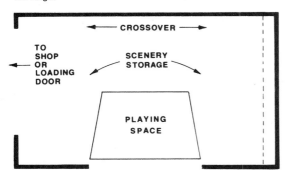

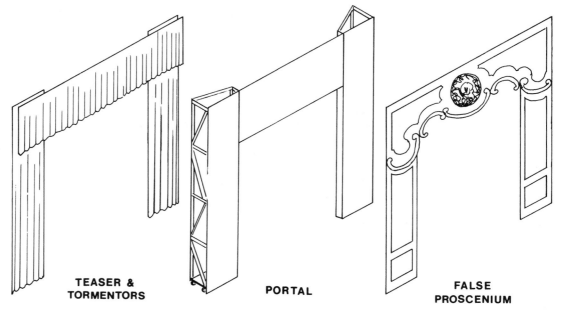

**TEASER &
TORMENTORS**   **PORTAL**   **FALSE
PROSCENIUM**

FIGURE 11–2   Means of framing a scene.

may be hung from the gridiron on tracks and adjusted by rope or manual control. Provision is sometimes made to mount tormentor lighting instruments on pipes located on the rear side. The top of the portal may be a framed unit articulating with the side frames or a drapery border. A third framing device is an **inner** or **false proscenium**. This is a cut drop or wood-framed unit created and decorated in a particular shape and style for the individual production.

The Auditorium. Equipment and staging elements, a necessary part of the "machine for performance," are also located in the auditorium of the proscenium theatre. An orchestra pit is sometimes provided in the front of the auditorium for live musical accompaniment. The pit should be large enough (sometimes it extends partially under the stage) for the number and appro-

priate combination of musical instruments and deep enough to prevent instruments from obstructing a view of the stage. The auditorium is also a major location for mounting spotlights for lighting the front portions of the stage. These locations include one or more **beam positions** (slots in the ceiling, or steel catwalks hung from above) and one or more **cove positions** (side-wall mounts for side lighting of the performance area). The **balcony front** is also a mounting location, if it is not too low in angle, and follow spotlights are sometimes positioned at the back of the auditorium. Sound- and light-control consoles are often placed in the auditorium where operators can see and hear the action for cues. A special light-control booth is found in many theatres. In large auditoriums, the sound panel that monitors the sound reinforcement system is best located within the auditorium proper. Speakers for this system are generally either located in a central cluster above the proscenium arch or distributed around the auditorium. While it has been traditional for the stage manager to operate the production from a control position backstage at one side of the proscenium arch, there has been a growing interest in recent years for the show to be managed from a booth at the back of the auditorium with a full view of the stage. The stage manager maintains contact with assistants and crews through headset communication.

In addition to the concern for extreme sight lines, audience view of the performance is enhanced by sloping the auditorium floor. The auditorium is ramped or tiered to improve the spectator's ability to see over those seated in front. Sometimes the slope is too flat or too steep. Of course, the size of the auditorium is a factor in the viewing angle. A staggered seat system allowing a view between the heads of spectators in the row ahead is a common practice. Seating plans should attempt to provide the best possible view of the stage for the audience. One seating plan eliminates all center aisles. Known as *continental seating*, the plan increases the distance between rows so a person can walk in front of the seats without disturbing seated spectators. This places aisles only at the sides of the auditorium, and the prime audience space is occupied with seats. (However, some fire codes require center aisles.) Many factors determine the audience capacity of a theatre, including the economics of operation and the type or types of performances intended for the facility. Usually, small auditoriums provide the optimum conditions for spoken drama where restricted distances permit audiences to discern readily the subtleties of speech and physical movement. Operas, musical productions, and spectacles can effectively play before larger audiences. Multipurpose theatres are the most difficult to design. When seating capacity approaches 2000 it becomes nearly impossible to achieve the ap-

propriate physical relationship and acoustics for the extremes of intimate drama and sense-provoking extravaganza.

The Arena Theatre

During this century interest in earlier staging forms led to the revival of the arena stage or theatre-in-the-round. Essentially, the stage (round, oval, square, or rectangular) is surrounded on all sides by audience seating in tiered rows (Figure 11-3). Actors use the aisles for entrances and exits; or, in more elaborate structures, they use vomitory entrances in steeply banked seating sections. This theatre form usually places the action close to the audience. The performer takes focus as a three-dimensional form in space, as sculpture, not juxtaposed against a vertical background as in the proscenium theatre style. These theatres must have sufficient height for proper lighting from all angles overhead. The simplest mounting system is a gridiron of pipe hung from the ceiling, although more convenient systems provide catwalks above the gridiron for access to light instruments. Besides the advantage of intimacy, arena theatres accommodate the largest audience with a minimum of building space. In addition, scenery costs are minimal. The floor is the largest area for scenic treatment. Vertical elements usually must be restricted to low scene units, furniture, and properties, although sometimes skeletonized or see-through structures and objects hung overhead are possible if they do not obstruct the view of the audience or interfere with the lighting. The layout of the setting must allow for a flow of action so the performers can play to audiences on all sides. Scenery for the arena stage must be constructed for close scrutiny by the audience. This requires appropriate construction and painting methods and care in execution. Shifting scenery is difficult in the arena. It generally must be accomplished manually by crews or cast members cos-

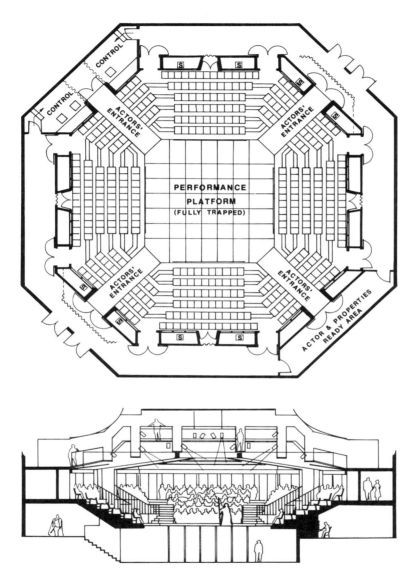

FIGURE 11–3 Arena theatre. Plan and pictorial section drawings of the Solvang Theatrefest theatre-in-the-round, Solvang, California. The 360-seat theatre includes a trapped stage floor, special actor entrances, and multileveled gridiron catwalks. Theatre designed by Richard L. Hay. Architects: Ross Associates and Flood, Meyer, Sutton and Associates of Santa Monica, California. (From drawings courtesy of Mr. Hay)

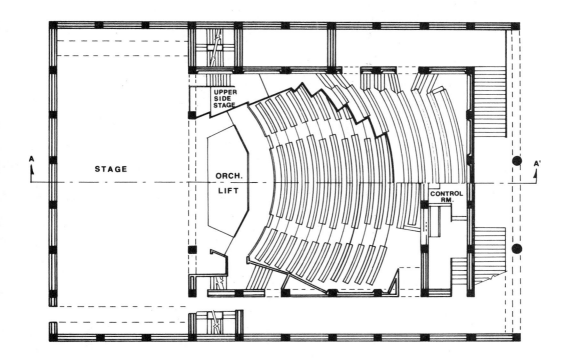

FIGURE 11–4 Modified proscenium theatre. A composite floor plan and section drawing of the 500-seat theatre for the Civic Center Complex of Modesto, California. The stage is extended by a forestage formed with an orchestra lift and surrounding caliper rim. The lift can also be lowered to the auditorium level and to the orchestra pit level. Note the side entrances to the forestage. Side stages are also provided on an upper level. Control rooms are located behind the main-floor seating. A port for follow spotlights is provided behind the balcony seating, and four auditorium beam positions for front lighting are hung above the auditorium acoustical ceiling clouds. Theatre consultants: Jerit/Boys, Inc., Oak Park, Illinois. Architects: Hall, Hoodhue, Haisley and Barker of San Francisco and Monterey, California. (From drawings courtesy of Jerit/Boys, Inc.)

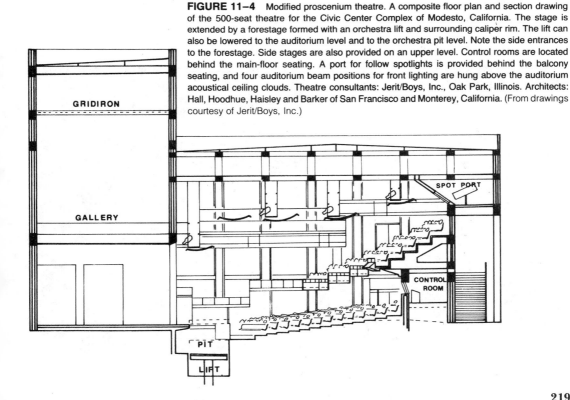

tumed as maids or butlers. A mechanical solution is an elevator stage which can lower to the basement to shift scenery or to exchange sets already placed on wagons.

The Modified Proscenium Theatre

Another theatre form conceived to bring the performer closer to the audience is a modification of the strict proscenium theatre (Figure 11-4). This was partially influenced by the new intimacy and subtle acting techniques developed in film and television performance. The physical changes are accomplished by the addition of an apron on the front of the stage or by platforming over the orchestra pit. This decreases the gulf between audience and actor common in many rigid proscenium theatres. When intimacy is desired for a production, the setting and playing area can burst through the proscenium arch to bring the action within a few feet of the first row of seats. Minimiz-

ing the appearance of the proscenium arch and not using the front curtain are additional means to reduce the actor/audience separation and detachment. For greater flexibility and convenience, a powered orchestra lift is often installed instead of cumbersome pit covers (platforms). The lift can be raised to stage level for use as a forestage, placed at the level of the auditorium floor for additional audience seating in regular proscenium style, or lowered below the floor for use as an orchestra pit. Some theatres have experimented with playing spaces in addition to the standard forestage, including small side stages projecting left and right along the side walls of the auditorium. This mode is sometimes called a *caliper stage*.

The Open-Thrust Stage

Interest in ancient theatre forms has led to the modern development of the open-

FIGURE 11–5 Open-thrust theatre. Scene during a performance of *Man of La Mancha* at the Pacific Conservatory of the Performing Arts Theatrefest, Santa Maria, California. Setting by Robert Blackman. (Photo courtesy of the PCPA Theatrefest)

thrust stage with the audience distributed on three sides (Figure 11-5). It was popularized in revivals of Shakespeare, especially at Shakespeare festivals, because of its similarity to features of the Elizabethan stage. Production experience has led to refinements of this theatre form in a number of workable new theatres including the Guthrie Theatre in Minneapolis. Some simple open-stage theatres have been designed by James Hull Miller. Unlike arena staging, the thrust form permits regular scenery along the nonaudience side of the stage. Therefore, it combines some of the pictorial aspects of the proscenium theatre (actor seen against a background) with the sculptural view of the actor in arena staging (three-dimensional actor in space). Operationally, this provides for the use of scenery (walls, platforms, and entrances) when necessary in the action, while at the same time placing more of the audience nearer the performers for more intimacy and involvement.

Besides providing for rear entrances, the vertical structure at the back of the simplest open-thrust stage is sometimes a permanent architectural facade or cyclorama wall. This usually requires most scenery to be constructed as freestanding units. Some stages provide a modest recessed area to permit the use of rear projections. Others break the wall with a proscenium arch leading to a real stage area equipped for some rigging and shifting of scenery. The gridiron above the auditorium must be extensive and flexible for lighting the stage from a variety of directions and angles. This gridiron is sometimes equipped to hang or fly limited scenic objects. Scenic treatment on the open portions of the stage is similar to that required on the arena stage. Action on the thrust stage often has the continuous flow of movement of Shakespearean drama and the fluidity of film. Owing to the restricted amount of scenery, the cost of production is reduced, but the cost of costume detail and increased lighting partially compensate.

The Multiform Theatre

Recognition of the advantages of the separate theatre forms but inability to afford more than one structure has inspired the development of theatres that can be converted into several configurations. Some of these alter seating and stage components to achieve two or three different but fixed arrangements by costly engineering and mechanical means. The Loeb Drama Center at Harvard University is one example of this type of multiform theatre. Seating units and stage sections can be rearranged electromechanically to create a proscenium shape, an open-thrust, and an arena form. The California Institute of the Arts Modular Theatre is mechanically able to achieve an even greater range of theatre configurations (Figure 11-6). The floor of this theatre is constructed of 4'-square modules that can be raised pneumatically (to a maximum of 10'). This provides an infinite number of elevation arrangements for audience seating and playing spaces. A system of wall panels articulates with the floor configurations, and a balcony surrounding the theatre provides audience access to the raised floor sections. The gridiron overhead is designed for convenience in mounting lighting instruments where needed. The grid is also equipped with portable motor winches for flying scenery.

A simpler type of multiform theatre, sometimes called the *black box* theatre, has become quite popular, especially with college and university theatre departments. This type can be arranged to suit any number of actor/audience relationships by manual movement. A flat-floored open room (60' × 60' is a compatible size) with sufficient height (15' from floor to grid is ideal) is quite adequate. Audience seating often consists of folding or stacking chairs placed on collapsible risers of various heights. Many different and subtle arrangements can be effected besides the standard configura-

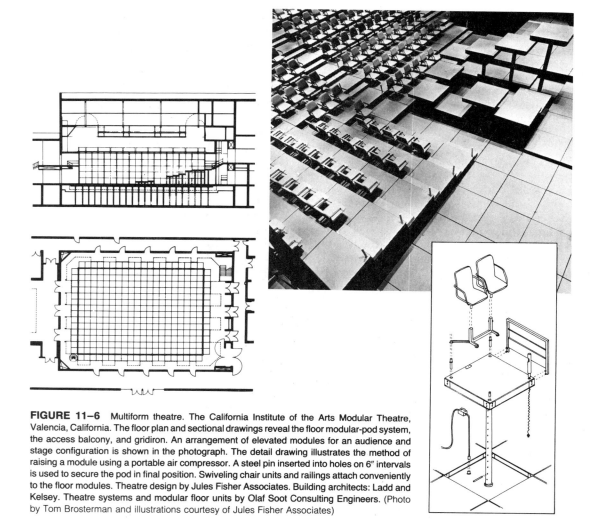

FIGURE 11–6 Multiform theatre. The California Institute of the Arts Modular Theatre, Valencia, California. The floor plan and sectional drawings reveal the floor modular-pod system, the access balcony, and gridiron. An arrangement of elevated modules for an audience and stage configuration is shown in the photograph. The detail drawing illustrates the method of raising a module using a portable air compressor. A steel pin inserted into holes on 6″ intervals is used to secure the pod in final position. Swiveling chair units and railings attach conveniently to the floor modules. Theatre design by Jules Fisher Associates. Building architects: Ladd and Kelsey. Theatre systems and modular floor units by Olaf Soot Consulting Engineers. (Photo by Tom Brosterman and illustrations courtesy of Jules Fisher Associates)

tions. The stage area can be uniquely shaped to meet the specific needs of the production, and the audience can be arranged one-sided, two-sided, three-sided, or four-sided in any pattern or manner (Figure 11-7). The overhead gridiron needs to be large enough and flexible enough to light the stage in an infinite number of locations as well as strong enough to support draperies and scenery elements. Of course, because of its limitations,

the multiform theatre usually does not satisfy all the demands of any one theatre form.

Television and Film Studios

Television and film studios are performance facilities in the pictorial staging concept of the proscenium theatre. However, the images we see on the framed screen are

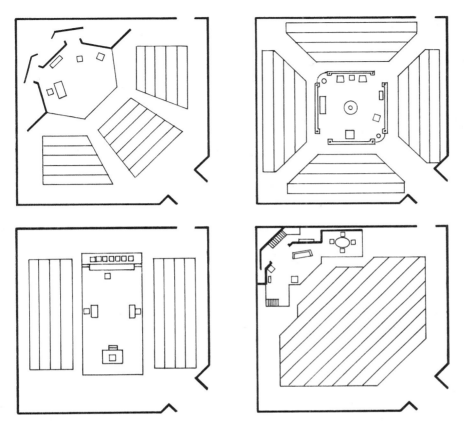

FIGURE 11–7 Manually arranged multiform theatre. Many different stage and audience configurations are possible.

selectively controlled by cameras and are often ordered by editing. Production needs must satisfy the eye of the camera and the conditions of either live or recorded performance. There are three general types of studios for film and television production: the live television studio, the television theatre studio with a live audience, and the soundstage for filming or videotaping.

Live studios are the smallest facilities used by networks as well as local TV stations. A studio 40′ × 50′ is adequate for small operations. The height of the room may be between 12′ and 15′, although greater height is better. Programming usually includes a series of regular shows—news programs and panel or interview shows—as well as specials. This requires some permanent two- and three-sided sets. Some may be fixed in location because of their size or type (a kitchen sink and counter), while others are portable or demountable. A variety of functional units and backgrounds are common and may include a set of folding panels, draperies, and a cyclorama. A gridiron is needed for lighting and may also support draperies or other scenic units. The floor must be smooth and kept free for camera movement. The surface must not be damaged by scenery and production equipment.

FIGURE 11–8   Production of *Antigone* at Northern Illinois University in a manually arranged multiform theatre. Scene design by the author. (Photo by George Tarbay)

Cameras are cabled to control units in a soundproof control room. Scenery often does not exceed 10′ in height for close-up and medium shots. The scenery and properties are designed for the camera view and to look effective close up.

Theatre studios are larger facilities used for productions which require audience participation or benefit from the response of a live audience. Game shows, specials, and variety and comedy entertainments are often performed in these studios. They are usually arranged in proscenium theatre fashion, banked audience seating on one side opposite the performance area. In fact, some are actual proscenium theatres with a proscenium arch. Some shows use a permanent set, but large productions with singers, dancers, or actors use considerable stage space and special scenery. Drapery or cyclorama backgrounds are commonly employed. The size of the stage and the scenery needs of a theatre studio require extensive rigging and mounting equipment for lights and scenery. Quick scene changes may require wagons and other equipment for shifting scenery.

Movies and videotaped dramas for TV are frequently produced on soundstages. Of course, when a script is translated into a series of sketches called the storyboard, it may be determined to shoot some scenes on location. These may be either exterior or interior scenes. However, use of the studio offers the advantage of a controlled environment. The settings can be built exactly to specifications, lighting can be created effectively, and weather will not interfere with the shooting schedule. It is not unusual for soundstages to be enormous rooms 100′ to 200′ across. Heights up to 35′ permit large sets for exteriors or two-story interiors. Soundstages must be acoustically protected from outside noises and vibrations. Individual settings are set up around the studio with sufficient open space for cameras to shoot each scene. Removable walls and panels are often necessary for shooting from various angles. The scenery is sometimes constructed outside and trucked to the studio for assembly, or it may be built in the room itself. A gridiron, catwalks, scaffolds, and towers are used for lighting the sets. Unlike live productions where there is continuous action between scenes, each scene for a film or videotaped story can be shot and reshot as often as needed, and time is available for costume, scenery, and lighting changes before shooting another scene.

THE STAGE FLOOR

The floor of the stage must conform to several requirements depending on the type or types of performances that are staged. The floor must be quite level, highly durable, and constructed to the live load standards of building codes. The stage floor of a proscenium theatre often must receive nails and stage screws used to support settings, and it must withstand considerable abuse from the weight of scenery and moving equipment. Tongue-and-groove flooring lumber in a wear-resistant soft wood (such as northern or yellow pine) best answers this need. Sometimes laid upon a plywood subfloor, it rests securely over wood sleepers placed on the concrete slab or steel beams of the floor structure. The surface of the floor is often painted or stained a dark color to minimize light reflection. A penetrating sealant is usually acceptable, but a waxed surface is too shiny and slippery. Because casters on heavy wagons can make slight dents in soft wood floors, it is usually desirable to provide caster tracks of tempered hardboard or formica. Units moved on air casters require the floor to be covered with hardboard or heavy plastic sheeting because the porosity of wood floors prevents the establishment of an air cushion.

Floors for dance performances usually require special bounce or resiliency to assist the movement of dancers and minimize physical injury. Additional spring is provided in floors specifically designed for dance through carefully constructed wood flooring systems, often resting on resilient pads. For instance, the floors of the dance theatre and dance studios at Bennington College, specified by architect Robertson Ward, Jr., are constructed on 2″ resilient cubes of precompressed fiberglass. Resilient dance floors are not common for multipurpose stages because they will not support the heavy loads of stage wagons and other equipment. Portable sectional units are sometimes used by traveling dance companies.

In addition, many dancers prefer a special surface on the floor. Vinyl dance floor surface materials are available for permanent installation or as portable, temporary coverings. These materials cover the pits and gaps in wood flooring and have an unchanging surface smoothness and mild resistance ideal for dance. And unlike wood, these surfaces are unaffected by continuous surface wear or temperature and humidity changes.

Television and motion picture studios need floors that are smooth, even, and hard-surfaced. They must not be easily marred or roughened by scenery or heavy equipment. Camera pedestals, dollies, and cranes must be able to roll smoothly without picture vibration. Polished concrete is common in many facilities. Large soundstages may have floating or isolated floors to protect from outside sounds and vibrations. Floor tile or seamless flooring surfaces are sometimes used on studio floors for improved smoothness and for ease of maintenance.

In a few theatres, provisions are included in the floor for scenery moving systems. These may include tracks countersunk in the floor for full stage wagons which roll into the wings and/or toward the rear of the playing space. Similarly, a revolving stage is permanently imbedded in the floors of some stages. Full stage revolvers usually exceed the width of the proscenium arch. Flush with the surrounding floor, they rotate on steel tracks which are often supported on piers and footings independent of the rest of the building.

Traps

A sizable number of dramas benefit from playing areas lower than the floor level (grave scenes, for instance) or from actor entrances and exits beneath the stage. To make this possible, removable sections of the floor, called *traps*, are provided in a large portion of the playing area on many stages (Figure 11-9). A stairway entrance from below the stage usually requires an opening of 7' to 8' in the floor. Thus, traps are often longer in one direction, rectangular in shape. The location and size of the opening in the floor varies with the particular needs of the production. For this reason, a degree of flexibility is usually provided in the supporting framework for trap lids. For instance, removing a demountable beam supporting two adjacent 3'-6' × 7' traps would fully open up a floor area of 7' × 7'. The room below the stage, known usually as the trap room, must be open and available for stairs and platforms when stage traps are removed.

FIGURE 11–9 Stage traps. A: Removable beam between adjacent trap lids provides flexibility to reorient traps either cross stage or up- and downstage.

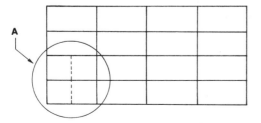

Stage Lifts (Elevators)

Elevators in the floor of the stage are costly installations but are often justified in compelling circumstances. Raised above the level of the stage, lifts are convenient means of providing elevations for a setting, eliminating the need for expensive and space-consuming platforms. The most sophisticated lifts tilt to provide raked playing levels. Lowered, they replace traps and instantly provide below-stage elevations. In addition, stage lifts provide a means of shifting scenery, properties, and actors above and below the stage. Lifts vary in size from small trap elevators to large plateau elevators capable of moving entire sets to storage areas in the basement. The latter type often has built-in tracks to accommodate rolling wagons. The elevators can then lower the wagons so they are flush with the stage floor or raise them from scene storage rooms in the basement. Remote-control consoles are needed to control direction, speed, height, and groupings of lifts for coordinate operation. Highly complicated lift systems are common in opera houses and Las Vegas showrooms where scenic and spectacle requirements are extensive. Most lifts are operated by hydraulic cylinders or screw-jack actuators. Cylinder pistons are usually powered by an electrically driven hydraulic pump. Electrically or hydraulically powered, the screw-jack system supports the platform on a series of vertical screw posts that raise and lower by threaded drive shafts.

DRAPERY TRACKS

Special drapery tracks are manufactured for the stage to carry the heavy weight of scenic drapes and curtains and to withstand the demands of production. Tracks are convenient suspension equipment for stage curtains and draperies due to the ease of moving them laterally into and out of the scene. In addition, when extended into the wings, tracks provide additional scene-shifting functions on stages without a fly loft, bringing in borders, cycloramas, projection screens, drops, and even framed scenery. A minimum of 20 percent of a track length should extend into the wings so draperies can be concealed from view when drawn.

Types of Tracks

Several types of tracks serve a variety of needs (Figure 11-10). They are available in various sizes depending upon the load to be carried. One of the most common is the **box channel track**. Curtain carriers in this type of track have two wheels, pass through a slot, and travel along the bottom edges of the channel. The **V-channel track** uses single-wheel carriers. The design of this track permits easy addition or removal of carriers at any location along the track. The **aluminum I-beam track** offers the advantage of being easily curved to virtually any radius by a hand operated bender. Two-wheel carriers ride on the lower flange of the I beam. Another type of track consists of two **C-channel carrier rails** suspended from 2″ O.D. pipe. Quiet in operation, it can serve as a straight track or can be curved to a radius as small as 4′. Traveler accessories for curtain tracks include hanging and mounting hardware, splicing clamps, double-track clamps, carrier end-stops, and pulley components for rope operation.

For smooth and silent operation, the best carriers have ball bearing wheels and rubber treads. Rubber bumpers prevent noise when carriers collect together as draperies are opened. A chain of three or four links extends from each carrier for drapery height adjustment at each point of attachment. Master carriers, used on the leading edges of draperies, are larger than single carriers and have twice the number of wheels and two chain attachments for the curtain (Figure 11-11).

FIGURE 11–10 Types of curtain tracks.

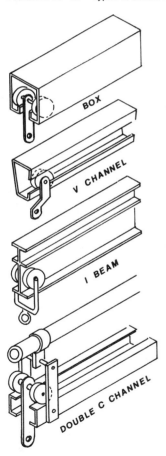

FIGURE 11–11 Master carrier.

Methods of Track Operation

The simplest method for drawing a drapery on a track is the **walk-on** system. While this can be achieved by pulling the lead edge of the material, it is usually best to pull a rope suspended from the master carrier. This prevents possible tearing of the fabric or loosening of the attachment to the track carriers.

A **rope drive** on a traveler consists of a continuous loop of rope to permit the drapery to travel in both directions on the track. This requires a dead-end sheave on one end of the track, two live-end sheaves on the operating end, and a floor block. The ends of the rope are secured by clamps to the master carrier so the rope directly pulls the lead edge of the drapery. Because a curtain that parts in the middle has two lead edges, the second master carrier is attached to the return side of the rope so the two halves of the curtain will close and open simultaneously (Figure 11-12).

As the rope is pulled to open a drapery, the carriers are brought together and the fabric is made to fold. In the regular process, called **front folding**, the master carrier collects each single carrier one by one and pushes them to the offstage position. A front-fold operation is often satisfactory. Sometimes, however, it is not desirable to destroy the appearance of the drapery by folding it on the onstage side.

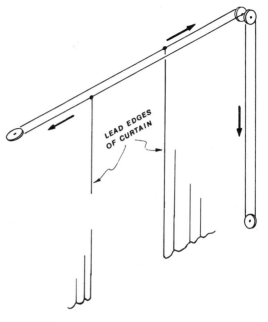

FIGURE 11–12   Rope drive for a curtain that parts in the middle. Opposite sides of the rope loop are clamped to the master carriers so the leading edges of the curtain will open and close together.

In addition, the collecting of the fabric by the master carrier adds increased weight to the pull of the rope. A **rear-fold** system solves these problems by folding the drapery on the offstage end of the track (Figure 11-13). A painted drop, for instance, would move offstage in a flat plane and gather up

FIGURE 11–13   Rear-fold curtain track.

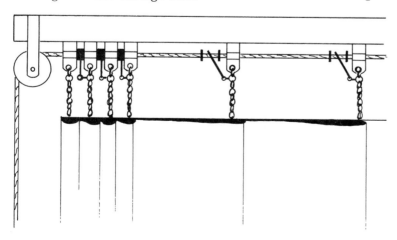

behind the scenes. Rear-fold carriers have attached guides which grab the rope when pulled to open a drapery.

Stage Track Systems

Tracks are used in several ways on a stage. The front curtain that opens to reveal the scene is sometimes a draw curtain, especially on stages with inadequate stage height. Tracks for removing curved cycloramas are valuable in some theatres and studios. Travelers are often used for the rear close in curtains as part of the drapery settings of multipurpose theatres. Drapery legs are sometimes attached to lengths of track so they may be adjusted for different positions. Another flexible tormentor device is a pivot arm (Figure 11-14). This is a length of pipe, to which the drapery is attached, that can pivot full circle as well as roll on a track.

Curved drapery track systems of the I-beam type are frequently used. The tracks can be shaped for several different drapery setting enclosures at various depths of the stage and interconnected in model railroad fashion. The curtain can be moved to different configurations, and with switching de-vices, they can be rolled onto storage tracks.

Stages without height for flying often benefit from a series of traverse tracks across the playing area and extending well into the wings. On a stage with limited means of shifting scenery, a track system can be a major asset as a convenient mover of draperies, drops, borders, and framed units.

TYPES OF CURTAIN RIGGING

Curtains are made of fabrics and other materials hung across the stage to mask or reveal a portion of the stage. They differ in method of rigging and operation.

The Traveler or Draw Curtain

This type of curtain is hung on a track and is drawn by a rope line as described above (Figure 11-15). Usually it is devised to part in the center to shorten the travel distance and operating time. This requires two sections of track joined together in the center for a 1'-6" curtain overlap. The length of each section of track must be carefully determined to provide for the desired

FIGURE 11–14 Pivot arm for drapery legs.

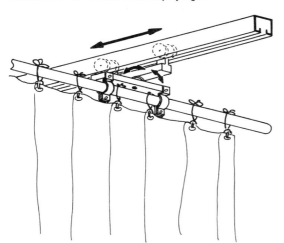

FIGURE 11–15 Draw curtain.

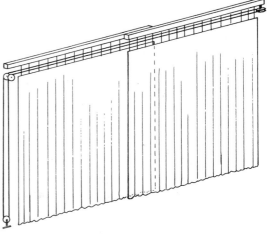

opening width of the curtain, the center overlap, and storage space for the folded material in the offstage position. Every 5' of curtain requires a minimum of 1' of track in storage. In some situations curtains are operated by a single- or variable-speed motor.

The Fly Curtain

A curtain tied to a regular pipe batten of the stage fly system is a convenient and efficient curtain system. Flying a curtain is unusually silent and uncomplicated. Furthermore, in its raised position, the curtain is not on the floor level to interfere with valuable production space. A fly curtain operated by hand on a counterweight system requires some practice by the crew member. A front curtain, for instance, is often of heavy fabric and frequently requires a fast closing for dramatic action. Practice is necessary to learn how to achieve a fast start, and how to stop it before the curtain piles up on the floor. In some theatres, the front curtain is rigged for both flying and drawing depending on the nature of the performance.

The Tableau (Tab) Curtain

A tab curtain opens with the two halves of the fabric moving diagonally to the upper two corners. This frames the scene with two drapery swags overhead and cascading jabots on the sides (Figure 11-16). Metal rings attached to cotton tape are sewn to the back of the curtain fabric along the diagonals. The two operating ropes are tied to the rings on the lead edges and pass through the remaining rings. Sheaves overhead direct the ropes to the operating side. For ease of raising, the fabric should not be too heavy, although small counterweights may be added on the ropes as long as they do not prevent the curtain from closing completely. Because the raised tab curtain remains in view

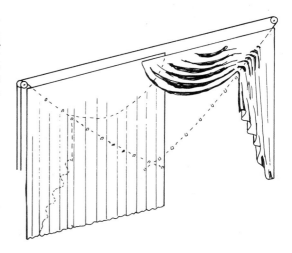

FIGURE 11–16 Tableau curtain.

to frame the scene, the resultant archway opening is often restricted in size.

The Contour Curtain

The contour curtain and its related form, the brail curtain, provide an arch of decorative swags when opened (Figure 11-17). A number of evenly spaced operating lines drop vertically through rings sewn to the curtain and attach to the chain in the bottom hem. Usually motorized, each line is fed to a motor winch drawn overhead. Operated at different speeds and stopped at different times, the winches create a variety of swag patterns when the curtain is opened.

The Roll Curtain

This is essentially a flat painted drop caused to rise by the turning of a roller at the bottom. It is sometimes used as an olio curtain (a painted drop for a front scene) for revivals of 19th-century melodramas or where lack of stage height prevents flying a drop. A muslin or canvas drop is attached to a sandwich batten at the top and secured to

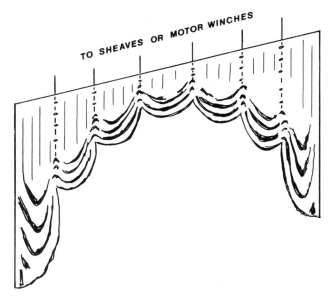

FIGURE 11–17   Contour curtain.

a pipe batten or to the ceiling. The roller, 6″ to 8″ in diameter, can be made of 1 × 3′s secured to circular disks of wood and covered with stiff cardboard or chicken wire and papier-mâché. The roller must be stiff enough not to sag in the middle with the increasing weight of fabric. The roller must be 3′ to 4′ longer than the drop. Ropes are wrapped around each end of the roller and pass over sheaves above leading to the operating side. As the ropes are pulled, the roller is raised and is caused to rotate, thus winding up the fabric as it travels upward (Figure 11-18). The rope should not be smaller than ½″ in diameter owing to the increased weight that is lifted as the roller collects the fabric.

GRIDIRONS

A gridiron or grid is an open framework hung beneath the roof of the stage. It supports rigging equipment for suspending or flying scenery, draperies, and lighting equipment. As a working floor permitting stagehands to adjust and maintain equipment, a minimum of 7′ of head room to the lowest obstruction (duct, piping, conduit) is

FIGURE 11–18   Roll curtain. As the operating line is raised, the curtain is wound around the roller.

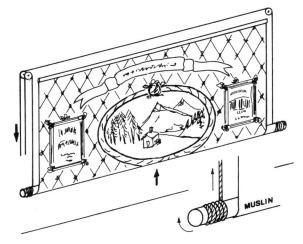

needed between the grid floor and the roof structure overhead. The grid must be supported by adequately designed structural beams of the building to provide sufficient load capacity for the machinery and suspended scenery.

Stages that do not have a gridiron usually present considerable rigging difficulties. To suspend drapes, scenery, or lights without a grid requires that sheaves or hanging devices be attached to the underside of roof beams or trusses. If the roof supports are not designed for this extra weight, the loading capacity is limited. Access to this equipment is often difficult, possible only by scaffolding or extremely tall ladders. This is a deterrent to the flexibility needed to relocate equipment and to provide special rigging for the special needs of a production. Furthermore, it discourages proper inspection and maintenance of the equipment.

Lack of a gridiron with overhead access is less of a problem in low-ceiling television studios and arena or multiform theatres. Although occasionally draperies and scene pieces need to be suspended, support from above is chiefly needed for mounting spotlights and other lighting sources. In these situations, a framework of pipe or an adjustable I-beam track system works as a substitute for an accessible gridiron. However, it is certainly an inconvenience to mount and adjust lighting equipment with rolling scaffolds or ladders from a floor cluttered with staging equipment.

An appropriate gridiron for small studios, arena, or multiform theatres consists of a series of interconnecting catwalks with sufficient open spaces and well-located pipes for instruments to light the playing area at proper angles. A similar grid treatment is used over many thrust stages. Provisions are sometimes included to fly or suspend scenery elements between catwalks when necessary.

The traditional gridiron over a proscenium stage is designed to support line sets attached to pipe battens that hang parallel to the proscenium arch. The prime locations for support on the grid are slots extending from the proscenium wall to the rear wall of the stage called **loft block wells** (Figure 11-19). Each well is formed by a pair of heavy steel channels back to back and separated by about 10″. The wells are spaced no more than 10′ apart. Loft blocks (sheaves) clamp to the top

FIGURE 11–19   The conventional gridiron.

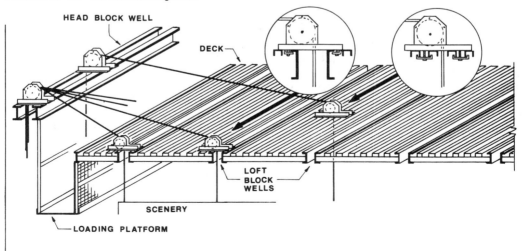

of the channels and direct a cable or rope through the well to connect to a pipe batten. Between the loft-block wells is an open decking of 3″-wide channels, flat side up, spaced 3″ apart and placed parallel with the wells. Loft blocks can also be clamped on the decking to drop a line within 1½″ of any location on the stage below. In some motorized rigging installations, loft blocks are underhung and attached to roof beams directly over the gridiron wells. This frees the floor of the gridiron of strings of cable, making it easier to work and move about. Steel grating and expanded metal have been used to replace catwalks and steel channels as deck surfaces on some grids. A stairway is needed to reach the gridiron from the stage floor.

FLYING SYSTEMS

Rope-Line Rigging

A flying system using manila rope lines is an early method of flying scenery and much of the terminology is adopted from the rigging of sailing vessels. The system consists of ropes which drop through **loft blocks** on the gridiron and are tied to the scenery (Figure 11-20). From the loft blocks the ropes pass across the gridiron to a multiple sheave **head block**, which directs the ropes down to a tie-off point called the **pinrail**. The pinrail is a large-diameter pipe securely anchored to the structure of the building. Vertical holes are drilled through the pipe for the insertion and removal of wood or metal **belaying pins**. The ropes are secured to the pinrail by wrapping them around the pins in a figure eight. The pins can be conveniently pulled out of the rail to quickly untie the attachment for a fast scene change. A double pinrail permits tie-offs for both the lower and upper trim of the scenery. The pinrail is located on the **fly gallery**, a balcony along the sidewall and above the stage floor 18′ or more. The fly gallery is the working area for flying and frees the stage floor of piles of

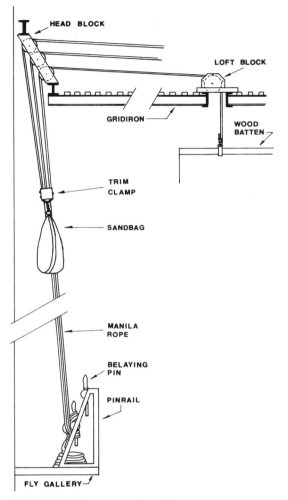

FIGURE 11–20   The rope-line rigging system.

rope and associated paraphernalia. Scenery that is too heavy for a fly operator to lift conveniently is partially counterbalanced by a **sandbag** attached to the ropes by a **trim clamp**. The scenery must always remain heavier than its counterbalancing sand so it will lower by gravity.

The rope system requires care in operation and maintenance. The necessary imbalance in counterweighting places great

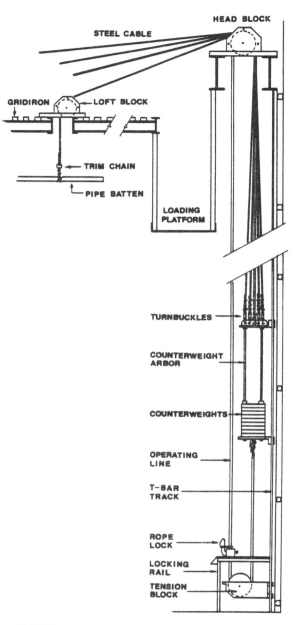

STEEL CABLE

HEAD BLOCK

GRIDIRON — LOFT BLOCK

TRIM CHAIN

PIPE BATTEN

LOADING PLATFORM

TURNBUCKLES

COUNTERWEIGHT ARBOR

COUNTERWEIGHTS

OPERATING LINE

T-BAR TRACK

ROPE LOCK

LOCKING RAIL

TENSION BLOCK

FIGURE 11–21   The counterweight rigging system.

importance in tying off the lines correctly. Scenery must be "muscled" to its high trim (storage position) before the sandbag counterweight can be attached. Similarly, extra assistance is needed when lowering the scenery after the sandbag is removed. The rope lines, which shrink and expand with temperature and humidity changes, need continual adjustment to keep the scenery in trim (parallel to the floor). The swinging sandbags overhead must be inspected regularly for possible tears in the canvas bag and for sand leaks. The ropes ($\frac{1}{2}''$ or $\frac{5}{8}''$ diameter in size) must be checked and replaced when necessary.

Few stages today rely on rope rigging as the principal flying system. However, because of its flexibility, the rope system is a common auxiliary method on a stage. Pinrails and fly galleries are often installed in theatres which have pipe batten systems. The rope-line system is particularly useful for spotline work (suspending an object such as a chandelier from a single line) or flying scenery at angles or locations not possible with the regular pipe battens.

The Counterweight System

The counterweight rigging system overcomes many of the disadvantages of the rope system. Steel cable replaces shrinkable rope for the hoist lines to support a pipe batten held in permanent trim; iron weights and guided frames replace sand and fragile canvas sandbags; and an operating line which can lower as well as raise scenery eliminates unbalanced counterweighting. The counterweight system is divided into line sets, each terminating on stage in a **pipe batten** parallel to the proscenium arch to which scenery, draperies, and lights are attached (Figure 11-21). Each batten is supported at equidistant locations by steel cables that run up to loft blocks on the gridiron, pass over a multigrooved head block near the stage wall, and then attach to the top of the **counterweight**

arbor, which is a frame for holding iron counterweights. The arbor rides up and down vertically in a prescribed path on **T-bar steel tracks** or **wire guides**. The head blocks are clamped to a pair of I beams beneath the roof. An **operating line** of ¾″ or 1″ manila rope forms a complete loop. Secured at the top of the arbor, it passes over a groove in the head block, drops down to the stage, passes over a weighted **tension block** near the floor, and returns upward to be tied off at the bottom of the arbor. The pipe batten is lowered by pulling the onstage side of the line, and raised by pulling the offstage side of the line. **Rope locks** for the operating lines are attached to a framework called the **locking rail**, which extends along the floor. When a pipe batten is lowered to the floor and scenery is attached, the arbor is loaded with counterweights from a loading platform located just beneath the gridiron. Nearly complete balance can be achieved between the weight of the scenery and the counterweights. The rope lock and its safety ring are designed to secure the operating line for these slight imbalances only.

The Double-Purchase System

On some stages there is insufficient wall height to provide for a full flight of the counterweight arbor. Often the locking rail cannot be located on floor level because wings or side stages extend beyond the walls of the fly-loft area. In these cases, the locking rail is located on a gallery off the floor. The double-purchase system is a modification of the counterweight system. The system provides a mechanical advantage of 2 to 1, requiring the counterweight to equal twice the weight of the scenery and move only one-half the distance of the scenery. Instead of terminating at the top of the arbor, the steel cables run through a block and return to be tied off just below the head block (Figure 11-22). The operating line follows the same path above the arbor and is diverted through a

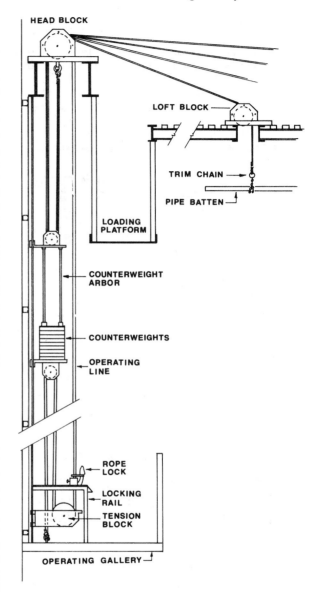

FIGURE 11–22   The double-purchase counterweight system.

block below the arbor to be secured to the gallery floor. The additional friction in the system plus the increased counterweighting are its chief disadvantages.

Power-Assisted Systems

It was inevitable that electric power would replace some of the human effort in flying scenery. Power-assisted counterweight systems are a relatively simple application of motorized rigging. Even in theatres equipped

FIGURE 11–23 Common fixed-speed, power-assisted rigging systems.

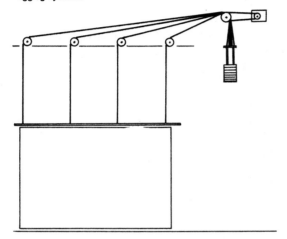

TRACTION DRIVE SYSTEM

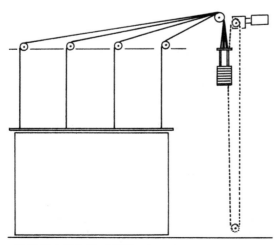

CLOSED-LOOP COUNTERWEIGHT SYSTEM

with hand-operated counterweight sets, a few objects are sometimes flown by fixed-speed power-assisted lines (Figure 11-23). Variable-speed equipment is higher in cost. In the **traction drive system**, lines from the loft blocks supporting the batten pass over a head block and attach to the counterweight arbor. Instead of an operating line, a motor and gear-reduction unit directly drives the head block. The motor can be small in size because power is necessary only to overcome inertia and friction in the system since counterweights fully balance the scenery. However, there is slippage in the passing of the cables over the head block. Therefore, the traction-driven head block is limited to items that have constant weight and can move at constant speed, such as a cyclorama, a fire curtain, or a drapery.

Another system, the **closed-loop counterweight drive**, replaces the operating line with a loop of cable or chain driven by a motor. With cable secured to a winch drum, or a roller chain fitting into sprocket wheels, there is no slippage. If accurate counterweighting is maintained in each new condition, a relatively small motor and gear unit is adequate. However, a larger gear and motor can be installed to handle a given amount of imbalance. A fixed-speed motor system of this type is sometimes used to fly a light bridge where some fluctuation of load occurs.

Motorized closed-loop counterweight rigging can also be provided with the advantage of variable speed control. This can be achieved on regular counterweight or double-purchase systems. One available system (Figure 11-24) features spotline versatility. This system uses swivel head blocks and loft blocks to permit the four to six lift lines to be positioned at any location above the gridiron and dropped to the scenery to be flown. These lines are variable in length and when positioned for use are adjusted for tension by trimming winches. When trimmed, the lines are mechanically locked to secure line lengths for that flying situation. The line set

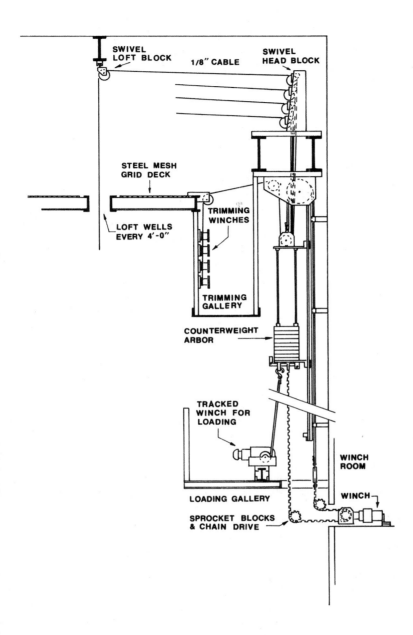

FIGURE 11–24 Motorized closed-loop rigging with spotline versatility. The system is based on the double-purchase system. Loft blocks can be positioned up and down the stage to fly irregular-shaped units. A movable winch on the loading gallery is needed to retrieve the empty arbor for counterweighting. The drive winch must be located in a soundproof room to the side or below the stage. The control console can be located on the loading gallery or at stage floor level.

is powered by motor drive and a closed-loop roller chain secured to the counterweight arbor. The control console with electric telemetry, variable speed control, and preset features is located on stage.

Although power-assisted systems can be useful, they have several limitations. They remain counterweight systems requiring loading weights from a loading platform, and a stage wall not too distant from the playing area, for the movement of arbors in T-bar tracks. Further, variable-speed capability and accompanying electric controls add considerably to the cost.

Full Power Systems

The ultimate in power rigging is to perform all mechanical and "muscle" functions required in flying with power-drive hoists. This eliminates manual operating lines, the need for counterweighting, and the locking rail and arbor track installations which line the side wall of the stage. While motorized hoists capable of lifting heavy loads have been in use for some time, only in recent years have complete power rigging installations been developed. What is desired is a system of power hoists that can not only move scenery vertically, but also can (1) support a complete load, sometimes unevenly distributed; (2) reverse directions; (3) vary in speed; (4) be preset for upper and lower trim; (5) be remotely controlled and interpatched for coordinating action; and (6) have fail-safe protection. These goals can be satisfied by existing electrical and fluid-power technology. Of course, the cost is high. However, with electrical rather than mechanical connections to the stage floor, the fly loft can be limited to the area immediately above the playing area rather than the full width of the stage. This reduces the construction cost of the facility.

There are essentially two approaches for pure power systems. One approach is to retain the function of pipe battens parallel to the proscenium wall for the attachment of scenery and other staging equipment. The result is powered line sets. The other approach associates the fixed-position batten rigging with an older two-dimensional scenic form and seeks to fly scenery of any configuration at any angle or position on the stage. This is accomplished by power spotline hoists that can drop lines from any location on the gridiron and be operated individually or in groups.

Electric-Winch Systems. An example of motorized line-set rigging has been installed in the Metropolitan Opera House. This installation has 109 battens, each cabled to a multigroove motorized winch. Each winch can carry a full load up to 1000 pounds at variable speeds and with a trim accuracy of $1/16''$. A patch panel plugs winches into any of thirty power supplies for electronic control at a control console. This saving in time and effort is vital for the enormous demands of grand opera repertory. Many motorized line sets have been installed on stages throughout the world.

Special versatility is provided by electrically operated spotline units. In some systems, spotline winches are mounted on the walls of the stage above the gridiron. Lift cables are fed through swivel loft blocks which can be attached to roof beams and dropped through the gridiron at any location. They may be synchronously operated in groups, at varying speeds, and can be controlled from a console on the stage. Another type of spotline winch is a completely portable unit. Power is supplied by flexible electric cable from a central channel above the gridiron. This permits the winches to be moved to any location on the grid steelwork, from which lift lines may be dropped to the stage. Those who advocate motorized spotline winches point out that besides the versatility of flying scenery in any position, a complete installation requires fewer winches than does a fixed motorized line-set system and results in a substantial savings in cost. In addition, portable spotline winches can be used on the stage floor for powering wagons. They are plugged into power outlets and control circuit receptacles. They must be designed with acoustical enclosures to quiet operational noise.

Figure 11-25 is a perspective drawing of the State Theatre at the Victorian Arts Centre in Melbourne, Australia. The rigging in this theatre includes 105 motorized line sets and 6 sidestage battens. The 15-HP variable-speed DC winches and winch drums that

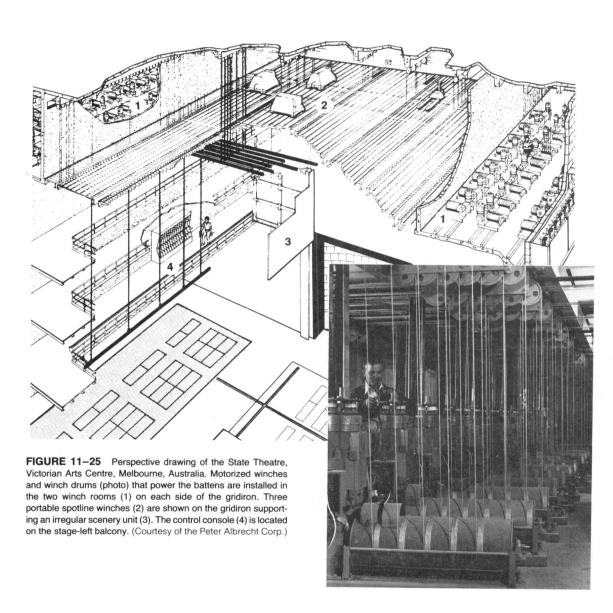

FIGURE 11–25 Perspective drawing of the State Theatre, Victorian Arts Centre, Melbourne, Australia. Motorized winches and winch drums (photo) that power the battens are installed in the two winch rooms (1) on each side of the gridiron. Three portable spotline winches (2) are shown on the gridiron supporting an irregular scenery unit (3). The control console (4) is located on the stage-left balcony. (Courtesy of the Peter Albrecht Corp.)

drive the battens are located in two sound-proof winch rooms adjacent to the gridiron. In addition, there are ten portable spotline winches located on the grid deck. Each is a 5-HP variable-speed DC motor winch capable of lifting 250 pounds at a speed of 300' per minute.

Control consoles, which provide electric/electronic control of the rigging machinery, can be located either on a gallery or at stage level. For operation, a winch is assigned to a control channel. The programed channel will display its current position, its preset trim position, the operational mode for a cue, and predetermined speed of travel. Each channel may be controlled manually or operated by master control. The master control can operate several winches with different trim positions and directions of movement.

The recent advent of computerized rigging controllers has advanced the control of electric winch systems. Unlimited by a given number of control channels, a computerized control system (Figure 11-26) allows individual control of each of the winches, permitting any number to run at one time, at different speeds, in different directions, and starting and stopping independently of each other. Winches within a group are kept in synchronization with one another. This is especially necessary when several winches are lifting a single element. Computer control has been extended to all moving scenery units: hoists, wagons, revolves, and elevators. It permits accurate repeatability of actions giving smooth, fast, and quiet transitions. The movements of stage machinery can be carefully choreographed in keeping with the flow of the production. Much like sensitive manual control, the computer can be programed to accelerate and decelerate a move-

FIGURE 11–26 The console of the Micro Commander, a computerized rigging control system that can provide individual control on each winch, allowing any number of groups to be running at one time at different speeds, in different directions, and stopping and starting independently of each other. (Photo courtesy of Hoffend and Sons, Inc.)

ment, allowing scenery to glide to a stop or to slow down before touching the stage floor.

Hydraulic Systems. Long used for stage lifts, the simple, efficient, and relatively quiet characteristics of hydraulic power has led to its application as a power source for hoists. Several types of hydraulic systems have been developed for stage rigging, although they have not yet proved to be as reliable as electric winch systems. They are generally pump-and-valve systems actuated by electric power.

Typical Proscenium-Stage Rigging

Despite the fixed orientation of pipe battens, line sets are the most widely used flying systems in proscenium theatres. These may be hand-operated counterweight, motorized counterweight, or pure power systems. It has also become common practice for the-

atres to install auxiliary systems for the additional advantages other rigging can provide. These may include a few motorized counterweight sets for certain permanent lines, some motorized spotlines or rope-line rigging especially for spotline purposes. In the case of the latter, some theatres install a complete fly gallery and pinrail as a valuable supplement to the regular pipe-batten rigging. Interest in the flexibility of motorized spotline systems is increasing even though the line set remains the best answer for certain regularly flown objects on stage.

A professional theatre generally requires a full complement of line sets, usually sixty sets or more. Educational and community theatres commonly have fewer. While it is difficult to generalize, the following is a typical pattern of line-set usage of a stage.

Line Sets Immediately Behind the Proscenium Arch. These objects are listed in order behind the arch (Figure 11-27).

1. Grand drapery border (may be decorative and fixed in height or may serve as a first teaser in trimming the top of the scene opening)
2. Front (act) curtain
3. Tormentors (drapery legs) or a complete portal (may or may not be flown)
4. Motorized light bridge or the first electric pipe batten.

Line Sets Throughout Most of the Stage. These are mostly free battens for use in flying scenery and masking borders, but interspersed are the second, third, and fourth electric battens.

Line Set at the Rear of the Stage. This is frequently a specially rigged curved batten for a cyclorama.

CYCLORAMAS

A cyclorama is a large scenic background designed to nearly or completely enclose a stage setting. Unlike the two-dimensional painted drop or sky drop, a cyclorama is U- or C-shaped, extending across the back of

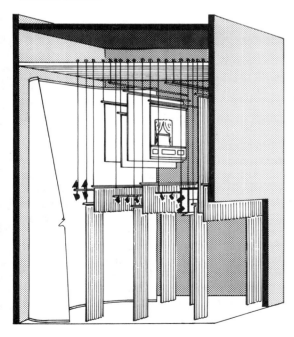

FIGURE 11–27 A view of a proscenium stage showing typical use of line sets.

the stage and curving downstage to mask all or a portion of the sides of a scene (Figure 11-28). It differs from a drapery setting hung in folds by being a smooth continuous surface without sharp corners. A cyclorama (or cyc) is often employed to represent a sky, real or abstract, or simply a limitless space or void. It is frequently lighted in colors and values to aid reality or mood. Shapes, patterns, and scenes are often cast on a cyc by lens and lensless projection equipment. The color of the surface is sometimes considered important for purposes of illumination. White, off-white, or light-blue material is more satisfactory for highly luminous backgrounds and daylight sky effects; a gray or medium-value surface for middle tones; and

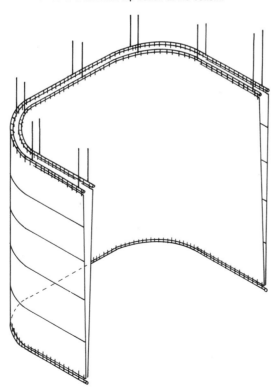

FIGURE 11-28 A cyclorama of canvas with a scrim hung in front. Tall cycloramas are sometimes dead-hung from the gridiron and are tied to a common trip batten at the bottom.

a black material for darkly lit backgrounds or, left unlighted, for total darkness or an endless void. For this reason, some designers and technicians maintain two or more cycloramas for selective production use.

Because a cyclorama is often considered a regular item of stage equipment, provisions must be made for its location and rigging. First of all, it must be large enough to surround the line sets (battens) on stage so they can be operative. The depth of the cyclorama should not sacrifice needed crossover space behind it for actors and crew. Second, the dimensions of the cyc are ultimately determined by the extreme sight lines of the audience (or camera). If maximum size is desired in a proscenium stage, the height of a cyc is governed by first-row vertical sight lines, and the sides of the cyc by extreme horizontal sight lines. In actuality, of course, providing a means of moving or shifting the cyc and gaining access from the wings for scenery and properties may argue for a cyc that is less than these ideal dimensions. In this case, borders and legs are often necessary for masking the extreme edges.

Types of Cycloramas

Cycloramas constructed of rigid materials such as plaster or plywood covered with cloth and painted may be found in some facilities. The immense weight of such structures often makes them permanent and immovable. Because plaster is an excellent light-blending surface, plaster cycs and plaster domes (curving overhead as well as to the sides) have been installed in some theatres despite space and movement disadvantages. A rigid, permanent cyclorama at one end of a film studio creates few, if any, problems because of the nature of film production. Studio cycs frequently curve to meet the floor to avoid the line of separation between floor and background (Figure 11-29).

Fabric is a common material for cycloramas. Black velour or duvetine hung flat is

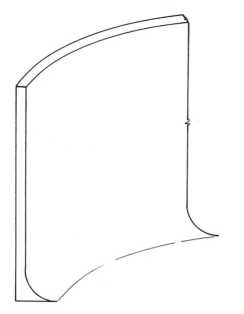

FIGURE 11–29 A permanent cyclorama is sometimes coved to the floor to merge the two planes.

effective for dark backgrounds. For lighter sky effects, muslin or canvas sewn with horizontal seams and dyed a light blue-gray is widely used. Other fabrics, textures, and colors are sometimes employed for special purposes. Cloth must be stretched tight for a smooth, wrinkle-free surface. A cyc of two fabrics, a layer of muslin or canvas with a separate scrim layer in front, affords a very satisfactory effect. The scrim, which is loomed in 30′ widths, tends to hide the seams and wrinkles of the other fabric and provides a textured surface for lighting.

Plastic cyc material is an alternative to fabric and provides an ideal surface for front and rear projection. Heat-joined seams become almost invisible, and the plastic is available in white, gray, or black.

The most practical means of shifting a cloth cyclorama is by flying it or moving it horizontally on an overhead track. In flying, the fabric is lashed or tied (grommets and tie lines) to special curved pipe battens at the top and bottom. The top batten is then raised by a special counterweight rigging set. Cables that lift the sides of the curved pipe must pass through mule blocks (see Chapter 13). If there is insufficient loft height for the flown cyc to clear the floor sufficiently for scenery (20′ or more is often needed), it may be necessary to trip the cyc. Bottom tripping is achieved by dropping the cables behind the cyc for attachment to the bottom batten. The top batten can be dead-hung from the gridiron by chains, which allow for height adjustment of the fabric. When flown, the bottom batten is lifted and the fabric folds in the middle. The line cannot be fully counterbalanced because of the difference in weight between the upper and lower trim positions. With a two-fabric cyc, the scrim and cloth usually require two separate top battens to maintain individual fabric tension, but they can be tied to a common trip batten. With the use of a curved track, a cyc can be removed horizontally. Some European systems roll the cyc compactly around a vertical cylinder at the end of the track. It can also be moved onto a storage track in the wings. Traveler cycs usually have a chain weight in the bottom hem.

THE CONTROL CENTER

Obviously, a production facility "machine" cannot operate efficiently without a control center and intercommunication. In a theatre production, the operational center is the stage manager's desk. At this desk, control is needed for work lights and signal systems, and sometimes power controls for stage equipment and similar operations are located here. Communication—a speaker or headset system—with all working areas of the theatre is needed for cues and production coordination.

In addition, a signal system of electric lights may be employed to communicate cues to crews. A page-cue system is used to reach actors in the dressing rooms and the green room. In the proscenium theatre, the stage manager has traditionally been located on the working side of the arch, where actors enter, where the flying equipment is operated, and where the stage manager can see the stage from the wings. The view of the stage is enhanced by placing a video camera in the auditorium and a monitor at the stage manager's desk. Monitors may also be provided for backstage crews unable to see the production.

In the thrust stage, arena, and multiform theatres, the best location for the stage manager is often in the control room with the lighting and sound operators, viewing the stage through a booth window. In recent years, there has been some rethinking about the stage manager's backstage position in the proscenium theatre. In some theatres, the stage manager has been located in or adjacent to the lighting booth at the rear of the auditorium to have a fuller view of the stage. An assistant stage manager handles the operation backstage. In television, production is managed from the control room. The director and technical director maintain headset communication with the floor manager, camera operators, and production crew.

FIRE-PROTECTION SYSTEMS

Certain equipment is required on the stage of a theatre to put out fire, to prevent the spread of fire, and to protect individuals from fire hazards. Among these are sprinkler systems, emergency lighting, fire extinguishers, fire alarm stations, hose and standpipes, and similar items. Prominent among these protective devices is the sprinkler system, which is designed to discharge water automatically at a given temperature. These systems and fire-prevention practices are presented in Chapter 4. In addition, most building codes mandate a means of isolating a fire onstage from the audience. The solution most often required is the use of a fire curtain and smoke vents. A fire curtain, made of special fiberglass material or steel, is located immediately behind the proscenium arch. Woven asbestos is becoming less common because of the hazards of inhaling asbestos particles. The fire curtain is guided by stretched steel cables on the sides located within steel channels called smoke pockets. These pockets prevent smoke from escaping around the edges. A fire curtain is rigged to fall automatically in case of fire.

One method of achieving this is to underbalance the counterweight arbor so the curtain falls by its own weight. Another means is to cause an additional weight to fall on an otherwise balanced line, thus overweighting the curtain and forcing it to fall across the arch. Either of these means is achieved by lines that pass across the top of the proscenium arch and down the side walls. Regularly spaced along these lines are fusible links that melt at a specific high temperature. When one of these links melts, the line is broken, causing the curtain to fall. In addition, the curtain may be dropped manually by cutting the line with a knife (if it is rope) or releasing it from a hook (if it is steel cable).

Fire curtain installations often include a hydraulic cylinder that slows down the freefalling curtain in its last 8' of travel. Accompanying the closing off of the proscenium arch is the opening of automatic smoke vents on the roof of the stage. Operated by gravity or spring action, the vents open when fusible links melt or by manual release. The combined action of the fire curtain and smoke vents is intended to keep fire and smoke from the audience by containment and exhaustion of smoke and fumes. Some local laws obligate a theatre to raise the fire curtain in full view of the audience before each performance as assurance of its presence and workability.

Changes in the New York City building code in 1968 provided a different mode of protecting audiences from stage fires. This system forbids the use of any barrier across the proscenium arch that would impede the passage of air to the stage. Instead, it requires a deluge sprinkler system capable of providing a water density of 3 gallons per minute per linear foot. In addition, it specifies emergency ventilation by fans to exhaust smoke and fumes rapidly from the stage. These new code regulations recognize and make accommodation for the thrust stage and other nonproscenium theatre forms.

SELECTED READINGS

THE AMERICAN THEATRE PLANNING BOARD, *Theatre Check List*. Middletown, Conn.: Wesleyan University Press, 1969.

PETER ALBRECHT CORPORATION, *Automatic Stage Systems: Catalog 11*. Milwaukee, Wis.: 1972.

AUTOMATIC DEVICES COMPANY, *Curtain Tracks-Curtain Machines: Catalog 11P*. Allentown, Penn.: 1973.

BURRIS-MEYER, HAROLD, and EDWARD C. COLE, *Scenery for the Theatre* (rev. ed.). Boston: Little, Brown, 1971.

BURRIS-MEYER, HAROLD, and EDWARD C. COLE, *Theatres and Auditoriums* (2nd ed.). New York: Reinhold, 1975.

J. R. CLANCY, INC., *Standard Specifications for Theatrical Rigging* (rev. ed.). Syracuse, 1988.

FORSYTH, MICHAEL, *Auditoria*. New York: Van Nostrand, 1987.

MIELZINER, JO, *The Shapes of Our Theatre*. New York: Clarkson N. Potter, Inc., 1970.

TRU-ROLL CORPORATION, *Stage Hardware Catalog*. Glendale, Calif.

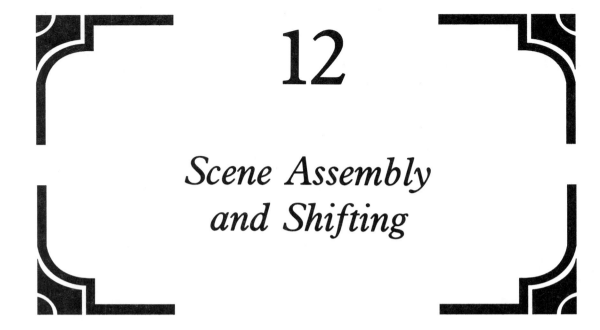

12

Scene Assembly and Shifting

The complexity and uniqueness of scenery is nowhere more evident than in the way it is assembled and shifted. Witness the fascination of an audience with the division of the scenic picture into integral units during a well-executed scene change. A fixed setting built directly on the stage is an exception. Scenery is usually joined, supported, and fitted for rapid assembly and disassembly. Scenic structures must be moved through the construction process in the shop, be conveniently transported to the stage, and frequently be shifted during performances. To achieve this, scenery is built in prefabricated units, constructed in finished sections, and equipped to be erected and joined together quickly. On many stages, only a limited amount of time is provided for hanging or setting up scenery, sometimes called **loading in**. And once scenery is mounted, only seconds are permitted for scene changes during a show, to avoid long interruptions in the continuity of the performance and in audience concentration.

The mounting and operation of scenery must be carefully considered from the outset, especially for a multiscene production. While still in the design phase, the production staff must determine how to get scenery and properties on the stage, how to remove them, and where they are to be stored backstage. Special methods are employed to join scenic units together easily and quickly. Ways are sought to handle, support, and transport large and awkward units. Scene shifts are plotted to be fast, quiet, accurate, and well organized. Scene changes in full view of an audience are often choreographed precision events. These, then, are some tasks relating to the assembly and shifting of scenery.

JOINING SCENERY

There are a variety of ways to join scenery units. The selection of joining methods depends on the strength needed and on requirements for separating the setting into convenient units for transporting, setting up, and shifting.

Permanent Devices

Scenery units can be joined permanently with standard hardware, including nails, screws, bolts, and metal plates. Permanent attachments provide strong joints, permit the concealing of cracks between scenic pieces, and simplify the assembly of units during the setup on stage. A set built onstage can usually be joined with permanent devices. However, scenery is often built elsewhere and moved to the stage. Therefore, it must be constructed in sizes and shapes that can be easily handled and transported. This is less of a problem where the shop is adjacent to the stage and separated by a large doorway. In this situation, flats that form a large straight wall, for instance, can be battened together as one unit and moved easily to the stage. However, when the shop is remote, large units must be constructed in smaller sections or must be built as foldable, demountable or collapsible structures.

Front Hinging

A straight wall can be constructed of flats or other framed pieces joined permanently with tight-pin back-flap hinges on the front (Figure 12-1). This permits the unit to fold conveniently for transporting, with the painted sides turned inside for protection. Further, the crack between the units can be masked with a cloth **dutchman.** Hinges are needed at least every 5' along the joint and within a foot of the top and bottom of the frames. Proper positioning of the hinges provides a secure joint and prevents the dutchman from loosening. The presence of the hinges is usually adequately hidden by the dutchman. However, the location of the scenery in relation to the audience, or the use of prominent side lighting, may result in

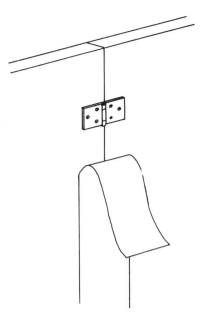

FIGURE 12–1   Front hinging and dutchman to mask joint and hinges.

a telltale bulge or shadow. If this is anticipated, it is best to countersink the hinges.

Special attention to the folding action is required when more than two flats are front hinged to form a straight wall. Flats that do not fold against each other are very awkward to handle. A 1″ × 2″ or 1″ × 3″ batten, known as a **tumbler**, must be hinged into one joint to allow the complete unit to fold compactly (Figure 12-2). Of course, the widest flat must be in the center position to accommodate the other flats when folded. With the use of tumblers, a multifold of several flats can be hinged together permanently.

Dutchmen are commonly used to mask cracks in all permanent scenic units. The cloth should be of the same fabric and texture as the covering on the flats. Each strip must be wide enough to mask the front hinges at the joint. Torn edges are necessary to conceal the dutchman; selvage edges will not disappear when applied and painted. Regular scenic paste is used to hold the

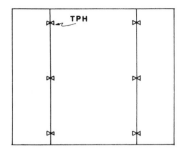

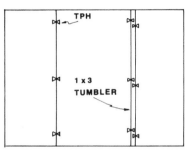

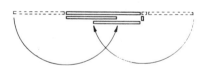

FIGURE 12-2 Planned properly, front hinging and the use of a tumbler permits the flats to fold compactly.

dutchman in place. Outer edges need to be well pasted and firmly pressed to the flat covers.

Lashing

The assembly and disassembly of a setting in a scene shift is made easier by a combination of permanent and temporary joining methods. The ideal is a series of easily handled scenic units which are connected to-

gether by temporary devices at only a few selected locations. It is a rapid process to break these connections and remove the permanently joined units from the stage by standard shifting means. Lashing is a common temporary joining method that involves the joining of two units by ¼″ cotton rope laced around lash cleats and tied at the end (Figure 12-3). The hardware must be precisely located, and a lash knot must be used to assure speed in making and breaking the attachment.

In joining two flats by lashing, the procedure is as follows:

1. The end of the lash line is secured at the upper right corner of the left flat by attachment to a **lash line eye** or through a ⅜″ hole drilled into the corner block. The rope is passed through the hole or eye and the end is tied with an overhand knot. The length of the rope should not exceed the height of the flat so it will not get caught beneath the flat or be stepped on during shifts.

FIGURE 12-3 Lashing.

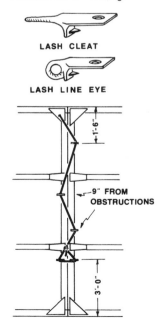

2. **Lash cleats** are mounted alternately on the inside of the adjacent stiles approximately every 3′. The top cleat should be placed within 1′–6″ of the top of the flat to keep the tops of the units from separating. Cleats must not be closer than 9″ to a toggle bar or other obstruction or it will be difficult to whip the rope around them. The bottom two cleats are placed opposite each other 3′ from the floor. This is a convenient height to tie off the line and eliminates the need of a rope which exceeds the height of the flat.

3. Once the flats have been brought together and aligned, the rope may be lashed to the hardware. Experience is necessary in learning to throw the lash line around the cleats. With some slack in the rope and a circular arm motion, a loop will travel up the rope and hook around the top cleat. This pattern is repeated until the rope is secured on all the cleats. The rope is passed around the bottom pair of cleats and pulled taut. The rope is then tied to itself just above the cleats. A lash knot is a form of slip knot which will untie by simply pulling the loose rope end. Any other knot will unduly delay disassembly of the scenery. Note the illustration of the lash knot later in chapter 13. Essentially, a tight loop is placed under the rope and another loop is passed through the first loop. The secret is to keep the rope taut while the knot is made and properly tightened.

Because of the inherent stability, lashing is most often located at corners of the setting. To minimize the chance of the audience seeing the junction between two units forming a corner, the butt joint should be parallel to the proscenium opening of the stage. The junction between the units will be less obvious, and offstage lighting will not reveal the joint. Corner lashing requires devices to keep the units aligned under the tension of the lash line (Figure 12-4).

Outside Lashing. When the angle of the back of the two units exceeds 180°, **stop cleats** must be located to protrude from the downstage stile and to secure the alignment of the joint. Three cleats, placed near the top, in the middle, and near the bottom are needed.

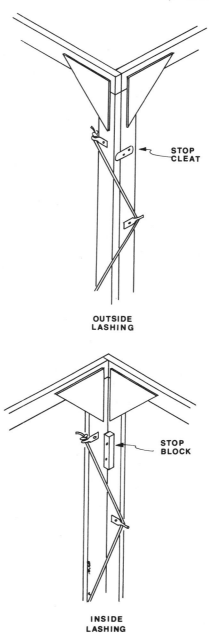

STOP CLEAT

OUTSIDE LASHING

STOP BLOCK

INSIDE LASHING

FIGURE 12–4 Lashing requires stop cleats at outside corners and stop blocks at inside corners.

Inside Lashing. When the angle of the back of the two units is less than 180°, **stop blocks** are necessary to maintain alignments. These are blocks of wood cut ¾″ × ¾″ × 3″ long. Three are necessary and are attached with screws to the stile.

Occasionally, flats that form a straight wall are joined by lashing. When this is planned, an overlapping batten or other ornamentation on the front side is often required to mask the vertical junction of the two units. Alignment of the units is assured by stop cleats on the back. Lashing is not limited only to flats. Almost any type of scenic construction can be joined by lashing if vertical battens are added to the back for the lashing hardware.

Loose-Pin Hinging

For strong attachments, loose-pin hinges are excellent temporary joining devices (Figure 12-5). They are used more as joining hardware than as hinges. The regular pins or pin wire are used to secure the hinge leaves together. Two or three hinges are often sufficient to join two scenic units such as two stair units, a stair unit and a platform, a

FIGURE 12–5 Loose-pin hinging.

stair unit and its masking/balustrade facade, and similar structures. However, because careful alignment is necessary for inserting the pins, loose-pin hinging often requires more time in a scene shift than lashing does.

Other Temporary Devices

A number of other devices are used to join scenic units for easy disassembly (Figure 12-6). The nature of the connection usually governs the selection of hardware. The low-

FIGURE 12–6 Other temporary joining devices.

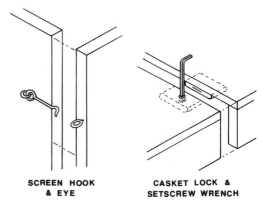

SCREEN HOOK
& EYE

CASKET LOCK &
SETSCREW WRENCH

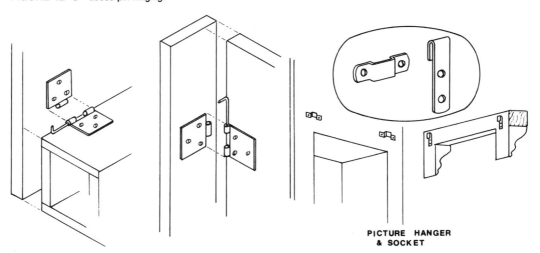

PICTURE HANGER
& SOCKET

ering of a flap of a **strap hinge** to hold a door or window unit in the opening of a flat is described in Chapter 9. This is useful for any framed structure inserted into another unit. **Screen-door hooks** and **screw eyes** are convenient attachments where stability is not a problem. They are employed in plug settings such as the temporary joining of a flat to the back of an archway thickness. **Picture hangers** and **sockets** are standard theatrical hardware used to attach objects to the front of flats. In addition to hanging pictures, small shelves, and other set dressings, these versatile hangers are effective in attaching cornices, panels, moldings, fireplace mantels, and other items for easy removal. A **casket lock** is a rugged joining device for butt-joint connections. Operable by a set-screw wrench, it can join together two platforms or large vertical objects that require separating for a scene change. A creative technician can determine, even invent, appropriate temporary joining methods for specific situations. Even when bolts are used for rigidity, **T-nuts** or hand-driven **wing nuts** offer some advantage in removing and assembling units with minimal time and effort.

STIFFENING SCENERY

Stiffening is the process of holding scenery units in a rigid shape or position. Sometimes stiffeners also double as joining devices, but they usually have the sole function of preventing the scenic units from bending, bowing, or losing shape. Scenery must be stiffened not only for its use in a scene but also for shifting by flying, rolling, or other means.

Permanent Stiffening

When several flats are used to form a straight wall, it is possible to secure them together with two or three 1″ × 3″ battens attached horizontally across the back and fastened to the stiles with screws. These battens will serve both joining and stiffening purposes. However, the size of this structural unit requires a large opening and easy access from the shop to the stage. It is more common to join the flats with front hinging (and dutchmen to conceal the junctions). The unit may then be folded for transport to the stage. A 1″ × 3″ **stiffening batten** is

FIGURE 12–7 Permanent stiffening.

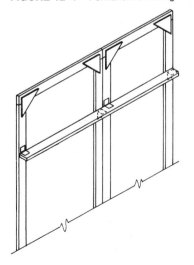
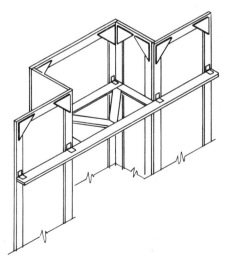

placed on edge across the back of the flats, usually near the upper third of the unit (Figure 12-7). The stiffener is attached to the stiles with loose-pin hinges. The hinges are placed alternately on the top and bottom of the batten to hold it perpendicular to the flats for maximum stiffening value. Removing the hinge pins allows the batten to be carried separately to the stage, where it is repositioned on the flats. Irregularly shaped scenic units require **stiffening frames**, which take the form of the structure. They are sometimes used vertically to conform with the shape of the unit.

Temporary Stiffening

For the purpose of shifting scenery, it is sometimes necessary to quickly remove a stiffener and fold up the wall for easy handling (Figure 12-8). This is made possible by **keeper hooks**. These are S-shaped hooks that hang on the toggle bars of flats and in the open end receive a stiffening batten. The batten and hooks are fully removable. The toggle bars on the flats must be located at the same height to accommodate the removable stiffener. To avoid loss of the keeper hooks in the rush of a scene change, they may be attached to the stiffener with screws. On walls that are not too wide, a **swivel stiffener** is appropriate. In this form the batten is attached to a stile, slightly off center and by a single carriage bolt. As the batten pivots to a horizontal position, it is held in position by keeper hooks attached to the toggle bars with screws. When the stiffener is raised to a vertical position, the flats can be folded and moved.

BRACING SCENERY

Scenery needs vertical support to stand upright and to endure door slams and other physical activity. The bracing system selected must be sufficient to prevent visible

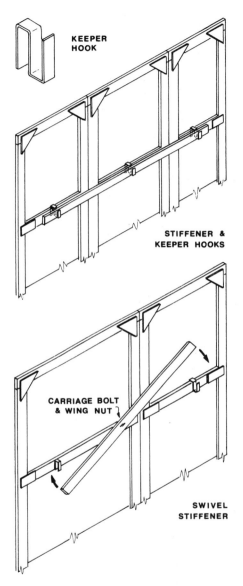

FIGURE 12–8 Temporary stiffening.

vibration of the setting. A setting that is not shifted can be braced permanently in place with a variety of structural supports. Sometimes, by design or by the inherent form of a scenic unit, bracing is a built-in feature of the structure. However, more often, bracing is a lightweight, easily removed or temporary attachment to the scenery.

Self-Bracing Units

Some scenic units are self-bracing. These are usually three-dimensional, freestanding pieces composed of elements joined at angles to provide internal support. Often bracing is an extension of the joining and stiffening framework. A fireplace, a folding screen, and a bay window frequently have this characteristic. The scenic needs of an open stage favor the conscious design of free-standing units (Figure 12-9). The openness of fragmentary scenery offers limited, if any, support from adjacent structures and few surfaces to mask conventional braces. A fragmentary doorway can be self-supporting if the door frame is structurally attached to a small platform beneath it. Self-bracing may be the solution for scenery used on a stage floor of concrete or hardwood, or the smooth floor of a TV studio, which cannot be penetrated with bracing hardware.

Many times self-bracing is an answer to difficult support problems. Added bracing can be given to a door that opens onstage, away from its offstage braces, if it is slightly recessed in the wall. The protruding wall sections help support the weight of the door shutter as it is opened. Scenery that is self-bracing is often time-saving in a scene shift, with no need to remove temporary braces. And those free-standing units that are too large, too heavy, or too awkward to handle can be constructed as rolling units.

The Stage Brace

A standard means of bracing scenery is the **adjustable stage brace** (Figure 12-10). The brace consists of two overlapping lengths of hardwood or telescoping metal tubes that can be adjusted in length and secured with clamp and thumbscrew. One end has a double hook that fastens to a **brace**

FIGURE 12–9 Self-bracing scenic units.

FIGURE 12–10 Adjustable stage brace.

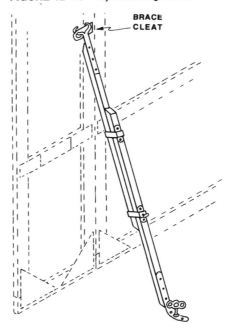

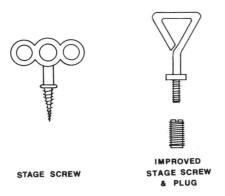

STAGE SCREW

IMPROVED
STAGE SCREW
& PLUG

FIGURE 12–11   Stage screws.

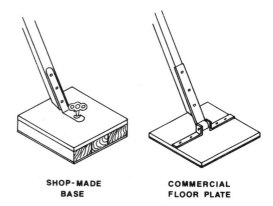

SHOP-MADE
BASE

COMMERCIAL
FLOOR PLATE

FIGURE 12–12   Weighted floor bases for stage braces.

cleat mounted on the scenery. A **rocker iron** at the bottom of the brace is secured to the stage floor with a **stage screw**. The brace cleat is attached to a stile in the upper third of the scenery. Once the stage brace is connected to the cleat, it is adjusted at an appropriate angle to the floor.

The stage screw is a hand-driven screw intended for use in softwood stage floors. An **improved stage screw** is made with bolt-like threads to fit into a threaded plug (Figure 12-11). The plug is driven into a ½″ hole drilled into the floor. This screw withstands repeated use without causing an ever-enlarging hole in the floor. The plug can be removed later or left in the floor for use again in the future. (Plugs can be permanently imbedded at regular intervals in a concrete floor when it is poured.) Sometimes floors do not permit the use of stage screws. In these situations, the stage brace may be secured to a weighted base having a nonskid surface (Figure 12-12). Shop-built bases are not difficult to construct. Stage braces are located as needed along expanses of scenery rather than at corners, which are generally self-supporting.

The Brace Jack

Another type of support is the brace jack, a triangular frame of 1″ × 3″ or 1″ × 4″ lumber stock (Figure 12-13). The jack can be constructed with cornerblock-reinforced butt joints. The long member of the frame should be at least two-thirds the height of the scenery. It is joined to a stile or to the toggle bars of scenery with loose-pin hinges. This will allow the jack, if convenient, to fold against the back of the scenery when the unit is shifted or stored. The brace jack is held to the floor with a foot iron and stage screw or by the weight of a sandbag or iron weight placed on the bottom rail. The use of weights makes the brace jack especially valuable on stage floors which cannot take stage screws. It provides more support than the stage brace because it attaches to the scenery at several points along the vertical edge of the frame. A jack for a profile or other isolated unit is sometimes constructed slightly less than 90°. The weight of the unit will be shifted slightly backward giving more stable support.

FLOOR ANCHORING

Scenery must sometimes be firmly secured to the stage floor. Repeated door slams and other actions cause walls to move out of position, to wobble, or to lean. This is particularly true of flown scenery or of units braced with a stage brace. Brace jacks provide bottom support to scenery, and therefore generally do not require additional floor securement. The **rigid foot iron** and **hinged foot iron** are standard hardware for floor anchoring (Figure 12-14). They accommodate a stage screw for attachment to the floor. The hinged foot iron folds flat and will not protrude on flown units when fly space is tight. As is the case with bracing of scenery, floors that cannot be marred with stage screws require specially designed devices to accommodate weights. Scenery mounted on rolling wagons for scene changes must be well secured to the wagon top. An alternative to floor hardware on permanent settings is the use of strips of wood securing the base of scenery to the floor with nails or weights.

Small wagons (platforms on casters) must be held to the floor so they will not roll beneath actors' feet. Sometimes a pair of **brake casters** on the offstage side of the wagon, if accessible, is an appropriate answer to this problem. Foot irons and stage screws provide a very secure anchor to prevent movement of the casters. At least two foot irons are necessary and must be mounted to the wagon ½″ or ¾″ above the floor to clear obstructions when rolling. Stage screws can be tied or hooked to the rear of the scenery so they will not be lost or misplaced in the scene shift. Of course, foot irons protrude from the edges of a wagon and may cause hazards

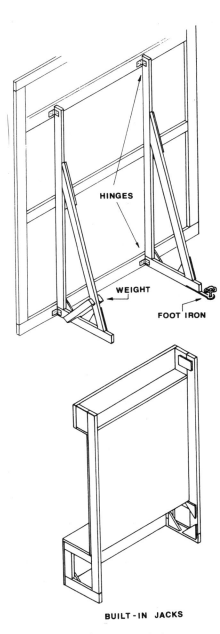

HINGES

WEIGHT

FOOT IRON

BUILT-IN JACKS

FIGURE 12–13   The brace jack.

FIGURE 12–14   Foot irons.

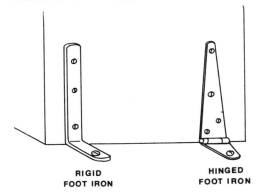

RIGID FOOT IRON

HINGED FOOT IRON

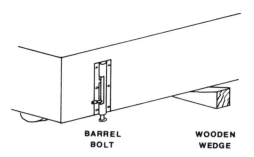

FIGURE 12–15 Other floor-anchoring devices.

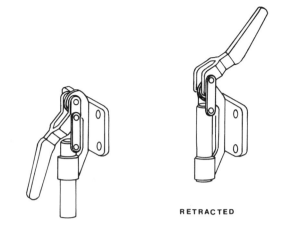

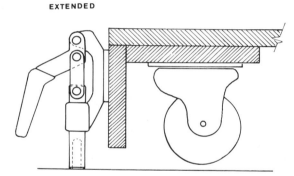

FIGURE 12–16 Platform clamp. De-Sta-Co Clamp #608, when extended, prevents a wagon from rolling by lifting the wagon off its casters. (Adapted from drawings courtesy of De-Sta-Co)

and difficulties in tight scene shifts. A very adequate anchoring is provided by large **barrel bolts** (Figure 12-15). They are attached to the wagon frame, and the bolts are lowered into predrilled holes in the stage. Before moving the wagon, the bolts are raised and locked in their top positions.

The foot iron, stage screw and barrel bolt methods give the strongest support to wagon movement. However, because they require precise alignment of hardware with predetermined holes in the floor, more time is needed in scene shifts. Two other methods can be employed which do not demand such alignment accuracy. The simplest is the use of **wooden wedges**, which are placed under the wagon frame on two or more offstage edges to remove wagon support from several casters. Wedges are effective in all but the most rigorous action on a wagon.

A very good method of securing a wagon is the use of the *De-Sta-Co* Clamp #608 (Figure 12-16). This clamp can be bolted on the offstage side of a wagon. By plunger action, a handle causes a rod to extend to the floor, raising the wagon off its casters. At least two clamps may be necessary for very active actor movement on the wagon. Foot action is often sufficient to set and release the handle. The plunger rod extends 1⅝″. It is internally threaded to accommodate a ⅜″ × 16 adjustable spindle if needed for greater extension.

SHIFTING OF SCENERY

In planning the settings for a multiscene production, methods must be considered for handling scene changes. This is determined by the scene designer early in the production design process. All approaches, technical and theatrical, are explored to arrive at the most effective solution for the production. Frequently, the choice is a complex shifting plan requiring exacting mechanics and coordination of rigging. On the other hand, a solution that reduces or eliminates scene shifting is sometimes more appropriate. Some plays, for instance, have been conceived for a **simultaneous setting**. This type of setting contains several different locales simultaneously on the stage. Each is individually used as the actors move from place to place. Settings for *The Miracle Worker* and *Death of a Salesman* simultaneously reveal several rooms and the outdoors of a home.

Space staging is another approach. This involves developing a neutral, unlocalized space on stage, sometimes with several levels or platforms. A specific place is created by

FIGURE 12–17   Unit set. Skeletal setting altered by additional units to serve both for the family room and the porch of *Fifth of July*. Designed by the author.

the dialogue, by the way actors use a portion of the space, or by the addition of props. A design concept known as a **unit set** often reduces the amount of scenery to be shifted. This utilizes a scenic element, perhaps a platform or a wall structure, which remains on stage to unify all of the different settings. The scenery might consist of a permanent structure that is altered in appearance by changes in plugs, a few additional units, furniture, and set dressings. **Fragmentary** and **cut-away settings** employ a minimal amount of scenery, which frequently lessens the task of a scene change. These and other types of settings are conceived primarily for design values, but they also can provide distinct scene-shifting advantages.

An inventive shifting plan generally requires several essential ingredients. One of these is a knowledge of technical shifting devices and how they can be adapted to a variety of situations. Another is the need for careful study of the script to learn the nature and development of moving from scene to scene. Is a setting used again? How much time can be allowed for the shift? Assistance for scene changes may be inherent in the script. Small scenes separating large scenes offer the opportunity for **alternation staging**; that is, locating some scenes in the shallow, downstage area while settings for large scenes are being changed upstage on the major portion of the stage. Scene shifts must be well organized and safely and speedily executed. A minimum of ten minutes is typical for an intermission between acts, but changes between scenes are often limited to thirty seconds to avoid prolonging the performance. Changes in full view of the audience save the time needed to lower and raise the front curtain.

Shifting Manually

A common method of moving scenery and properties is by hand. Scenery, of course, is often large, awkward to handle, and easily damaged. Therefore it is important to know the techniques for handling, moving, and stacking scenic units. A standard 14′ flat is not heavy, but the center of weight is well above the height of a crew member. Mishandled, the cloth covering can be torn or loosened and the lightweight frame can be warped or broken.

Raising Flats. One person can usually raise a single flat without heavy added decoration to its vertical position. The flat is first lifted so that one edge is resting on the floor. Moving to the bottom of the flat, you steady the pivot point with your foot while both hands on the upper stile flip the unit quickly and smoothly upright (Figure 12-18). This will not be possible in raising large flats, flats with heavy three-dimensional trim, or several flats joined together. One or more persons are needed to **foot** the scenery by steadying the bottom rail with their feet. Other crew members can then lift the top of the unit and **walk** it upward hand over hand along the stiles (Figure 12-19).

Running Flats. A flat is balanced in the upright position by holding it with hands spread vertically. One hand grasps the stile above head height and the other hand crosses the body at the waist to hold the lower part of the stile (Figure 12-20). With this same grip, the flat can easily be moved. The lower hand lifts the edge of the flat slightly allowing the rear of the rail to slide

FIGURE 12–18   Flipping a flat.

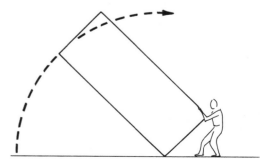

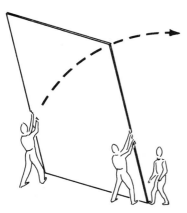

FIGURE 12–19 Walking a heavy flat upright.

Stacking Flats. Backstage, flats are stored temporarily until they are run on stage for a scene change. They should be placed in an upright position in stacks against a wall or other support. A stack should be compact and as vertical as possible to prevent the stiles from warping and to reduce the amount of floor space needed for storage. Flats are stored face-to-face to protect the painted front surfaces. Be careful of projecting nails and other objects which can damage adjacent flats. Flats with protruding decor or surfaces should be stacked separately from other flats. It is best to organize stacks according to shift needs and to distance from their location on the set. Identifying members are usually painted on the back of flats, and they are stacked in order of their setup in the coming shift.

Lowering Flats to the Floor. A flat or series of flats without added weight or decor can be **floated** to the floor by placing a foot against the bottom rail and letting the unit fall (Figure 12-21). Air pressure provides a cushion beneath the fabric covering allowing the units to drop to the floor gently and without damage. The floor space must be adequate for the height of the flat, which must fall squarely to take advantage of the air cushion. It is advisable to protect yourself from the dust raised when a flat is floated.

along the floor as you move forward. The upper hand continues to balance the unit. Having a portion of the flat on the floor helps to stabilize the unit. It is inadvisable to raise a tall flat entirely off the floor because it is very difficult to control the balance. Moving a flat in this manner is known as *running* because with moderate speed air pressure on the sides of the flat aids in the balancing process. Running a particularly large or heavy flat may require another crew member on the trailing edge to push and to assist in maintaining balance.

FIGURE 12–20 Running flats.

FIGURE 12–21 Floating a flat.

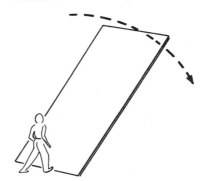

Heavy flats, especially those with additional framing or architectural trim, must be lowered to the floor by walking. While one or more persons foot the bottom rail, others walk the unit to the floor hand over hand along the stiles.

Handling Heavy or Awkward Units. Some scenic structures to be manually shifted may be difficult to handle and transport. Units of this type must be examined and solutions found to assist in moving them. Structures that cannot be handled conveniently and safely often delay a shift or are easily subject to damage. Sometimes handles, a length of rope, or an added batten will facilitate grasping and lifting of a unit (Figure 12-22). Handles or special support battens also may improve the ability to steady a top-heavy wall. Furniture glides will make a unit slide on the floor more easily. If these or other devices do not provide sufficient help, another shifting method may be more appropriate.

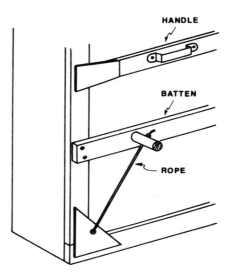

FIGURE 12–22 Ways to carry heavy or awkward scenery.

Shifting by Rolling Methods

Rolling devices provide an easy and convenient way to mobilize scenery on the floor. While they are especially suitable for three-dimensional, heavy, and large structures, they are adaptable to nearly every type of scenic unit from entire settings to the smallest part. The amount of offstage space for storage is the only limitation in using these shifting systems.

Casters. Casters are the most common means for horizontal movement of scenery. Do not settle on the cheapest. High-quality casters are essential to support scenic loads, to move easily, and to run quietly. Casters for a rolled unit should be selected for durability, rated load capacity, and diameter of wheel. Wheel diameters from 3″ to 6″ are the most useful for scenery. Wide rubber wheels or rubber-tired wheels are preferred for quiet operation. **Rigid casters** move back and forth in a single plane; **swivel casters** are multidirectional (Figure 12-23). **Brake casters** permit the wheels to be locked to prevent them from rolling when a unit is placed in position for use.

Wagons. A wagon in its simplest form is a castered platform. In fact, standard platforms can be easily converted into wagons. The parallel is the only platform system with a framing that is unsuitable for the attachment of casters. Low wagons (6″ to 8″ in height) are widely used. They can be achieved with platform frames and tops (without leg posts) by the addition of framing members to which casters are mounted.

FIGURE 12–23 Casters.

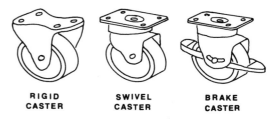

RIGID CASTER   SWIVEL CASTER   BRAKE CASTER

On platforms made of lumber, for instance, 2″ × 6″s are nailed between members of the platform frame flush to the underside of the platform top (Figure 12-24). The mounting plates of the casters are then secured to the broad surface of the 2″ × 6″s with large screws or carriage bolts. Concealed within the platform frame, swivel casters must be positioned 3″ to 4″ from framing members to have freedom of movement. Casters with a minimum wheel diameter of 3″ are usually sufficient for small wagons. It is sometimes necessary to add facing boards clearing the floor by ¾″ to conceal the casters. Higher wagons are constructed from legged platforms. To adapt a 2″-lumber platform, 2″ × 6″ plates are added to the bottom of the legs for caster attachment. To secure these plates and to keep them from twisting, they are firmly attached to 2″ × 4″s placed along the outside of the legs. When this lumber is positioned properly, the base of the wagon has the same perimeter as the wagon top, simplifying the task of mounting flats, plywood, or other sheet material as a facing surface.

Metal framed platforms are also easily converted to wagons (Figure 12-26). Relatively little additional framing is necessary to fit casters to these structures. The mounting plates of casters can be welded to a platform formed of welded steel tubing or secured to special welded brackets. Casters are easily bolted to platforms framed with slotted steel angle. On platforms made of pipe and slip-on pipe fittings, a strip of lumber to which casters are bolted can be attached to the bottom of the pipe legs with pipe flanges.

In constructing wagons, it must be determined what size and number of casters will be used. This is based largely on the total load carried by the wagon. Generally, the distribution of casters every 4′ is adequate for typical scenic loads. When selecting the appropriate wheel diameter, it is advisable to check the rated load capacity of the caster as provided by the manufacturer. The overall height of the caster must be known to achieve the specific height of the wagon. Normally, swivel casters are used on small wagons that, in the course of a shift, must roll in several directions. However, rigid casters are best on wagons that move in a single direction. On heavy units, swivel casters tend to lock up until all the wheels are aligned in the direction of the thrust, making it difficult to start them in motion.

FIGURE 12–24   Converting platforms to wagons.

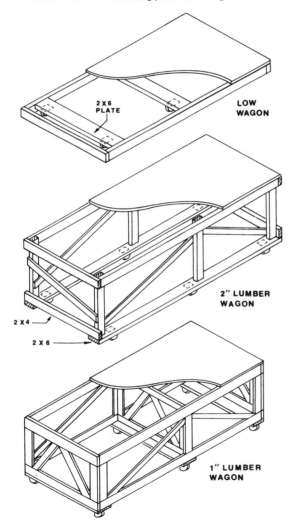

2 X 6 PLATE

LOW WAGON

2″ LUMBER WAGON

2 X 4

2 X 6

1″ LUMBER WAGON

FIGURE 12–25 Wagon units used for large turning scenic structures in *Merry Wives of Windsor*. Scene design by Kenneth Bunne. (Photo by George Tarbay)

Wagons are ideal for moving three-dimensional scenic units and heavy properties. A bay window (with or without a window seat) or a major entrance way may often be on a level higher than the rest of the setting. The wagon may represent the raised hearth for a fireplace unit or a raised pedestal of an alcove or wall niche. A flight of stairs with necessary landings is frequently part of a wagon unit. Wagons are often not large, being tailored to the dimensions of the heavy or three-dimensional structures they carry. On the other hand, multilevel settings may require larger wagons. These are often achieved by bolting several platform units together.

Tracks placed on the stage floor are sometimes necessary to accurately guide a wagon in its pattern of movement. This may be necessary for wagons moving partial or complete settings. Even with rigid casters, after repeated movement a wagon frequently tends to drift away from its intended position. A groove can be provided on the floor by narrow strips of beveled wood or steel angle irons. A piece of angle iron attached to the under side of the wagon frame rides in this groove and keeps the wagon aligned in position (Figure 12-27). This tracking system will not work, of course, if it interferes with other rolling units or with the action of the performers. In permanent installations a groove is sometimes cut directly in the stage floor.

Wagons can be moved or driven in a number of ways. Manual operation—pulling or

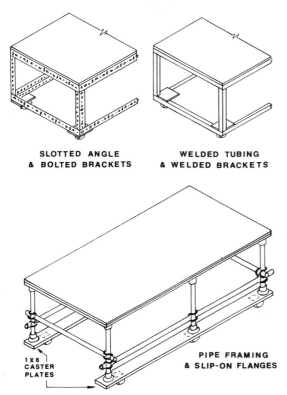

SLOTTED ANGLE
& BOLTED BRACKETS

WELDED TUBING
& WELDED BRACKETS

1 X 6
CASTER
PLATES

PIPE FRAMING
& SLIP-ON FLANGES

FIGURE 12–26 Metal framed wagons.

FIGURE 12–27 Wagon guide-track using steel angle.

pushing—is the simplest method. To do this it is often necessary to have mechanical aids that will place the pulling and shoving pressure properly on the wagon base. Handles, push sticks, and pulling devices may be helpful. On a low wagon, for example, eye or ring hardware can be installed at strategic locations to accommodate tow ropes or steel pull bars, providing a safe and controlled moving action. This is better than pushing on scenic walls, which are not designed for this pressure. Heavy wagons and those requiring unseen power sources are often cable-driven. A hand winch provides considerable mechanical advantage to drive large rolling units. The winch is mounted on a steel frame at a comfortable height and secured firmly to the floor in an offstage position (Figure 12-28). A loop of cable passes from the winch drum through floor sheaves and is directed close to the floor beneath the wagon and around a sheave in the extreme onstage position. One side of the loop is attached to the wagon. By winch control, the wagon can be moved on or off the stage with little effort. It is an effective device in a shift seen by an audience when the visibility of the stage crew is not desired. Thin aircraft cable minimizes the chance of visibility to the audience. Electric motor winches (fixed or variable speed) are also available to drive the cable. Theatres equipped with hydraulic

FIGURE 12–28 Wagon driven by cable and hand winch.

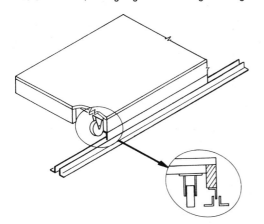

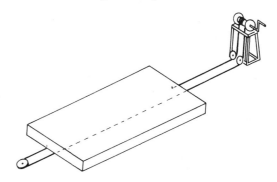

power may prefer this work source. Air casters are examined later in this chapter.

The one disadvantage to cable-driven wagons is that the cable and the onstage sheave may impede other functions on the stage floor. For this reason, some productions use a temporary floor installed above the regular stage floor. The space under the temporary floor conceals the cable and sheaves. Metal brackets mounted under the wagons extend through guide slots in the floor to attach to the cable (Figure 12-29). This system also permits the use of thin wagons—sheets of ¾" plywood on furniture glides—for shifting furniture and prop items (Figure 12-30). For this purpose, the top surface of the temporary floor must be a tempered hardboard or other hard-surface material.

Full-Stage Wagons. A full-stage wagon is large enough to hold an entire setting complete with furniture and other props. Its advantage in a scene change is obvious. The shift is limited to rolling the wagon to its position onstage. With a minimum of two wagon stages, one setting can be set up on a

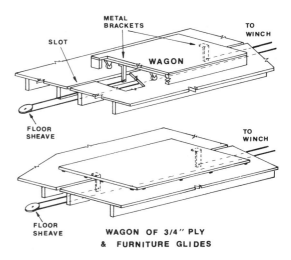

FIGURE 12–29 Temporary floor to conceal wagon drive-cable and sheaves.

wagon in the offstage position while a scene is playing on the other wagon (Figure 12-31). Shifting from wagon to wagon results in fast scene changes for productions requiring several large settings. Generally, theatres must be specifically designed for full-sized

FIGURE 12–30 Broadway Scenery. Setting for *Dreamgirls*; designed by Robin Wagner. Aluminum tower/wagons move on and offstage by motorized winches through cable drives beneath the temporary floor on the stage. Another set of winches rotate the towers. Alternation of the stage space is made further kinetic by aluminum bridges that raise and lower to the floor. (© 1983, Martha Swope Photography)

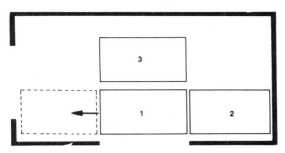

FIGURE 12–31 Full-stage wagons.

stage wagons. Certainly, considerable clear offstage space is needed for wagons. The Metropolitan Opera House in New York has three complete wagon stages located in offstage areas known as **wagon houses** to the right, left, and upstage of the playing area. The upstage wagon contains a revolving stage. Large wagon stages are specially constructed of heavy lumber or metal. Those constructed of lumber may require metal reinforcement at framing joints and for the attachment of casters. To move easily, they often require large casters, sometimes flanged wheels that roll on steel or hardwood tracks embedded in the stage floor. On any stage with sufficient space, it is possible to construct a temporary full wagon of several small wagon units bolted together and mounted on large rigid casters. Guide tracks are nearly always essential for large wagons.

The **jackknife stage** is a full-stage wagon requiring less stage width (Figure 12-32).

Two wagons are usually used. Each is pivoted at a downstage corner to swing a quarter of a circle into a different offstage wing. The stage depth must exceed the width of the wagons. A heavy bolt or metal pin can serve as the pivot. The pin must be well secured in the corner of the wagon and dropped into a reinforced hole in the floor. Rigid casters must be mounted perpendicular to radius lines from the pivot point to assure smooth and easy movement of the wagon. Another method of rolling an entire setting is a **split wagon** (Figure 12-33). This is a full-stage wagon in two sections. A portion of the setting is mounted on each section, which are joined when brought together in the playing area.

Revolves and Arcs. A revolving stage is another excellent method for shifting large and heavy scenic units. Large revolves can handle entire settings. A revolve with two settings placed back-to-back has the shifting potential of two full-stage wagons. Two or more settings can be permanently mounted on the revolve, or a setting can be erected on the back of the revolve during the performance of a scene in front. In addition, small revolving units for moving partial settings are also useful. Interior settings are particularly suited to shifting by a revolving stage, as are permanent three-dimensional settings (levels and upright structures) designed to present multiple facades to an audience. Settings placed on a turntable generally must

FIGURE 12–32 Jackknife stage.

FIGURE 12–33 Split wagon.

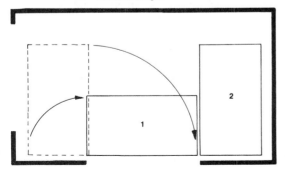

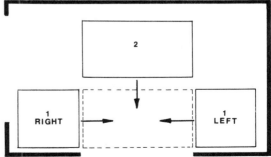

be the same height for masking purposes. Otherwise, draperies, drops, or framed units must be flown in to augment a setting. This is often necessary for exterior scenes or fragmentary settings. On the downstage corners of a setting, separate or fold-out masking returns may be needed.

There are several types of revolving units. Some theatres have permanently installed revolving stages built into the stage floor. These are usually larger in diameter than the proscenium width to handle the largest setting and to easily provide for return masking at the sides (Figure 12-34). Permanent turntables are usually motor driven, variable speed, and capable of being rotated in either direction. Portable turntables can be constructed in any size and shape. The dimension of the stage sometimes restricts the maximum size of units. A single disc is not the only answer for revolve shifting. Two small turntables or an arc unit are especially adaptable for a shallow stage (Figure 12-35). A setting can be broken into several parts for shifting. Any combination of discs, arcs, and rings can be devised. The number, type, and combination of portable units are mostly determined by the scenic and shifting demands of the production. The revolve can be irregular in shape to fit the particular shape of the settings (Figure 12-36). However, circular turntables are required when

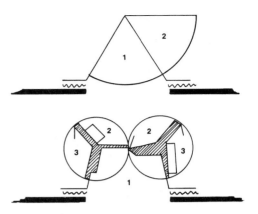

FIGURE 12–35 Use of turntable segments and small revolves.

the surrounding floor must be built up with platforms to the height of the revolve.

Portable turntables usually must be constructed in sections and bolted together on stage. The size of these sections usually depends on transportation, touring, and storage requirements. The division of a disc into wedge-shaped sections is very common. A unit of this type may become permanent equipment to be stored and used again. Another approach is to construct the heart of the revolve with stock platform units joined to specially made segments around the outside. An unusual-shape revolve exclusively for a particular production may require custom construction.

The pivot of a revolve may be achieved simply by a rod or pipe extending into a well-greased flange secured to the floor (Figure 12-37). This will serve to hold the position of the turntable as it turns. On the other hand, a large ball or roller bearing, which will support some of the weight as well as reduce friction and noise, is often preferred. A pivot of this kind can be adapted from a turret assembly or vehicle wheel-bearing. Rigid casters are positioned perpendicular to lines of radius from the pivot point. The floor of the stage must be even to avoid a wobbly turntable and to ensure level rota-

FIGURE 12–34 Full-stage turntable.

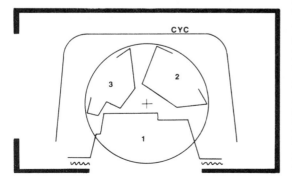

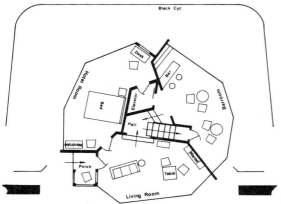

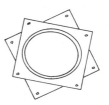

PIPE IN A
FLANGE

BALL BEARING
PIVOT

FIGURE 12–37 Pivots for revolves.

proved bearing surface for easy turning. Another solution, especially useful on uneven floors, is reversed castering. In this method casters are mounted on the floor and roll along tracks attached to the underside of the revolve. When leveled and shimmed properly, the turntable will roll easily and quietly.

Properly constructed, most portable turntables can be driven manually. This is frequently an appropriate and convenient method if the operator can remain unseen. Tow ropes hooked to cleats may assist the process. A revolve can also be turned by cable-drive systems. A loop of cable wrapped

FIGURE 12–38 Portable revolving stage with rim cable drive and electric motor power. Control includes both speed and direction.

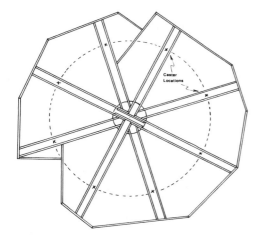

FIGURE 12–36 Irregular revolve (approximately 30′ in diameter) used to shift three sets for *Three Men on a Horse.* The lower drawing is a view of the major framing of the revolve showing 2″ × 6″ caster wells and a weight-bearing pivot.

tion. It may be necessary to lay ringed track surfaces (¾″ plywood) on the stage with added shims (thin blocks of wood) in low spots as determined by a level. On particularly heavy turntables, the rubber wheels often sink into the softwood floors, increasing the difficulty of rolling the unit. Tracks with a hard, smooth outer layer such as formica or tempered hardboard provide an im-

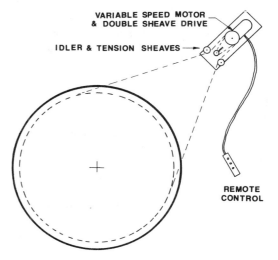

VARIABLE SPEED MOTOR
& DOUBLE SHEAVE DRIVE

IDLER & TENSION SHEAVES

REMOTE
CONTROL

one turn around the edge of a disc is directed by an idler sheave to a hand winch. Large turntables are powered by electric motor systems which drive cables wrapped around the rim (Figure 12-38). Another type of motorized system mounts on the revolve and actuates a drive wheel that rolls on the skirted edge of the revolve.

Outrigger Wagons. A wagon by necessity adds a higher level to the playing area. But a special structure, the outrigger wagon, allows the action to be played on the stage floor. The outrigger is essentially a wagon frame without the top. It is custom constructed to the backside shape of a freestanding scenic unit (Figure 12-39). Casters are mounted on the frame in a manner similar to regular wagons. Bay windows, recessed alcoves, and similar three-dimensional structures can be mobilized with outrigger wagons. The outrigger need not be large to provide adequate stability for the scenery.

Castered Jack Systems. Many times it is advisable to remove scenery from its caster support during performance rather than to bother with the problem of anchoring the unit to keep it from moving. Two simple systems offer this possibility. The **lift jack** consists of a length of lumber hinged to scenery. One or more casters are mounted on the board (Figure 12-40). When you step on the rear edge of the board, the casters act as a fulcrum to lift the scenery upward. The caster plate is then locked into position from above by a hinged strip of lumber. In this process, the scenic unit is raised onto its casters for shifting. Pressure on the end of the caster board again permits the brace to be released, and the set is removed from caster support. The lift jack is highly versatile and is adaptable to many forms of scenery. It can fit behind or under objects, even in tight spaces, but is used mostly for three-dimensional units such as bars or counters, stair units, and platforms.

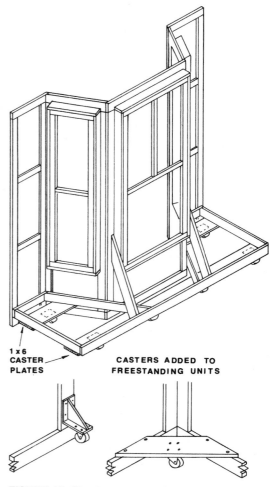

1 x 6 CASTER PLATES

CASTERS ADDED TO FREESTANDING UNITS

FIGURE 12–39   Outrigger wagon.

The **tip jack** is a rolling device intended exclusively for scenery that is not freestanding (Figure 12-41). When it is necessary to shift a wall unit by rolling, this is an easy solution. A tip jack is a triangular frame similar to a brace jack. It has an added plate and casters on the bottom rail, and the vertical stile joins at an angle less than 90°. A minimum of two jacks is needed. They are joined to the back of scenery with loose-pin hinges and cross-braced together in a rigid position.

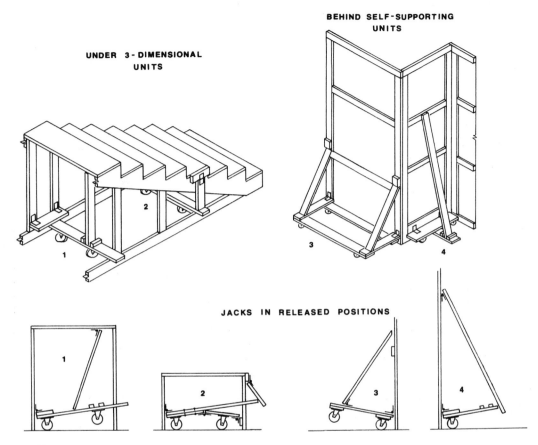

UNDER 3-DIMENSIONAL
UNITS

BEHIND SELF-SUPPORTING
UNITS

JACKS IN RELEASED POSITIONS

FIGURE 12–40 Types of lift jacks.

When the scenery is tipped back onto the jacks, support is entirely on the casters, and the unit may be rolled offstage. When it is rolled onstage into place, it is tipped into its vertical position, taking its weight off the casters, and is joined to the rest of the setting. The angle of the jacks must be determined by the scenery to be rolled. For proper balance, the center of weight must fall between the front and back casters on the jacks. Scenery with a heavy cornice or other top decor will permit a steeper angle than will a wall with a predominance of architectural trim at the bottom.

Other Castered Structures. Scenery to be fitted for rolling does not always necessitate special devices. Some three-dimensional objects have structures so inherently suitable for rolling that they require little more than the addition of casters. Objects that are relatively small, heavy, and difficult to carry can become **tip-over** units (Figure 12-42). Small platforms, rocks, bars, and similar objects can be rolled offstage by tipping them onto their offstage sides where casters are mounted. Flown objects such as chandeliers can be lowered into castered crates for easy removal from the setting.

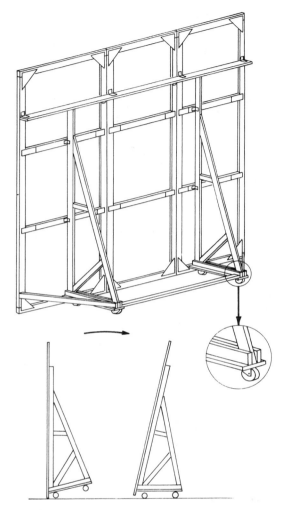

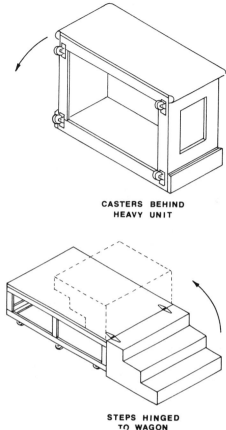

CASTERS BEHIND
HEAVY UNIT

STEPS HINGED
TO WAGON

FIGURE 12–42   Tip-over units.

FIGURE 12–41   Tip jack.

Air Flotation. A revolutionary and successful system in many industrial applications for horizontal movement of heavy loads is replacing the wheeled caster in scene-shifting situations. Sometimes called the air caster, this system lifts a load on a thin cushion of air. The result is a nearly friction-free surface requiring little effort to move the heaviest objects. An air caster is a doughnut-shaped inflatable bag of rein-

forced fabric and neoprene (Figure 12-43). When inflated by a compressor or air storage tank, the bag overflows, causing it to rise slightly and to "float" the load off the floor. Standard air-caster units range in size from 12″ to 48″ in diameter. Load capacities are exceedingly high: a 12″ air caster has a rated load of 2000 pounds. Three or four air casters, minimum, are needed to lift any object. The weight of a load should be equally distributed to the casters for best performance. A low-pressure, high-volume air supply is needed to power the system. In fact, a house-

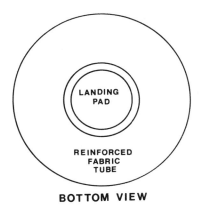

BOTTOM VIEW

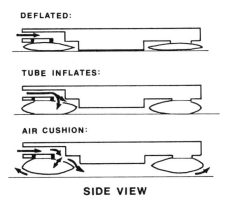

SIDE VIEW

FIGURE 12–43 Air caster.

hold-type vacuum cleaner compressor will float unusually heavy loads.

To reduce noise in a scene shift, of course, it is best to have the air compressor in another room. Flexible hoses supply air to the air casters. Hoses leading to each caster must be the same length since air casters function satisfactorily only with equally distributed pressure. The required volume of air is determined by the nature of the floor. A major limitation is that a smooth, nonporous floor surface such as sealed concrete, vinyl flooring, or metal sheeting is needed. Cracks, unsealed softwood, and surface pits destroy the air film and inhibit movement; but pits and cracks can be filled and taped, and plastic sheeting can cover rough surfaces.

Some noise from air casters is inevitable, and can be considerable on floors that are not smooth. Yet under the best conditions it is tolerable for most scene-change situations. The cost of air casters is not as high as might be expected. The major expense is an air-supply system, but this also has considerable value in other shop and stage power applications. Furthermore, the short duration of scene changes permits the use of compressed air tanks to power air caster units. There is no doubt that air flotation is an ideal system for horizontal movement of scene shifts. A minimum push propels heavy objects in any direction with greater ease than regular casters. When the air is removed, the scenery rests on its own support.

Treadmills. Another system for horizontal movement is the treadmill. Similar to a "moving sidewalk," the treadmill is an endless horizontal belt used to move scenery, properties, and sometimes performers laterally across the stage. Its potential was well demonstrated in the highly acclaimed Broadway musical *Annie*. The flexible belt is often constructed of narrow slats of wood. It passes around motor-driven drums at each end. A treadmill is raised above the stage sufficiently to allow the belt to pass underneath.

Shifting by Elevator Methods

Stage lifts (elevators) are generally permanent installations found in opera houses or presentation theatres (such as Radio City Music Hall and the showrooms of Las Vegas). To justify the sizable investment, lifts must have considerable use. Besides serving as raised stage levels replacing platforms, they also are used to shift scenery from the basement to the stage for a scene change. Sometimes a lift works in tandem with full-stage wagons. An entire setting might be mounted on a wagon in the basement, rolled to the lift, and raised to the stage above. Alternation is achieved with two wagons and wagon houses in the basement. Although costly, this is a highly effective way to change complete scenes on a permanent arena stage.

Individual **trap lifts** are used to move properties, small scenic units, and performers up to the stage floor. A stage without an elevator system can have a small elevator fitted into a floor trap. After removing a trap section, a special platform can be constructed in the trap room below to fit the opening required. It is guided by wooden tracks at all corners and lifted by a motor winch and cable. The cable passes through sheaves under the platform frame and is directed to the winch drum. A **disappearance elevator** is a unique lift used for the sudden appearance or disappearance of an actor or property through the stage floor. Counterweights on the double-whip rigging will sufficiently hold the elevator in the stage position. When the actor steps on the elevator and the lock is released, the elevator falls rapidly, then slows to a stop as the angle of the supporting lines change (Figure 12-44). The action is usually accompanied by a flash of light and smoke from flash powder.

FIGURE 12–44 Disappearance elevator.

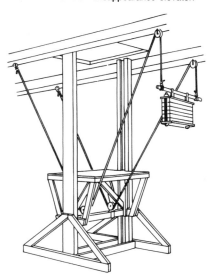

Shifting by Flying Methods

The number of existing stages with sizable fly lofts attests to the common practice of shifting scenery by flying. The process of raising scenery the short distance above the stage is achieved with rapid and quiet efficiency. Furthermore, scenic units are stored in a convenient location and do not occupy valuable space on the stage floor. The various flying systems are described in the previous chapter. The technical advances in flying equipment represent efforts to overcome problems in older systems and to better meet the needs of contemporary staging. While many procedures presented here apply chiefly to line-set rigging, especially the counterweight system, which remains the dominant form of rigging, some problems and practices are necessary concerns for all flying methods.

Because equipment used in flying is often complex and its purpose is to raise scenery directly over the playing space, the use of this shifting system is a major responsibility. Poor planning, miscalculation, and inept operation can lead to hazardous conditions. Safe and effective flying begins with careful planning. Each shift must be thoroughly plotted and each operation analyzed. The weight of the scenery requires close estimation for appropriate hanging hardware and the load capacity of the rigging equipment. Thorough instructions must be prepared for the fly operators. The hanging schedule needs to be well conceived and carefully followed. Supervision should be conducted by an experienced fly operator following all safety practices. No one should work with rigging without a basic understanding and training with the equipment (standard rigging principles are presented in Chapter 13). It bears repeating that equipment should be in good condition and regularly inspected and maintained.

Basic Hanging Scenery. The first step in mounting scenery on a counterweight system (Figure 12-45) is to lower the desired

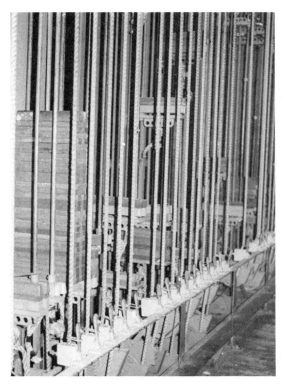

FIGURE 12–45 The counterweight system showing the locking rail, rope locks, tension sheaves, operating lines, counterweight arbors, and weights.

batten (line set) to its lowest position above the stage floor. This is done by releasing the safety ring and rope lock and pulling the operating line. The scenery is then attached to the batten at its proper location in the setting. Now counterweights may be added in the arbor to balance the weight of the scenery. A fly operator must climb up to the loading platform to perform this task. Iron weights are generally in two sizes, 1″ thick (12 or 20 pounds) and 2″ thick (24 or 40 pounds). The number added is based on an estimated weight of the scenery. The stage area beneath the loading platform must be clear of people when the arbor is being loaded. The scenery is then raised off the floor to test the counterbalance. It may be

necessary to add or remove weights to attain perfect balance. When balanced, the scenery should be run to the top of the gridiron to check its clearance with other lines. It also must be set in trim by adjusting the lines that secure it to the batten so it is parallel and flush to the floor when lowered in place. The lower trim (the location on stage) and upper trim (the storage position) are marked by white tape wrapped around the operating line just above the rope lock. The scenery is labeled on the locking rail for ease of finding the line in a scene change. The flown unit is now ready for use.

To remove scenery from a line set, the process is reversed. After lowering the scenery to the floor, the weights are removed first, before the scenery is disconnected. Obviously, failure to follow this sequence can result in an unbalanced line and considerable risk to people and property. Sometimes a stage does not have a loading platform and you must add weights at the stage floor level. This requires the aid of a power winch. The winch cable is attached to the bottom of the arbor before the batten is lowered to the floor. Once secured to the batten, the scenery is raised by the winch to the top of the loft so the arbor can be loaded from the stage level. When the line is balanced, the winch cable is disconnected.

Hanging Framed Scenery. In preparation for flying, framed units are fitted with appropriate hardware. Flying hardware is equipped with steel rings for attachment to rope, steel cable or snap hooks needed for lifting (Figure 12-46). The **ceiling plate** is used to fly ceilings and other horizontally positioned units. **Hanger irons** are used on vertically flown frames such as flats. The bottom hanger iron is bent into a hook to fit under the bottom rail of a flat frame. Both top and bottom irons are needed for suspending nearly all framed scenery to keep the joints of the frame in compression. The line supporting the scenery is secured to the ring of the bottom hanger iron (for lifting action) and passes through the ring of the

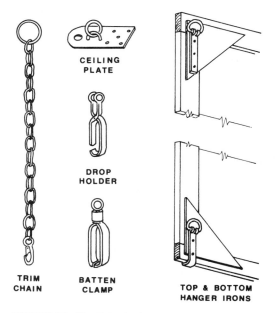

CEILING PLATE

DROP HOLDER

BATTEN CLAMP

TRIM CHAIN

TOP & BOTTOM HANGER IRONS

FIGURE 12–46 Flying hardware.

top hanger iron (to hold the unit upright). Only in the case of lightweight borders and small structures should scenery be supported by top hanger irons only. A framed unit is attached to a pipe batten by a **trim chain**, rope, or steel cable. A trim chain is a short length of chain (18″ to 48″) with a steel ring at one end and a snap hook at the other. The ring slides along the pipe, and the snap engages the ring of flying hardware. Thin aircraft cable sprayed flat black is used when exposed suspension lines must be invisible. A bent hook replaces the top hanger iron when the lift line must be flown out after the scenery is lowered to the stage (Figure 12-47). When hanging two-dimensional structures, the scenery is first placed face down on the stage floor with the top directly below the batten to which it will be hung.

When scenery is lifted in the air, it is trimmed level by adjusting the attachment of the lines at the bottom hanger irons. **Turnbuckles** are sometimes used for accurate adjustment. Since battens may be as

close together as 6″, scenery of some thickness or with projecting molding or other architectural trim may interfere with adjacent line sets. In addition, the added weight on one side will cause a wall to fly in a slightly tipped position. On some units it may be possible to adjust the flying hardware to the center of balance. In any case, it is best to recognize in advance that some lines may be blocked and cannot be used. Some spotline systems use trusses instead of battens because there are fewer lift lines.

Hanging Battened Drops. Drops and borders with sandwich battens can be attached to pipe battens or spotlines. Support to the batten is usually needed every 6′ to 8′. A

FIGURE 12–47 Removable snatch line for scenery that must be detached from the line set.

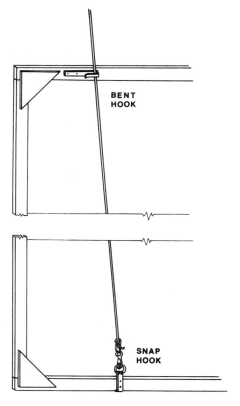

BENT HOOK

SNAP HOOK

mark on the wooden batten should indicate the center of the drop to aid in positioning. After the cloth is unrolled, the batten is placed under the line set for flying. It is suspended by ropes passed through holes drilled in the batten or by **drop holders**. **Floor stays** secure the bottom batten to the floor (Figure 12-48). Adjustments in the lines may be necessary to place a drop in trim. The face side of the fabric must be protected in hanging and removing.

Hanging Soft Drops and Draperies. Soft goods are attached to the pipe battens by tie lines secured to grommets in the reinforcing webbing at the top of the fabric. A drop must be unfolded with the top edge stretched out beneath the batten. The center of the drop (as marked on the webbing) is aligned with the center of the batten. The middle tie line

FIGURE 12–48   Rigging a battened drop.

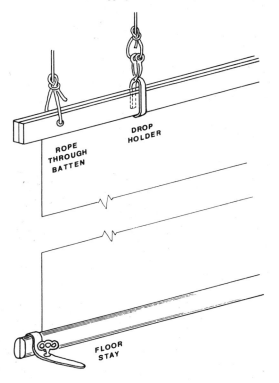

ROPE THROUGH BATTEN

DROP HOLDER

FLOOR STAY

is tied first, followed one-by-one by lines on each side. Keep the fabric taut as the tying progresses to the outer edges of the drop. Only bow knots are used, which can be untied rapidly by a pull on a loose end of the ropes. Draperies (with or without sewn-in fullness) are usually hung at the ends first. Center tie lines are then tied, subdividing the fabric so fullness is distributed equally across the drapery. When hanging drops and draperies, keep them face up on the floor so the front surface will stay as clean as possible.

Flying Safety. With necessary precautions, the rigging and flying of scenery is a reliable and effective method of shifting. Scenery must be hung and flown with care and precision by crew members who are cautious, alert, and know the equipment. Learn and practice the following safety rules:

1. Become fully acquainted with the operation and safe practices of flying before using the equipment, and let no one use the system who is not qualified.

2. Remember the hanging procedure—scenery mounted first, then the counterweights and the dismantling process—counterweights unloaded first, then the scenery.

3. Frequent checks and inspections of all flying components are essential to maintain safety in equipment. Know what to look for and be observant at all times.

4. When working on the gridiron, be sure all pockets are empty and tools and other items are secured to you with tie lines.

5. Clear the stage area below when someone is working on the gridiron or the loading platform and when scenery is raised or lowered. The warning of "heads up" is used to alert personnel of work in process above the stage.

6. The rope lock can handle only a few pounds of unbalance and is used to avoid drifting of the line. It should not be used to control a heavily unbalanced line set.

7. Never handle an unbalanced line alone. Get help. A runaway line can cause severe damage.

8. Become accustomed to the feel of operating a line. Any resistance may be the result of a hang-up or an entanglement with scenery or another line. Release the pressure until you find the cause of the difficulty.
9. Whenever operating a line, be in a position to observe the action of the equipment. If you cannot, have another person watch it for you.
10. Precision, accuracy, and timing are important in a scene shift, but speed is unnecessary, dangerous, and leads to loss of control.

Shifting by Track Methods

Without a fly loft above a stage, flying is not a scene-shifting option. At best, low ceilings only permit items to be suspended overhead, with perhaps occasional roll drops or tripped scenery. In addition to shifting scenery by rolling on the floor, you should explore overhead track methods. The standard curtain tracks can have considerable value in scene changes. In addition to draperies, a straight track extended into the wings can hold a soft drop or a border that is walked on or pulled by rope drive. With a curved I-beam track, soft scenery can be stored on track spurs in out-of-the-way corners of the stage. Even framed scenery units can be rolled on tracks if there is sufficient offstage space to store them. Imaginative use of tracks gives some shifting versatility in loftless stages and avoids the pitfall of immovable, dead-hung scenery.

SELECTED READINGS

Burris-Meyer, Harold, and Edward C. Cole, *Scenery for the Theatre* (rev. ed.). Boston: Little, Brown, 1971.

Gillette, A. S., and J. Michael Gillette, *Stage Scenery* (3rd ed.). New York: Harper and Row, 1981.

J. R. Clancy, Inc., *Theatrical Hardware, Catalog 59-A.* Syracuse, N.Y.: February 1982.

Mutual Hardware Corp., *Theatrical Equipment and Supplies, Catalog 91.* Long Island City, New York, 1991.

13

Scenery Rigging

The equipment, materials, and procedures involved in hanging and flying scenery are all elements of rigging. While general flying techniques for scene shifting have been examined in the previous chapter, it is also necessary to acquire an understanding of basic rigging practices and safety procedures. Lack of knowledge about safe rigging practices is a major cause of rigging accidents. Equipment and hardware are designed and developed for specific purposes; knowing their potentials and limitations is essential to gain efficiency in rigging and to avoid hazards. Rigging information and practices are presented here. The scene technician should also be aware of local regulations and manufacturers' requirements.

FIBER ROPE

Fiber ropes are constructed of either natural or synthetic fibers. Rope is rated for specific strength based upon size, type of fiber used, and form of stranding. For most rope, fiber filaments are twisted in a right-hand direction to form strands, and the strands are then twisted in a left-hand direction to form rope. Rope is generally constructed of three or four strands. This twisting is known as the *lay* of the rope. It can be laid tightly (hard-laid) for stiffness and for greater resistance to abrasion, or be laid loosely (soft-laid) for pliability and greater strength. Usually, a medium lay is preferred. The twist in rope causes it to turn or spin when lifting a load. Adequate care of rope includes coiling and uncoiling it properly to remove loops and kinks that can damage it. New rope should be withdrawn from the inside of the shipping coil and unwound in a counter-clockwise direction. After stretching and bending, rope becomes more pliable. Braided rope does not spin or kink, so it is used where spinning an object would be objectionable.

Natural-Fiber Rope

Three-strand **manila rope** is the most satisfactory natural-fiber rope for rigging purposes. It is durable, strong, and withstands heavy usage. It is available in several quality grades. Yacht grade is the finest, and hoisting grades are numbered 1, 2, and 3, in descending order of quality. Manila rope sold in hardware stores is usually the poorest grade, low in strength and short in life. Manufacturers of high-quality rope often identify it with a colored string in one strand or with some other type of marker. Ropes are chemically treated to repel moisture and to resist dry rot and mildew; nevertheless, these are the most common causes of rope deterioration, and good maintenance is needed to prolong the rope's life. Manila rope that is ¾″, ⅞″, or 1″ in diameter is used for the operating lines of counterweight systems. Both ½″ and ⅝″ rope are common for rope-line and spotline systems. Fly operators should wear cotton work gloves to protect their hands from rope splinters. **Braided cotton rope** lacks the structure for hoisting strength but is well adapted for rope drives (½″ diameter) on curtains and draperies and as tie lines (⅛″ diameter) for hanging drops and draperies.

Synthetic-Fiber Rope

Ropes made of synthetic fiber include nylon, polypropylene, polyethylene, and polyester (*Dacron* and *Terylene* are trade names). Unlike manila rope, which is composed of short overlapping fibers, synthetic ropes are made of fibers that are continuous throughout the length of the rope. For this reason they are stronger than natural-fiber ropes. In addition, synthetic ropes are generally unaffected by rot, mildew, or fungus, and have good resistance to chemicals. They are considerably more expensive than manila rope, but their strength and long life are worthy compensations. Synthetic ropes are increasingly replacing manila rope in construction and rigging. Nylon and polyester are the strongest of the synthetic ropes. However, the high degree of stretch (10 to 40 percent) makes pure nylon rope a disadvantage. Polyester and blends of polyester with other fibers offers the best for stage applications and have three times the strength of manila rope. New rope constructions provide greater strength, stability, and resistance to abrasion. With a braided sheath over a braided or parallel filament core, these soft flexible ropes do not twist or turn under load, have less permanent stretch, and offer more surface area for wear and grip.

Safety Factor

The breaking-strength characteristic of new rope is specified by rope manufacturers. Approximate strengths are listed in Figure 13-1, but actual manufacturers' listings should be consulted for specific rope. For safe working loads on fiber rope, a considerable factor of safety is necessary. The actual strength of rope is weakened or reduced in ordinary usage and wear. Loss of strength in rope occurs from bending over sheaves, drying out, rot, mildew, heat from friction, abrasives, knots, ground-in dirt, and many other causes. Further, sudden stops or jerks from shock-loads adds an extra strain to rope. For these reasons, safety factors are essential and must be considered in the usable capacity of the rope. Safe working loads should never be exceeded. A minimum safety factor for hoisting scenery or personnel should be not less than 8 to 1. With a 10 to 1 safety factor, for instance, ¾″ manila rope with a breaking strength of 5400 pounds would provide a working load of 540 pounds. A 6 to 1 ratio is adequate for other uses of rope.

FIGURE 13–1 Breaking strength of rope.

APPROXIMATE BREAKING STRENGTH OF 3-STRAND ROPES (IN POUNDS)				
Diameter	Manila	Nylon	Polypropylene	Polyester	Polyethylene
1/4"	600	1,500	1,250	1,500	1,250
3/8"	1,350	3,500	2,500	3,500	2,500
1/2"	2,650	6,250	4,150	6,000	4,000
5/8"	4,400	10,000	6,500	9,500	5,250
3/4"	5,400	14,000	8,500	12,000	7,500
7/8"	7,700	19,000	11,000	17,000	10,500
1"	9,000	24,000	14,500	21,000	12,500

APPROXIMATE BREAKING STRENGTH OF BRAIDED SYNTHETIC ROPES (IN POUNDS)				
Diameter	Nylon Cover Nylon Core	Nylon Cover Polypropylene Core	Polyester Cover Polypropylene Core	Polyester Cover Polyester Filament Core
1/4"	2,100	—	1,900	2,000
3/8"	4,400	3,400	3,700	4,500
1/2"	7,500	7,400	6,900	7,900
5/8"	12,000	10,500	12,000	14,000
3/4"	17,500	16,000	14,300	17,600
7/8"	24,000	20,750	19,000	26,300
1"	28,500	24,000	28,000	31,600

Use and Maintenance of Rope

With proper care and use, rope has a long and dependable life. Below is a list of the fundamentals of rope care.

1. *Never overload a rope.* Use safety factors of 8 to 1 for hoisting and 6 to 1 for other usage.
2. *Avoid exposure to chemicals and heat.* Acids, strong alkalis, paint, fumes and gases, and excessive heat can cause serious damage to rope.
3. *Keep ropes clean and dry.* When ropes become dirty, wash them in cool water and hang them up to dry. Imbedded dirt acts as an abrasive. Do not drag a rope along the ground.
4. *Provide proper storage.* Store rope in a dry, cool room. Hang it up in loose coils in an area with good air circulation.
5. *Coil and uncoil rope properly and avoid kinks.* Know how to compensate for the twist in rope. Avoid kinks. In removing new rope, reach inside the coil and unwind the rope in a counterclockwise direction. Used rope should be recoiled in a clockwise direction.
6. *Protect rope from weather, dampness, and sunlight.* Moisture and extreme temperatures promote decay and loss of strength.
7. *Avoid abrasives.* Sharp or rough edges and surfaces weaken rope.
8. *Avoid sharp bends.* Severe bends from tight knots and sharp angles can weaken a rope by as much as 50 percent. Use thimbles when attaching ropes to hooks, rings, or eyes.
9. *Use correct sheaves for rope.* A sheave should have a smooth groove the width of the rope and a diameter at least six times the rope diameter.
10. *Bind or whip loose ends.* Prevent the ends of rope from untwisting or fraying, and strands from slipping, which causes uneven distribution of the load.

Inspect Rope Regularly

Rope should be checked to assess its safety and load-carrying ability. Look for external wear, cuts, broken strands, and frayed areas. Abrasions and reductions in diameter will indicate weakened areas. Dark, brown spots are often the result of chemical damage or burns. Rope that is unusually dry, soft, and flexible is probably old and has lost its elasticity. Open up the strands with a slight twist and examine the interior of the rope. It should be clean and bright. Deterioration is evident if there are broken yarns, loose threads, or dirt or dust caused by internal wear. If the weakness is limited to one spot, it should be cut out. If there is any doubt about the condition of the rope, it should be removed from service. Cut it up into short lengths so it will not be used for hoisting purposes by mistake.

Rope Knots

A good knot is one that provides adequate strength, will not slip, and can be tied easily and quickly. In discussing knots we refer to the end of the rope used in tying a knot, a loop or bend in the rope (usually formed by the end), and the rest of the rope (called the standing part). Figure 13-2 shows some of the most common knots used in stage rigging.

1. *Overhand knot.* A loop is formed in the rope, and the end is passed through it. It is used to keep a rope from passing through a lash eye or in conjunction with a bow knot on tie lines of a drop or drapery. It is also the basis of other knots.
2. *Figure-eight knot.* A loop is made, and the end passes over the standing part, then down under and through the loop. It can be used at the end of a rope to prevent the strands from unlaying and to keep a rope from slipping through a sheave.
3. *Square knot.* This is used to tie together two ropes of the same diameter. One rope is

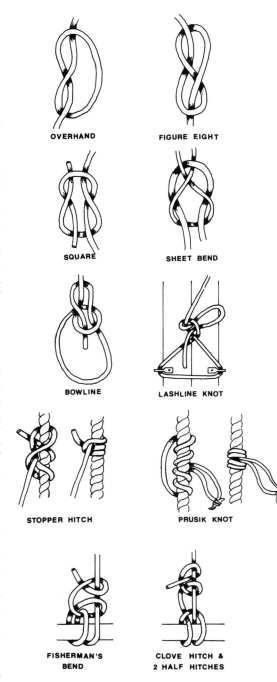

OVERHAND   FIGURE EIGHT

SQUARE   SHEET BEND

BOWLINE   LASHLINE KNOT

STOPPER HITCH   PRUSIK KNOT

FISHERMAN'S BEND   CLOVE HITCH & 2 HALF HITCHES

FIGURE 13–2 Common rope knots.

passed around another, and the process is repeated by reversing the direction of the rope ends. The live and dead ends of the rope should come out of the loops on the same side. Pull tight.

4. *Sheet bend.* This knot is used for joining ropes of different sizes. A loop is made in one rope. The other rope is passed through the loop, then up behind its standing part, and down through the loop again. Draw it tight.

5. *Bowline.* A bowline is a strong knot that forms a nonslipping loop yet remains easy to untie. To tie, a loop is formed over the standing part. Pass the end of the rope up through the loop, behind the standing part, and down through the loop. Pull it tight.

6. *Lashline knot.* The rope used to join scenery by lashing is tied with this knot. The rope is passed under the two bottom lash cleats. A loop is formed and is passed under the standing part above the cleats. A second loop is passed through the first one, and the rope is tightened. Pulling the free end will immediately release the knot.

7. *Stopper hitch.* This is used for tying a snubbing rope to operating lines. The free end is looped around the operating line over the standing part. Then three or more full turns are made around the operating line. The knot is tightened by adjusting and sliding the rope turns upward and pulling the rope tight.

8. *Prusik knot.* This is another knot to secure a rope to an operating line or set of lines. A rope is tied together to form an endless loop. The loop is passed two or more times around the operating line. The ends are passed through the loop and tightened.

9. *Fisherman's bend.* This is a useful knot for securing support lines to a pipe batten. Pass the end twice around the batten. The end is then passed around the standing part and through the loops. The knot is drawn tight, and another half hitch is made. Draw it tight.

10. *Clove hitch.* A loop is passed around a batten, then over the standing part for another loop, passing the end between the loop and the batten. It should be finished with two half hitches around the standing part. A clove hitch is a quick way of tying a rope to a batten or post and is easy to untie and to adjust.

CABLE (WIRE ROPE)

Cable is constructed of individual wires laid into strands that are spun around a center core. Classifications of cable are identified by numbers such as 6 × 19, 6 × 7, and 8 × 19. The first number indicates the number of strands; the second number is the number of wires per strand. There are numerous types of cable designed for specific purposes or tasks. Wire rope for the lift lines of flying systems must have sufficient strength for maximum loads, must take repeated flexing through sheaves, and must resist abrasion, distortion, and rotation. Standard **hoisting cable**, 6 × 19 in construction and made of plow steel, is appropriate for flying systems. It is flexible and tough, and it resists abrasion and fatigue. Cable made with more wires per strand is more flexible but often has a lower breaking strength. Flying systems are usually rigged with ¼″, 5⁄16″, or ⅜″ hoisting cable, depending upon the load capacity desired for each batten. Another type of wire rope is stronger and more flexible. This is **aircraft cable**, which is made of specially processed wire of high tensile strength. The most flexible is the 7 × 19 construction. Aircraft cable in 3⁄16″ and ¼″ diameters is often used with winch systems because smaller diameter sheaves and winch drums may be employed. Thinner aircraft cable, painted black, is useful for invisible flying and levitation. It is available in galvanized or stainless steel. The galvanized finish is easier to coat with black paint.

Aircraft cable covered with matte black vinyl is available in some diameters. The 1⁄32″ vinyl must be stripped off before applying sleeves or cable clips. Sheaves used with aircraft cable must be hardened steel to prevent wear. An 8 to 1 safety factor is the minimum for working loads on cable in flying systems. This is necessary to account for the stresses placed on cable, which result in reduced strength, and for the potential for extra stress caused by live or shock loads. With a safety ratio of 8 to 1, ¼″ 6 × 19 hoisting

FIGURE 13–3 Breaking strengths of cable.

CABLE TYPE	DIAMETER (IN INCHES)	BREAKING STRENGTH (IN TONS—2000 LBS)
Hoisting cable*	¼	2.4
(6 × 19)	⁵⁄₁₆	3.8
	⅜	5.4

CABLE TYPE	DIAMETER (IN INCHES)	BREAKING STRENGTH (IN POUNDS)
Aircraft cable	¹⁄₁₆	480
(7 × 19 galvanized)	⁵⁄₆₄	650
	³⁄₃₂	1000
	⁷⁄₆₄	1260
	⅛	2000
	⁵⁄₃₂	2800
	³⁄₁₆	4200
	⁷⁄₃₂	5600
	¼	7000

*These figures are based on the lowest quality of plow steel and core construction used in the 6 × 19 hoisting cable classification.

cable (with a 4800-pound breaking strength) would have a safe working load of 600 pounds. Rated breaking strengths of new cable are listed in Figure 13-3.

Cable Attachments and Hardware

Fittings are installed at the ends of cable to permit connection to flying components. Selecting cable attachments and installing them properly is vital for strength and safety. Only forged fittings of weldless construction should be employed. A loop is formed at the end of the cable to accommo-date the attachment of fittings. A **thimble** must be used in the loop to prevent sharp bending, flattening, and wear to the cable. **Cable clips** are a common means of clamping cable (Figure 13-4). One type of clip consists of a U-bolt and a saddle joined tightly with nuts. The U-bolt is placed on the dead or short end of the cable, and the saddle on the live or load end. "Never saddle a dead horse": The reverse application of cable clips can reduce the strength of the connection to 40 percent. Fist grip clips cannot be installed incorrectly. For minimum strength, two cable clips are necessary on cable less than ½" in diameter, three clips on a cable ½", ⁹⁄₁₆" or ⅝" in diameter, and four or more on ¾" cable and larger. In applying cable clips, the amount of cable turn-back varies with the cable diameter. Check with specifications supplied by clip manufacturers. The steps involved in installing cable clips are enumerated below.

1. Apply first clip one base width from the dead end of the cable—U-bolt over the dead end.

FIGURE 13–4 Cable clips.

U-BOLT   **FIST GRIP**

STEP 1

STEP 2

STEP 3

FIGURE 13–5 Applying cable clips.

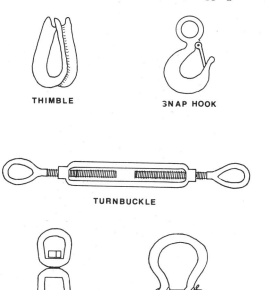

THIMBLE   SNAP HOOK

TURNBUCKLE

SWIVEL   SHACKLE

FIGURE 13–6 Common cable attachments.

Tighten nuts evenly to recommended torque.

2. Apply second clip nearest the loop as possible. Turn nuts firm but do not tighten.

3. Apply other clips equally between the first two. Tighten all nuts to recommended torque. Apply initial load and retighten all nuts again (see Figure 13-5).

High-pressure **swages**, or **Nicropress sleeves**, sometimes replace cable clips. Industrial terminal assemblies swaged to cable by hydraulic presses are permanent and 100 percent effective. Nicropress sleeves are oval in shape and are applied by a **Nicropress tool** and checked by a gauge.

Rings, snap hooks, turnbuckles, shackles, swivels, and eye bolts are some of the hardware used in rigging. Figure 13-6 lists some standard cable hardware. They are just as important as the cable and rope used with them. These and all other fittings should be forged steel and be rated for load capacity by the manufacturer. Standard items found in hardware stores often are not of hoisting quality. Welded-steel passing-link chain is used in the rigging and suspension of scenery. Short lengths of chain at the end of cable supports are valuable as batten levelers. Trim chains are composed of lengths of

passing-link chain with a ring at one end and a snap hook at the other. Attached to a batten, they enable the trim of the scenery to be adjusted by placing the snap into the appropriate link.

Sheaves and winch drums are major items in preserving the life and efficiency of cable. They must be constructed of steel as hard as the cable to avoid damage to the cable by excessive wear. Bending tolerances specify minimum drum and sheave diameters for cable of varying sizes and construction. The angle of cable feeding onto drum or a sheave, known as the **fleet angle**, must not exceed about 1.5° from the center line to prevent rubbing and crushing of the cable (Figure 13-7). The grooves in sheaves must be of the proper size, shape, and depth for the cable. Spacer bolts, which hold the side plates of a block or sheave, should be positioned to prevent cable from jumping out of its groove. To reduce friction and cable wear, sheaves need self-lubricating ball or

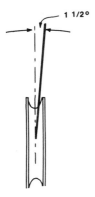

FIGURE 13–7 Fleet angle.

tapered roller bearings. These and many other factors must be considered in designing stage rigging. Few technicians have specified and installed the flying systems on their stages. However, they need to become familiar with the installation, confirm its conformity to safety standards, know how to maintain it properly, and use it efficiently and safely.

Use and Maintenance of Cable and Hardware

Cable and cable hardware have the potential for long and satisfactory service if they are maintained and used properly.

1. Always use the correct cable, fittings, and hardware, and know manufacturers' guidelines and recommendations.
2. Never exceed the safe working loads of rigging components.
3. Avoid conditions that will cause abrasions, rubbing, or flattening of cable.
4. Avoid kinks in cable. Should they occur, the weak spots are permanent and the cable should be replaced.
5. Follow manufacturers' recommendations for lubricating cable, sheaves, and other components.
6. Minimize shock loads on cable. They cause additional stress to cable and hardware.

7. Store cable in coils and on reels in dry, clean areas.
8. Perform regular inspections of rigging equipment, and replace damaged items when needed.

Conduct Safety Inspections

Safety checks of cable and cable flying systems should be a task performed whenever specific equipment is used. In addition, a program of periodic inspections should be established on a year-round basis. For a thorough, systematic inspection, a checklist of items to examine will prevent omissions (see sample checklist in Figure 4-3). Cables require close scrutiny for broken wires, wear, corrosion, reduction in diameter, kinks, protruding wires, and other evidence of damage. On end fittings, examine the thimbles and look for signs of slippage. Are there cracks in swages? Loose cable clips? All loft blocks and head blocks should be inspected for sheave wear and for condition of mounting clamps and bolts, bearings, and axles. In similar fashion, the counterweight arbors, the tension sheaves, the locking rail, and all pipe battens require careful inspection. The same is needed for parts of motorized winch systems.

BLOCK-AND-TACKLE RIGGING

Combinations of ropes and sheaves are basic machines designed for lifting and pulling (Figure 13-8). The most basic form, the **single whip,** consists of a single sheave to redirect a rope in lifting a load. This form is central to stage flying systems. However, we more commonly think of multiple reeved systems, which provide mechanical advantage in work applications. The **running block,** for instance, consists of a sheave (to which the load is attached) running on a rope that has one end tied to an upper support. The weight of the load is divided between the two halves of the line giving a 2 to

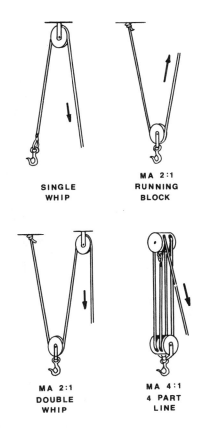

SINGLE WHIP

MA 2:1 RUNNING BLOCK

MA 2:1 DOUBLE WHIP

MA 4:1 4 PART LINE

FIGURE 13–8 Block-and-tackle systems.

1 mechanical advantage (MA). A 200-pound load requires a 100-pound pull. This advantage is achieved only by pulling twice as much rope for the distance traveled by the load, and there is an equal loss in speed of movement. **Double whip** rigging adds a stationary block to conveniently change direction of the line of a running block. It also has a mechanical advantage of 2 to 1.

Greater mechanical advantage is offered by more complex block-and-tackle systems. These use two blocks with single, double, or triple sheaves. One block is stationary, and the other, which is attached to the load, is a movable or traveling block. The mechanical advantage of any multiple reeved system is equal to the number of rope lines support-

ing the movable block. Four lines indicates a 4 to 1 mechanical advantage. Once again, distance and speed are sacrificed for this lifting advantage. In addition, tackle rigging is not 100 percent efficient. Friction from the sheaves adds to the load weight by an amount equal to 3 to 10 percent per sheave depending on the type of bearings used.

HANDLING THE UNBALANCED LOAD

Occasions occur when a flown person or piece of scenery must be removed from a counterweighted line set without the time and opportunity to remove the counterweights. This immediately leaves an unbalanced line and the dangers associated with it. Several rigging solutions can handle this situation.

Power Drives

Stages that have full power flying systems (electric winch or fluid power systems) have no problem with variable loads. The power source lifts scenery without the need of counterweights. On stages without the luxury of power rigging, a power-driven winch can be attached to a regular counterweight line set to handle unbalanced loads (Figure 13-9). A fixed or portable winch is a valuable accessory with a counterweight system. Sheaves can redirect the cable from the winch drum to support a line set. It can be attached to the top of a loaded arbor or to the bottom of an arbor in place of counterweights equaling the weight of the scenery.

Substitute Weight

Scenery that is not very heavy can be replaced on a line or line set by a substitute weight. Line balance is then retained. This is accomplished by a sandbag or iron weights that equal the weight of the scenery. The substitute weight can be rolled on a small

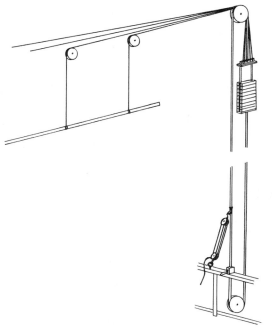

FIGURE 13–10 Block-and-tackle snub line.

FIGURE 13–9 A motor winch with cable directed by a mule sheave to the bottom of a counterweight arbor. This is useful for loading arbors from the stage floor or for hanging unbalanced loads.

wagon to the batten or line and attached by a rope snatch line or trim chain. The weight must be attached before the scenery is removed. It should be disconnected only when the scenery has been reattached.

Block-and-Tackle Snub Line

Control of the overweighted counterweight arbor can be handled with a block and tackle (Figure 13-10). A short rope is attached with a prusik knot to the operating line near the locking rail. The moving block of the tackle is hooked to this snub line, and the stationary block is secured to the locking rail. When the scenery is removed from the batten, the block and tackle, with its mechanical advantage, controls the lifting and lowering of the overweighted arbor. When the scenery is attached to the batten, the block and tackle is removed from the snub line.

Carpet Hoist

The carpet hoist uses the counterweight arbor of an adjacent line to provide the counterweights needed to equal the scenery flown. The batten and lift cables of the adjacent line set are disengaged from the arbor. (They may be removed or simply tied off to the gridiron.) This leaves the arbor and attached operating line free to assist the line on which the scenery is flown. Brackets are mounted on the arbor of the scenery batten, which will engage the arbor of the free line set. Thus, when the scenery is attached to the line set, the arbor of the free line rides

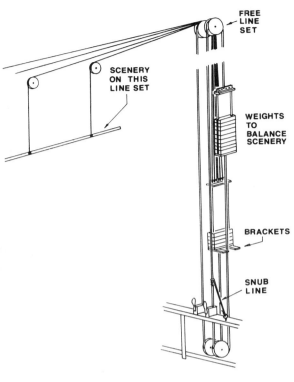

FIGURE 13–11 Carpet hoist.

Use of Multiple Battens

The process of hanging and flying scenery on a line set has already been described. There are times, however, when more than one batten is necessary to fly a particular unit of scenery. This is often desired for large, three-dimensional structures, for ceilings, and for set units hung at angles not parallel with a line-set batten. A scenic unit of considerable thickness or depth (a wall containing an alcove, for instance) may require suspension from two battens for flying. On a counterweight system, two fly operators will be needed to raise and lower the unit. However, if the line sets are not far apart, the counterweight arbors can be bolted together and controlled by only one of the operating lines or by an auxiliary motor winch. Scenery flown on two or more line sets of a motorized batten system can be synchronized and operated by a single controller.

Ceilings for settings also require more than one batten. In flying a single-frame ceiling or roll ceiling, one batten must be attached to the downstage edge of the ceiling and another to the upstage edge. The two battens chosen must permit the ceiling to hang in its proper position. Lengths of rope (snatch lines) or trim chains secure the battens to the ceiling plates on the ceiling. To raise the ceiling, the front and back lines must be lifted together. Once the scenery is mounted on stage, the ceiling is lowered to rest lightly on top of the walls of the setting.

The book ceiling is constructed to be flown by three adjacent line sets directly in the center of its position in the setting. (See Figure 8-22.) This permits the ceiling to be folded compactly when raised into its storage position. Unlike the flying of other ceilings, this action allows all other line sets of the rigging system to be used for scenery in other scenes. The center batten is attached to the middle of the ceiling frame with snatch lines at least one-half the depth of the ceiling. Snatch lines from the front and back battens are twice as long and pass through

along with the scenery batten (Figure 13-11). When the scenery is lowered to the floor, the arbors are high above the floor. Before the scenery is removed from the batten, the free arbor (carrying the weights to balance the scenery) is held overhead by securing the operating rope with a snub line to the locking rail. The empty batten is balanced with its own arbor weights and can be raised. After the scenery is attached to the batten again, the snub line is released, adding the free arbor and its weight to the flying unit again.

RIGGING TECHNIQUES

Several principles and practices are useful in solving other production needs.

single blocks tied to the center line before terminating at the downstage and upstage edges of the ceiling. The book ceiling will fold when you raise the middle batten, and all three lines are operated together to lift the unit to high trim. To minimize the imbalance in flying the ceiling on a counterweight system, the middle-line counterweighting should equal one-half the weight of the ceiling, and the outer lines one-fourth its weight.

One of the principal limitations of batten flying systems is the difficulty of handling scenery that is not parallel to the stage opening. Multiple lines are often necessary for angled scenery unless it can be (1) hung from the batten with a hook and pivot line, (2) removed from the batten before final positioning, or (3) left attached to the batten but with ample slack in the line. The latter two approaches necessitate dealing with an unbalanced line.

Spotlining

Many objects cannot be flown effectively with batten rigging systems. Spotlines are useful to raise a single object such as a person, a chandelier, or small scenic item, or to fly angled scenery units (Figure 13-12). Because of the frequency of such rigging, stages that have counterweight batten or power batten systems often include provisions for spotline equipment. A few motorized spotlines, or a pinrail and fly gallery for rope-line spotlining, are found in many contemporary stages. A single rope-type spotline is not difficult to install. It is essentially a rope extending from the locking rail or fly gallery to a head block above, across the gridiron to a loft block, and down to the stage in the selected position. Special stage blocks grooved for rope are necessary and should be equipped with clamps to secure them at any location on the gridiron. If more than one lift line is necessary, additional loft blocks and a multigrooved head block will

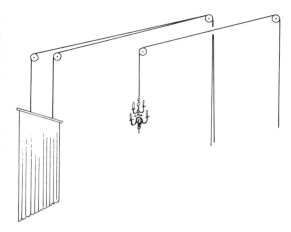

FIGURE 13–12 Spotlining.

be required. The lines can be secured to a trim clamp just below the head block to provide only one rope for the operating line. A tie-off cleat will be necessary in the absence of a pinrail. A sandbag counterweight can be added if necessary, or mechanical advantage can be included to control the weight of the flown object.

Bridling

The number of lift lines is sometimes insufficient to support the top of a flown object or batten. Bridling is a means of increasing the frequency of pickup support (Figure 13-13). Two ends of a rope can be tied to scenery and the lift line tied to the center, thus

FIGURE 13–13 Bridling.

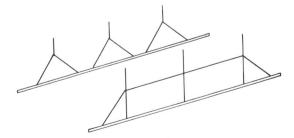

reducing the number of lines to raise an object. Bridling is also needed when adding extensions to a regular pipe-batten line set.

Breasting

Sometimes an object or piece of scenery must move or be relocated from its regular flown position. This is accomplished by a breasting line. Depending upon the nature of the object or movement, either a spotline or a batten set can serve in breasting (Figure 13-14). In the simplest form, the object is dead-hung from the gridiron. The breasting line is attached to the top of the object or to its support line at an angle. Pulling the line causes it to move upward and to one side. As the breasting line is pulled, it supports increasingly more of the weight of the load. Therefore, some mechanical advantage or counterweights may be necessary to handle the change of weight.

Muling

In some rigging situations special blocks are employed to change the direction of a fly line (Figure 13-15). This is known as mul-

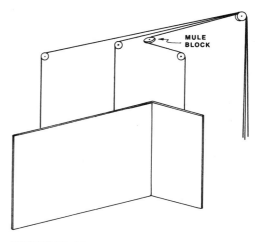

FIGURE 13–15 Muling.

ing. A common example is the downstage arms of the cyclorama. Muling blocks are mounted sideways on special brackets to redirect the cables from the headblock to the loft blocks. This permits the lines to feed properly onto the sheaves, preventing damage and excessive wear. Muling is frequently needed to change the path of lines around obstructions and to avoid the chance of fouling.

Tripping

Scenery is sometimes too tall to be flown high enough from the top. Tripping is a way of lifting scenery from the bottom or a middle location. It is a solution primarily for soft scenery. For bottom tripping, a set of lines is placed behind a drop and is attached to the bottom batten (Figure 13-16). When lifted, the fabric forms a fold or loop. If the top of the drop can be raised as well, the drop can be lifted in half the normal distance of a regular flown unit. Tripping from the middle of a drop is achieved by a special batten secured by tie lines and webbing at a mid-height location. On some stages, cloth sky cycloramas are so tall they are dead-

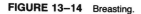

FIGURE 13–14 Breasting.

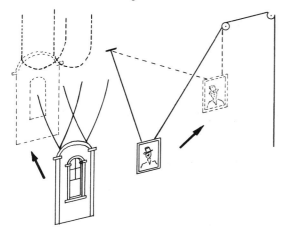

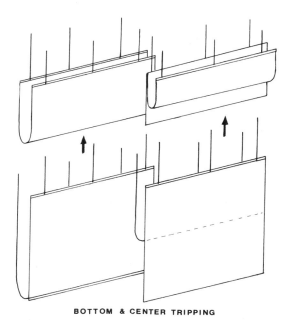

BOTTOM & CENTER TRIPPING

FIGURE 13–16 Tripping.

hung by chains and bolts to the gridiron and are raised off the floor by a trip batten.

LEVITATION

The suspension or flying of an object or a person without apparent support is achieved by a variety of special rigging techniques. Being an illusion, levitation requires an appropriate lack of lighting on the cable and a proper background to mask and distract attention from the invisible support lines. Above all, careful rehearsal is vital when an actor or an object must move or seem to fly across the stage.

Flying props and scenery is often not a complicated process. Sometimes small objects, pictures, and decorative items must hang in space in the manner of suggestive or fragmentary settings. Black nylon trickline (or fish line) is an ideal support line and is available in 20-, 40-, 70-, and 108-pound

test sizes. A dark background aids in concealing the exposed line. Large or heavy scenery to be suspended without visible support must be hung with thin aircraft cable (painted black), using the appropriate safety factor. Before the advent of aircraft cable, piano wire, which has great tensile strength, was a widely used flying wire. It is not recommended any longer. Being single-strand wire, it weakens easily by the kinks, bends, and heat of inexpert handling.

Sometimes small objects must hover, drift, or soar through the air. This might be a bird flying through a scene, the vase sailing across the room in *Blithe Spirit,* or the top hat in Giraudoux's *The Enchanted,* which falls from a man's head to the ground as if by a gust of wind. A unique solution must be found for the special needs of any illusion, but probably each will be a variation of pendulum action, the basis of most flying effects. The influence of gravity on pendulum motion is easily understood. In a single plane, a weight at the end of a string, when displaced to one side, will swing through the point of equilibrium in the other direction. The falling hat demonstrates the simplicity of the action. A trickline is rigged as a spotline over sheaves to an operator offstage. It falls diagonally downward from the loft block to the top hat worn by the actor. A tug on the line removes the hat from his head, and pendulum action causes it to swing across the stage, where it is lowered to the floor before reaching the return cycle of the pendulum.

Flying of actors is the most complex form of levitation. It may involve merely the lifting or lowering of an actor, or it may be more complicated (a person floating in space, the virtuoso flying of Peter Pan, or the group flying of an aerial ballet). The appropriate flying system is selected for the particular situation. Flying routines must be carefully developed and rehearsed by the flyer and the operator. Consistency of action is vital for believability and for safety. The operator must be in a position to observe

FIGURE 13–17 Actors in flight. Scene from *Peter Pan* with flying by Foy. (Photo by George Tarbay)

the flyer's movements at all times. The actor must learn not to anticipate a flight before receiving a signal—a slight tug on the line—from the operator. Precise timing and coordination are important. All ropes, cables, associated hardware, and attachments must be of the proper size and strength (with safety factors) for flying. Sheaves require spacer bolts to prevent the cable from jumping out of the grooves.

Frequent safety checks should be made of all equipment. Flying harnesses are made of heavy webbing straps that extend over the shoulders and under the crotch of the actor (Figure 13-18). A waistband fits around the center, and all is sewn and riveted to heavy leather at the back of the harness where the cable is attached. Like a parachute harness, a flying harness must give support to the appropriate portions of the anatomy, lifting the body primarily from the buttocks, the stomach, and the waist. Undue pressure across the chest restricts actor movement and can cause cracked ribs. The cable must

be attached to the back of the harness above the center of balance so the actor will fly at a slightly upright angle. Normally, the flying cable should be $5/64''$ in diameter or larger. To reduce the visibility of its attachment to the harness, the cable terminates in a solid-thimble reinforced loop, and a custom-made hook is attached to the harness. The harness and all flying components must be labora-

FIGURE 13–18 Flying harness.

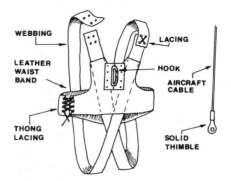

tory tested for safety. For safety reasons, only specialists should provide and install flying rigs. The appearance of naturalness in flying depends heavily on the attitude, posturing, and body control of the performer.

What follows is a list of some of the special rigging systems used for levitation (see Figure 13-19).

Single Pendulum System

This basic pendulum rigging is useful for very simple flights. It can be used for light-weight performers only, because the operator lifts the entire weight without any mechanical advantage. Usually, pendulum systems require a gridiron with a minimum of 40' to 45' in height to offer enough horizontal movement and lifting height. In pendulum motion, precise movements can be planned. By starting a flight from one location, the flyer will "land" repeatedly at a predetermined point at the end of the pendulum swing. The flight would be unreliable if the flyer attempted to control distance, speed, and direction by pushing off at the start of the flight. Peter Foy is a specialist in theatrical flying and has developed ex-

FIGURE 13–19 Levitation systems.

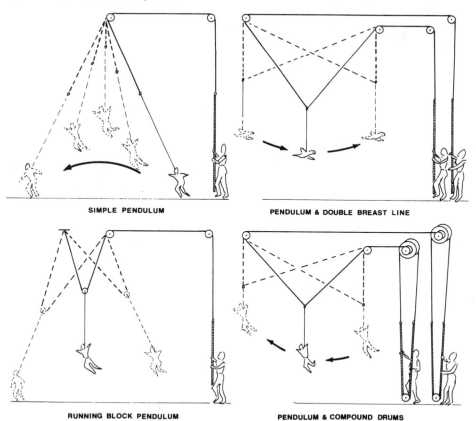

SIMPLE PENDULUM

PENDULUM & DOUBLE BREAST LINE

RUNNING BLOCK PENDULUM

PENDULUM & COMPOUND DRUMS

cellent equipment and techniques for flying people and is frequently employed to stage flying sequences throughout the world. He increases efficiency of the system by the use of thin (1/8″ diameter) and highly flexible aircraft cable running through the sheaves.[1] It connects with the flying cable just above sight lines and with a length of 3/4″ operating rope on the offstage side. Even then, a pure pendulum rig provides only limited control of movement and distance.

Pendulum and Breast-Line Systems

Both increased lateral movement and movement control are provided by adding a single or double breast line to the pendulum. The object can be dead-hung from the gridiron and moved by a single breast line for limited movement or hung from two breast lines for a more complete flight across the stage. The weight of the lift by the fly operators will change as the flying object shifts from one line to the other.

This system is more common for flying small objects than for people. As with all pendulum systems, movement is more predictable if the flyer does not attempt any additional movements.

Pendulum and Mechanical-Advantage Systems

Mechanical advantage is needed for the fly operator to handle heavy loads. To achieve this, some control is sacrificed, because the operator must pull more rope than is achieved in flyer movement. A **running-block pendulum** rig provides a 2 to 1 mechanical advantage. Improved efficiency in this system is achieved by replacing the heavy rope and running block, which causes slack in the line at takeoff, with lightweight aircraft cable and cable sheaves. The cable tie-off and loft block must be far enough apart to prevent the cables from twisting

around each other. A superior method to achieve mechanical advantage is the **compound drum system**. The flying cable is fed to the small drum, and the endless control rope runs over the large drum. The amount of mechanical advantage is determined by the difference in diameters of the drums.

Pendulum and Two Compound Drums

This system provides considerable control of distance and speed of flying. With two suspension points, long flights are possible and movements can be choreographed and paced in time to music and action. Great skill is necessary in handling the change in suspension points, which can result in uncontrollable high-speed flights. The two drum operators must be well trained and in constant communication. Only highly skilled operators should handle this system.

The "Track-on-Track" System

The "track-on-track" system was designed to provide flying movement in theatres with low grid height. It is more complicated and difficult to install. One operator controls horizontal track movement of a flyer; another handles the lift line. While it offers less-realistic, less-spectacular flying effects, it provides infinite movement control and very graceful flights.

SELECTED READINGS

AMERICAN IRON and STEEL INSTITUTE, *Wire Rope Users Manual* (2nd ed.). Washington, D.C.: November 1985.

AUTOMATIC DEVICES COMPANY, *Curtain Tracks-Curtain Machines, Catalog 44*. Allentown, Penn.: 1973.

BURRIS-MEYER, HAROLD, and EDWARD C. COLE, *Scenery for the Theatre* (rev. ed.). Boston: Little, Brown, 1971.

DICKIE, D. E., ed. *Rigging Manual* (1st ed.). Toronto: Construction Safety Assn. of Ontario, 1975.

GILLETTE, A. S., and J. MICHAEL GILLETTE, *Stage Scenery* (3rd ed.). New York: Harper and Row, 1981.

GLERUM, JAY O., *Stage Rigging Handbook.* Carbondale and Edwardsville: Southern Illinois University Press, 1987.

J. R. CLANCY, INC., *Theatrical Hardware, Catalog 59-A.* Syracuse: February 1982.

MACWHYTE WIRE ROPE COMPANY, *MacWhyte Wire Rope, Catalog G 18* (2nd ed.). Kenosha, Wis.: 1981.

ROSSNAGEL, W. E., *Handbook of Rigging* (3rd ed.). New York: McGraw-Hill, 1964.

14

Properties

Properties are generally the smaller objects that complete the visual setting, including all furniture, floor coverings, window and wall furnishings. Objects used by the actors are also props, as well as sound and visual effects that are not electrical. The definition of a prop is determined in the actual production situation. For instance, an item such as a parasol or a sword may be identified as a costume accessory if it is used by only one actor, but the same item may be a prop if it is used as business by several actors. Similarly, large props may be identified as scenery if they must be rigged or shifted in a special manner. The question of what is a prop in a given production becomes a concern when it must be determined which union or crew must provide it. Decision in this matter is made by the stage manager or technical director.

An enormous number of crafts and skills are involved in providing properties for a given production. Thus, capable property specialists must have a wide range of knowledge, versatile talents, and research abilities. The solution to the creation of props requires resourcefulness, sensitivity to the needs of actors, problem-solving inventiveness, and creative skills. Contrary to those who may regard the providing of props as an unimportant task, it is one of the most essential technical areas to be executed for a production. Next to costumes, properties are closest to the physical activity of the actor, and therefore vital to the actor's expressiveness. Props require decisive judgment and imagination, for nothing is more glaring and conspicuous than inappropriate props or props that do not work flawlessly in a scene.

TYPES OF PROPERTIES

For the convenience of discussion in referring to properties, they are divided into sev-

FIGURE 14–1 **Television Scenery.** Properties play a vital role in creating an environment. Setting for the NBC Live Theatre presentation of *A Member of the Wedding*. Production designer: Roy Christopher. (Photo courtesy of NBC-TV)

eral general classifications based on the size, use, and function of prop items.

Set Properties

This term is used to identify the largest items used in a setting. Included in this category are furniture, rugs and other floor coverings, large kitchen appliances, outdoor benches, tree stumps, rocks, bushes, and similar items. These objects are generally supported on the stage floor, but not constructed as part of the stage setting as are some fireplaces, built-in bookcases, and china cupboards.

Hand Properties

This identifies small objects that are handled by the actors as part of their business.

Hand props include such items as letters, pens, dishes, trays, books, weapons, packages, umbrellas, manuscripts, and similar objects. They may be items carried onstage by actors or picked up for use from tables, desks, bookcases, and other locations on the setting.

Decorative Properties

These are properties that are used to decorate the setting and make it look complete. They generally are not used by the actors. They include window curtains and draperies, pictures, mirrors, wall hangings, and small objects throughout the setting. Fireplace mantels, bookcases, desks, bureaus, buffets, and china cabinets must contain objects to make the environment seem lived-in. Scenic designers are well aware of the vast importance of props used to dress the setting. A bouquet of flowers, candlesticks, ivy on a wall, logs in a fireplace, flowers on a trellis, a clock on a mantel, and similar objects are vital to the expressiveness and documentation of a scene. They require careful selection and preparation.

Trick or Breakaway Properties

This category refers to properties that must perform in certain ways. They include breakaway bottles, shooting firearms, chairs that must collapse, a sword that breaks, as well as other trick or breakaway effects. In television and film production, many of these effect properties, along with the more sophisticated effects required in these industries, are handled by the special effects department. Chapter 15 presents some of these effects. Those special properties that are electrically wired are often the task of electricians. These include electrically wired candles, torches, fireplace logs, and similar devices.

PLANNING PROPERTIES

There are no shortcuts or easy methods of planning properties for a production. You must try to be thorough and precise in the planning process. The development of the production in rehearsal, and the frailties of the communication process among the production team, will necessitate changes, clarifications, and constant updating of even the best-made plans. The properties chief should be wary of overconfidence, always questioning and reconfirming the properties required for the production. As with any technical element in production, nothing is certain until it has been seen and actually tested in performance. Properties, so closely related to the actors and their physical action, must function and operate extremely satisfactorily to be effective. The following steps are essential in the planning process.

Read the Script Carefully

The drama must be read several times. The first reading should be done to capture the overall meaning and quality intended for the audience. Study of details and structure of the script should be done in subsequent readings. Each time the drama is read, decide in advance specifically what you want to learn. First and foremost, it is important that the property person analyze the script as carefully as the director, the designer, or principal actor. Without this knowledge, a person will have difficulty understanding the qualities needed in the properties for the production. Second, learn to study the drama for a clear understanding of the properties required, how they are used, their description, and their importance to the plot.

Prepare a Descriptive Listing of the Properties

A complete list of properties must be prepared for the production (Figure 14-2). This list is begun by study of the script. List items found in the author's description of each scene, the stage directions, the dialogue, and the physical actions of the drama. Remember that, often, many properties are only implied. For instance, the use of a fire poker in a scene may require the existence of a fireplace complete with other fireplace equipment. Some standard acting editions of scripts include a listing of props in their final pages. These may be useful as double checks to the list you are preparing.

However, you must realize that these were the properties used for a different production, a different setting, and a different director. Properties for any production will depend upon the director's interpretation and the setting planned by the scenic designer. In fact, the next step in preparing the complete property list is to consult with the director and the designer. Each item on

---

The Gentleman from Athens by Emmet Lavery

Set Props

Sofa, 5' to 6', American Georgian style, camel back, green fabric (see designer)

Armchair to match sofa, same upholstery

Wing chair, gold upholstery

Table, drum type, pedestal base, approximately 2' in dia., walnut or mahogany

Writing table, Sheraton style, walnut or mahogany

2 straight chairs, Sheraton or Hepplewhite style

Coffee table, about 3' long, Hepplewhite style, leather top

Typewriter, 1940s model

Typewriter table, office type, metal

Fancy desk, oversized, garish modern, padded & upholstered sides in tan *Naugahide*

Liquor cabinet, about 3' wide, walnut or mahogany

Hand Props

Briefcase, large, official looking

Pen-and-ink desk set, gold pen would be best

18" bust of Socrates

Racing form (Igor)

Pencil and notebook, pocket size

2 supper trays with covered plates, food, silverware, cup and saucer

12 telegrams (Daniel)

Punch bowl, glass

Newspaper (Mike)

Newsreel camera

Large tripod for camera

Microphone and cable

2 photographers' floodlights and cables

Cigars, large (Mike)

Cutouts from newspapers

Large white envelope

Affidavits, very official looking

Book, large

3 telephones, 1940s black

Lease, 9½" × 14"

Assorted legal papers

Liquor bottles and liquor: cognac, whiskey, brandy, and scotch

6 assorted liquor glasses

House bills, various sizes

Magazines, 1940s (Mary)

Decorative Props

2 candelabra (see designer for style)

Oil painting, over mantel, a Gilbert Stuart portrait, check space dimensions

Bell rope, gold cloth with tassel, 3" wide

Calendar

Window drapery (see designer for fabric)

4 pictures on back wall (see designer with selections)

Christmas greens and holly, hung on mantel and hallway entrance

Fireplace screen, brass

Fireplace tools, brass

FIGURE 14–2 Complete list of properties for a production.

the list should be discussed individually, and additional items should be added. The director will be able to explain the general approach to be followed in staging the drama and will be able to provide some insight into the nature of the action and the use of the properties. The designer will have developed a setting that should finalize the set props and determine the nature of the decorative props. The property person will need copies of the ground plans of the settings in order to know the location and approximate size of the properties in each scene.

The complete prop list cannot be prepared in a short time. In one sense it is an ever-developing list, subject to changes that occur in rehearsals of the cast. In fact, the list may not be absolutely final until after the technical rehearsals. The list must be flexible and altered as the production develops. In the meantime, it is important to have an adequate description of each item. This includes the size, shape, and measurement of each object; the needed color, appearance, and weight; and above all, how each is to be used by the actor. The fact that an actor must stand on the table, that a sofa must be tipped over, that a chair must collapse in a certain way, or that muffins are eaten during dialogue is vital knowledge in the selection, procurement, and fabrication of the properties.

Perform Necessary Research

A thorough description of the props is seldom complete without some research. This is generally a study of historic periods for items such as an 1850s snuff box, a Rococo armoire, or a Norwegian Victorian stove. Never be satisfied with only one example or description, or simply with the most typical or stereotyped item. Frequently, other examples may have qualities or characteristics more appropriate for the particular action, mood, or style of the drama. Make drawings or obtain pictures during the research for confirmation with the designer and director and for use by the property crew.

Attend Occasional Rehearsals

Once the director begins to block the action of the drama, it is valuable for the property person to begin to attend some rehearsals. Don't be satisfied with explanations of how the actors are using the properties. Nothing substitutes for watching the action yourself and learning how the items are handled, used, or operated by the cast. Changes in the type or location of props or a change in the blocking may be necessary for a scene to work effectively. Your presence at rehearsal from time to time will help identify those or other problems requiring different solutions. The property person should attend the regular production-staff meetings and maintain contact with the stage manager for regular reports of the progress of the rehearsals. You will also be called upon to provide essential rehearsal properties for the actors. Major furniture and other set props should be approximated in size

and shape. Substitutes are used in lieu of the actual hand props.

Organize the Property Procurement and Construction Schedule

As soon as approval is reached on prop needs, the property manager should begin the process of procurement and fabrication. Properties frequently take considerable time to acquire and construct. A meeting with the prop crew is necessary to explain the needs, to study pictures and drawings, and to review how the props are to be used. A construction schedule will need to be prepared to assure completion of the work before the first technical rehearsal. Some props (a stuffed owl or an 18″ bust of Socrates) may require considerable search. Property people soon acquire a list of phone numbers of specialty shops, companies, and individuals helpful in searching for unusual items. For other props, solutions and methods must be found for their manufacture. These decisions must be made, and in some cases time must be allowed to test the resultant prop under conditions similar to the action of the drama.

SOURCES FOR RESEARCH

Almost every production, period or modern, requires some research in properties and set decoration. Before you select or create properties, it is imperative that you have a knowledge of both the artifacts used in the period and the circumstances of the drama. Indeed, an understanding of the manners, customs, and lifestyle of a given time or occupation is necessary.

Most needed is information on furniture, antiques, and home decoration, and hundreds of books and materials are easily available. Novices will want, first of all, to consult general introductions and period outline sources for brief descriptions of a period, styles of ornament, or chief characteristics of the furniture and decoration before launching into more extensive volumes. Furniture encyclopedias and comprehensive studies of historic furnishings are useful and valuable in personal libraries. The best provide considerable descriptive text and numerous illustrations and photographs. Never be satisfied with only one example or a general description of a piece of furniture; seek a number of examples and variations in the style. Once acquainted with the particular styles and the artists and craftspeople of the period, research will become fruitful. More depth of information is found in publications limited to furnishings of a particular country, a specific period style, or an individual designer. Photographs of complete interiors are extremely useful in visualizing the composite effect of interior furnishings and decoration of a period. Photographic histories and miniature interiors are also very helpful.

Sources that present interior and architectural decoration are frequently limited to the most fashionable and lavish of the time. The finest in fashion in any age can be afforded only by the wealthy. Be careful to seek items that reflect the customs and style of living of the individuals in the drama. Sociological histories and publications dealing with everyday life in various periods usually provides better information about the life of the average individual. In recent years, interest in the history of popular culture has focused on the preservation of popular magazines and the reproduction of old mail-order catalogues.

Nearly all current magazines are useful sources for prop personnel. These include architectural, interior, and home furnishings magazines; magazines that rely heavily on photographs to record contemporary and past events; hobby, travel, vacation, and adventure magazines; and trade journals. Woodworking publications sometimes provide detailed drawings, dimensions, and proportions of period objects. These are invaluable for building reproductions.

Museums in major cities generally have collections of furniture and decorative arts for firsthand observation. Sometimes they have reconstructed rooms typical of past ages. Nearly every city and town is active in preserving buildings, including their interiors and the cultural arts of the past. A visit to these historic sites is a rich experience in understanding the life and interior furnishings of the past.

Keep a Card File and Scrapbook

Since you cannot purchase every good book you find, it is wise to keep a card file for the titles of books that are particularly useful. Many prop people also keep scrapbooks of newspaper stories, drawings, pictures, magazine articles, exhibit catalogues, and similar material for future use.

ACQUISITION OF PROPERTIES

After the period of planning and research, it is soon time to acquire the needed property items. It is wise to begin immediately on the hardest-to-find objects and those pieces that may require considerable time to construct or that may require some experimentation. Both time and cost must be considered in the acquisition process. Although the method of procuring some objects is clear from the start, for many items decisions must be made whether to buy, build, borrow, or rent them. In some cases it may be necessary to establish an alternative method of procurement if the desired method cannot be achieved.

Property Stock

Many producing organizations, particularly those with heavy or ongoing production schedules, maintain a stock of properties. The purpose of a property stock is to collect items that will likely be needed for productions in the years ahead. This results in the reduction of costs for properties in the future, as well as in the time and effort necessary to locate them. On the other hand, a prop collection requires space, often a precious commodity in a production facility, and some regular maintenance. These are important factors when deciding what to add to or retain in the stock. Unless availability of space is not a problem, it would be unwise to keep very unusual items not likely to be used again. The type of props that should be kept in stock will depend on the range of productions regularly staged by the organization. Among small items commonly stocked because of frequent use are books, liquor bottles, glassware, silverware, pictures, candlesticks, dishware, artificial flowers, artificial fruit, vases, and canes.

Two types of furniture are valuable to collect. One of these is a variety of sturdy rehearsal pieces: basic tables, benches, stools, chairs, and sofas. The other is furniture, especially period or reproductions of period styles, with some potential for use in settings. Matching sets of furniture are frequently more useful than single items of a given style. It is helpful to establish goals, listing the kinds of furniture most frequently required, to guide purchases and donations. Victorian, French Provincial, Elizabethan or Tudor, English 18th century, Early American, and Duncan Phyfe are a few of the common styles that should be considered for adding to stock. A prop stock can grow rapidly if donations are actively solicited. If a stock exists, it is the first place to go in search of items for the coming production.

Renting or Borrowing Properties

Renting and borrowing greatly expands the range and variety of properties available to the producing group at a relatively low cost. Most large cities have prop rental companies to serve the needs of theatre, industrial theatre, film, TV, film commercials, and the display industry. Many have extensive collections of furniture, hand props, and decorative props. There are also a few companies that rent modern furniture for apartments. In addition, antique and secondhand furniture dealers are available in nearly every community who will rent items for theatre production. It is helpful to become well acquainted with these sources in your vicinity. Visit them regularly to maintain familiarity with their normal stock and to cultivate a sound relationship with them. Not only could they be a valuable source for props some day, they may also be helpful in locating a needed item they do not have themselves.

For many groups, extreme budget limitations require considerable borrowing of props. A loan policy with another producing group is often an excellent practice. In effect, it increases your own available stock by the size of the other organization's collection. However, borrowing from commercial stores, dealers, or individuals is frequently risky business. Privately owned items often have antique or heirloom value or sentimental associations for the owner. Damage to items borrowed will not help the producing group's reputation and public image. Borrowing from stores can have a similar effect.

Further, after use in a production, new furniture often can no longer be sold as new. A secondhand dealer can often find one more scratch on the table after it is returned than when it was originally loaned. You may be charged for repairs or be forced to purchase the piece. Many theatre property stocks have grown through the addition of "borrowed" items that had to be purchased. Additionally, a borrowed object may adversely affect the production. Particularly in amateur groups, loaned objects have a way of not belonging to the scene. Actors, cautioned that the antique buffet or Victorian chair is borrowed from the Joneses and must be protected, have a tendency to avoid the object or to treat it with unrealistic care. In such cases the props will not seem to "belong" in the setting and will not effectively assist the production.

There are several obligations in renting and borrowing props. First of all, reasonable protection of the object must be provided while it is in your possession. It should be covered and secured when not in use. It must be returned promptly after the production. Inadequate care and failure to return the item at the time arranged are the fastest ways of ruining your organization's reputation and reducing the chances of renting or borrowing from that source in the future. Be sure the terms of the loan or rental are fully established at the beginning so you know firm costs and other obligations. Transporting the props to and from your facility is another concern. If damage occurs in transport, who is financially liable? It may be desirable to obtain insurance coverage or to pay a commercial carrier to deliver and return the props.

Purchasing Properties

Many properties can be obtained only by buying them. Among these are things that are consumed—not only foods and other perishables, but also items that are destroyed or otherwise used up in the course of the production. It is helpful to know where to locate hard-to-find items, such as large statuary, artificial flowers, and similar items. Display suppliers and magic and novelty shops are invaluable for small specialized trick and decorative props. Secondhand stores, resale shops, flea markets, and junk dealers are particularly valuable for prop purchases. Expect costs to be high in antique shops and be more reasonable at secondhand dealers and at warehouse outlets selling slightly damaged goods. The best bargains are usually obtained at the resale stores of the Salvation Army, Goodwill Industries, and similar agencies.

The purchase of furniture is often advisable if the item is worth adding to the organization's stock of prop furniture. Used furniture can be relatively inexpensive. A well-styled chair, even an antique with a broken arm or leg, will sell for a lower price. Then it can be repaired, reglued, and reupholstered satisfactorily in the prop shop. You need also to look at the potential of low-cost furniture of the most eclectic design. The general proportion of a piece or the shaping of the legs or back may be sufficient to enable you to turn it into a handsome, high-styled item of furniture. It is also worthwhile to consider purchasing new furniture, particularly reproductions of period styles. Old furniture, especially antiques, is often fragile from wear and age and demands continual repair and maintenance. New furniture will take more abuse and seldom costs more than items regarded as antiques. Be certain, of course, that the piece is a good enough reproduction, in proportion and detail, for scrutiny by your audience. You may be able to reduce the cost of new furniture by ordering muslin covering in lieu of regular upholstery material, or just the frame or unfinished frame, recognizing that you will provide the particular upholstery or finish to meet the needs of production.

Constructing Properties

Things that must be constructed include objects not available for acquisition in other ways. These may be unusual objects or items that do not exist or are unavailable except as museum pieces (ancient Greek or Roman objects, for example). Items that must be overproportioned, such as fantasy, distorted, and unusual-style objects will require manufacturing. All food items and perishable props, or items consumed or destroyed in the production, must be prepared or constructed. Trick props and breakaways must be devised, and often furniture must be manufactured to meet the unusual needs of the action or the particular dramatic style.

PROPERTY CONSTRUCTION AND RECONSTRUCTION

Furniture Framing

Sometimes it is necessary to manufacture furniture in the prop shop. It is usually advantageous to build if you cannot find or afford what is needed, if it is less expensive to build, or if a particular proportion, shape, scale, or style is necessary for the production. Certainly, shop-built furniture can be lighter in weight, and body support units (beds, upholstered sofas, and chairs) can be firmer, distinct advantages for production purposes. However, before deciding to build furniture, the prop department should be certain the cost is warranted, that there is sufficient time for construction, that adequate shop tools exist, and that property personnel have the necessary skills to construct the units.

Certain kinds of furniture can be constructed without great difficulty (Figure 14-3). These include some types of case furniture (furniture that contains objects, such

as bookcases, desks, hutches, cabinets) and primitive, rustic, or rectilinear furniture (simple benches, stools, tables). Overstuffed furniture, which has much of its construction hidden, is easier to build than exposed wood units. Some contemporary furniture influenced by the "form follows function" standard can be easily constructed, while Rococo (Louis XV) furniture with its elaborate carving and decoration would be more difficult to build in an average prop shop. Highly stylized, overscaled, and distorted items usually must be shop-built projects.

Repair and reconstruction of furniture is a distinctly common practice. When repairing or modifying furniture, it is usually best to follow the existing construction. The framing of the item to be repaired should be studied before attempting to make repairs. Wood joints on good furniture are often glued mortise-and-tenon joints (such as used in joining stretchers to leg posts), glued dowel joints (such as used to join rails and aprons to the legs of chairs and tables), and glued dovetail joints (used in drawer construction). Loose joints should be reglued

FIGURE 14–3 Shop-built furniture. The frame of a chair and settee for padding and upholstery and a table.

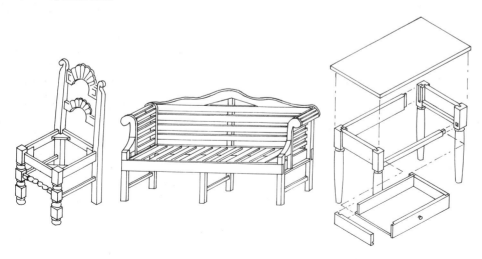

with good quality wood glue and well secured with bar clamps until the glue has dried.

A stronger epoxy glue may be necessary if the wood is unusually dry and cracked. Broken dowels should be replaced with grooved hardwood dowels for maximum strength. Usually side-rail and leg joints on tables and chairs are reinforced with glue blocks or corner blocks to strengthen the furniture frame at the point of greatest strain. The screws in these blocks may need to be retightened or the blocks replaced.

Somewhat simpler construction is often possible when building new furniture in the prop shop, but attention must be given to providing strong joints. While true joiners and cabinetmakers cannot be surpassed in skillfulness, with care, patience and adequate power tools an amateur can perform amazingly well. The most difficult task is to cut the joints absolutely square. Only a few major joints need to be adopted by technicians in building furniture (Figure 14-4). With contemporary tools they are not difficult to make, and strength is added with modern adhesives. The **open mortise and tenon joint** and the **dowel joint** are excellent for corner joints and are easily achievable. A reinforcing block gives an added measure of strength. **Open dowel joints,** which require little skill, can be used instead of these standard joints. **Dado joints** are ideal for shelves in a bookcase and in drawer construction. The **rabbet joint** can replace the time-consuming dovetail joint. Screws should be used rather than nails in constructing furniture. Commercial steel drawer glides are ideal to keep drawers from sticking when operating. Countersunk screw holes and gouges can be filled with wood putty and sanded for a smooth surface. If plywood is used in building furniture, it is best to hide the edges exposing the layers of ply. **Miter joints** or narrow wood strips can mask these edges.

The exposed wood of constructed and reconstructed furniture will need appropriate wood finishing. The standard method is through application of stain to give the appropriate color, followed by a protective coating of shellac, clear varnish, or lacquer. All surfaces must be sanded smooth, first of all. Care is needed in selecting the stain color for an appropriate wood tone or effect, particularly if the piece must match other furniture in the setting or replace part of a single furniture item. When stained, pine and fir, especially plywood veneer, have very pronounced grain patterns that prevent successful simulation of furniture hardwoods. To reduce the absorption rate of the stain, they require a preliminary coating of shellac cut 50 percent with denatured alcohol before staining. Stain is applied by brushing or wiping, then removing the excess. Because woods will absorb stain at different rates, the method of application and the duration of time before removal helps to control absorption. Be careful of end grain, which absorbs stain quickly and will become much darker than the other surfaces. After a light sanding, shellac or clear varnish (gloss or semigloss) is applied for the protective coating.

Furniture can also be finished (stained and/or grained) by the shellac-glaze method.

FIGURE 14-4 Common wood joints for furniture.

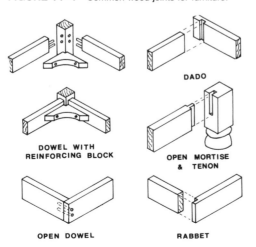

DADO

DOWEL WITH
REINFORCING BLOCK

OPEN MORTISE
& TENON

OPEN DOWEL

RABBET

Sometimes called **French enamel varnish** (FEV), this uses fabric, shoe, or leather dyes in a base of shellac cut with an equal amount of denatured alcohol. Being alcohol soluble, the finish can be stripped to bare wood at the end of the production with a wiping of alcohol-soaked cloths. Sometimes, furniture is painted. Certain French styles are painted with enamels in light pastel tints for a high gloss finish. Before applying paint, a coat of shellac is needed to seal the pores of the wood.

Upholstery

The simplest furniture upholstery system employs durable fabric held firmly over a thin pad. The seats and backs of straight and occasional chairs are made more comfortable in this manner. It is not difficult to reupholster these units, and rubber or plastic foam is available in various thicknesses for use as padding. Chopped foam is also available for creating tufted or curved upholstery surfaces. Overstuffed furniture, however, requires a more complicated upholstery system. A system involving coil springs often is used for sofas and overstuffed easy chairs. Although improvements have been made in some contemporary furniture, seat cushions have traditionally been constructed in the following way. A knowledge of this method is needed when repairing overstuffed furniture.

Base. Strips of 3 ½″ jute webbing are stretched and tacked across the bottom rails of the seat (Figure 14-5). The strips are placed both lengthwise and crosswise in an interlaced manner. A webbing stretcher or webbing pliers is used to pull the webbing taut before securing it to the frame with #8 upholstery tacks.

Springs. Coil springs are placed where the strips of webbing cross each other (Figure 14-6). The bottom of each spring is sewn to the webbing with heavy thread or twine.

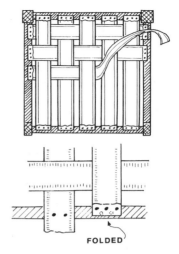

FIGURE 14–5 Attaching webbing to the frame. Webbing is interlaced and double-tacked after folding for secure attachment.

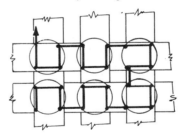

FIGURE 14–6 Securing springs. Springs are stitched to the webbing in a continuous pattern (top view). A wire is added to reinforce the exposed edges.

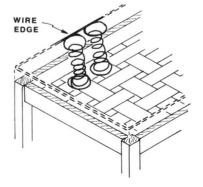

The thread need not be cut between springs if each spring is securely sewn at four locations and the thread is knotted on the last stitch before proceeding to the next spring. The upper coil of the first row of springs must extend over the front seat rail. This edge is strengthened by attaching a wire edge to the front and side springs to give the seat a firm and durable front edge. This wire is sewn or wired to the top coil of each spring. The tops of the springs are then tied both crosswise and lengthwise so they will act in unison. Heavy twine is used, securely knotted to the springs and held firmly to the seat frame with #11 tacks. Burlap is stretched across the springs and tacked to the frame. For added strength, the top of the springs is sewn to the burlap.

Stuffing. A layer of padding is placed on top of the burlap (Figure 14-7). In older furniture curled horsehair, moss, or cotton was used; foam is more common today. The stuffing is often stitched to the burlap to keep it in place.

A padded roll of stuffing is added to the front of the seat and to the edges of the back of the furniture to eliminate sharp edges and to prevent the stuffing from working away from the edges.

Covering. The padding is covered first with a layer of muslin to hold the material in place. The final upholstery material is placed over the muslin covering and securely tacked to the frame. When reupholstering a piece of furniture, it is wise to keep each piece of the old upholstery fabric to serve as a pattern for the replacement cover, noting how each was secured to the frame. Covers and seams in the upholstery cover frequently include cording. This is done by sewing bias strips of the fabric over cotton welt cord. Braid, gimp, or fringe is used as an edge decoration to hide the tacks. Refer to the fabric yardage chart (Figure 6-27) to determine approximate yardage for furniture upholstery and slipcovers. Additional yardage may also be necessary with patterned fabrics.

Loose Cushions. Some overstuffed furniture includes loose cushions instead of padding added directly over the springs. These may be the inner-spring type or made of sheets of foam.

This same process is followed in upholstering the backs of sofas and chairs, although smaller springs are used. The arms of the furniture are created with the same base of cross-meshed webbing, but no springs.

In upholstering shop-made furniture, it is best to avoid using coil springs or even flat sagless springs. It is time-consuming and expensive, and requires considerable skill. Furthermore, coil spring construction is generally so soft the actor sits in a very low and unattractive position and finds it awkward to get up. Such furniture often requires a board placed under the cushion to stiffen and heighten the seat. New constructed units can be built with a rigid foundation covered with foam or other padding material, to be more comfortable for the actor.

Hand and Decorative Properties

There is no finite list of the kinds of properties required in theatre production. Each script has its own unique set of properties.

FIGURE 14–7 Covering the springs.

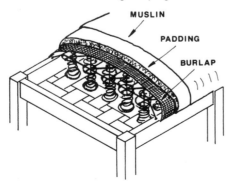

MUSLIN

PADDING

BURLAP

FIGURE 14–8 Decorative properties play an important role in the scenic environment. A scene from *Road to Mecca* at Northern Illinois University. Scene design by Alan Donahue and properties by Kathryn Hubbard. (Photo by George Tarbay)

Furthermore, each dramatic situation prescribes a particular way each property must perform or function for the action. This, in part, determines how each prop should be created or fabricated. The test of the property person often lies in the ingenuity employed in determining the appropriate construction solution for each prop piece. For example, an urn can be fabricated of paper, papier-mâché, Celastic, wood, clay, plaster, fiberglass, foam, or metal, to mention only a few materials. The right solution depends on the use of that object in the production.

Food and Drink. Food can become a real problem in a production, especially scenes requiring the actors to eat an entire meal. There is seldom sufficient time to devour much food, and the dialogue must continue with the maximum of convenience and ease for the actors. This means that eatables must be easily chewed and swallowed. Food cannot be hot, heavily seasoned, tough, hard, chewy, dry, or sticky. Often it is necessary to prepare substitutes to represent the items that are too difficult to eat. Fresh bread, jello, whipped potatoes, whipped cream, canned vegetables, and similar palatable foods can often be shaped and colored to imitate hard-to-chew dishes. Whipped, airy foods that melt in the mouth are ideal. The steam from hot dishes can be created by a little dry ice on a warm plate. Food must be freshly made for each performance and must be satisfactory in appearance and taste for the actors. Food that is nonpractical—not eaten by the actors—can be easily created. Artificial fruit and other novelty store items are effective. Cakes, pastries, a roast chicken, or a piece of meat can be fabricated in urethane foam, plaster, papier-mâché, or other materials.

Beverages of all kinds are standard prop requirements. It is nearly impossible to eliminate liquids in a drinking scene. Actual tea and coffee are easy to provide. Liquor and wine should usually be simulated. Mixtures of tea, food coloring, coffee, cider, and lemon juice can be prepared and examined to match the color of a particular alcoholic drink. Ginger ale works well for champagne, and proper handling offstage will make the carbonation produce an appropriate "pop" in the uncorking. If actual beer is inappropriate for the production, the use of nonalcoholic or near beer is a good solution. Near beer is available in typical beer containers for opening on the set. All bottles, glasses, and cups must be kept thoroughly clean and fresh drinks prepared for each performance.

Flowers, Plants, and Foliage. Real flowers are usually avoided as theatrical properties; they are expensive and have a limited life. Commercial artificial flowers, made of plastic, paper, or cloth, are generally effective. While the best quality are costly, they will last indefinitely in stock if properly stored and maintained. The best artificial flowers are soft and pliable, such as those made of cloth (especially silk), foam, or rubberized material. If they are to be handled naturally by the actor, they cannot be stiff and crackling in sound nor hard and noisy when dropped. The nature of the floral arrangement will influence the solution to the problem. It may be a short-or long-stem bouquet, a nosegay, a corsage or boutonniere, a wreath, a garland, or flowers on a bush, a potted plant, or a trellis vine. The particular species must be examined carefully to learn the shape and characteristics of the petals and leaves. The components may be cut out of colored cloth, felt, or paper and glued to wire wrapped in tape or cloth. Actual florist's tape and covered stem wire greatly aids the

process. Rose and carnation-like blossoms are easily made from white or pink facial tissues or crepe paper. It requires a special folding technique held together by a twist of soft wire.

Plants and Small Trees. Live plants have difficulty surviving in the windowless confines of a stage. Imitations can be fabricated without great difficulty and will remain consistent in appearance. Artificial plants are widely available in department stores, florist shops, and display dealers. Because of their natural look, real branches of trees and shrubs are often best for the trunks of small trees and plants. They may be secured in a pot filled with sand or plaster.

Leaves, Vines, and Foliage. Sometimes palm fronds, preserved fern leaves treated for preservation, are available through local florist and display suppliers. In addition, craft shops often have artificial vines, garlands, leaves, and similar supplies useful in creating foliage and vines. Sometimes real leaves and cut lengths of ivy or other vines can be employed, especially in a mass effect on a trellis or a wall, although they may need replacement if the production period is extensive. Leaves can be made of a variety of materials. The nature of the foliage must be considered. Are the leaves large? Are they shiny, or soft and frizzy? Felt, velour, flocked paper, thin foam, crepe paper, stiff paper, plastic, and canvas are some of the choices of material. Once cut out, the leaves may be glued to covered wire and stiffened or held in shape by shellac, glue-sized starch, or a glazing material.

Hedges. Exterior settings frequently rely heavily on large bushes, shrubs, and neatly trimmed hedges for their illusion. A few types of artificial shrubs are available commercially, but they are extremely expensive. Fortunately, the construction of hedges and shrubs trimmed in rectangular, cube, sphere, and cone shapes is not difficult. This includes junipers, yews, and privet hedges grown and cut in rectilinear hedge rows, and individual shrubs such as upright junipers, arborvitae, boxwood, and other ornamental evergreens common in formal gardens. The latter are often trimmed in the shape of precise cones, balls, or tiers of diminishing spheres. One method of constructing these units is similar to decorating parade floats. It involves building a lightweight frame to support chicken wire shaped to the correct contour. Paper napkins or crepe paper are then stuffed into the openings of the wire to create a rough foliage-like surface (Figure 14-9). Spray painting or brush texturing can give the desired final appearance to the hedge. Another method of construction creates the shape of the shrub in a ground row made of plywood (or other construction board). Individual leaves, leaf clusters, and small branches are then taped, glued, or stapled to the surface. Some variations in the prime color will aid the illusion of depth.

Grass. When necessary, the effect of grass can be achieved as a floor covering, for little knolls, or as base trim for exterior set units. Grass mat, sold in sections up to 6′ × 10′ has been a traditional grass surface. It contains a simulated grass material attached to a burlap backing. More sophisticated and costly, grass carpeting is a short-cropped plastic grass on a rubber base. Also sold through display outlets is a grass-coated paper and a loose grass material for scattering or for applying to surfaces with a binder.

Weaponry. When staging fights and duels, actual swords and foils should be used for human safety, for the proper sword durability, and for the clanking sound of metal. Obviously, the actors must have fencing training, and all fight scenes must be well choreographed and rehearsed by a specialist. Real dagger stabbing, however, is dangerous unless (1) the point and edge of the blade have been dulled by a grinder, (2) the actual stabbing and fall have been thoroughly routinized, and (3) the action is well masked from the audience or camera. Rubber daggers and disappearing daggers (the blade slides into the handle when pressed against an object) are far safer. However, the actor must learn to fall properly while clutching any dagger so it will not cause injury. Swords and daggers that are decorative and nonpractical can be manufactured in the prop shop. This also includes battleaxes, spears, maces, and halberds. Excellent simulations can be crafted of metal bar stock or entirely of wood and coated with metallic paint for the proper appearance of metal.

Firearms not fired are generally not difficult to provide. Quality theatrical replicas are available in a wide variety of rifles, muskets, and pistols. With some care, simulations of most types of firearms can be manufactured in the shop. Guns that must be fired on the stage are special problems and require extremely careful rehearsal and control. The safest solution is to use the type of starting pistols and caps employed in athletic events. There is less risk with shots from a starting pistol. If real guns and blank cartridges must be used, several precautions are essential. First, the gun should never be shot at someone at close range. The powder and wadding will cause damage to objects near the muzzle. There must be adequate clear space so the emitting materials will not harm

FIGURE 14–9 Shrubs and hedges can be made of chicken wire stuffed with paper.

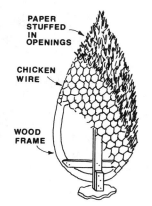

PAPER STUFFED IN OPENINGS

CHICKEN WIRE

WOOD FRAME

people or scenery. Special short loads may be obtained from gunsmiths if the regular blanks are too loud in the theatre. A backup gun may be necessary if the pistol used by the actor tends to misfire. Real firearms must be carefully loaded and regularly cleaned by a prop person thoroughly trained in firearm safety. Tight supervision and security are both necessary at all times to prevent theft of the weapons and to keep unauthorized individuals from handling them. When in doubt, seek authoritative advice on safe handling practices of firearms. Legal firearms must be registered with the local police department. Other types of "gun shots" and explosive effects are reviewed in Chapter 15.

Rocks, Stumps, Logs.

Rocks, Stumps, Logs. Many three-dimensional objects used in exterior settings are classified as properties. Those that are irregular (not rectilinear) in shape command our special attention. Three-dimensional items purely decorative and nonpractical are certainly the easiest to manufacture. Once the actual contour of the object is determined, an appropriate sculptural construction method/technique already described in this text may be employed in fabricating the item. Spray urethane foam, papier-mâché, and Celastic are some of the standard answers to these structures. Some display firms sell realistic-looking foam rocks in several sizes and types. If, however, the object must be weight-bearing, a different approach is necessary. The weight-bearing structure must be created first, using a platform construction technique. Following this step the irregular and non-weight-bearing surfaces can be fabricated. With either type of structure, size and magnitude often results in a heavy unit that's awkward to shift. Lightweight materials such as cardboard, fiberglass, or foam may be desired. Or a large object can be built in smaller units. The ease in shifting and handling also benefits by a built-in caster system or by concealed handles to pick up and carry large and awkward objects.

Pictures and Mirrors. The selection of framed or unframed pictures, paintings, photographs, diplomas, certificates, and plaques to adorn a wall, a table top, or a mantel should not be done haphazardly. As with all properties, such objects must relate to the drama and its characters. The size, scale, coloring, and style of pictures must be appropriate to the setting. Inexpensive prints of works by known artists of the past and present will reflect the taste of the characters. These prints may be used to simulate original paintings, but avoid known masterpieces that audiences would recognize as belonging to museums or special collections. It is often necessary to tone down the vividness and contrast of some paintings and photographs so they will not be highly pronounced or distracting in the entire scene. A picture rented or borrowed (with or without picture glass) can be softened in contrast by a facing of dark netting. This also prevents distracting reflections from the smooth surface of the glass. Sometimes it is necessary to have a painting of a particular subject, painter, style, or size for the setting. It may be necessary to create it in scene paint. If the audience or camera distance and position allow, a moderately skilled artist can create an "old master" in a few hours. Because mirrors are heavy, they are sometimes simulated by Upson board or hardboard painted in silver or aluminum paint or covered with a mirrored plastic.

It is usually best to remove the glass from framed pictures. In fact, glass in any form can be a problem in settings that are shifted or toured or which must stand considerable physical action. Glass is easily shattered unless it is mounted in a reasonably rigid frame and handled with extreme care. When it breaks, the bits of flying glass can be extremely dangerous. What's more, the hard and smooth surface can create glaring reflections to the audience or camera. The same occurs with highly polished woodwork, silver service, marble, and other shiny surfaces when filming a scene. *Krylon Dulling*

Spray can eliminate shiny surfaces from causing reflective glares. They also can be broken up with a thin coat of wax, a daubing of putty, a covering of black netting, or any other type of thin coating that acts to diffuse reflected light rays.

The choice of frames for pictures and mirrors must be appropriate in quality and style. Frames should be chosen based on authenticity of the period, and generally can be located, constructed, and painted without great difficulty. It is important to mount pictures securely to the walls of the set. Never hang them from the cloth cover of a flat. On such scenery, toggle bars are needed to support both the top and the bottom of the picture. The picture can be secured by bolts or screws to the toggles of a soft flat or to the plywood of hard flats. For easy removal, a picture hanger and a socket, standard theatrical hardware, are used to attach pictures and other objects to scenery.

Lighting Fixtures. Chandeliers, wall sconces, floor and table lamps, candelabra, and other light sources are requirements in almost all dramatic settings. Many of these items can be purchased from antique dealers or rented from property houses. Modern and traditional electric fixtures and components are purchasable. Also available are electrified reproductions of Colonial, Victorian, and early 20th-century lamps. A variety of globes, shades, plastic chandelier crystals, chains, and so on can be bought for the make-it-yourself light sources. It is also valuable to collect fixture components, especially for chandeliers and wall sconces. Purchase and rental cost of these units is high, so it is frequently necessary to construct them. When the design is known, it is usually possible to create a chandelier or sconce out of standard materials. Electrical conduit and plastic pipe can be bent and shaped for the cluster of socket mounts; strings of plastic crystals, beads, and pendants, and globes and shades can be used as final decorative treatment. Imagination and moderate creative skills can generally produce a stageworthy piece. Kerosene, gas, and oil lamps; candles; lanterns; and torches are sometimes difficult problems. The existence of actual flame in a stage setting provides a potential danger that requires special caution.

Indeed, in some areas it may either be prohibited or require the presence of a member of the fire department backstage. In any case, if real flame is used, a stagehand who has been specially trained to act responsibly in preparing and handling the effect should be holding a fire extinguisher offstage while the flames are burning onstage. Whenever possible, it is advisable to wire the units for electric or battery power. Where the bulbs can be concealed, as in a lantern or by a shade, the conversion can be quite effective. Sometimes a burning candle is satisfactorily achieved by a flashlight bulb daubed with a few strokes of colored transparent acetate ink. The batteries can be concealed in the base of the candlestick or in the hollow tube representing the candle. An on-off switch can be placed at the base. Torches are the most difficult problem; they are not satisfactorily achieved by electricity. A can of *Sterno* sprinkled with salt to create a more visible yellowish fire is often effective. A canister of propane fuel such as used for camp stoves and lanterns can be built into the torch to good effect. A decorative frame around the flame is also helpful in preventing contact with flammable objects. This and other use of fire on stage is discussed further in Chapter 15.

Conventional Theatrical Properties and Practices. Over the years, the property profession has evolved a set of standard conventions and practices. They are truly theatre properties and routine property procedures. Included among these are commercially supplied items such as paper stage money; breakaway bottles; stage blood, which can be removed easily from costumes and props; and even the ever-comic rubber chicken. Coins are frequently made from the round metal knockouts of electrical boxes or by painting poker chips. Faced with the task of filling up numerous shelves of books, book fronts are constructed of painted wood strips glued to an upright frame. The prop crew learns how to tie bundles and seal envelopes so they can be easily opened by the actor. Placing a little water or wet sand in ash trays helps extinguish cigarettes and cigars. Smoking materials (tobacco, matches, and lighters) are commonly needed in plays. Be sure they are used and disposed of safely. Magic illusions, breakaways, and other trick properties are considered in Chapter 15.

Three-Dimensional and Molded Objects

Creating sculpture, three-dimensional objects, and ornamentation challenges the craft skills of the property person. Each project must be analysed to determine the best construction solution. Chapter 9 presents some techniques and materials used in three-dimensional construction. Most methods fall within one of the following approaches.

Sculpting and Carving. Many objects are achieved by carving or sculpting from wood, polystyrene foam, or sculpture's clay. The material is shaped and/or carved to reproduce the object desired. Small objects can be made of **epoxy putty,** which is mixed from aluminum particles and fiberglass fibers in an epoxy base and is molded into shape. When cured in 2 hours at room temperature, this material is strong and has excellent bonding properties.

Creating a Sculptured Object on a Frame. Some objects require the creation of a structural frame to which a skin surface is applied (Figure 14-10). Foundation frames can be constructed of wire, wood, or metal. Commonly, the frame is covered with wire netting and then a skin of Celastic, papier-mâché, or plaster cast cloth (plaster ban-

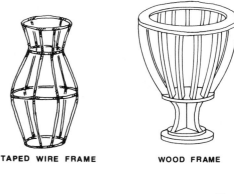

TAPED WIRE FRAME   WOOD FRAME

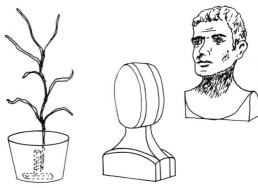

WIRE FRAME FOR   WOOD OR FOAM FOUNDATION
A POTTED PLANT   FOR A BUST

FIGURE 14–10 Common foundations for surface skins, applique, or molding materials.

dages). Sometimes, only a wire armature is needed as the heart of an object sculptured with papier-mâché, epoxy putty, clay, or other material.

Applique. A common way of creating ornamentation is the use of applique or applied buildups on a surface. Lumber, foam, fiber, or vacuum-form ornaments can be added to furniture, fireplace mantels, and other property items for three-dimensional enrichment. This provides interesting architectural and ornamental details, and otherwise nondescript items will be decorated in the appropriate style chosen for the production.

Altering an Existing Object. Many property items can often be created by altering existing objects. Careful search can result in the use of "found" objects that can be assembled and decorated to form the item needed. An existing statue can be altered with plaster cast tape, putty, or Celastic. A window mannequin can become the base for a statue by dressing it in a garb of muslin and sizing or felt and shellac. Bottles can be reshaped to become elaborate urns. A common bowl can be enriched to become an ornate chalise.

Creating an Object From a Mold. Making a copy of a three-dimensional object or a relief ornament by casting material over it is a simple way of creating a property object from a mold. In this case, the actual sculptured model becomes the positive mold. The copy (casting) can be made by applying Celastic, papier-mâché, or plastic cast cloth over the object. The appropriate release agent must be applied first so the casting will not adhere to the mold. When dry, the casting of a relief or half-round object is easily removed. Ornaments, half bottles, and book fronts for set dressings can be produced this way. On a full-rounded object, the casting must be cut in the back to be removed and the halves rejoined at the seams. Sometimes, castings can be made by placing the objects directly in a vacuum-form machine to make copies.

Negative molds are usually necessary when a number of copies of the sculptured object are needed. A relief or half-round object requires only a one-piece mold, while a full-round object requires a two-piece mold (the front and back of the object). The first task is to make the model. The model for a relief ornament is usually built up on a piece of hardboard 2″ to 4″ larger than the object. Wood, plastic foam and metal are often cut and shaped to build up the largest portions of the mold. The final surface is then sculpted with **plastelene modeling clay.** Fingers and tools are used to mold the clay. Dipping your fingers in a little alcohol now and then will keep the clay soft for sculpting. With the completion of the model, the mold can be made. The model is coated first with layers of liquid latex, at least five coats, allowing each layer to dry before applying the next. A frame of lumber is placed around the model 1″ taller than the thickest part of the relief and secured to the hardboard with screws (Figure 14-11). This frame will hold plaster of paris, which gives support to the latex and completes the mold. Plaster of paris is prepared by mixing dry plaster slowly into water in a porcelain or plastic container. The plaster should be stirred gently until it is dissolved. Only a few minutes is allowed before it starts to set. The plaster is poured into the box over the latex. Short pieces of burlap added into the wet plaster gives it strength. Tapping on the box helps to make bubbles in the plaster rise to the top. After an hour or two, the box may be inverted and the model removed from

FIGURE 14–11 Making a negative mold.

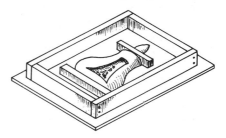

SCULPTED MODEL
IN MOLD FRAME

MOLD READY
FOR CASTING

the mold. After cleaning the mold and the latex lining, another day is necessary for the plaster to dry thoroughly before making castings. Silicone rubber and polyurethane rubber compounds can also be used in making flexible molds. They do not need plaster support but can be poured over the model in one process. Being flexible, they are easy to remove when making castings of rigid materials. However, because of the higher costs of these rubber compounds, they are often used only for small molds.

Having created a negative mold, you are now ready to make castings. Plaster of paris can be mixed and poured into the mold, and, when dry, it can be removed and mounted on the surface of a prop with construction mastic. Hollow castings can be made in the mold with Celastic or papier-mâché. Plaster cast tape can be used similarly. The tape can be cut in short pieces, dipped into water and pressed into the mold. Pour-in-place polyurethane foam can also be used in casting (see Chapter 7) as well as fiberglass. Appropriate mold release agents must be employed.

Many materials for casting and sculpting are available from medical technology. These include dental plaster and molding materials and fabrics or tapes for casts. Polyurethane or thermoplastic impregnated fabrics and tapes used for body casts are activated by water and/or heat. *Cuttercast, Vara-form,* and *Polyform* are trade names of resin-coated cotton fabrics and can be cut easily and molded over most any type of material. Setting time is usually only a few minutes, and, when hardened, they are extremely rigid. *Scotchcast* and *Scotchflex* (3M products), are knitted fiberglass tapes, 2" to 5" wide, impregnated with polyurethane resin. They are water activated and inexpensive products. Petroleum jelly is needed as a release agent in the mold.

Many properties require a rough or textured surface. Automobile body putty and carpet adhesive are especially useful in texturing props. These materials can be thick enough to apply with a putty knife and shaped with sculpting tools. Raised ornamentation and window leading can be achieved effectively with paste-like thickened adhesives in a plastic squeeze bottle. Pastes can be prepared with flexible adhesive (*Phlexglu* is one trade name) thickened with cabosil, metallic powders, or powdered graphite. In addition, equal parts of polyvinyl glue and clear acrylic gloss medium can be similarly thickened for "squeezing" out ornamental patterns.

INTERIORS

Throughout the ages, architectural structure and interior design have profoundly affected furniture and the decorative arts. Indeed, the very materials and construction of human-created enclosures, and the space and nature of the environment they provide, is both a reflection of a civilization and an influential force on the lifestyle of the age. Most of the forms of furniture and decoration originated in architectural structure. It is interwoven with the modes and manners of human activity. Those involved in theatrical properties need to understand structural and decorative forms and principles.

The Orders of Architecture

As classical architecture developed, it resulted in different styles or **orders.** The Doric, Ionic, and Corinthian were the three orders of architecture of Greek buildings. While the orders differ in proportion and detail, each consists of a **column** and an **entablature.** Elements of the column are the **base,** the **shaft,** and the **capital.** The entablature, created by the beam (or lintel) and added ornament, consists of the **architrave,** the **frieze,** and the **cornice.** Later, the Romans replaced the block on which the column rested with an elaborate **pedestal.** Like the column, the pedestal was delineated with **base, shaft,** and **capital.** Formed at the ends of classical buildings, the **pediment** is the triangular area created by the roof line and the cornice. These elements have had a profound effect on subsequent architecture, interiors, and furniture throughout the ages (Figure 14-12). Their influence is evident by the presence of pilasters and paneled wainscoting of interior walls as well as in the casings and pediments of doorways and windows, over mantels, and on case furniture. Cornices, and sometimes complete en-

FIGURE 14–12 Architectural details in interiors.

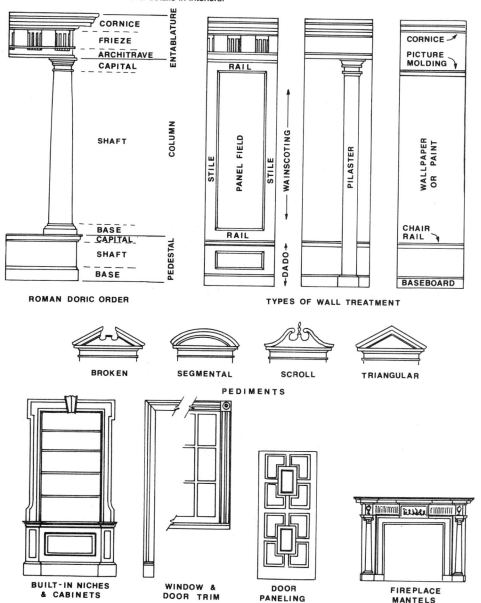

ROMAN DORIC ORDER

TYPES OF WALL TREATMENT

BROKEN   SEGMENTAL   SCROLL   TRIANGULAR

PEDIMENTS

BUILT-IN NICHES & CABINETS

WINDOW & DOOR TRIM

DOOR PANELING

FIREPLACE MANTELS

FIGURE 14–13 Common ornamental motifs.

ACANTHUS ANTEFIX ANTHEMION ARABESQUE
ARCADE BOSS CARTOUCHE CORNUCOPIA DENTILS
DOLPHIN EGG & DART ESCUTCHEON FESTOON FINIAL
FLUTING FRET GRIFFIN GUILLOCHE HONEYSUCKLE HUSK
LINENFOLD LOTUS LOZENGE LUNETTE MODILLION
PALMETTE PENDANT REEDING RINCEAU ROCOCO
ROSETTE SHELL STRAPWORK SWAG VOLUTE

tablatures, separate the tops of walls from ceilings. The pedestal is the origin of the lower-wall treatment called the dado.

Moldings and Ornaments

Forms of moldings were established to provide interest and accent in architectural ornamentation. Classical Greek moldings were freehand creations and exceedingly graceful. The Romans modified them in simpler shapes and by mechanical curves. Moldings serve to terminate areas and to divide or accent surfaces for added sharpness and interest. Contemporary moldings, available in a variety of shapes and styles, are invaluable in interior and furniture decoration.

An ornament may be described as an embellishment to a surface to provide contrast by means of color, texture, or relief. It may be applied to the surface (applique), it may be cut into the surface (incised ornament), it may be carved to project from the surface (relief), or it may be painted on the surface. Ornamental forms or motifs have been created or reproduced in modified ways throughout history. They intrinsically reflect a particular style and therefore characterize the people and the times. Ornaments that closely copy forms of nature are called **naturalistic**, those that idealize life are called **conventional**, and those that are purely imaginary are known as **abstract**. A pattern or design is an organized arrangement of motifs. They may be ordered in many ways to become panels, borders, or diaper patterns, which spread in all directions. Common abstract motifs include such geometric forms as the circle, square, triangle, diamond, and star. The acorn, urn, pine cone, shield, wheat husk, spiral, heart, and wheel are other examples of decorative forms. Figure 14-13 reveals a few examples of ornamental motifs used frequently in architecture, interior decoration, and furniture.

Window Treatment

The treatment of windows is a major means of decorating an interior, providing color accents and softening the hard straight lines of the room. It also performs practical functions. Window coverings help to control the light from outdoors, to regulate the penetrating heat from the sun, and to maintain privacy. Formal period windows are usually treated with several layers or coverings (Figure 14-14).

1. *The glass curtain* is a translucent curtain hung nearest the window glass. It is made of lace, net, gauze, voile, or other sheer fabric appropriate to the room.
2. *The draw drapery* is an opaque drapery (lined or unlined) hung on a traveler track or on rod and rings. Appropriate fabric includes taffeta, satin, velour, and silk shantung.
3. *The overdrape* is a decorative feature that masks the top and side edges of the window. Brocade, damask, velvet, velour, and chintz are some elegant fabrics for this purpose.
4. *The valance* is a cornice decoration piece at the top of the window designed to mask the means used to hang draperies and curtains. It may

FIGURE 14–14 Formal window treatment.

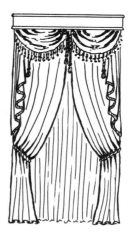

or may not be employed with an overdrapery, according to the particular period.

One or more of these coverings may be suitable for an informal room treatment, depending on the period style. There are many different styles and arrangements for windows (Figure 14-15). Roller shades and Venetian blinds are also commonly used to create privacy and control light. Curtains and draperies may extend to the floor or only to the sill. The former is the most common practice. **Priscilla** curtains are ruffled, sometimes with a ruffled overdrape, and often hung with overlapping swags across the window, held back with ruffled tiebacks at the sides. **Tiered** curtains (sometimes called cafe or cottage curtains) are composed of upper and lower curtain tiers hung on rods. Either or both may be opened as desired. Usually, curtains and draperies are hung in straight panels. Bay windows or two or more immediately adjacent windows are frequently treated as one when hanging draperies and overdrapes.

Overdrapes may be primarily a decoration at the top and partially down the sides of the window, or they may extend to the floor. When they are full-length, they are usually pulled to the side and held with tiebacks. They may be pulled back in a relatively straight, tailored way or into a gently curved swag, depending upon the effect wanted. Tiebacks should never be placed at the center of the window height, but preferably above or below center, roughly a third of the distance from the top or bottom. Tiebacks are often the same material as the drapery, that is, sewn in a belt-like fashion and lined with buckram or other stiffening material to hold their shape. A ring is sewn to each end to be held by a hook. Tiebacks are also made of metal or wood in various ornamental shapes. Braided rope and tassel tiebacks are commonly used as well. The top of an overdrape may be hung in swags, drapes, or pleat patterns, creating an interesting and decorative effect. The lower edges often are treated with fringe, braid, or other trimming. Braided rope and tassels are also effective. Short side panels of overdrapes are sometimes shaped as jabots, pleated at the top and cut to hang in a diagonally overlapping manner.

Window curtain tracks should be heavy enough to perform well. In older periods, drapery rods and rings were used. They are commercially available and often have decorative end ornaments. The regular wooden rings on a 1¼″ wood round work satisfactorily. A spray of silicone will reduce friction to allow the rings to slide easily.

Valances are frequently flat plywood frames ornamented with a shaped lower edge and applied moldings or designs. Sometimes they are cloth covered in a rich and decorative fabric. If the valance is an extension of the architecture, it may be

FIGURE 14–15   Some window treatments.

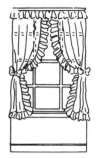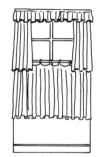

treated as a cornice, with a molding or band applied on the top edge.

Glass curtains should generally have at least 100 percent fullness. The top is **shirred**, that is, compressed with several rows of long gathering stitches. Rings may be sewn to the top edge, or a channel may be sewn at the top through which the rod may be inserted. Curtains and draperies must be hemmed top and bottom. Draperies should have a minimum of 75 percent fullness. The top hem of about 5″ can be stiffened with buckram or Pellon. French pleating or box pleating is then provided. The material should be gathered in small folds about every 6″ for French pleating and sewn together 4″ or 5″ from the top of the fabric. Bottom hems should have at least 2″ to be able to insert drapery chain or BB-shot weights.

FURNITURE

A basic understanding of the structure, function, and decoration of furniture is valuable in becoming more furniture minded. The first task in studying furniture is to develop a vocabulary that will aid recognition of forms, styles, and construction of furniture.

Furniture Woods and Finishes

From the beginning, wood was found to be the natural substance for furniture. It is an unusually strong organic material, relatively light in weight, easy to work, easy to join together in a variety of ways, and attractive in appearance. Woods are divided into *hardwoods* and *softwoods*, although this does

FIGURE 14–16 The importance of carefully selected furniture, especially with minimal scenery or in an arena theatre, is seen in this production of *Gigi*.

not provide a clear distinction regarding the comparative hardness. Softwoods derive from evergreen trees such as pine, fir, hemlock, and spruce. Hardwoods are maple, oak, walnut, and the broadleaf or leaf-shedding trees. Most furniture is constructed from the hardwood group, although some (such as basswood and poplar) are not as hard as some softwoods. Historically, the choice of woods has depended upon local availability or prevalent fashion. Maple, a distinctly native-American hardwood, played a major role in Early American furniture. In terms of style, the English Renaissance can be divided into specific ages: the Age of Oak (1500–1680), the Age of Walnut (1680–1710), the Age of Mahogany (1710–1770), and the Age of Satinwood (1770–1820).

Oak has been one of the most prominent woods for furniture. It is hard, durable, coarse grained, and blond in natural color. It is suitable for carving and one of the least expensive of hardwoods owing to widespread availability. It is the typical furniture wood of the Gothic and early Renaissance periods. **Walnut** has been widely used because of its great strength and workability. It ranges from light brown to dark brown. Fine grained and excellent for carving, walnut is one of the most beautiful woods and takes a high polish. Expensive because of limited supplies today, it is often used in veneers. **Mahogany** is a reddish-brown wood of medium hardness. It is imported from South America and Central America chiefly, and was first introduced in the 18th century. It is a beautiful wood for furniture and cabinetry and polishes with ease. **Lauan**, sometimes called Philippine mahogany, is not a true mahogany. Woods from various fruit trees, such as pear, apple, and cherry are known as **fruitwood**. They are usually hard and durable and are common in certain French periods and in provincial furniture. **Maple** is a fine-grained wood that is extremely hard and strong. It is difficult to carve but is frequently shaped and turned on a lathe for spindles. Its natural color is light tan or yellow brown, but it is often stained to a red brown shade. **Red gum** is an inexpensive hardwood that is sometimes used for low-cost furniture as a substitute for walnut and mahogany. **Pine, redwood**, and other softwoods are rarely used for quality furniture except for outdoor or recreation purposes. **Rosewood, teakwood, zebrawood**, and **tulipwood** are among a variety of imported woods to find a use in furniture. Some, like zebrawood, are used primarily for ornamental cabinetwork. Teakwood, on the other hand, is widely used in the Orient, and in recent years for Danish furniture.

Veneer has increasingly replaced solid wood in furniture over the years. Solid sheets of wood have a tendency to split and are costly because of the diminishing availability of some woods. Plywood veneer is amazingly strong and resists warping. The crosswise graining of alternate layers (three or five ply) is the secret of the strength of plywood. Laminated veneer was conceived and practiced hundreds of years ago. John Belter's superior furniture of the 19th century was almost exclusively laminated construction. But the 20th century developed the gluing materials and technology to make veneer a major product for furniture. Veneer furniture is made by careful selection and matching of veneer patterns. **Book matching** involves opening two adjacent sheets of veneer like a book and gluing them side by side, producing a symmetrical pattern. In **end matching**, adjacent sheets are joined end to end to create a continuous pattern. **Four-way matching** is produced by combining book and end matches. Also common are **repeated patterns**, adjacent sheets placed side by side in interesting combination forms such as checkerboard and herringbone.

Furniture receives a variety of finishes. Colonial furniture was often left natural with only an oil or wax as a protective surface, resulting in a soft mellow patina. Most furniture is stained to bring out features of the grain. This requires a clear varnish, lacquer, or shellac to give a protective gloss or semigloss finish. Varnish with stain in it is often used to darken the furniture beyond the color of the wood. French furniture (Louis XV and Louis XVI) was painted in high gloss oils or enamels in light pastel tints.

Furniture Decoration

Furniture is decorated with numerous ornaments and decorative motifs as discussed in the previous section. In general, it can be said that furniture woods are decorated in six distinct ways:

1. *Shaping.* An outline such as an urn-shaped splat in the back of a chair is cut out of wood with a saw.
2. *Carving.* Because carving is essentially a hand craft, carved furniture is expensive.
3. *Piercing.* Holes or patterns are cut out of the center of wood.
4. *Turning.* Wood is cut on a lathe.
5. *Applique.* A general term in this context for inlay, marquetry, intarsia, banding, added moldings, or other forms of imbedding or adding to the surface with wood, metal, ivory, tile, or shell.
6. *Bending.* Wood is soaked and steamed, then shaped in steelforms to be dried in a kiln. This results in bentwood furniture and molded plywood furniture.

Common Forms and Components of Furniture

Names have evolved to identify different types of period and modern furniture. Similarly, terms are given to the various parts of furniture. Many of these terms are derived from the method of construction (a turned and tapered leg); the appearance, shape, or form of furniture (a chaise longue equals a long chair); a decorative motif (an urn-shaped splat); the way furniture is used or operates (a tilt-top table); or the individual,

place, or circumstance of furniture origination (the Windsor chair). The following common forms and components of furniture will help the technician start acquiring the vocabulary and knowledge of furniture construction, styles, and decoration.

Seating Units. Figure 14-17 illustrates some of the common components of a chair. A central vertical feature on the back of a chair is called a **splat**; all horizontal members are **rails**. The top rail is often ornamented and may be known as a crest rail. A chair with several rails is a ladder-back chair. Vertical turnings, as seen in a Windsor chair, form a spindle back. Shields, hearts, lyres, and ribbands are motifs used for splat-back chairs. Chair seats may be flat, shaped, or scooped out; molded, upholstered, or carved. Arms sometimes stop at the arm stumps, or they may extend beyond and terminate in a scroll or other ornamental form. Chairs vary considerably in proportion and ornamentation throughout the centuries. They range from the armless side chair to the upholstered wing chair and the ornate and stately throne. Multiple seating units include settles, settees, sofas, and bornes.

Tables. The rail beneath the front side of a table top (similar to the front seat-rail of a chair) is called an **apron**. Aprons frequently receive special ornamental treatment. Tables are designed to serve a specific need. A trestle table is a knock-down table, and a console table has an unfinished side because it is placed against a wall. The butterfly, gate leg, and Pembroke tables are types of **drop-leaf** tables. These and some occasional tables are shown in the accompanying illustration (Figure 14-18).

Case Furniture. A piece of furniture containing items is known as *receptacle* or *case furniture.* This includes hutches, buffets, bookcases, secretaries, desks, cabinets, chests, and similar furniture (Figure 14-19). Because many forms of case furniture are intended to be placed against a wall, the back

FIGURE 14–17 Seating units.

panel is often left unfinished. Breakfronts, sideboards, and secretaries are sometimes quite tall.

Furniture Legs, Feet, and Stretchers. Furniture legs may be carved, turned, or shaped. They are often identified by this treatment or by the decorative motif created. As with a human or animal leg, we refer to the parts of a leg on furniture as the knee, the ankle, and the foot. As a terminating feature, the foot is given emphasis. In period furniture, certain ornamentation is common at the knee. Although some styles of furniture omit them, stretchers are a common means of providing support to furniture legs. Some examples of legs, feet, and stretchers are illustrated in Figure 14-20.

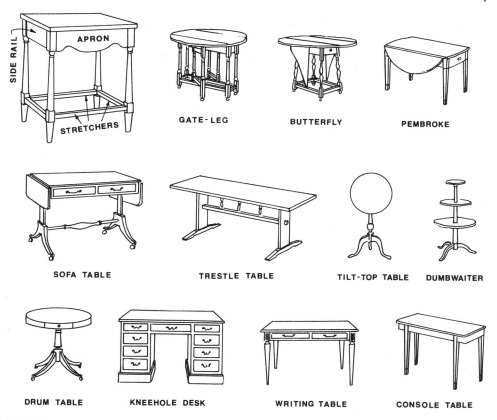

FIGURE 14–18 Some types of tables.

Furniture Accessories

Equipping a setting with furniture is seldom complete until all accessories are provided. An accessory is an item that belongs with furniture to complete the atmosphere of the locale. Sofas and large chairs frequently require pillows, slip covers, quilts, or antimacassars. Antimacassars are doilies or lace-like cloth strips placed over the back and arms of furniture to protect them from soiling. Since tables serve particular purposes, we expect normal objects on them, such as lamps, table cloths, books, sewing baskets, bowls of fruit, and flowers. Desks and writing tables are identified by suitable accessories placed upon them. Case furniture must be appropriately filled with the items for which they were designed. Fireplace mantels should have a selection of objects, such as vases, clock, and photographs. Beds, pianos, hearths, and liquor cabinets are other items that need accessory treatment.

Period Furniture Styles

The study of furniture deals with historic or cultural *periods* (when furniture and the decorative arts were shaped by public taste) and with *style* (referring to the work of particular designers or schools of design).

FIGURE 14–19 Examples of case furniture.

FIGURE 14–20 Examples of furniture legs, stretchers, and feet. Legs: (A) straight, (B) tapered, (C) bell, (D) trumpet, (E) spiral, (F) cup and cover, (G) cabriole. Stretchers: (A) H-shaped, (B) serpentine, (C) X-shaped, (D) box-shaped. Feet: (A) bun, (B) block, (C) claw and ball, (D) spade, (E) turnip, (F) ball, (G) Spanish or tassel, (H) pear, (I) cloven, (J) scroll, (K) bracket.

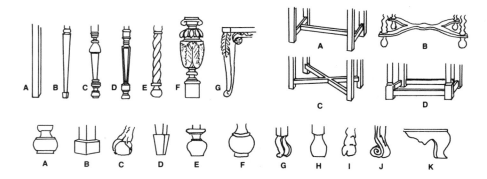

FIGURE 14–21 A chronology of periods and styles.

Antiquity		Middle Ages	
Egyptian	4500 B.C.–332 B.C.	Early Christian	A.D. 300–A.D. 800
Greek	2000 B.C.–30 B.C.	Byzantine	A.D. 476–A.D. 1200
Roman	300 B.C.–476 A.D.	Romanesque	A.D. 500–A.D. 1100
		Gothic	A.D. 1100–A.D. 1500

England	France	America	Other Countries
16th Century			
Tudor (1500–1558) Elizabethan (1558–1603)	Early Renaissance (1484–1547) Middle Renaissance (1547–1589)		Early Renaissance (1500–1600) in Italy, Spain, Holland, Germany.
17th Century			
Jacobean (1603–1649) Cromwellian (1649–1660) Restoration (1660–1689) William & Mary (1689–1702)	Late Renaissance (1589–1643) Baroque (1643–1700) Early French Provincial (1650–1700)	Early American (1608–1720)	Late Renaissance (1600–1700) in Italy, Spain, Holland, Germany. Flemish influence is strong.
18th Century			

Queen Anne (1702–1714)
 Early Georgian (1714–1750)
 Middle Georgian (1750–1770)
 Late Georgian (1770–1810)
   Chippendale (1740–1779)
   Hepplewhite (1770–1789)
   Sheraton (1780–1806)
   Adams Brothers (1760–1792)
	French Regency (1700–1730)
	 Rococo (1730–1760)
	 Neo-classical (1760–1789)
	 Directoire (1789–1804)
	 Middle French Provincial (1700–1800)
		Georgian (1720–1790) copies of English, Dutch, and French styles.	Furniture greatly influenced by French, Dutch, and English styles.

19th Century			
English Regency (1810–1837) Victorian (1830–1890) Eastlake (1879–1895)	French Empire (1804–1820) Restoration (1830–1870) Late French Provincial (1800–1900)	Federal (1785–1820) Duncan Phyfe (1790–1830) American Empire (1800–1830) Greek Revival (1820–1860) Victorian (1840–1880) Eastlake (1879–1895)	Biedermeier (1800–1850) in Germany and Austria.
20th Century			
Arts and Crafts (1900–1920) Modernistic (1925–1940)	Art Nouveau (1890–1905) Art Deco (1925–1940) Modernistic (1925–1940)	Mission (1895–1910) Modernistic (1925–1940) International Modern (1925–)	International Modern (1925–) Germany and Austria. Scandinavian Modern (1930–) Sweden, Denmark, Finland and Norway.

Knowledge of periods and styles is vastly important to be able to provide exciting and meaningful properties for a production. A production is considerably enhanced by the appearance, character, and functioning of its furniture. While historical accuracy is important, it is secondary to capturing the quality and the unique mode and manner of a period that will be most useful to the style of the production. To help the property technician develop proficiency in identifying period furniture, a chronology of periods and styles is provided (Figure 14-21). Furniture, like the other human artifacts, is continually evolving. Dates of styles are often arbitrary, and trends pass into periods of transition before new styles emerge. Acquire a knowledge of furniture styles and build a library and file of useful sources.

MAINTENANCE OF PROPERTIES

Properties require care and maintenance to ensure proper condition while serving the needs of production. This includes the time they are in use as well as when they are in storage waiting for some future service.

During the Production

Proper security for properties between rehearsals and performances cannot be overemphasized. Prop cabinets and shipping boxes should provide appropriate and well-marked space to store items securely. Some objects may require special types of containers for proper protection. Refrigeration is necessary to preserve perishables. Furniture, pianos, and other large props usually need to be covered. Rules should be established for the company to discourage people from the temptation of handling or "trying out" properties offstage. After every performance, each prop should be examined to check the need to repair or replace the item. This will require the availability of the necessary tools and materials to maintain properties used in the production. It is also important to have a backup or an extra supply of items that may be broken or destroyed accidentally.

While in Property Storage

It is all too common, unfortunately, for prop storage facilities to look like the aftermath of a siege by Attila the Hun. Lack of space, lack of time, and inadequate storage facilities for properties contribute to this. However, proper storage and organization of items is the first requirement for the protection of props. A system of storing items should be clearly established to maintain the safe condition of props. Furniture should not be stacked in a way that is likely to cause damage. Shelving, racks, and wall hangers are desirable for small furniture and properties. If possible, furniture should be repaired while in storage. If not, then broken arms or legs should be preserved for repair when the item is pulled out of storage for use. The room should be kept clean and free of dust; some items may require special covers or protective storage containers. Whenever possible, attempt to prevent extreme temperature changes, excessive humidity or dryness, and water damage. To maintain a really useful property collection, a degree of control of items must exist. Active collections may require a checkout system for borrowers and a requirement of proper maintenance of items borrowed.

SELECTED READINGS

Aronson, Joseph, *The Encyclopedia of Furniture.* New York: Crown, 1965.

Dryden, Deborah M., *Fabric Painting and Dyeing for the Theatre.* New York: Drama Book Specialists, 1981.

Dubois, M. J., *Curtains and Draperies, A Survey of Classic Periods.* New York: Viking, 1967.

FEIRER, JOHN L., and GILBERT R. HUTCHINGS, *Advanced Woodwork and Furniture Making* (4th ed.). Peoria, Ill.: Chas. A. Bennett Co., 1972.

GOVIER, JACQUIE, *Create Your Own Stage Props*. Englewood Cliffs, N.J.: Prentice Hall, 1984.

GROTZ, GEORGE, *The Furniture Doctor* (rev. ed.). Garden City, N.Y.: Doubleday, 1983.

JAMES, THURSTON, *The Theatre Props Handbook*. White Hall, Va.: Betterway, 1987.

JAMES, THURSTON, *The Prop Builder's Molding and Casting Handbook*. White Hall, Va.: Betterway, 1989.

KENTON, WARREN, *Stage Properties and How to Make Them*. New York: Drama Book Specialists, 1974.

MOTLEY, *Theatre Props*. London: Studio Vista, 1975.

PRAZ, MARIO, *An Illustrated History of Furnishings*. New York: Braziller, 1964.

SPELTZ, ALEXANDER, *The Styles of Ornament*. New York: Dover, 1959.

WHITON, SHERRILL, *Interior Design and Decoration* (4th ed.). New York: Lippincott, 1974.

15

Special Effects

The term *special effects* generally brings to mind images of magical illusions and secret devices that amaze audiences, but they are more often routine practices and tediously rigged apparatuses that produce unheralded responses. While closely related to scenery, properties, and lights, special effects are unique because of some requirement that commands special attention. Although sometimes exciting spectacle-for-the-sake-of-spectacle is demanded, special effects usually enhance the performance by being believable, advancing the story, and being instantly understood. The special-effects field is probably most closely associated with television and film production, in which sizable departments are required specifically for such work. The eye of the camera permits a wide range of effect techniques such as optical tricks, electronic devices, special graphics, and miniature scene re-creations.

Although effects allowed by the camera are often not possible in live theatre production, it is beneficial to become acquainted with the practices in other media and to keep abreast of developments in science and technology. Imaginative solutions to effects problems sometimes derive from new techniques, new materials, and experimentation. Above all, the best effects are usually those that are simple and easily achieved, reliably repeatable, and safe. Whenever possible, avoid special-effects solutions that are complicated, untested, or hazardous.

BREAKAWAY AND MECHANICAL-ACTION EFFECTS

Things that must break, collapse, or fall are standard effects for furniture, railings, walls, doors, and other objects. Usually, it is best to precut these items or to construct them in separate, "broken" units. The components can be held together temporarily with (1) easy-to-break toothpicks or wooden match sticks, (2) pins that are pulled just prior to the action, or (3) magnets such as used for cabinet door catches. The sections of a breakaway chair can be held together with match-stick dowels or pegs and the smallest amount of glue. The location and angle of the precut sections must be chosen correctly for the chair to collapse under weight or pressure applied. A few hinge joints are valuable because they allow components to fold apart during the collapse. Be sure to camouflage saw cuts with a little paint so the coming action is not anticipated.

In film production, structural breakaways and action objects are sometimes activated by air valves or by small explosive or electric-solenoid devices. However, there are many simple ways to trigger separations and movements. Note the following examples of the use of gravity, lever control, compressed air, spring activation, and pendulum action. (See Figures 15-1 to 15-3.)

Effect	*Solution*
A vase falls from a fireplace mantel.	***Lever action.*** A lever operated from behind the scenery pokes a peg up through a hole in the mantel causing the vase to tip and fall.
A ghost, a breeze, or a mysterious force causes an object to move off a table.	***Pendulum action.*** A trick line (black nylon fish-line) is connected to the object. The line rises above the stage diagonally, passes through a pulley overhead and down to the operator. A tug on the line raises the object and it will "fly" in pendulum action until it hits the floor.

FIGURES 15–1 to 15–3 Some mechanical-action devices.

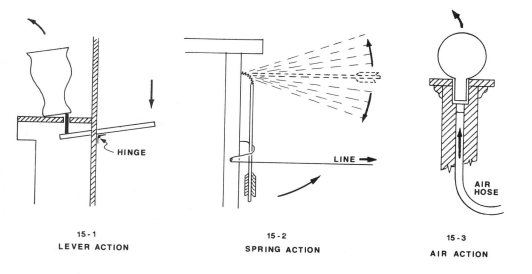

15-1
LEVER ACTION

15-2
SPRING ACTION

15-3
AIR ACTION

An arrow is shot at a wall or object in the scene.	*Spring action.* The point of the arrow is connected to the object with a spring. The arrow is held flat and concealed against the object with a trick line. The line is released, the arrow pops up and quivers as if striking the object.
A picture falls from the wall or swings to an oblique angle.	*Gravity action.* A pin that supports the picture on the wall is pulled out by a stagehand.
The finial or knob of a stairway newel post falls to the floor.	*Compressed air.* Concealed in the newel post is an air hose leading to a tank of compressed air. Opening the air valve blows the knob off the post.

Additional techniques for the falling and flying of objects with invisible line are in Chapter 13. Trick line is a valuable means of triggering physical actions. A jerk on a line wrapped around a set of books on a shelf will cause them to fall to the floor (commonly used in *Blithe Spirit*). A table can be rigged to collapse if a set of legs hinged at the top is pulled out at the bottom by an invisible line. Do not overlook a device as simple as a spring mouse trap as a trigger device. Precautions must be taken to prevent falling and collapsing objects from being dangerous to the performers.

When an actor must be struck with an object, extreme care is necessary to prevent injury. Lightweight materials are best. Balsa wood furniture, as used in movie westerns for fight scenes, is safe but expensive. Ure-thane and polystyrene foam are ideal materials for objects that must break in a fight. Many objects might be appropriately made of flexible foam. A bull whip made of soft woven yarn is an appropriate substitute for the real item.

Sometimes small prop items, such as pottery bowls and small statuary, must be broken or smashed in performance. They may need to be purchased in quantity for this purpose. If the cost is too high, objects can be made of unfired pottery or plaster of paris. Real glass should never be broken on-stage. The risk to the performers of damage from flying fragments is much too great. Precut plastic objects can substitute for glass in many instances. Breakaway bottles and drinking glasses are available from theatrical suppliers (Figure 15-4). They shatter realistically and will not harm the actors, but the cost is relatively high and they are rather fragile.

Simulated glass items can also be cast. One of the oldest methods is a candy mixture similar to rock candy and taffy. Candy glass can be made with 3 cups of sugar, a cup of white Karo syrup, 2 cups of water, and ¼ teaspoon of cream of tartar. Once well

FIGURE 15-4 Breakaway bottle that shatters safely on impact. (Photo courtesy of Rosco Laboratories, Inc.)

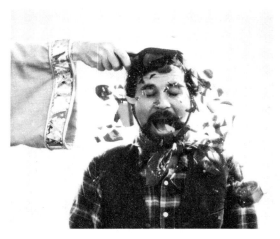

mixed, it is heated to about 300°F (use a candy thermometer). It must be poured into a well-greased mold slightly chilled. A cookie sheet serves for glass panes. A bottle mold or a bowl will require swilling the hot mixture to coat all sides evenly. The crystalline object must be kept cool until used because it becomes sticky to the touch. When broken, there is no danger. Stepping on fragments merely grinds the material into finer particles of sugar.

Bottles, vases, and glass bowls that must break can also be made of hot paraffin wax swilled in a plaster mold (a two-piece mold is usually needed). The mold is soaked in cold water before casting. After each of several swillings, the mold must be inverted to allow the excess wax to drain out. This prevents a buildup of wax at the bottom of the object, which would be dangerous if the object is used in a fight. The final object can be varnished for added realism. In television and film, special mixtures of plastic resins are used for breakable window glass. The material is heated and poured over a smooth flat surface. Certain hydrocarbon thermoplastic resins heated and poured into a flexible mold have been used in smaller shops to create breakaway panes of glass. With the proper mixture of resins, the final material is fragile but is not harmful when broken by hand.

On occasion, items with mechanical animation are needed. The 19th-century theatre utilized such devices to enhance reality. A waterfall might be a muslin loop painted with white-crested falling water. The cloth is held taut by two rollers and driven by a hand crank or a motor. Such an effect would not be inappropriate for the musical *Little Mary Sunshine*. A scene containing working machinery may require moving gears, cranks, and other components. Units that must vibrate or rock can be mounted on springs or rockers. Camp fires and logs blazing in a fireplace are sometimes animated. For a minimum effect, gaps between simulated logs are filled with color media which con-

FIGURE 15–5 Chiffon "flames" that flicker by the air of a fan.

ceal flickering lights below. Further fire action can be provided by adding slender blades of flames made of colored silk chiffon that will wave above the logs by the air of a small fan below (Figure 15-5).

ATMOSPHERIC AND ENVIRONMENTAL EFFECTS

A number of practices in the several media aid in simulating the atmosphere or environment of a scene. Film and television also have filters and other camera devices that satisfy many circumstances. Complicated effects may require creating the atmospheric display in a miniature set, a technique that can be employed for a film scene, or with special lighting and scenic projections.

Smoke and Fog

Several ways exist to create smoke and fog. One of these is **dry-ice fog**, which produces a white vapor of carbon dioxide (CO_2). Being heavier than air, it is a low-hanging ground fog. It is completely nontoxic, odorless, and harmless and also believable in appearance. The vapor can be produced by lowering a wire-mesh basket of crushed dry ice into water that is heated near or at the boiling point. Dry-ice smoke machines are commercially available, although it is not dif-

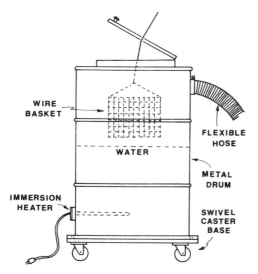

WIRE
BASKET

FLEXIBLE
HOSE

WATER

METAL
DRUM

IMMERSION
HEATER

SWIVEL
CASTER
BASE

FIGURE 15–6 Dry-ice fog machine.

ficult to build them (Figure 15-6). A garbage can or steel oil drum can be used for the water chamber. The water can be preheated or an electric immersion heater can be installed in the chamber. The dry-ice basket can be fabricated of hardware cloth or perforated metal. The basket can be secured to

a rod or cable, which passes through the lid of the water chamber. Lowering the rod will plunge the basket of dry ice into the heated water. A hole and fitting in the water chamber can accommodate piping and/or hoses (3″ or larger is desirable) to direct the smoke to the appropriate location in the scene. The smoke is not unlimited: the dry ice and heated water must be replenished. If the fog must be sustained for some period of time another fog unit may be necessary. The loud bubbling noise of this system, sometimes called a rumble pot, may be distracting to the performance. Another method of producing CO_2 fog is spraying hot water or live steam directly into a basket of dry ice.

Probably the most commonly used theatrical fogs are **chemical fogs**. Special fog machines are designed to mist water-glycol fluid mixtures, which are capable of simulating many different types of haze, fog, and smoke. Several machines are on the market and may be purchased or rented from theatre suppliers (Figure 15-7). The fog liquid is placed in the machine, and, after a short heating period, a large puff of smoke can be generated. Manual and remote control systems are available. High-volume machines are the most costly. Noise is generally

FIGURE 15–7 Fog/smoke machine featuring internal pump, external fog juice tank, and modular electronic controls. (Photo courtesy of Rosco Laboratories, Inc.)

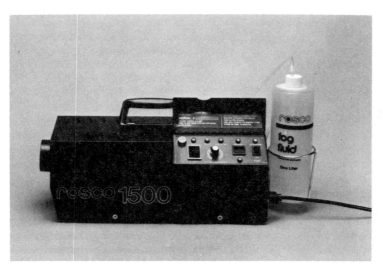

limited to the whoosh of the escaping vapor. Some machines provide a basket accessory in front of the nozzle for dry ice, which converts the vapor into a low-hanging fog. Early formulas were petroleum-based compounds, which were irritating to the eyes and may have had acute toxic effects. Improved water-based mixtures of glycols are safe if ingested and safe during short lengths of time when used normally in a setting. However, fog vapors may be irritating to people with asthma or respiratory ailments. Be sure to use fog or smoke compounds in safe concentrations, for only short periods of time, and in well-ventilated areas.

Another white smoke can be produced with **sal ammoniac** (ammonium chloride) in a porcelain heater cone or in an aluminum pan on a hot plate. The smoke rises slowly and can last for up to 10 minutes, depending on ventilation. Adding a little cinnamon can eliminate the chemical odor. Only small quantities of the powder should be used indoors unless the area is well ventilated because chloride-containing smokes can be irritating to the lungs. Sal ammoniac is the least irritating of chloride smokes; other chloride forms should be avoided altogether.

Smoke and fog techniques must be tested in the setting to determine the appearance and duration of the effect. Drafts, breezes, or air from the building fans or ventilators may affect the life and dispersal of the vapor. Solutions may be necessary to correct any adverse control of the fog.

Rain and Water Effects

There are times when scene projections of rain and other simulations of water are insufficient. The real thing is needed. On exterior locations in film work, rain can be achieved by an overhead perforated water pipe or the spray from a hose held in the air. Indoors, in the studio or on the stage, this presents a problem. The flood of rain

on the floor must be collected and directed to a drain. Heavy plastic sheeting can accomplish this, but extreme care must be taken to prevent damage to the floor and, more important, to avoid contact with the electrical wiring. For this reason, the best solution on stage is a catch pan directly beneath the perforated pipe or hose to collect the water. It is also advisable to confine the rain outside a window or other opening of the setting. A hose should lead from the pan to a drain, or a pump can be used to recycle the water to the hose above. Waterproof paint may be necessary on adjacent scenery to prevent damage by water. The collecting pan can be lined with appropriate padding to produce the kind of rain sound desired.

Running water is often a necessity for faucets, pumps, and fountains. The faucet of a sink or wash basin can be attached by hose to a bucket or plastic bag placed high behind the scenery so that it is gravity fed. It will be necessary to have a bucket to catch the water from the sink drain. Old-fashioned hand pumps, such as needed in *The Miracle Worker*, can also be functional (Figure 15-8). They must be placed on a small platform to conceal a bucket of water. The pump pipe extends down into the bucket. A valve in the pipe permits the water to rise in the pipe and out the spout with each pumping action. Fountains with running water may enrich a scene. Units with circulating pumps can usually be found or constructed.

Snow, Ice, and Frost

The material for falling snow must be light in weight and capable of catching the light while falling. Two materials fit this criteria particularly well. One is paper confetti (tiny disks of paper). The other is made from polyethylene sheet. Transparent and similar to the polyethylene bags used by dry cleaners, this sheet material is shredded and processed through a hammer mill. The milling gives it a white color. Both types of snow

FIGURE 15–8   A functional water pump in *The Miracle Worker*, a production of California State University–Fresno. Setting by Richard L. Arnold.

are lightweight, thus they fall slowly, twisting and turning to reflect the light. Snow machines at film production centers are large hopper devices with slots in the bottom through which the snow material passes when an electric motor rotates a long rod. The **snow cradle** is a simpler version of this device. This can be a long narrow fold of muslin with slots cut along the bottom fold (Figure 15-9). It is hung from two battens. When the cradle is rocked gently, snow sifts through the holes and falls to the floor. ("Rose petals" of chopped crepe paper can also be used in the cradle.) Another snow device is a cylinder of ½" mesh hardware cloth mounted on one batten and rocked with rope lines. Electric fans may be employed to blow snow in a realistic manner.

A snow scene may also require a white floor cloth. Piles of snow and snow banks may be necessary. While some of this can be realized as a painted effect, substitutions may be necessary. Ground polystyrene foam can be purchased in the appropriate size for snow-covered objects (do not use Styrofoam dust, which is hazardous if inhaled). Another kind of clinging snow is the flocking used as artificial snow on Christmas trees. Commercial flockers can perform the work, or flocking equipment can be rented. Pres-

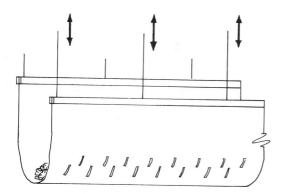

FIGURE 15–9 A snow cradle. Raising and lowering one side of the cradle will provide a steady fall of "snow."

surized spray cans of artificial snow and frost material are also available to apply to objects as snow or as window frost. Icicles (and ice cubes) can be cast in acrylic or can be made by dipping cellophane strips into hot paraffin.

Other Environmental Effects

In film production, breezes are achieved by quiet wind machines. These are large fans used to blow costumes and other materials in the scene. Both direction and speed control are provided. They are also used to blow snowflakes or to simulate a dust storm. Bubble machines can fill the air with a continuous stream of moving bubbles in such scenes as the mermaid's lagoon in *Peter Pan*. Cobweb machines are available to spin out cobwebs for an unkempt or abandoned environment. Fuller's earth or talc can be used for the dusty old book. Attention to these details will usually enrich the total scene.

SOUND EFFECTS

Sound first became recognized as a technical art in the fields of radio, television, and film. Audio engineers developed public appreciation of good sound and sound reproduction through constantly improving techniques and equipment in the controlled environment of sound and recording studios. Only in recent years has the demand for quality sound forced live theatre to recognize sound as a separate and necessary production field. Sound technology includes the techniques of sound reinforcement, the selection and use of microphones, the design and placement of equipment for the acoustics of a specific facility, effective control through sophisticated mixers and operating equipment, introductory and bridge music for the dramatic scenes, and the creation of specific effects in the dramatic action.

Our concern in the context of this text relates primarily to sound effects. Sound plays as vital a role in creating a setting as do its visual cousins, scenery and properties. During the golden age of radio drama, we learned how sound alone could establish environment through background effects, or dramatically heighten tension by a stab of music. It is becoming increasingly common that a sound designer plans the total effects for a production to meet the needs of the script and the director's interpretation. Duties include specifying the material to be used, supervising the recording sessions, determining equipment, and directing sound in rehearsal when it is coordinated with the other elements of production. The sound technician carries out the designer's plan in preparation and in production.

Sound Equipment

To provide effective sound effects, especially in the expansive space of an auditorium, a first-rate sound system is a necessity. A good system requires high-fidelity equipment that is easy to operate, rugged, and reliable. It must be specified by sound experts and satisfy the acoustical requirements of the auditorium. Quality equipment is costly but will provide superior service when handled and maintained properly.

The tape recorder is the center of a theatre sound system, since sound effects are generally played on tape in contemporary practice. This is preferable to the old practice of using records that can be scratched and are difficult to cue. Tapes on reel-to-reel recorders are durable, each sound can be recorded for the proper duration, and sound effects can be recorded in sequence for the production. Theatre tape recorders must be top quality, quiet in operation, and maintain cueing accuracy. A second tape recorder is useful when there is a rapid succession of sound effects or when sounds must be reproduced simultaneously from different speakers on stage.

Power amplifiers are the most costly elements of the sound system. An amplifier magnifies the electrical signals from the tape recorder (or microphone) to provide the power needed by the loudspeakers. A sound system usually contains several amplifiers and pre-amplifiers. Loudspeakers finally convert the electrical impulses into audible sound for transmission to the audience. Auditorium loudspeaker systems are usually placed in a central cluster near the front of the room or in a distributive system of speakers throughout the house with appropriate delay devices and are frequently used for music between acts. However, most production sound effects are broadcast from speakers placed behind the stage set on stage. This requires a variety of speaker outlets backstage so that speakers can be located to provide a directional sense for the sound. Essentially, requirements for producing sound effects in a production only necessitates a system with playback function. Thus, when other equipment is provided, it generally serves other functions. Microphones, for instance, will have some use for sound effects but serve primarily for sound reinforcement. Other pieces of equipment, such as record players and reverberation devices, are useful for recording sound effects. Not all sound equipment is compatible; equipment must be selected to function together in a given system with matched impedance and proper wattage.

Technology is rapidly changing sound design and production. One of the first steps was the development of digital recording where sound is converted into a binary number system for storage on tape or disc then changed back to its analog form for playback. Synthesizers, samplers, and other digital equipment can be synchronized with MIDI (music instrument digital interface), making communication possible between all equipment. This has increased the opportunities for creating new sounds and music, editing, altering sounds, blending sounds, creating and storing loops, and almost instantaneous playback cueing. In the near future, computer technology is expected to further advance the field, increasing the options of creativity and control for sound designers and technicians.

Frequently, a sound control booth is located at the rear of the auditorium for the sound operator. A window in the booth that can be opened is often desirable so the operator can listen to sound levels directly in the auditorium.

Function of Sound Effects

In general, sound effects aid the production in three ways:

1. *Documenting time, place, and action.* This includes the city, country, and location of the scene; the specific climate conditions; the time of year and day; the specific events in the dramatic action.

2. *Providing specific atmosphere.* This enhances the believability of the environment. Street sounds, fog horns, bird sounds, and similar effects are often used for this purpose.

3. *Giving emotional reinforcement.* This includes music or other sound beneath dialog or sounds of short duration used to punctuate the pauses of dramatic speeches.

Short-duration effects, such as door bells, telephone rings, and car horns, are common in drama. They generally are required by the action and therefore command audience attention. Sometimes they serve to enhance dialog and intensify the mood (as would a clap of thunder after King Lear's "Blow, winds, and crack your cheeks"). All such effects must have a function in the action and they require precise cueing to be effective.

Long-duration sounds used for atmosphere include rainfall, noisy traffic in the street, a loud party in the next room, or outdoor sounds in an exterior scene. Playing these sounds at a steady volume nonstop through the scene is rarely effective. The sound competes with the actors' dialog and generally distracts from the action. The best plan is to establish the environment at the beginning of the scene, then either fade the sound out entirely when the actors begin, or lower the sound under the dialog where as background it will be reduced to a subliminal level of our consciousness. The effects may be reintroduced from time to time when reference is made to the environment or when the sound may effectively reinforce the action. A character pausing reflectively to look out the window might provide the opportunity to reintroduce the sound of rain. The din of the party in the next room would fade up and out with the opening and closing of the adjoining door when characters enter and exit. Remember, silence may be as effective as sound.

Acquiring Sound Effects

Once the desired sounds have been determined and planned in detail, they must be acquired or created. There are several ways to obtain appropriate effects.

Available Recorded Effects. Commercial recordings are available for a host of everyday sounds. These recordings are described in catalogs and may be purchased on records, tapes, or discs. They include sounds of automobiles, animals, firearms and explosives, weather, human and industrial sounds, as well as standard fanfares and short music selections. The nonmusical sounds are, for the most part, highly realistic.

Live Effects. Mechanically created sound effects may be the preferred choice for certain sounds before a live audience. The acoustical quality of the room often makes some manually produced effects more convincing than can be achieved by recorded sound. This may be due to the recording and playback limitations of sound equipment or to the distribution of sound from the loudspeakers in the auditorium. In addition, it may be wise to create an effect manually if it is more convenient to cue. For instance, the sound of a telephone or door bell can be cued more easily and more consistently by using a real bell and push button. Sometimes even long-duration effects such as thunder and wind can be better coordinated to the scene by manual control because of the changes in timing of live dialog in repeated performances. Live sounds often accompany some special effects and cannot be surpassed. This would be true in the firing of blank cartridges in firearms and explosions in flash boxes. Throughout the history of theatre and in early radio and television, many mechanical sound effects were perfected that, if used properly, are highly effective. A partial list of these can be found in Figure 15-10.

Special Recorded Effects. Special music written for a show should be recorded with high-quality equipment, whenever possible in a recording studio. For other sounds, the sound technician may find it desirable to record sounds on location to capture an appropriate real-life sound. This is not as easy as it seems because of the difficulty of isolating the sound from other background noises. It may be more appropriate to create simulated effects before the microphone. Books on sound list many successful illusions that can be developed with little difficulty. The crumpling of cellophane for fire and breathing into the microphone to create thunder

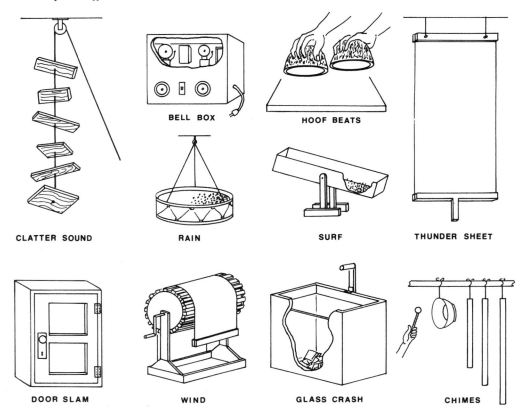

CLATTER SOUND BELL BOX HOOF BEATS

RAIN SURF THUNDER SHEET

DOOR SLAM WIND GLASS CRASH CHIMES

FIGURE 15–10 Some mechanical/live sound effects. Rope attached to pieces of wood is released to produce a clatter sound; a bell box with a transformer provides a variety of door and telephone rings; coconut halves and appropriate surface produce hoof beats; thunder is simulated by shaking a sheet of galvanized metal; rice rolled on a drum head or shallow pan suggests rain; a long narrow box filled with rice is tipped for the sound of the surf; a door in a frame or box will create effective door slams; canvas is stretched over a wooden drum that, when turned by a crank, simulates the sound of wind; a sheet of glass placed in the safety of a box is struck by a hammer device for an authentic glass crash; chimes and other objects produce chime sounds when hit with a drum stick.

are examples of such simulations. It is unfortunate that we rely too often on realistic sound effects instead of recognizing the unique style and mood of each drama. How can we justify the same realistic door slam for two dissimilar plays? Equipment available today permits us to create unique sounds. Equalizers, filters, synthesizers, echo and reverberation devices, and other special electronic processing allow us to create new sounds or to alter original sound quality. A little experimentation, even playing sounds at different speeds, is worth the time and effort in developing good sound effects.

PYROTECHNIC AND EXPLOSION EFFECTS

Pyrotechnic devices are materials for producing fire, flashes, smoke, and explosions. Because the dangers of fire and fireworks are considerable, all other solutions should be explored before pyrotechnics are employed. Even the mildest explosive ingredient requires the utmost care.

Federal laws administered by the Bureau of Alcohol, Tobacco and Firearms and the Department of Transportation classify and govern the manufacture, use, transportation, and shipping of explosive and fireworks ingredients. Further, the use of these materials is also governed by state and municipal regulations. While special effects pyrotechnics may not be classified technically as explosives, since most are primarily intended to create flash, loud bursts, smoke, or sparkle effects, they are listed as flammable solids, hazardous materials, or dangerous fireworks. Many states and cities require special licenses for pyrotechnicians, certifications, or permits to use firework substances. The State of California has extensive fireworks regulations and rigid requirements to obtain a license in its several pyrotechnic operator classifications. Unauthorized persons are prohibited from handling pyrotechnic materials. Even the use of blank cartridges by an actor in a production requires a local or state permit. Shipping and transporting these substances are subject both to federal and state laws. Know all laws governing pyrotechnic displays before contemplating their use in production.

The formulas for pyrotechnic effects contain substances that are extremely hazardous. They consist of several chemicals combined together to be ignited by a flame or an electric spark. Many safeguards and techniques must be followed to mix these compounds safely. This includes how they are mixed, the accuracy by which they are measured, the purity of the substances, how they have been stored, and the temperature and humidity of the atmosphere. No inexperienced, unlicensed person should prepare these dangerous mixtures. Experienced pyrotechnicians wear proper clothing, conductive-soled shoes, personal safety gear, and exercise extreme caution and precise procedures in the work. We are probably most familiar with pyrotechnic special effects in motion picture production. They are widely

used in this media especially under the relative safety of outdoor locations. Even under the most controlled condition of film making, government regulations lay out strict requirements and safeguards. The effects are produced by licensed pyrotechnic special-effect operators. Knowledge, care, and experience are needed to develop pyrotechnic effects, to mix the ingredients, and to supervise safety precautions.

Actual flame or fire may be required in a scene. Some types may be prohibited inside a studio or theatre. When fires are allowed, fire laws usually require specific precautionary measures. For fire safety alone, real fire in a setting should be considered only if satisfactory substitutes cannot be found. Then careful safety procedures should be exercised. When a candle flame or torch is used, for instance, movement and action must be well planned and rehearsed to prevent igniting costumes, scenery, or other materials. Fire extinguishers should be held ready for emergencies. Canned Sterno (jellied alcohol) and camp-stove propane fuel are relatively safe for torches and other flaming effects. In outdoor locations for a film, the illusion of a fire scene is planned with great attention to safety. Fire is confined in steel fire pans or in sheets of flames from jets strategically placed behind objects or piles of debris. Gas valves control the height of flames. Nearby objects that might be consumed by out-of-control flames are treated with fire-resistant paint or with flameproofing material.

Sometimes dramas call for colored fire. A red fire is required in the comedy *You Can't Take It With You*, and a blue fire is ignited in an ash tray in John van Druten's *Bell, Book and Candle*. Fires of this nature can be developed by a mixture of chemicals. It is best to obtain them premixed by a chemist or to acquire instruction for their use and preparation. Pyrotechnic fires are all hazardous, and ingredients should be treated as forms of gunpowder.

Some of the most common pyrotechnics effects are flashes of light. They are created by **flash powder**, a mixture of magnesium and an oxidizing agent that produces a brief bright light when ignited. Explosions, bombings, and electrical sparks or short circuiting may be simulated, and magical appearances and disappearances may be aided, by flash powder. Smoke and an explosive noise accompany the intense flash of light. Flash powder is available through theatre supply companies. Besides a regular mixture, it may also be acquired in a formula that provides a brilliant flash and a little smoke or a great deal of smoke and very little flash. A **flash pot** is used to produce the effect (Figure 15-11). This is a strong metal box containing two electric terminals. Thin fuse wire is placed between the terminals and over the powder. An electric current is used to melt the wire, thus igniting the powder. Another simple flash material is magician's flash paper, fragile sheets that produce small instant flashes of light.

More spectacular pyrotechnic effects can create loud percussion sounds, columns of flames, or fountains of sparkles. Materials and devices for producing fireworks of this type should be provided by licensed pyrotechnicians. To create these effects, special powder formulas, well-designed stainless steel pots, and a remote-control firing unit are needed. Components for these effects are available from firms specializing in pyrotechnic displays. Always be sure instruction manuals and safety precautions are provided.

FIGURE 15–11 Flash pot.

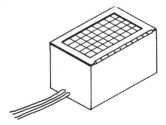

TRICK, LEGERDEMAIN, AND ILLUSORY DEVICES

Occasions arise when special items must be acquired or constructed for tricks and illusions. The simplest are gag, sleight of hand, and the magic devices available in stores specializing in novelty and trick merchandise. Mr. Applegate in *Damn Yankees* uses a magical appearance of a lighted cigarette. A shotgun that shoots out an open parasol is used in *Who's Afraid of Virginia Woolf*. More complicated illusions require sophisticated equipment and rigging. Among these are mysterious disappearances, levitations, escapes, and other tricks commonly performed by magicians. Of course, many illusions of this nature can be performed by standard scenic practice such as projections, lighting, transparencies, invisible-line rigging, disappearance traps, and flash pots. Seance scenes (as in Menotti's opera *The Medium*) are developed effectively with these devices. However, many magician's illusions require mysterious cabinets, boxes, chests, and other carefully constructed apparatus. It is true, these are often well-guarded secrets unavailable to lay people. Nevertheless, variations of many standard tricks and illusions that have application to theatre production can be found in books on magic, or obtained from dealers in the trade. Methods of building sword boxes, tables with false bottoms, disappearance chests, devices for levitation, and a host of less-spectacular tricks and illusions can be found (Figure 15-13). Many are optical effects that use mirrors to conceal items or to facilitate magical appearances of rabbits, scarfs, or people. The use of a mirror under a table or projecting ledge will serve for the "melting" of the Wicked Witch of the West in *The Wizard of Oz* (Figure 15-14). Properly constructed, these illusions can directly serve production needs. However, it often takes some imagination to apply the principles involved in an illusion to a specific production requirement.

FIGURE   15–12 A magician's sword box for the musical *Carnival*. Box designed and constructed by Kenneth Bunne. (Photo by George Tarbay)

SPECIAL LIGHTING EFFECTS

It would be difficult to overstate the importance of production lighting. Its invaluable function in giving the physical setting dramatic atmosphere as well as in creatively revealing the performer is very much a part of the visual scene. The study of lighting is extensive and is not included in the selected focus of this text. Nonetheless, it is necessary to acknowledge those lighting effects that serve special scenic functions.

Rear Illumination Effects

Some settings utilize rear illumination as a visual element. The simplest is the use of lighted signs, such as in the hotel sign in *Hot*

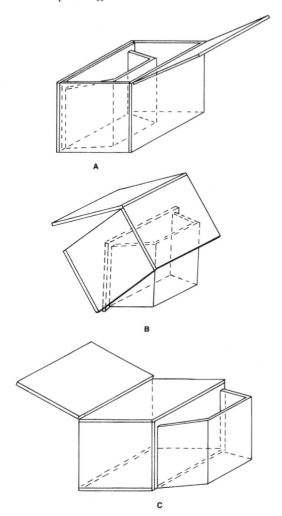

FIGURE 15–13 Disappearance box. (A) Opening the lid reveals a hidden chamber. (B) The box is tipped over for scrutiny of the audience. (C) The lid is opened to show the box is empty.

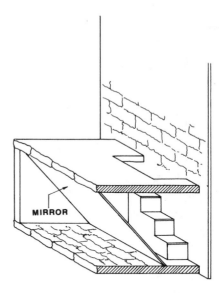

FIGURE 15–14 A mirror at 45° angle hides the "melting" of the witch. It reflects the floor painted to resemble the wall behind, creating the illusion of an open ledge.

L Baltimore. These may be constructed as an enclosed shadow box. The opaque material on the front is cut out to form letters or designs. A sheet of translucent plastic or cloth stretched across the opening is lighted by wired lamps inside the box. Translucent windows are common in interior settings when offstage light and shadow patterns are valuable to enhance a scene. A standard illusion for an elevator is a sliding door containing a rear-lighted translucent window. The elevator's movement is created by raising and lowering a roller shade behind the window, suggesting the raising and lowering of the elevator car to other floors when the door is closed. The variety of both translucent and transparent plastic—fiberglass, vinyl, acrylic, polyethylene—creates many possibilities for rear-illuminated scenery. For instance, colorful, see-through trees can give the appropriate lightness and dream-like fantasy for *A Midsummer Night's Dream.*

Rear illumination effects have long been used on drops and ground rows. Muslin is perhaps the most common translucent scenic fabric. Portions of a painted drop can be made opaque by a heavy base coat and back painting, while other portions can retain translucency by thin coats of paint or dye. In an exterior scene, this permits a spotlight to backlight the sky areas between opaque buildings and trees, windows in buildings, or street lamps. This enriches the illusion, suggesting a change in the time of day or altering the pictorial emphasis. Similarly, ground rows can be constructed for rear illumination with translucent openings in foliage or as windows in buildings of a city skyline.

Flashing Effects

The reality of the environment is sometimes enhanced by flashing-light effects. A flashing neon sign can add excitement to a downtown street scene or a cheap shabbiness as seen through a hotel-room window. The British musical revue *Oh What a Lovely War* utilized an electronically controlled news panel sign composed of rows of individual lamps; controlled in sequence, the lamps spelled out words traveling across the panel, flashing messages to the audience. Sudden flashes from light sources, explosions, and firearms can be achieved by photographic flash bulbs or shutters on spotlights. The effect of lightning can be achieved by quick-acting shutters on a spotlight or by photographic strobe or other flash systems. Louvered shutters, similar to the mechanisms used on Navy signal lights, are manually operated. Using an electric arc floodlight for a lightning flash is a dangerous practice because of the risk of fire from the open arc.

A continuous strip of flashing lights, called **chaser lights,** is sometimes used for marquees, for archways, for ornamented facades, and for outlining performance runways. Timer mechanisms, often with variable-speed controls, pattern the lamps to go off and on in a chase sequence. Creating the effect of flashing lights on a sophisticated computer console also requires control of multiple light sources. Another kind of flash

FIGURE 15–15 Revue Entertainment Scenery. The use of flashing lights for scenic environment in a Las Vegas revue. (Photo courtesy of the Stardust Hotel)

device is the **strobe light.** Strobes produce a bright blinking light, adjustable in speed, which appears to stop the action momentarily, creating a slow-motion or old-movie effect. Another type of flickering light can be created by the use of a **spinner** positioned in front of a spotlight. While these are available commercially, they are not difficult to fabricate. The simplest is a disc of lightweight aluminum cut in the shape of blades. A small motor is attached to the pivot point to turn the blades (Figure 15-16). The motor of an old food mixer is appropriate, and its speed can be controlled by a dimmer. The lobsterscope is a hand-driven spinning device. Two holes in the metal disc rotate past the light source mechanically giving an effect similar to the electronic strobe light. A number of other flashing effects are used at discotheques, night clubs, and rock concerts.

Projection Effects

Light projections supplement and in some cases replace traditional scenery. Both lens and lensless projectors are used for making images.

Linnebach Projectors. A Linnebach projector has no lens or reflector. Being lensless, it is essentially a shadow projector capable only of creating colored abstract patterns without sharp edges or clarity of detail. Most Linnebachs have large, flat openings that use a glass slide and can project an image on

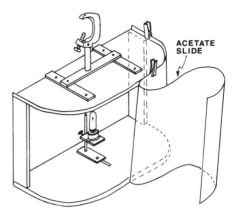

FIGURE 15-17 A Linnebach projector for a curved cyclorama.

a large sky drop. These are available from lighting equipment suppliers. Curved cycloramas require Linnebach projectors with curved openings and slides made of clear cellulose acetate (0.010″ thickness is adequate) (Figure 15-17). Either type of Linnebach can be constructed locally without difficulty or great cost. It requires some sheet-metal work, a method of holding the slide in place, a lamp base, and a concentrated filament lamp. Colored dyes and paints are available for painting patterns on plastic and glass.

Lens Projectors. Scenic lens projectors are often very expensive items of equipment because they are usually designed to cover a large surface, thus requiring extremely wide-angle lens systems and high wattages (5000 watts is not unusual). Cooling fan units are necessary to protect the lamp and slide. A remote-controlled multislide changer is a valuable accessory. Medium-sized and more moderately priced scenic projectors consist of a plano-convex spotlight with fan, a slide carrier (for two slides), and an objective lens system. These range in wattage from 1000 to 2100 depending upon the type of lamp used. Scenic projectors usually use 3½″ × 4″ slides, and some models require larger sizes. The 35-mm projector

FIGURE 15-16 A spotlight with a spinner operated by a small appliance motor.

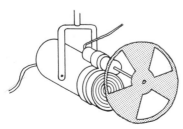

FIGURE 15–18 Scenic projector with a spiral machine and an objective lens system. The projector can also be fitted with slide carriers, a flicker machine, a prism machine, a kaleido machine, a disc machine, and a film machine for other types of motion or projection effects. (Photo courtesy of The Great American Market)

paint or prepared in other ways are sometimes the most effective. Colored foils and overlay films used in transparencies for overhead projectors can create interesting slides. Designs can be etched in a coat of flat black paint on the glass slide. Tiny pin pricks in thin aluminum will create a starry night. Slides sometimes must be supported in a sandwich of projection-slide glass.

Motion Devices. Motion effects have also been used in lens projectors. Formerly known as sciopticon effects, they consisted of round mica discs patterned for such moving effects as clouds, flames, rain, and snow. Rotated by electric motor or clock mechanisms, they are attached to the front of spotlight-type projectors. Today, the range of motion-devices includes spiral effects, film loops, slide carriers, and disc patterns (Figure 15-18).

Often the most effective projection effects on a large background such as a cyclorama consist of a combination of light sources. This might include a broad pattern from a Linnebach, colored washes from floodlights and striplights, a lens projection of sharp focused objects (clouds, stars), and

with a wide-angle lens should not be overlooked where a smaller image and a lower wattage will be sufficient. Lens projections provide clear, detailed images, and photographic slides are often used when absolute realism is sought. However, slides created in

FIGURE 15–19 Industrial Theatre Scenery. Multiscreen projection used for an entertainment presentation at an industrial meeting. Industrial shows are staged at industrial conferences, new product introductions, sales meetings, and annual conventions. Design by Terrance McClellan. (Photo courtesy of Williams/Gerard Productions)

when needed, a motion or spinner projection. Each is controlled by dimmers to achieve the desired composite effect. The result is a richer, more varied image and a greater depth of illusion. Changes in the composition through selective fades and pile-on of images can provide numerous and subtle variations in the picture as the developing dramatic action requires.

Multiscreen projection consists of screen surfaces hung or placed in a variety of locations in the scene. Because they are small, they can be illuminated by standard 35-mm carousel projectors. In contrast to a large cyclorama, small screens can be more readily lighted by rear projection. A number of high-quality plastic rear-screen materials are on the market. Frequently, unusual materials are more appropriate for multiscreen projection. The coordination of a number of projectors usually requires a remote control console.

Template patterns, commonly called **gobos,** are projection slides which fit into the aperture of ellipsoidal spotlights (Figure 15-20). They are useful in providing shadow images on a wall, on the floor, or on some other surface of the scene. Inexpensive preformed gobos are available at theatrical suppliers, and custom patterns can be made from thin sheets of aluminum or other metal. Versatile and low in cost, gobos are a prime means of enriching the environment with projected effects.

Luminescent Effects

Phosphorescent and fluorescent light effects have special qualities. Phosphorescence is the storing of light energy after exposure to a source. Phosphorescent paint will glow in the dark. Fluorescent paints and dyes are seen when lit by an ultraviolet light source commonly called "black light." The effects can be most interesting and may provide the appropriate visual illusion for a given production circumstance.

315 Reversed Trees

316 Fantasy Castle

319 Circles

320 Scribble

FIGURE 15–20 Projection patterns (gobos) for ellipsoidal spotlights. (Photo courtesy of The Great American Market)

Laser and Holography Effects

Laser technology has been used for scenic projections and offers more exciting potential in the future. Laser-developed projections have been employed in special light shows and in a number of theatre productions, including the projected image of Tinker Bell in the Broadway production of *Peter Pan* with Sandy Duncan. The laser is a unique light source. It produces a coherent light, with waves all of the same length, in phase (wave crests and troughs are aligned) and compacted into an extremely narrow beam. One application of laser-beam projection synchronizes light patterns to music and sound. The tiny laser beam is directed to a mirrored surface activated by vibrations of a sound speaker. The reflected beam creates intricate line patterns and designs on a screen. Single or multiple colored images can be achieved depending on the equipment and control methods used. Because a laser can severely damage the retina if the beam directly enters the eye, lasers must be used with extreme caution. Laser equipment is federally regulated and licenses must be obtained to purchase it.

Holography is the most intriguing product made possible by the development of the laser. A hologram creates a three-dimensional image in space that realistically changes in perspective when viewed from different angles. The image is highly believable and offers rich potential for scenic illusions. In developing a hologram, the laser beam is cast on an object or scene as well as on a photographic plate used to record the image (Figure 15-21). A hologram is the recording on the film of the interference pattern formed by the light waves reflected from the object and from the reference beam. When the film is developed, you see only a grayish transparency. However, illuminated again with the reference beam, replicas of the wavefronts that reflected from the object are produced and the image is reconstructed. At present, sizable holographic images are extremely costly and require very powerful and energy-consuming lasers. However, rapid developments in holography continue, and shortly it should have significant application in scene technology.

DISASTER EFFECTS

Highly challenging and enormous in scale are phenomena we might best describe as

FIGURE 15–21 A hologram. (A) Recording a hologram. (B) Reconstructing the image.

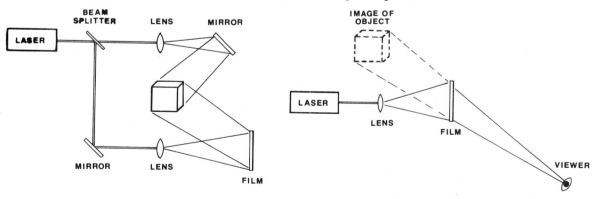

disaster effects. Much as we might wish writers had not thought of them, they exist and require our creative energies. Disasters include avalanches, erupting volcanos, thunderstorms, dust storms, cyclones, explosions, bombings, and that most dreaded word of all, conflagrations (disastrous fires). For motion pictures, the best solution often is to create the illusion in miniature in the controlled studio environment. Of course, many must be executed in full scale at location sites. The conditions of the film industry are more conducive to special effects of this nature. There is time to set up a disaster scene properly, and more control of equipment and materials is possible. Scenes are filmed one at a time, and with retakes, ineffective performances can be eliminated. Audio interference is no problem because sound can be dubbed in later. Adequate protection is easier to provide for the actors. Powerful fans create wind storms, snow machines spew out winter blizzards, and large chunks of soft foam rocks provide avalanche scenes with great realism.

Some of these can be applied to live theatre, but most cannot. The confines of the stage and the presence of an audience generally prohibit their use. For a stage production, it is often more effective to *suggest* the disaster through a combination of effects. Background lighting can dim; bold light projections can increase in prominence; spinners or flashing lights can convey the nature of the disaster or the motion or atmospheric disturbance of the event; sound effects can begin to swell; smoke can be added if needed; and mechanical devices can trigger the falling, rocking, or swaying of objects. A disaster effect should be planned carefully and should grow in intensity with the action of the scene.

SELECTED READINGS

BURRIS-MEYER, HAROLD, VINCENT MALLORY, and LEWIS S. GOODFRIEND, *Sound in the Theatre* (rev. ed.). New York: Theatre Arts Books, 1979.

CLARK, FRANK P., *Special Effects in Motion Pictures.* New York: Society of Motion Picture and Television Engineers, 1966.

COLLISON, DAVID, *Stage Sound.* New York: Drama Book Specialists, 1976.

FINELLI, PATRICK M., *Sound for the Stage.* New York: Drama Book Specialists, 1989.

HOPKINS, ALBERT A., *Magic: Stage Illusions, Special Effects and Trick Photography.* New York: Arno Press, 1977. (First published in 1898 by Munn and Co.)

KOCK, WINSTON E., *Lasers and Holography.* New York: Doubleday, 1969.

PARKER, W. OREN, HARVEY K. SMITH, and R. CRAIG WOLF, *Scene Design and Stage Lighting* (5th ed.). New York: Holt, Rinehart and Winston, 1985.

RYDELL, WENDY, and GEORGE GILBERT, *The Great Book of Magic.* New York: Harry N. Abrams, 1976.

SAXBY, GRAHAM, *Manual of Practical Holography.* London: Focus Press, 1991.

TURNBULL, ROBERT B., *Radio and Television Sound Effects.* New York: Holt, Rinehart and Winston, 1951.

WILKIE, BERNARD, *Creating Special Effects for TV and Films.* New York: Hastings House, 1977.

WILKIE, BERNARD, *The Technique of Special Effects in Television.* New York: Hastings House, 1971.

16

Shop Management

It is amazing the number of abilities and skills required in the management of a scene shop. Proficiencies in all construction techniques, drafting, and problem solving are readily recognized as necessary attributes for the job. In addition, the shop manager or technical director frequently serves as a personnel supervisor, an efficiency expert, a purchasing agent, an equipment repairer, a safety officer, an inventory clerk, and more. This listing illustrates the array of accepted responsibilities that are needed to operate a shop efficiently. Unfortunately, except in commercial scene shops, serious attention is not always given to shop management. However, all industrial ventures, even a shop with a modest production load, can improve in function and efficiency by regular study, evaluation, and review of its operation.

EQUIPMENT AND MATERIALS MANAGEMENT

Maintaining Equipment

Tools and machinery will function correctly and safely only when they are properly maintained. The first step in maintaining equipment is to avoid misusing it. Know how to use each tool properly. Consult the instruction manual if necessary to confirm how to adjust a tool for a particular purpose. If adequate shop supervision is provided, workers can be trained to use tools correctly. Improper usage not only is hazardous to the equipment, but is often dangerous to the worker.

Care and maintenance of tools requires a servicing program. The most basic service need is simply the sharpening of saw blades and bits that become dull. Blades and bits should be replaced whenever signs of dullness are evident. Beyond this, preventative maintenance requires regular inspections and equipment checks. To accomplish even the simplest servicing, you must be familiar with the equipment. File folders containing the instruction manual, servicing and maintenance procedures, parts list and specifications, safety information, serial number, manufacturer, warranty, and similar data should be kept on each major tool. If these are not available, they can usually be obtained by contacting the manufacturer. The shop manager must understand equipment instructions and be able to provide the regular servicing. A maintenance schedule should be drawn up to regularize inspections of tools. This will greatly limit equipment failure and wasteful downtime during the construction period. Service checks include examining all adjustment knobs and levers, replacing dull blades and bits, lubricating with the proper lubricant, cleaning dirt and rust off of components, examining equipment alignment, tightening loose bolts and screws, and replacing worn and faulty parts. Equipment service instructions describe specific maintenance procedures.

Maintaining the Stock of Supplies

Work is possible in a shop only if it is stocked with the materials for construction. Some shops acquire special supplies only when needed for a given production. This practice is acceptable as long as the need and the quantity of materials can be determined from the drawings in sufficient time to obtain them for the start of the construction period. The shop manager must keep a list of supplies and the estimated time required for the purchase and delivery of scenic materials. However, many items must be in stock at all times because of the day-to-day regularity of use or because of the extended time

necessary to acquire them from suppliers. Running out of nails, paint, or glue will only interrupt and delay construction. What follows is a partial list of material categories commonly stocked in a scene shop.

Paint supplies
Dyes
Nails (common, box, finish)
Staples (for both hand and power staplers)
Screws (for wood and metal)
Scenic fabric and screening (muslin, canvas, screen wire)
Tape (spike, masking, duct)
Standard plastic materials
Glues and adhesives
Common lumber supplies (1″ stock, plywood, Upson board)

Bolts
Standard stage hardware
Common regular hardware
Sandpaper (regular and power sanders)
Wire, cable, tape
Drawing supplies
First-aid supplies
Knife blades, saw blades, bits
Lubricants
Protective material (air filters, masks, gloves)
Spare equipment parts

It is highly advisable for the shop manager to develop an inventory list of regularly needed supplies based on past experience. This list should include the minimum quantities of each item that should be on hand at all times. Several times during the year, an inventory should be taken to determine which supplies need replenishing. This preventive action will greatly reduce the chances of running out of building materials during construction. In some cases, the resupplying of stock materials is a planned activity during a hiatus period each year when scenery is not being constructed. A microcomputer with an inventory software program is an excellent way to keep track of an extensive stock of supplies. Some supplies, such as nails, paint, and glue, are fully consumed and require continual replacement. Other items—bolts and door hardware, for instance—are reusable. Producing groups that dismantle and save materials from settings after a production are able to salvage casters, hinges, and other items. Once a certain quantity of these relatively indestructible items is acquired, additional purchases may be infrequent. Further, even salvaged lumber, fabric, and other less-durable materials will reduce the need for new supplies. Appropriate bins and racks are needed to accommodate salvaged lumber and other materials.

Hazardous Materials

For the health and safety of personnel and facilities, the proper handling and storage of hazardous substances is paramount. Store flammable and toxic materials in nonbreakable containers separated to prevent possible chemical reactions. All items must be carefully labeled and accompanied with hazard warnings, safety signs, and handling precautions. Obviously, shop personnel must be properly advised on how to handle these materials safely. Flammable solvents should be stored in approved safety containers and solvent-soaked rags placed in waste-disposal cans. Hazardous wastes are identified as materials or liquids that are flammable, corrosive, violently reactive chemically, or toxic. Disposal of these polluting waste materials should be handled only by a pollution control company.

PURCHASING

Scenic designers and technicians need to be well informed about scenic materials and the acquisition process. Budget limitations for a production must be taken into account when developing a design. This requires a knowledge of the cost of materials and of suppliers. Collecting catalogs, current price lists, and names of distributors and manufactur-

ers is important. Directories, indexes, and trade magazines are valuable references. By all means, know what local merchants regularly stock or can special-order for you. Keep up-to-date with price changes so you may develop a realistic budget estimate for a production.

Availability of Materials

The lead time for receiving new supplies should not be forgotten. Special as well as standard scenic materials which must be ordered from distant suppliers should be identified early so orders can be processed and the items can arrive in ample time. Distributors have a limit on the quantity of a material they stock. A realistic estimate of delivery time must include the time needed to process a purchase order, the location of the supplier, the size of stock maintained, and the method of shipping. While occasional emergency orders are necessary, the cost is usually higher, especially if special shipping is necessary, and construction may be jeopardized by the delayed arrival of the materials. Emergencies are generally the result of inadequate planning, failure to predict needs in advance, or incorrectly estimating the rate of consumption of regular supplies in stock. It is advisable, when planning to use an unusual material or a large quantity of an item, to check on its availability from reliable suppliers. Promises of delivery from wholesalers or manufacturers without direct confirmation can lead to construction delays and costly substitutions at the last minute.

Determining Estimated Costs

Before completing the design for a setting, an early cost estimate is needed to determine whether the desired scenic plan will stay within the production budget. An estimate is developed by computing standard costs of materials with anticipated measurements of the setting (Figure 16-1). This requires some skill and judgment to arrive at figures that are as realistic and complete as possible. The estimate should include the approximate cost of shipping and any potential price increases. The inventory of supplies on hand should be checked to determine the quantity of materials already available. Commercial shops will need to estimate construction time, labor, and overhead costs.

Preparing a List of Needed Supplies

When the design and working drawings are completed, an accurate list of materials to purchase can be prepared. Quantities should be determined by standard units and unit costs: board feet for regular lumber, lineal feet for decorative lumber, square feet for sheet materials, and lineal yards for fabric. A minimum of 50 percent fullness and hem allowances should be included in fab-

MATERIALS ESTIMATE

Production "Close Ties" Dates 10/12-20, 1992

Estimate by R. Arnold Total $ 1,780.81 Date 6/14/84

LUMBER	QTY	UNIT	COST	AMT
1X3 Clear	200	BF	1.65	330.00
1X3 #2	30	BF	.51	15.30
1X4 Clear	66	BF	1.70	112.20
1X4 #2	50	BF	.53	26.50
1X6 #2	258	BF	.60	154.50
1/4" PLY AC	2	Shts	14.32	28.64
3/4" PLY AC	14	"	21.01	294.14
1/2" PLY AC	3	"	15.85	47.55
MOLDING NOSE 1 3/4"	25	LF	.14	3.50
1/2" DOWEL	10'	LF	.12	1.20
1/4" MASONITE	10	Shts	10.00	100.00
			$	1113.83

FABRIC	QTY	UNIT	COST	AMT
Muslin	18	yds	3.45	62.10
Black Scrim	6	yds	30.00	180.00
			$	242.10

METALS	QTY	UNIT	COST	AMT
1" Pipe ID	42'	FT	.32	13.44

PLASTICS	QTY	UNIT	COST	AMT
1" Styrene foam	1	Sht	6.50	6.50
Vinyl rug 12'x15'	20	sq yds	5.20	104.00
			$	110.50

HARDWARE	QTY	UNIT	COST	AMT
Regular				60.00
Corner plates	10	ea	1.53	15.30
Mending plates	8		1.32	10.56
Btm Hanger irons	6		1.68	10.08
			$	95.94

SPECIAL	QTY	UNIT	COST	AMT
Stove buy				85.00
Plumbing for sink				30.00
			$	115.00

PAINT	QTY	UNIT	COST	AMT
Vinyl	5	gal	18.00	90.00

FIGURE 16–1 A materials estimate sheet.

rics for curtains and draperies. Fabric yardage tables are available for estimating the quantity of fabric required for upholstery and slipcovers for various types of furniture. Individual lengths and sizes of materials should provide as little waste as possible. Specifying 12′ lumber for a group of 10′-high flats, for instance, would be wasteful. On the other hand, it is advisable to provide some extra in the total quantity of any item to allow for construction errors, such as a spilled container of paint or an incorrect cut in lumber or fabric.

Methods of Purchasing

A uniform method of purchasing protects an organization from waste, unauthorized purchases, and inadequate accounting records. A purchase-order system managed by the business manager or purchasing department provides accountability and control. The technical director or shop manager submits a requisition to the business office specifying materials needed. From this, a purchase order is issued to a vendor and constitutes the commitment of funds. The purchase order includes a description of the material, sizes, quantity, unit and total price, method of shipment, expected date of delivery, and terms of payment. Often the purchase order is delivered to the vendor when an authorized technician picks up the supplies. Otherwise, it is mailed to the supplier, and a copy of the order is held in the shop until the materials are delivered. Once the materials are unpacked and verified, the shop manager authorizes the business office to make payment on the order.

FIGURE 16–2   High School Scenery. Setting for *The Crucible*, with a suggestive and moody silhouette and lighting projection. Scene design by Thomas G. Hines. (Photo courtesy of Barrington High School, Barrington, Illinois)

The need for the immediate purchase of small quantities of supplies often requires special arrangements. One method is the establishment of renewable or open purchase orders at a few local stores and nearby theatre suppliers. This permits the shop manager to place telephone orders or authorize direct purchases of standard supplies needed on a regular basis. A petty-cash system is also valuable, especially for purchases that are too small to process through a regular purchase order. With this system a person may be authorized to make a small purchase in cash and be reimbursed from the petty-cash account by submitting the sales slip or receipt. This is valuable in dealing with cash-and-carry merchants, in acquiring specialty prop items, or in buying from dealers where infrequent purchases do not justify a regular account.

Purchasing agents are trained and experienced in making wise and economical purchases. They work to obtain the lowest prices and discounts for you as well as to expedite orders to meet your deadlines. However, they need help to perform their work effectively. This includes precise and complete specifications of materials. Power tools and custom-made staging equipment especially need detailed specifications. Indicate when compatibility with existing supplies and tools (paints, staples, and so on) prohibits substitutes. Catalog numbers and a list of recommended vendors should be provided. Most of all, purchasers need sufficient time to seek good prices and negotiate for discounts.

Volume orders generally provide the largest discounts. Costly orders often require the submission of sealed bids from several vendors and the acceptance of the lowest bid. Whenever possible, order in large volume—a season's supply of standard material, for instance—and allow several weeks for the purchaser to place the order. Plan far enough ahead to avoid emergency purchases. A rush order will not be economical. Be aware that some companies have a minimum-order policy and will charge extra for small orders.

A purchase is not complete until the merchandise arrives and the supplier is paid. When the supplies are delivered, they should be examined immediately to be certain they conform to the specifications of the order. Certify the satisfactory receipt of the order promptly so the bill will be paid without delay. Dependable service means selecting vendors who have a history of experience and reliability in their field of merchandise. Their willingness to provide good service will depend on how well they are treated. Pay bills on time; avoid rush orders and unrealistic delivery dates. Establishing and following a responsible purchasing and accounting procedure will result in economical management.

SUPERVISING THE CONSTRUCTION

At the heart of shop management is the day-to-day activity of constructing scenery and properties for the production. This requires careful planning and supervision.

Scheduling the Work

An organized shop operation requires the development of a construction schedule. A planned calendar distributing the work sequence over the working period establishes goals to meet and keeps the progress of construction moving. Without such a plan, there is no guide to the pace of preparing the production. This often results in a rush of activity and long hours of work in the last days before the opening. This cannot assure satisfying results, and working excessive hours when exhausted is dangerous to workers and equipment. With some experience, you can establish a calendar of construction for the particular production. With the completion of construction drawings and receipt of supplies, a 4-week construction schedule might appear as follows:

1st Week: Construction of scenery and properties—basic fabrication
2nd Week: Construction of scenery and properties—joining and covering
Trial setup of scenery
3rd Week: Addition of set dressing and small properties
Scene painting
Assembly of setting and major properties on stage
4th Week: Addition of set dressing and small properties
2 technical rehearsals
3 dress rehearsals
5th Week: Performances

A specific schedule of construction for a given production should list the activities on a daily basis. Deadlines can be established for particular segments to coordinate the work sequence so whole scenic units will be ready at the scheduled time for assembly, painting, or trial setup. A few unscheduled days may be appropriate as a catch-up time or safety factor in the work process. A work sequence and calendar must be determined by a careful analysis of the construction and the ability of the work force. A list of the work steps should be prepared, grouped in scenic units to estimate time and difficulty of construction. Projects requiring considerable construction time will need to be started early in the work schedule. The order of construction should be prioritized. Some items, such as platforms and some property or special-effects devices, may need to be built first so they can be used in rehearsals if substitutes are impractical. The calendar will need to consider sufficient time for complex painting jobs, the rigging and hanging of a setting, and the needed setup time required by the lighting designer.

After studying the drawings, the shop supervisor usually prepares **work orders** and **cut lists**. Work orders divide the work into logical groupings and in the proper sequence of operation. It lists the various steps of the work and often requires a check and signature to confirm completion of a job. A cut list is made for each scenic item constructed and consists of the actual quantity of material, size and length of material to be cut, and special work requirements of the job (Figure 16-3).

Large set and multiset productions often are the most difficult to schedule in the shop. Frequently, several operations must be

FIGURE 16–3 A cut list.

Cut List						
Production _Harvey_ Scene _2_ Drawing No. _13_						
Unit _G_ Compiled By _J. M_ Cut By _K. B_ Date Cut _11/13/92_						

No.	Item	Size	Length	Cut From	Special Work	
2	Stiles	1"×3"	13'-7"	1×12		✓
2	Rails	1"×3"	4'-6"	1×12		✓
3	Toggles	1"×3"	4'-1"	scrap		✓
2	Braces	1"×2"	2'-6"	scrap	end cut at 45°	✓
4	Cornerblocks	10"×10"		scrap ply		✓
1	Muslin	4'-10"	14'-4"	new stock		✓
6	Keystones	8"		crap		✓

scheduled simultaneously. If there is limited storage space in the shop, it may be necessary to build one set first, which can then be delivered to the stage or to a storage area out of the shop area. The limits of the work space often dictate the sequence of construction. The construction of large units will restrict space for other types of construction. It may be necessary to schedule a number of small projects while a large drop is being painted on the floor. The order of construction must also consider the efficient use of personnel. Whenever possible, each craft area should have continuous activity, and projects should be well coordinated for the next step in construction. Projects should be set up to use workers' time efficiently. The production of multiple items should be organized for mass production with appropriate templates or assembly-line techniques. The number of weeks required in the construction schedule will depend on the complexity of the setting, the size of the shop, and the number and skill of the shop workers.

Protecting the Environment

There has been a growing effort in recent years to improve the management of resources for protecting our environment. Properly disposing of hazardous wastes and participating in recycling programs for paper, glass, and aluminum, for instance, are examples of environmental responsibility. There are also many other ways we may not have explored. Conserving electrical energy use and cutting back on water consumption are obvious steps we could take. Reducing the amount of throwaway trash that ends up in landfills can be helped by using more reclaimable raw materials. For example, wood and steel used in scenery can be salvaged and used again. When scraps become too small, steel can be recycled and wood can be used for fuel. When striking a production, a little more care and time can salvage lumber, steel, muslin, and hardware for future productions. In addition, our own health and safety as well as the environment benefits if we substitute nontoxic materials for more toxic and polluting substances whenever possible.

Keeping the Scenery Inventory

Maintaining a stock of scenery reduces production costs, reduces labor, and cuts production time. Basic scenery units can be altered or changed at less cost and time than building entirely new ones. Standard flats, drops, platform tops, stair units, and draperies are common items worth sorting. However, to be of maximum use, information about the scene units in stock must be readily available as the designer and technical director plan the setting. This is accomplished if each item in stock is described on a card in a card file or in a computer file. The information should include an identifying number of the item, its measurement, description, condition, and location in storage. Flats can be filed by height; other items by category. As the setting is planned, cards can be pulled from the file or labeled in the computer if the units will be used in the set. At the end of the production, information must be changed to show alterations, and the cards returned to the file. Annual inventory of the scenery stock is valuable in maintaining a usable stock and accuracy of the file.

The Shop Office

The shop manager and technicians need an office adjacent to the shop facility. This room is the operational center of the shop. A drafting area or a place to review plans and drawings is valuable. Meetings can be held here to lay out the projects and to prepare work schedules and calendars. Shop purchases are planned here, and records are maintained on suppliers and manufacturers. Files should include equipment information, parts lists, and maintenance and safety instruction for shop tools. Inventory files on scenery in storage, and lists of supplies and materials regularly stocked are necessary. Time cards and records of workers may be kept in the room. The office may also be located near a design and drafting room, locker rooms for shop personnel, and a supply room.

SCENERY AND PROPERTY STORAGE

The economical advantages of maintaining a stock of scenery and properties has already been examined. The cost of the warehouse facility and maintenance of the stock must also be considered in the economics of storage. The determination of what to save is based essentially on the potential use of items in coming seasons. Highly unusual or specialized scenic units are discarded or stripped to basic materials. However, scenery in standard sizes and shapes, easily alterable units, and common properties are often worth saving if storage space is available.

A scenery stock needs to be well labeled to conform to the inventory. The number should be clearly tagged or painted on the scenic unit. As settings are planned, available units in stock should be easily located to be assessed for use in a production. Unusual-shaped scenic structures can be partially composed of standard units in stock with only a few, if any, specially constructed pieces. A file of properties in stock is not always worth the trouble. However, if the stock is sizable, matching sets of furniture might be itemized on cards, with a polaroid photograph of one piece to indicate the style of the furniture.

The Storage Facility

In the planning and constructing of production facilities, appropriate storage rooms often have a low priority. This frequently results in inadequate storage areas or none

whatever. Considering the need and value of an active scenic and property stock, this is a rather short-sighted view. Many organizations must store items in cramped basements or out-of-the-way areas not designed for storage. Others are forced to use warehouse space some distance from the production facility. These adapted and makeshift spaces seldom meet storage requirements. The ideal storage facility should be a dry, well-ventilated space to prevent mildew, water stains, and warping. Extreme temperatures should be avoided. The space should be reasonably clean and free of rodents. The storage area needs to be fire resistant and be equipped for fire-protection devices such as sprinklers. Finally, it is preferable if the storage is accessible to the shop and stage. Storage at a distant location will add time and transportation costs to the construction of a setting. Accessibility also refers to the size of doors, passageways, and elevators leading from the storage facility to the shop.

Storage Principles

Some thought and attention is needed in laying out and maintaining an efficient storage system. Establish guidelines or principles to plan the arrangement of the storage area.

Storage Should be Organized. Locate items in logical categories within the confines of the storage areas.

Keep Items Visible. Avoid stacking items, which makes them difficult to find. Mark out aisles on the floor to provide wide passageways and easy access to all items in storage.

Make the Most of the Storage Space. Plan the use of space to maximum effectiveness. If there is height in the room, store objects vertically. It is useful to build racks and decks of ready-to-assemble metal so lightweight objects can be placed on upper levels and tall items can be placed upright. These flexible rack structures can be varied and altered as the storage undergoes change. A hoist and track may be necessary for lowering items to the floor. Use rolling carts or mobile units to transport or relocate items easily.

Protect Items in Storage. Protect objects from damage not only how and where they are stored, but also with necessary protective coverings or placement in appropriate containers.

Keep the Storage Area Clean. The rooms should be regularly cleaned, objects should be checked for proper organization, and aisles should be kept open and free of clutter.

Methods of Storage

Objects in storage are extremely varied and will require different methods of storage. These can be established within the configuration of the warehouse facility.

Flats and Other Framed Units. A scene dock for vertical storage of flats takes the least amount of floor space. A scene dock consists of vertical frames of wood or pipe attached to the floor and ceiling (Figure 16-4). Twenty or more flats can be stored between dock frames spaced approximately 3′ apart. The dock must be high enough for the tallest flats. The frames need not exceed 5′ in width. A clear aisle of 6′ is needed to insert and remove scenery from the scene dock. The inventory number should be painted on both stiles of a flat at a height easily readable from the floor. If room height is insufficient, a storage dock can be constructed to store flats on their sides. This will require a larger open space in front to remove scenery.

Rolled Objects: Drops, Borders, Ceilings, and Carpets. Long rolled items are best stored on specially constructed wall racks or adjustable bracket shelving such as Unistrut assemblies. Support is needed every 4′ to 6′. The items may be stored the full height of

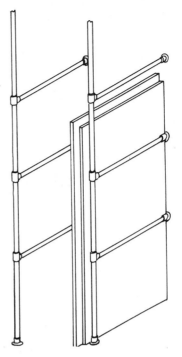

FIGURE 16-4   The scene dock.

the wall if provision is available to lift them. The rack must accommodate the longest drop. Identification tags corresponding to the inventory file should be tied at one end of each piece. Curtain tracks can also be stored on these racks. The length of rolled drops requires a location with clear access to loading doors and to the stage.

Folded Drops, Draperies, Borders, and Scrims. Folded fabrics should be stored in canvas bags or trunks for protection. These can then be placed on large shelving units to keep them off the floor. Large, rolling, industrial laundry hampers provide excellent storage for heavy stage draperies and borders. This reduces unnecessary handling and damage to the fabric. The hampers can be rolled directly to the stage when draperies are to be hung. All materials should be tagged with inventory identification.

Platform Frames and Tops, Door and Window Units. As for flat storage, vertical racks for framed units of this type will be economical in use of space and will provide easy access to the units.

Three-Dimensional Units. Fireplaces, stairs, and other three-dimensional units require a large, open floor space owing to the nature of their construction and their weight. They can be arranged in categories. Avoid stacking items, which may damage them and make them hard to locate.

Furniture and Large Properties. Sofas, bureaus, cabinets, stoves, and other heavy furniture props are best stored on the floor. However, long rows of deep shelving can provide storage for lightweight objects such as chairs and small tables (Figure 16-5). Fur-

FIGURE 16–5 Shelving for furniture storage to maximize storage space and avoid harmful stacking.

FIGURE 16–6 Hand prop storage.

niture warehouses have multitiered shelving and rolling lifts to raise and lower furniture. All furniture should be fully visible and aisles ample in size to remove items. Stacking furniture is not advisable, as many are easily scratched, marred, and broken. Furniture should be arranged in matching sets in general categories (garden furniture, kitchen furniture). Good upholstered pieces may require dust covers. Keep the storage area clean of dust and debris.

Hand Properties. Adjustable shelving units are ideal for storing and displaying hand props (Figure 16-6). The shelves can be adjusted from time to time as quantities of items vary. Hand props are best organized in categories or departments. Dishware, bar supplies, musical instruments, plants and flowers, artificial fruit, office supplies, weapons, pictures, and plaques are logical headings. Numerous small items might be stored in covered boxes or trunks.

SELECTED READINGS

Brown, Robert K., *Industrial Education Facilities.* Boston: Allyn & Bacon, 1979.

Burris-Meyer, Harold, and Edward C. Cole, *Theatres and Auditoriums* (2nd ed.). New York: Reinhold, 1964.

Carter, Paul, *Backstage Handbook.* New York: Broadway Press, 1988.

Carter, Paul, *Backstage Forms.* New York: Broadway Press, 1990.

Irvin, Daniel W., *Power Tool Maintenance.* New York: McGraw-Hill, 1971.

Power Tool "Safety is Specific." Power Tool Institute, Inc., 5105 Tollview Drive, Rolling Meadows, IL.

Ramsey, Charles G., and Harold L. Sleeper, *Architectural Graphic Standards* (8th ed.). New York: John Wiley, 1988.

Royer, King, *The Construction Manager in the 80's.* Englewood Cliffs, NJ: Prentice Hall, 1981.

Supervisor's Safety Manual (7th ed.). New York: National Safety Council, 1991.

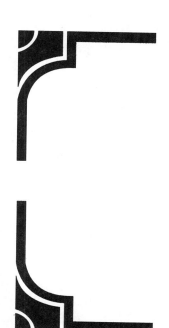

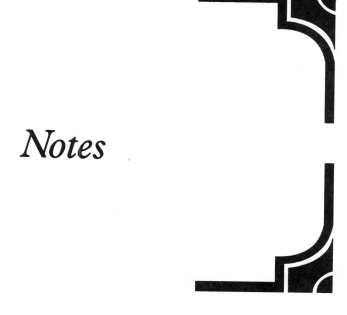

Notes

CHAPTER 3

[1] The line weights in the USITT Graphics Standard are as follows:

Thin: 0.010″ to 0.0125″ width
Thick: 0.020″ to 0.025″ width
Extra thick: 0.035″ to 0.040″ width

The extra-thick line would be used only infrequently for emphasis or as a plate border or a section-cutting plane line.

CHAPTER 5

[1] Robert Scales, "Pneumatic Fluid Power Systems Basics," *Theatre Crafts*, Vol. 15, No. 3 (March 1981), p. 28.

CHAPTER 9

[1] Alexander F. Adducci, "A Comparative Analysis of Five Structural Component Part Systems for Use in Platform Construction on the Stage" (Unpublished Master's thesis, Northern Illinois University, 1966).

[2] Robert C. Jackson, "Stressed-Skin Scenery for the Theatre," *Theatre Crafts*, Vol. 12, No. 1 (January–February 1978), pp. 24–25, 57–58.

[3] Tom Corbett, "Laminating Stage Platforms Using Honeycomb Paper," *Theatre Design and Technology*, Vol. 16, No. 4 (Winter 1980), pp. 11–16.

CHAPTER 13

[1] Peter Foy, *The Art of Theatrical Flying* (brochure), Las Vegas, Nev., 1973.

Index